Was the Red Flag Flying There?

Was the Red Flag Flying There?

Marxist Politics and the Arab-Israeli Conflict in Egypt and Israel, 1948–1965

Joel Beinin

UNIVERSITY OF CALIFORNIA PRESS
Berkeley · Los Angeles

University of California Press
Berkeley and Los Angeles, California

© 1990 by
The Regents of the University of California

Library of Congress Cataloging-in-Publication Data

Beinin, Joel, 1948–
    Was the red flag flying there? : Marxist politics and the Arab-Israeli conflict in
Egypt and Israel, 1948–1965 / Joel Beinin.

    p. cm.
    Includes bibliographical references.
    ISBN 0-520-07035-6 (alk. paper).—ISBN 0-520-07036-4 (pbk.: alk. paper)
    1. Israel—Politics and government. 2. Nationalism and socialism—Israel.
3. Communism and Zionism. 4. Egypt—Politics and government—1952– .
5. Nationalism and socialism—Egypt. 6. Jewish-Arab relations—1949–1967. I. Title.
DS126.5.B359 1990
956.9405′2—dc20   89-49036
                                                                                      CIP

Printed in the United States of America

1 2 3 4 5 6 7 8 9

The paper used in this publication meets the minimum requirements of
American National Standard for Information Sciences—Permanence of
Paper for Printed Library Materials, ANSI Z39.48-1984. ♾™

To my son, Jamie,
who may inherit a better world
if he struggles for it

Contents

List of Tables	xi
List of Abbreviations	xiii
Acknowledgments	xvii
I. Introduction	1
Comparing Egypt and Israel	5
Revisionist History of the Arab-Israeli Conflict	7
Was MAPAM a Marxist Party?	15
Nations, the Construction of Hegemony, and Political Discourse	17
Structure of the Book	19
Narration and Politics	21
II. The Creation of Israel: Zionism as Anti-Imperialism	24
The Unification of the Marxist-Zionist Left	25
MAPAM and the 1948–49 War	31
The Palestine Communist Party's Road to Binationalism	40
The Communist Educational Association	41
The Palestinian Arab Intelligentsia and the National Liberation League	42

Two Paths to Endorsing Partition of Palestine	43
Toward the Communist Party of Israel	48
The Palestine Question and the Egyptian Communists	55
The Marxist Left After Partition	63

III. The Political Economy of Hegemony — 66

Labor and Capital in the Zionist Movement	67
The Seamen's Strike and Israel's International Orientation	73
Confirmation of MAPAI Hegemony	76
Deradicalization and Depoliticization of the Kibbutzim	79
The Old Regime and the Egyptian National Movement	84
The Coup of July 23, 1952	86
The Revolutionary Command Council and the Working Class	88
The Workers' Movement and the 1956 War	91
Guided Capitalism	93
The Communist Intelligentsia's Accommodation with Nasserism	97
Arab Socialism	99

IV. A Window of Opportunity? 1949–1955 — 102

The Jewish Question in Egyptian Communism	103
The Rise of the Indigenous Intelligentsia	110
"The Question of Yunis"	113
Was There a "Zionist Deviation" in the DMNL?	114
A MAPAM–MAKI United Front?	117
Elections to the Constituent Assembly (First Knesset)	120
Marxism Engaged in a Jewish Problematic	122
The Rise and Decline of the Left in MAPAM	125
The Left Socialist Party	134
Defense of the Rights of the Arab Minority	137

V. Internationalism in Practice: Relations Between the Egyptian and Israeli Marxists — 144

The International Peace Movement	145
The Rome Group and DMNL–MAKI Contacts	148
Yusuf Hilmi's Peace Initiative	153

Contents

VI. The Consolidation of Nationalist Politics: 1955–1958 ... 160
    The Illusion of Success ... 162
    Bandung and the Czech Arms Deal ... 164
    The Suez/Sinai War and MAPAM's Capitulation ... 172
    The Nasserist-Communist Alliance ... 177
    Unification of the Egyptian Communist Movement ... 185
    The Twentieth Congress of the Communist Party of the Soviet Union and National Communism ... 190
    MAKI's Arab Period ... 193

VII. The Triumph of Nationalism: 1959–1965 ... 204
    Breakup of the Nasserist-Communist Alliance ... 205
    Dissolution of the Egyptian Communist Parties ... 208
    Nasserism, MAPAM, MAKI, and the Palestinian Arab Citizens of Israel ... 212
    Defeat of the Left in the 1959 Knesset Elections ... 218
    A New Beginning—or the Beginning of the End? ... 223
    MAKI and Jewish National Communism ... 231
    Toward the Split in MAKI ... 235
    Decline of MAKI's Influence in the Jewish Working Class ... 239
    Mobilization of the Palestinian Arab Citizens of Israel ... 243

VIII. Conclusion ... 246
    Marxism, Zionism, and Arab Nationalism ... 248
    Political Discourse and Political Action ... 253
    Epilogue: Toward a Palestinian State and Beyond ... 255

Notes ... 259
Chronology ... 293
Glossary ... 295
Bibliography ... 297
Index ... 309

List of Tables

1. Social Composition of EMNL, Iskra, and DMNL Membership	57
2. Capital Imports to Israel, 1949–65	71
3. Arrests for Communist Activity in Egypt, 1949–58	108
4. Sales of *Al-ittihad*	216
5. Fourth Knesset Election Results (November 3, 1959)	220
6. Fifth Knesset Election Results (August 15, 1961)	230
7. MAKI Membership, 1958–65	241
8. Circulation of MAKI Press, 1956–63	242

List of Abbreviations

BIBLIOGRAPHICAL CITATIONS

AA   Arkhion Haʿavodah Vehehalutz, Lavon Institute for Labor Research, Tel Aviv (Shmuʾel Mikunis and MAKI papers)

AM   *Al hamishmar*

HH   Hashomer Hatzaʿir archive, Merkaz teʿud veheker shel hashomer hatzaʿir, Givʿat Haviva, Israel

I   *Al-ittihad*

KA   *Kol haʿam*

KM   Kibbutz Meʾuhad archive, Efal, Israel (MAKI papers)

M   *Al-masaʾ*

POLITICAL TERMS

AWC   Arab Workers' Congress

BANKI   Brit Hanoʿar Hakomunistit Hayisraʾelit—The Young Communist League of Israel

CEA   Communist Educational Association

CPE	Communist Party of Egypt
DMNL	Democratic Movement for National Liberation
EMNL	Egyptian Movement for National Liberation
ETZEL	Irgun Tzva'i Le'umi—National Military Organization
GFETU	General Federation of Egyptian Trade Unions
IDF	Israel Defense Forces
LEHI	Lohmei Herut Yisra'el—Fighters for the Freedom of Israel
LSP	Left Socialist Party
MAKEI	Hamiflagah Hakomunistit Ha'eretz Yisra'elit—The Communist Party of the Land of Israel
MAKI	Hamiflagah Hakomunistit Hayisra'elit—The Communist Party of Israel
MAPAI	Mifleget Po'alei (Eretz) Yisra'el—The (Land of) Israel Workers' Party
MAPAM	Mifleget Hapo'alim Hame'uhedet — The United Workers' Party
MISHMISH	al-Munazzama al-Shuyu'iyya al-Misriyya — The Egyptian Communist Organization
MK	Member of Knesset [Palestinian Arab]
NAHSHAM	Nahwa Hizb Shuyu'i Misri—Toward an Egyptian Communist Party
NLL	National Liberation League
PCP	Palestine Communist Party
PLO	Palestine Liberation Organization
RAKAH	Hareshimah Hakomunistit Hehadashah—The New Communist List
RCC	Revolutionary Command Council
SHABAK	Sherut Bitahon Klalit—General Security Services [of Israel]

List of Abbreviations

SHELI	Shalom Leyisra'el—Peace for Israel
UAR	United Arab Republic
UECP	Unified Egyptian Communist Party
UNSCOP	United Nations Special Committee on Palestine
WPCP	Workers' and Peasants' Communist Party

Acknowledgments

Much of what I know about politics in Egypt and Israel I have learned from Mohamed Sid-Ahmed and Re'uven Kaminer. Although they have been motivated by a similar political and social vision for several decades, they have never faced each other. In a better world they would have met long ago and drawn strength from learning of each other's efforts. Perhaps they still will. Each of them will find echoes in these pages of the many discussions we have had over the years, although each will also find more than a little to disagree with. More important than the knowledge they have shared with me, both of them have, in their own way, given me an enduring sense of place and purpose in their country. No one has encouraged me to feel intellectually more connected to Egypt than Mohamed Sid-Ahmed. The entire Kaminer clan has been a second family in Israel to me and my family.

Yusuf, Iqbal, and Nawla Darwish have repeatedly welcomed me most warmly in Egypt, sharing their home, their historical memories, and current insights; encouraging me to pursue my research interests; and providing physical and emotional sustenance. In the process they have taught me about aspects of Egypt that cannot be understood from reading alone.

This book owes much to the kind support of many others who allowed me to interview them (they are listed in the bibliography) or shared with me historical documents in their possession. Joyce Blau permitted me to see the papers of Henri Curiel in her home in Paris, and Yusuf Hazan provided me with copies of the publications of the Rome group. Maxime Rodinson allowed me to use the collection of papers and publications of the Egyptian communist movement, which he amassed over several years. Abu Sayf Yusuf provided copies of some documents of the Popular Democracy group and of the united Communist Party of Egypt. Nawla Darwish gave me access to her father's papers while I was engaged in earlier research on another project. Reflecting on Yusuf Darwish's biography was one of the original stimuli that led to this book. Rif'at al-Sa'id has discussed the history of the Egyptian left with me for over a decade and has periodically shared documents he has acquired. Re'uven Kaminer lent me his large collection of MAKI and MAPAM publications. Shmu'el Amir showed me his papers relating to the formation of the Left Socialist Party and helped me to understand that process. Me'ir Lamm granted me permission to see the MAKI papers deposited at the Kibbutz Me'uhad archive, and Moshe Felzenstein and other members of the staff allowed me to use the papers even though they were not fully sorted and cataloged at the time. No'am Kaminer and Asher Davidi were especially helpful at the Lavon Institute for Labor Research. The staff at the Hashomer Hatza'ir archive in Giv'at Haviva was friendly and always invited me to share coffee and cookies with them at break time, despite their apprehension that I might be a "hostile witness," as one of them put it.

Research for this book was supported by grants from the American Research Center in Egypt, the National Endowment for the Humanities, the Pew Foundation, and the Stanford University Department of History. The first draft was composed while I was a fellow at the Stanford Humanities Center. The Center's previous director and associate director, W. Bliss Carnochan and Morton Sosna, presided over an extraordinary institution that provided a congenial and supportive atmosphere for thinking and writing.

Benjamin Beinin, Estelle Freedman, Barbara Harlow, Re'uven Kaminer, Zachary Lockman, Timothy Mitchell, Richard Roberts, Michael Shalev, and Mohamed Sid-Ahmed read and commented on all or parts of drafts of this book. Amos Funkenstein kindly offered to read the final draft. He expressed both his generous appreciation and penetrating criticism in an intense and stimulating conversation that I will long remember. The comments of an anonymous reviewer for the University of California Press and of the editorial committee were also helpful. Lynne Withey, Mary Lamprech, and Anne Geissman Canright of the University of California Press were humane, supportive, and efficient while rendering exemplary editorial assistance. Zachary Lockman's friendship and intellectual acumen have become so central to my consciousness that it is difficult to imagine functioning without them. One of my first oral presentations on the communist movement in Egypt was to an expanded meeting of the editorial committee of *Middle East Report*. Hanna Batatu, Rashid Khalidi, and others disagreed with me vigorously on that occasion, but stimulated me to continue thinking about the questions that were raised.

My wife, Miriam, shared with me many of the life experiences in Israel and Egypt that made it possible and necessary to write this book. She has provided companionship and support without which it would have been impossible to complete this work. My son, Jamie, accompanied me on a research trip to Israel and so gave me the opportunity to see it anew from a child's perspective.

It has been challenging to write a book while standing both with and against its subjects. Many of those I have written about are longtime friends, parents of friends, friends of friends, or friends of parents; and my own past is closely entangled with the subject of this book. Writing it has been my way of sorting matters out. No one who has helped me along the way shares responsibility for my errors or conclusions unless they choose to.

CHAPTER I

Introduction

This book is an attempt to reconceptualize the history of the Palestinian/Arab–Israeli conflict through the lens of the history of Marxist politics. The purpose for doing so is to examine the process by which the hegemony of nationalist politics was established and to affirm the historic existence of an alternative politics while analyzing the causes of its failure. Three Marxist political formations in Egypt and Israel are treated comparatively and relationally: the communist movement of Egypt (primarily its three major tendencies); the Communist Party of Israel (MAKI); and the United Workers' Party of Israel (MAPAM), which attempted, but ultimately failed, to sustain a dual commitment to Marxism and Zionism.

Both before and after the 1948–49 Arab-Israeli war these political formations advocated a peaceful resolution of the Palestine question and the Arab-Israeli dispute on the basis envisioned by the United Nations partition plan of November 1947: recognition of the right to self-determination of both the Palestinian Arab and Jewish peoples, formation of an Arab and a Jewish state in Palestine/Eretz Israel, and peace based on mutual recognition between Israel and the Arab states. As a hegemonic nationalist political discourse was consolidated in both countries in the mid-1950s the Marxists began to modify their original stands to varying degrees. By the mid-1960s the Marxist parties had failed to persuade the people of either Egypt or Israel to adopt their approach to the Palestinian/Arab–Israeli conflict, yet their positions still placed them beyond the boundaries of the prevailing national consensus. As a consequence of their isolation they gradually abandoned their distinctive internationalist opposition to the hegemonic nationalist discourse, and ultimately their organizational integrity as well. In 1965 the two Egyptian communist parties dissolved themselves and instructed their members to join the party of the Nasserist regime, the Arab Socialist Union. MAKI split into exclusively Jewish and mainly Arab components: MAKI and the New Communist List (RAKAH). Jewish MAKI adopted a Zionist outlook and eventually dissolved. RAKAH continued to be a fundamentally oppositional force in Israeli politics, and has recently reclaimed the MAKI name. But because it was increasingly identified as an Arab party, it became isolated on the margins of Israeli politics. MAPAM ceased to be an opposition party posing an alternative to the Zionist consensus when it joined the coalition government led by the Israel Workers' Party (MAPAI) in 1955 and retroactively approved the 1956 war.

Because the Arab-Israeli conflict became the salient issue in national politics in both Egypt and Israel by the mid-1950s, the Marxists' stand on this issue provides an entry point into the broader question of the role of the Marxist parties in a political arena shaped by a nationalist struggle. Eric Hobsbawm has written that communist parties, the predominant organizational form of the international socialist movement from 1917 until relatively recently, were the children "of the marriage of two ill-assorted partners, a national left and the October revolution."[1] In the Middle East and other parts of the world colonized by European powers, the left was not only national, but also strongly nationalist. Marxism became a political force as a component of the anticolonial national liberation movement in the post–World War II period.

As Henri Curiel, founder of the Egyptian Movement for National Liberation (EMNL), said, "If the salvos of October brought Marxism to China (according to Mao), those of Stalingrad brought it to Egypt."[2] Marxist political action was critical in mobilizing and radicalizing the postwar Egyptian nationalist movement. Consequently, the Marxist conception of imperialism gained widespread currency among the intelligentsia, and organized labor became a highly visible component of the nationalist upsurge. Yet because Marxism never became socially or organizationally consolidated, the Free Officers were eventually able to assume leadership of the nationalist movement—a role that the Marxists thought was destined for them. The military regime eventually suppressed the Marxist organizations while nominally adopting many of their slogans and programs.

In the Palestinian Arab community, with the salvos of Stalingrad resounding in the background, the new national orientation of the Palestinian communists and their critique of the leadership of the Palestinian national movement, whose traditionalist politics of notables was exposed as ineffectual with the defeat of the Arab Revolt of 1936–39, made Marxism a significant social and political force for the first time.

The salvos of October originally brought Marxism to the Jewish community (*yishuv*) in Palestine and strongly influenced labor Zionism—the hegemonic tendency in the Zionist movement from the 1930s to the 1970s. Within labor Zionism, the largest current was MAPAI—precursor to the Labor Party. Although MAPAI's leader, David Ben-Gurion, had flirted with Marxism early in his career, long before the party's organizational consolidation he had adopted an anti-Marxist, reformist, social democratic outlook that explicitly subordinated class struggle to the necessity of maintaining an alliance with wealthy Jews outside Palestine and with the British (and later the U.S.) government to realize Zionist objectives. MAPAI's historic, and until 1965 successful, opposition to Arab membership in the Histadrut (the General Federation of Hebrew Workers in the Land of Israel), in which it was by far the largest party, was a salient expression of its rejection of the traditional Marxist-internationalist approach to resolving the Palestinian-Zionist conflict on a working-class basis.

The component elements of MAPAM did consider themselves Marxist and were nonetheless given organizational and financial resources and land to settle on by the World Zionist Organization and the Jewish Agency. Within the labor Zionist movement, then, kibbutzim, trade unions, workers' culture, and of course socialism and class struggle were conceptualized in Marxist and non-Marxist variants—and not always with a sharp distinction between them. Consequently, Marxist ideas were not alien or illegitimate per se within the *yishuv*, especially after the Soviet Union supported the UN partition plan. In addition, the antifascist struggles of the European communist parties in the 1930s and the Soviet Union's heroic role in defeating Nazism brought the Palestine Communist Party (PCP) out of isolation, created widespread sympathy for the Soviet Union, convinced many in the *yishuv* that Marxism was the most consistently antifascist world outlook, and radicalized the Jewish working class in both the kibbutzim and the cities. The hegemonic status of labor Zionism, the prominence of MAPAM, and the short-lived legitimacy enjoyed by the Communist Party led many local and foreign observers of Israeli politics immediately after the formation of the state to conclude that the Jewish working class might adopt a revolutionary perspective and become the vanguard of socialist revolution in the entire Middle East.[3]

In contrast to the post-1967 balance of political forces, during the late mandate and early statehood years of Israel the components of Marxist MAPAM were a far more important factor in the political arena than Yitzhak Shamir's LEHI (Fighters for the Freedom of Israel) or Menahem Begin's ETZEL (National Military Organization), which were shunned as terrorist secessionists from the national consensus by many (but not all) liberal and labor Zionists. Ben-Gurion adamantly refused to consider admitting the Herut (Freedom) Party that Begin established after the dissolution of the ETZEL to any government coalition. Begin joined a government for the first time only on the eve of the 1967 war. The centrist General Zionists (later the Liberals) and the religious parties were significant before 1967 mainly because they had considerable support among American Zionists and because Ben-Gurion preferred them to MAPAM as government coalition partners. That an alliance of the Likud (with the historic Herut as its central component) and the orthodox Jewish religious parties could become the dominant force in Israeli politics, as was the case in the 1970s and 1980s, appeared inconceivable before 1967.

Thus, in both Egypt and Israel after World War II the Marxists sought to situate themselves within the nationalist movement but were too weak to lead that movement. Many Marxist ideas became popularized beyond the ranks of the Marxist parties, but non-Marxist socialists representing a broad alliance of class forces became the dominant force in the nationalist movements. This situation was fundamentally due to the structural characteristics of the working class and its relationship with other classes in the nationalist alliance. In Egypt, the working class was small and politically undeveloped; in Israel, although it was large and organized in a sophisticated complex of institutions, it was also organically dependent on capital.

While it is impossible to write the history of any national communist movement without taking into consideration the leading role of the Soviet Union in the international movement and other international determinants, this book emphasizes the indigenous national factors in the rise and decline of Marxist politics in Egypt and Israel. The particular conjuncture of the rise of the anticolonialist, anti-imperialist movements of the third world, the baroque excesses of late Stalinism, and the cold war have made it especially difficult to disentangle the national and international components of Marxism in the Middle East. Most commonly, the communist parties have been regarded as functions of Soviet foreign policy, and little attention has been given to the indigenous social forces that made them important actors in the national political arena despite the generally small size of their membership.[4] Moreover, the Marxists' commitment to internationalism in opposition to the dominant nationalist orientation in Egypt and Israel has been regarded as an unnatural suppression of the "real" nationalist impulses of the party members, imposed on them by the requirements of Soviet policy or other temporary tactical considerations.[5]

In addition, as part of the common legacy of the economist and reductionist Marxism of the second and third internationals, the Marxist parties themselves had an inadequate understanding of nationalism and its political power. Basing themselves on the writings of Stalin and Mao, they had an instrumental view of national liberation struggles as a necessary preliminary stage that would inevitably be superseded by the politics of class struggle. Therefore, the Marxists shared and legitimized a nationalist political discourse without realizing that by doing so they were participating in creating the conditions for the delegitimization of their own internationalist and class-based political project.

To summarize the argument, it was primarily the internal structure of the Zionist movement and the Israeli state it established on the one hand and the nationalist, anti-imperialist class alliance forged by Gamal Abdel Nasser on the other that marginalized Marxist politics and thus the Marxist approach to the Palestinian Arab–Israeli conflict. Moreover, the Marxists were to a certain extent complicit in the processes that led to their failure, and this was reflected in their ideological and theoretical conceptualizations as well as the social composition of the parties and the relations between their different class and ethnic components. This analysis is neither a historic indictment of the Marxist political formations nor a self-righteous critique of ideological "errors" that, if "rectified," would have led to success. It is simply an argument that Marxist political movements are the product of the history that they themselves sought to understand and shape, and that they can be properly understood only in that context.

COMPARING EGYPT AND ISRAEL

It may seem odd to treat Egypt and Israel in the same analytical framework, because at first glance their political systems, cultures, and historical trajectories seem quite different. This book does not compare the two countries and their Marxist political formations along fixed axes. Zionism and Arab nationalism cannot be treated symmetrically because of their fundamentally dissimilar relations to the Western imperial powers that have dominated the Middle East. Therefore, this is an effort to construct what Perry Anderson has called a "relational history": a history that "studies the incidence—reciprocal or asymmetrical—of different national or territorial units and cultures on each other."[6] Despite the lack of symmetry between Egypt and Israel, the processes by which nationalist ideologies became the hegemonic political discourse in the two countries were both similar and dialectically related. This suggests that the fates of the Egyptian and Israeli Marxists were, to some degree, interrelated and bounded by the same historical forces.

But why compare the Marxists in Egypt and Israel? There were also communist movements in Syria, Lebanon, Iraq, and Jordan that in large part shared the world outlook of the Israeli Marxists. While the Syrian-Lebanese and Israeli communists had little contact after 1948, the Iraqis and Jordanians were linked to the Palestinians and Israelis in ways that might invite a relational analysis. The Communist Party of Iraq, like the communist movement in Egypt, had a disproportionately large number of Jewish members, many of whom joined MAKI after immigrating to Israel in 1950–51. The Communist Party of Jordan was founded in 1951 by Palestinian Arabs, and most of its supporters until 1967 were residents of the West Bank—former Palestinian territory occupied by Jordan that according to the UN partition plan was to have become part of the Palestinian Arab state. But only the Egyptian communists attempted to maintain contact with their Israeli counterparts, even though this was most often done problematically and indirectly through Henri Curiel and the group of Egyptian-Jewish communist émigrés he led in Paris.

Perhaps more importantly, until the signing of the Egyptian-Israeli peace treaty in 1979, Egypt was Israel's most formidable Arab adversary. Before the establishment of the Palestine Liberation Organization (PLO) in 1964 and its reorganization after 1967, autonomous Palestinian action in the conflict with Israel was often intentionally eclipsed by the role of the Arab states. Consequently, Israel and Egypt were considered the two primary actors in the conflict. For these reasons, I have chosen to concentrate on the Marxists in these two countries, although I do briefly mention the communist parties in other Arab countries when appropriate.

REVISIONIST HISTORY OF THE ARAB-ISRAELI CONFLICT

The account of the origins, causes, and issues at stake in the Palestinian/Arab–Israeli conflict that the Marxist parties shared was shaped by entirely different terms of reference from those prevalent in their societies. During the 1930s the PCP had adopted an Arab-centered approach that explained the Arab-Jewish conflict in Palestine as one between an indigenous and a settler-colonial population. This approach lingered on in the Palestinian Arab National Liberation League (NLL) and the Egyptian New Dawn group. By 1947–48, though, the Marxists adopted the view that the tensions between Arabs and Jews in Palestine were instigated by British imperialists as a divide-and-rule tactic that would allow Britain to continue occupying the country. While some incidents in the history of the Palestine mandate do support this thesis, essentially it was a functional myth that allowed the Marxists to organize and act in the belief that there were no contradictions between the "real" national interests of both peoples and that any apparent contradictions could be resolved by uniting against the common imperialist enemy. Other components of the Marxist account have a much more solidly supported historical foundation.

The Palestinian Arabs, of course, have always told a story about the history of their conflict with Israel that is different from the Zionist version most commonly known in the West, but it has, until recently, been largely ignored. Research in the Israel State Archives and other public and private Israeli archives conducted in the last decade, mainly by Israelis, has decisively debunked many components of the Zionist and, to a lesser extent, Arab nationalist mythologies.[7] Unfortunately, neither the Egyptian nor any other Arab government has made materials on the post–World War II period in its national archive available for historical research. As a consequence, the focus of revisionist historical work has been on Israel and its actions.

Among the Israeli revisionist historians, Simha Flapan adopted the most comprehensive and intentionally provocative approach by attempting to refute seven foundation myths about the birth of Israel that have been central to Zionist historiography—namely, that (1) the Zionists accepted the UN partition plan and planned for peace; (2) the Arabs rejected partition and launched war; (3) the Palestinians fled voluntarily; (4) all the Arab states united to expel the Jews from Palestine; (5) the Arab invasion made war inevitable; (6) Israel faced militarily superior Arab forces in the 1948–49 war; and (7) Israel has always sought peace, but no Arab leader has reciprocated.[8] Flapan's work is weakest on issues related to Arab political intentions and the Arab military campaign against Israel; nevertheless, detailed and profusely documented studies by Benny Morris and Avi Shlaim have corroborated many of Flapan's arguments, especially those relating to Israel's intention to avoid fully implementing the UN partition plan, the expulsion of the Arab population, and the willingness of some Arab states to avoid war and to conclude a peace with Israel.[9]

In Zionist discourse the function of the myths Flapan criticized is to represent the central issue of the dispute as Israel's consistent desire for peace counterposed to "the Arabs'" refusal to recognize Israel's "right to exist." If this characterization is correct, then by definition all of Israel's military actions against the Palestinians and Arab states have the status of legitimate self-defense. For the Marxists, the core of the dispute is that the Jewish people realized its right to national self-determination by establishing the state of Israel, whereas as a result of collusion between Israel and Transjordan and the complicity of Britain and later the United States, the Palestinian Arab people's right to self-determination was not realized. Moreover, Israel and pro-Western Arab states, especially Jordan, have continually obstructed Palestinian Arab self-determination since 1948.

Those Palestinians who remained in Israel were, according to the Zionist consensus, a potential fifth column that had to be carefully supervised, and Israel undertook this task with as much regard for democratic norms as was compatible with its legitimate security considerations. For the Marxists, in contrast, the Palestinian citizens of Israel are an oppressed national minority whose livelihood and political rights were despoiled by the Israeli state. Sabri Jiryis's classic account of the expropriation and oppression of Israel's Palestinian Arab citizens first appeared in Hebrew in 1966.[10] By then the Israeli public was largely unconcerned with this issue; a common critical response to the book was to dismiss Jiryis as an ultranationalist extremist ungrateful for the legal education he received at the Hebrew University. Moreover, since the first English edition was published by the PLO after Jiryis left Israel and became an advisor to Yasir Arafat, his book was not given widespread international credibility. It was subsequently "balanced" by a scholarly apology for Israel's treatment of its Palestinian Arab citizens bearing the same title.[11] More than a decade later, studies by Elia Zureik, Ian Lustick, and Charles Kamen substantially confirmed and elaborated on Jiryis's story and made it more widely known and accepted.[12]

Both Zionist and Arab nationalist historiography have cherished the myth that the Arab states have invariably presented a solid front against Israel, rejecting Israel's offers to resolve the conflict peacefully. But as Flapan and Shlaim have shown, Jordan colluded with Israel before and after the 1948–49 war to prevent the emergence of a Palestinian Arab state, and Syria was briefly prepared to consider signing a peace treaty terminating the state of war in 1949. Although there was a substantial gap between Israeli and Egyptian views of the conflict and the basis on which it might be resolved, Egypt did not pursue a policy of unmitigated hostility to Israel that led inevitably to the "second round" of 1956.[13] Although still no comprehensive study continues the revisionist line of argument into the 1950s and many critical documents for this period remain classified, more than enough is known to establish the framework for an alternative historical narrative.

During the years between the first two Arab-Israeli wars, Israel's borders, the status of the Palestinian refugees and their political future, and Israel's relations with its Arab neighbors were unfixed and widely perceived as susceptible to revision. The armistice agreements signed between Israel and its Arab neighbors in early 1949 did not establish recognized international frontiers. In particular, Egypt rejected Israel's claims to the Negev because Israel occupied the region after unilaterally breaking a cease-fire on October 15, 1948. UN Security Council resolutions of November 4 and November 16, 1948, ordered both armies back to the positions they occupied on October 14, but were unheeded. On December 11, the General Assembly reiterated this call and also directed Israel to repatriate the Palestinian refugees. In April 1949 the UN Conciliation Commission for Palestine convened the Lausanne Conference in an attempt to reach a negotiated end to the conflict. There Israel briefly agreed, under pressure from the United States, to the return of one hundred thousand refugees. This offer was dropped and never made again when it became clear that the Arab states would not, in exchange, recognize Israel's territorial gains during the war and relinquish the principle that all the refugees had a right to return to their homes. Thereafter, the official Israeli stand was, "Not one refugee shall return."

Despite the diplomatic impasse at Lausanne, during the early 1950s a monolithic and intransigent view of the conflict did not prevail unchallenged in either Israel or Egypt. From 1948 to 1956 the two countries engaged in extensive diplomatic exchanges, which included talks between the Israeli and Egyptian ambassadors to the UN in 1951 and

1952; regular contacts between diplomats in European capitals, especially Paris, through 1955; an exchange of letters and an effort to convene a meeting between Moshe Sharett and Gamal Abdel Nasser in late 1953; and mediation efforts by third parties including British Labour M.P. Maurice Orbach in 1954, Elmore Jackson of the American Friends Service Committee in 1955, U.S. presidential envoy Robert Anderson in 1955–56, and Maltese Labor Party leader Dom Mintoff in 1956.

Before and after the military coup of July 23, 1952, Egyptian government officials, political leaders, and public figures issued many statements suggesting that a peaceful resolution to the conflict and coexistence with Israel were possible and desirable, though official statements were often oblique and contradictory.[14] Yet no Egyptian or Arab leader ever publicly accepted either the validity of Israeli territorial gains beyond the borders allotted by the UN partition plan or the notion, virtually a self-evident truth in Israel by the early 1950s, that Palestinians who had fled or been expelled during the 1948–49 war had forfeited their rights to their homes and lands.

Publication of Moshe Sharett's personal diaries revealed that the faction of MAPAI led by Prime Minister David Ben-Gurion and his young lieutenants—prominent among whom were Moshe Dayan, chief-of-staff of the Israel Defense Forces (IDF) from 1954 to 1957, and Shimon Peres, director-general of the Ministry of Defense in the 1950s and architect of the Israeli-French alliance—consistently exacerbated military tensions on Israel's borders and avoided opportunities for negotiations with Arab states in which Israel might be expected to concede territory or repatriate a significant number of Palestinian refugees. They developed the politico-military doctrine of activism: a policy of preemptive strikes, massive retaliation, and creating "facts." Repeated demonstration of Israel's decisive military superiority, they believed, would force Arab recognition of Israel on Israeli terms; if not, it would create possibilities for Israeli territorial expansion.

Security became a national cult in Israel after 1948. Ben-Gurion made the IDF the central institution of the state and consolidated his control over it by occupying the premiership and the ministry of defense and eliminating all potential rival sources of authority.[15] In November 1948, even before the end of the war for Israel's independence, he disbanded the elite Palmah unit of the prestate era because he distrusted its MAPAM-dominated officer corps. By 1950 most MAPAM members in the senior echelons of the officer corps were pushed out of the IDF. Ben-Gurion promoted his young activist protégés to central positions in the security establishment.

Unit 101, an unorthodox commando company created to conduct reprisal raids for violations of Israel's borders under the command of Ariel Sharon, was the symbol of activist ascendancy. In the early 1950s thousands of Palestinian refugees infiltrated into Israel. Some came to see their families or recover their property; some committed acts of sabotage and terror. Frustrated by its inability to stop infiltrations, the IDF established Unit 101 in August 1953. The unit attacked targets unrelated to the source of border violations and inflicted casualties on innocent civilians far out of proportion to those suffered by Israel. Although most infiltrators came from Jordan, reprisals were also directed against Egypt in order to weaken the regime of Israel's most formidable Arab adversary.[16] Unit 101's inaugural action was a raid on the Palestinian refugee camp of al-Burayj in the Gaza Strip, in which nineteen refugees were killed—including seven women and four children—and eighteen wounded.[17] On October 14, Unit 101 attacked the West Bank village of Qibya, killing fifty-three civilians, wounding fifteen, and blowing up forty homes in retaliation for the murder of an Israeli woman and her two children. Ben-Gurion announced on Israeli radio that the raid, described by the head of the UN Mixed Armistice Commission as "wanton destruction" and an "atrocity," had been carried out by outraged civilian vigilantes, "mostly Jewish refugees from Arab countries or survivors of Nazi concentration camps," and not the IDF. Subsequently the IDF proudly took responsibility for the action.[18] In the aftermath of Qibya Ben-Gurion resigned his post as prime minister, to be replaced by Moshe Sharett.

The members of Unit 101 became Israel's new culture heroes, and the unit's "successes" encouraged a reckless mentality in military circles. As a result, in July 1954 a group of Egyptian Jews previously organized as an Israeli spy ring was ordered to bomb British and American institutions in Egypt. The objective was to convince the British government that Egypt was an unstable radical nationalist state and that British forces therefore ought not to be withdrawn from the Suez Canal Zone. The amateurish bombers were quickly apprehended and put on trial, with Israel denying any connection to the group. In fact, Sharett did not know of the order to initiate acts of terror. Israel denounced the trial of the terrorists and subsequent execution of two of them as a "show trial." The Histadrut daily, *Davar* (The word), called it a "Nazi-inspired policy." In the midst of this hysteria, Ben-Gurion was recalled to the government as minister of defense. His response to the executions was to order a massive attack on Gaza on February 28, 1955, in which thirty-nine Egyptians and Palestinians were killed and thirty wounded. This raid began the sequence of events that culminated in the Suez/Sinai War.[19]

In 1960, the revelation of the likelihood that a Ben-Gurion protégé, military intelligence chief Binyamin Givli, possibly with the approval of Dayan, Peres, or others close to Ben-Gurion, had given the order to activate the ring of Jewish saboteurs in Egypt without the approval of Sharett or Defense Minister Pinhas Lavon broke a major political scandal in Israel. It became known as the "Lavon affair" after Ben-Gurion attempted to force Lavon to accept sole responsibility for the incident. This affair brought down the Israeli government in 1961, undermined Ben-Gurion's political authority, and contributed to his removal as prime minister and replacement by Levi Eshkol in 1963.[20]

Ben-Gurion understood, as no other Zionist political leader did, that the capacity to deploy a powerful recognized army would immeasurably strengthen the Zionist project, transform the balance of forces between the *yishuv* and its Arab neighbors, and allow Israel to shape the political agenda. The existence of an all-encompassing conflict with undifferentiated Arab "others" was the formative experience for the Israeli polity, determining its collective identity and international orientation and contributing significantly to its economic viability. The persistent creation of political and military facts heightened the conflict, gradually undermined the Israeli peace constituency, and legitimized the official Israeli conception of peace as a condition in which Israel maintained absolute military supremacy over its neighbors and the right to veto any regional developments it defined as threatening. In this context the Zionist project continued to develop as a set of economic, political, and military practices and a discourse consolidating its interpretive power even as the Arab-Israeli conflict was transformed from a local communal conflict to a regional front in the cold war.

Lack of documentation makes it increasingly difficult to extend the revisionist account of Arab-Israeli relations beyond the 1956 war. But this lacuna is not critical to the argument of this book if the thesis (articulated in great detail by Kennett Love and Donald Neff)[21] that the events of 1955 and the Suez/Sinai War constitute a critical turning point in determining the future course and scope of the Arab-Israeli conflict is valid, as I believe it is.

Israeli representation of Arab refusal to accept its territorial conquests and the permanent displacement of the refugees as unmitigated hostility has been reinforced in the West by a combination of a guilty conscience about the victims of the holocaust, Christian millenarianism, fear of Nasserist Arab nationalism, the political influence of the Zionist lobby in the United States, and a growing American commitment to the notion that Israel was an irreplaceable "strategic asset" vital to maintaining U.S. power and influence in the Middle East. Consequently, the official Israeli story became the hegemonic interpretation of the conflict in the United States and Europe as well as in Israel.

It is impossible to make sense of the historical trajectory of the Marxist left and the issues that occupied it without referring to the revisionist history of the Palestinian/Arab–Israeli conflict summarized above. Indeed, two members of MAKI, Moshe Machover and Akiva Orr, made a pioneering contribution to this historiographical project—for which they have not received due recognition—by compiling an account of the conflict from Israeli newspapers and other published Hebrew sources that, while not free of flaws, shares much with the growing body of literature by professional historians and others.[22] While I have relied on the revisionist historiography and the outline extrapolated from it above, I have not recapitulated all the evidence for the arguments. Those who wish to pursue specific issues more fully may study the works cited in the notes and the documentary sources on which they are based.

The main thrust of revisionist historiography has been to shift the burden of responsibility for the Palestinian Arab–Israeli conflict much more toward the Israeli side than has commonly been accepted in either Israel or the West. Within this framework it is also possible to indicate some themes that may challenge the prevailing consensus of nationalist Egyptian historiography regarding Egypt's approach to the conflict, although here the documentary evidence is even scantier than for Israel. The most important of these themes would be the point previously mentioned: that Egypt was not unequivocally and consistently hostile to Israel from 1949 to 1956, and certainly not to its existence as a state—although Israel's borders were, for Egypt, a matter of dispute.

While the vast majority of Egyptians who had an opinion on the matter felt that establishing the state of Israel constituted an injustice toward the Palestinian people, popular Egyptian sympathy for the Palestinians rarely pressured governments to adopt strongly anti-Israeli stands. The monarchy shamelessly exploited the Palestine question to enhance its own power and prestige, internally as well as in relation to its Hashemite rivals in the Arab world. Monarchist propagandists misinformed the Egyptian people about the social character of the *yishuv* and the military situation both during and after the 1948–49 war.

Both under the Egyptian monarchy and after July 23, 1952, anti-Zionism was sometimes demagogically commingled with anti-Semitism by the regimes and their mouthpieces. Both regimes absurdly equated Zionism with communism. The Nasser regime did not seek a more serious understanding of the sources of Israel's strength and what this strength might mean for Egypt and the Arab world any more than the old regime did, and thus the Egyptian people's misunderstandings about the nature of Israel and Zionism were perpetuated. Nonetheless, European-style anti-Semitism was little in evidence in Egypt before World War II. Overt discrimination or persecution against the majority of Egyptian Jews, who were neither communists nor Zionists, did not become common until after Israel attacked Egypt in 1956.

Egypt and the Arab world interpreted Israel's extension of its borders beyond the boundaries of the UN partition plan as definitive proof that Zionism was inherently and indefinitely expansionist. How else could all the Jews of the world be resettled in Israel as Zionism sought to do? Certainly, an expansionism does underlie the dominant Zionist ethos. As early as 1937, when the Royal Commission's proposal to partition Palestine was under discussion, Ben-Gurion explained to his son that his support for partition did not mean that he accepted the partition borders as the final boundaries of the Jewish state. Ben-Gurion outlined his elaborate vision, which included a prominent military component and foresaw the ultimate expansion of the Jewish state throughout all of Eretz Israel. As he wrote, "Erect a Jewish state at once, even if it is not in the whole land. The rest will come in the course of time. It must come."[23]

Nonetheless, there were perhaps two moments in Israel's history when territorial expansion had little popular support and was not a major factor in the perspective of its political leadership. During the early 1950s, Israel was too occupied with absorbing the mass immigration and integrating newly acquired territory to consider further expansion. Until the reorientation symbolized by the formation of Unit 101 in 1953, the IDF had a defensive outlook that the activists criticized as defeatist. After the Israeli withdrawal from Sinai and Gaza in 1957, mass immigration slowed down and the economy began a period of rapid expansion that offered the possibility of an improved standard of living for many. Zionist élan declined, and most Jewish Israelis sought "normalcy," including a general satisfaction with the territorial status quo. This spirit prevailed until shortly before the 1967 war.

During these two periods—which are difficult to date precisely because activism and expansionism were never entirely absent from Israeli political culture or subjected to a fundamental critique by their Zionist opponents—it is possible to imagine that a more consistently peace-seeking Egyptian regime less committed to Arab nationalism might have been able to reach an accommodation with Israel similar to the one achieved in 1979. This would not necessarily have meant a resolution of the Palestine question. Indeed, ignoring Palestinian Arab demands would likely have been a necessary condition for Israel's acceptance of any Egyptian-Israeli accommodation, just as it was for negotiating the peace treaty of 1979.

WAS MAPAM A MARXIST PARTY?

Traditionally, Zionism has been regarded by both its adherents and its opponents as an impermeable boundary dividing the Israeli left into, on the one hand, a small and marginalized non- or anti-Zionist fringe (primarily the communists) located beyond the limits of the (Jewish) national consensus and, on the other, the Zionist left, which shared the basic world outlook of the Zionist consensus, participated fully in Israel's national political life, and, consequently, shared responsibility for Zionism's treatment of the Palestinian and Arab peoples.[24] Obviously, there is a clear ideological divide between Zionism and anti-Zionism, and after the 1956 war MAKI and other non-Zionist political forces (such as Uri Avnery's Semitic Action group) clearly did become isolated in Jewish society. But the rigid boundary line between the Zionist and non-Zionist left was, I believe, historically constructed through consolidation of the political hegemony of MAPAI.

During the early 1950s, MAKI and MAPAM voted together in the Knesset on several critical issues, cooperated in organizations like the Israel Peace Council and the Israel–Soviet Union Friendship League, and occasionally organized joint demonstrations around working-class economic demands and other issues. On several occasions members of one party resigned or were expelled and joined the other. At least until the Slansky trial in 1952 and the expulsion of Moshe Sneh and the Left Section, MAPAM regarded itself as a loyal member of the international socialist camp headed by the Soviet Union. Indeed, MAPAM leader Ya'akov Hazan once announced in the Knesset that the Soviet Union was "the second homeland of the Jewish people."[25] While MAPAM always acknowledged its difference with the Soviet bloc and the international communist movement on the question of Zionism, many party members devoted great energy to expressing this difference in the most minimal form possible. Ben-Gurion often regarded MAKI and MAPAM in the same light and polemicized against them in a similar fashion.[26] Since the emergence of mass movements opposing Israel's invasion of Lebanon in 1982 and its repression of the Palestinian *intifada*, the tactical-political boundary between the Zionist and non-Zionist left has once again become less sharply delineated, suggesting even more strongly the need to historicize the conditions in which it did become an inviolable divide.

MAPAM's Marxism can be questioned in another sense. The party was founded as a coalition of forces, including elements who regarded themselves as revolutionary Marxist-Leninists differing with the international communist movement only on the Jewish national question (Zionism), as well as other components who considered themselves Marxist, had a strongly pro-Soviet international orientation, but rejected Leninism as a party organizational principle and allowed themselves a wider latitude for dissent from the line of the Soviet Union and the international communist movement. The orthodox Marxist-Leninists were an important minority in MAPAM and prominent among its public spokespersons and professional organizers, though they were never able to impose their line on the entire party.

In Egypt, the Democratic Movement for National Liberation (DMNL) and the New Dawn group, although they had no ideological differences with the international communist movement, did not officially organize themselves as communist parties until 1955 and 1957, respectively. Their radical nationalist strategy and unorthodox organizational practices made them suspect among many of their sister parties, especially the Communist Party of France. Thus, both countries had pro-Soviet Marxist parties that did not precisely fit the mold shaped by the Comintern's twenty-one conditions.

Marxism is a historically formed social and political movement broader than the particular organizational form that the Comintern sought to impose and not a reified demon emanating from the Soviet Union. A history of Marxism as a political movement should, therefore, consider actually existing parties and not disregard those that diverge slightly from the orthodox model. I will therefore treat MAPAM as a Marxist party and try to demonstrate that its decline was the result of the same forces that led to the communists' decline, although MAPAM's Zionist commitments made it more readily susceptible to those forces.

Introduction

NATIONS, THE CONSTRUCTION OF HEGEMONY, AND POLITICAL DISCOURSE

I have referred to a hegemonic nationalist political discourse in both Egypt and Israel and will continue to use this concept, so let me clarify what I mean by it. Benedict Anderson has described nations as "imagined communities."[27] They must be constructed and reproduced by both social relations and institutions that operate within, and thus reinforce, national boundaries and discursive practices that interpret cultural and political phenomena, past and present, in a national framework. Individuals and collectives must be made to feel part of the nation by receiving material as well as spiritual sustenance from it. I consider the material components of the construction and reproduction of national communities in Egypt and Israel in three analytical categories: the political economy; the military dynamics of the Arab-Israeli conflict, including the social role of the army; and international orientation. Social relations, social institutions, and the social forces whose interests they serve can best be understood by using the tools of political economy and class analysis, which is the approach I have adopted in discussing these matters.

Although I believe that the interpretive order that sustains national consciousness is bounded by material conditions, it is not automatically derived from the character of the economic relations within a national community. Antonio Gramsci has argued that ruling classes do not simply coerce subaltern social groups into accepting the prevailing regime; rather, subaltern groups regard regimes as legitimate because their power is reinforced throughout civil society by educational and cultural norms, and especially by the activity of the organic intellectuals who articulate and elaborate the interests of a given class within the context of the national culture. For Gramsci, hegemony is established through the noncoercive components of class rule. These components have an autonomous life and do not simply reflect class relations and economic interests, but neither can they be detached from them. It is in this sense that I use the term *hegemony*, although I extend the application to relations between dominant and subaltern national communities, specifically to the relations between Jews and Arabs in Palestine/Israel and to relations between Arabs and Jews within the pan-Arab national community.

Gramsci attributed great import to the particularities of Italian national history and culture in analyzing the historical construction of the hegemony of its ruling class. His example has nourished a current in Marxist theory that has continued to emphasize the specific national context of Marxist political movements despite the internationalist commitments of the Marxist world outlook. To understand the hold that nationalist political ideas maintain over people without resorting to coercion and the role of these ideas in configuring the limits of possible political alternatives, it is necessary to analyze the structure of the interpretive order that reproduces a particular national representation of historical and current events.

Gareth Stedman Jones has argued that the language of politics can determine the range of options that social movements will regard as available to them.[28] Anyone who has engaged in more than occasional discussions with Zionists and Palestinian nationalists about the Arab-Israeli conflict will know that the two parties frequently do not share the same interpretive framework and that language is a powerful marker delineating what can and cannot be conceptualized in each camp. The two sides do not even agree on whether the territory in dispute is called Palestine or Eretz Israel. This is what I mean by a political discourse: a structured framework of interpretation embedded in a matrix of social power that culturally limits how issues are conceptualized, defines what options can be regarded as legitimate, and, in the case of a nationalist political discourse, reinforces the boundary markers separating one national community from another.

The Marxism of the second and third internationals did not take nationalism and national political culture seriously, even though both internationals were ultimately undermined by nationalism in different ways. Nations were acknowledged to exist, and Stalin even developed a definition of a nation that was dutifully reproduced on almost all occasions when "the national question" was discussed. But most Marxists did not regard nations and nationalism as "real" because of their belief that national liberation struggles were a stage on the road to proletarian revolution, that "the proletariat has no country," and that proletarian internationalism was based on a firmer, more material reality than nationalism. As a result, Marxists typically had an instrumental approach to nationalism and did not recognize the autonomous power of nationalist politics.

In opposition to this view I wish to suggest that political discourse is more than a tactical question. Persistent use of nationalist imagery and language ultimately contributes to erecting a barrier to internationalism. As a component of hegemony, a political discourse, if it is not fundamentally challenged in an organized public manner over a protracted period of time, can become an autonomous force that impedes the articulation of an alternative politics. It was not simply because the Egyptian and Israeli Marxists used the wrong language that they became marginalized in the political debate over the Palestinian/Arab–Israeli conflict, of course. But by examining political discourse we may demonstrate to just what extent the Marxists were formed by their national environments and functioned within their boundaries. Consequently, the line of demarcation between hegemonic and counter-hegemonic political projects was not always as clear as many on both sides of the divide imagined it to be.

STRUCTURE OF THE BOOK

Chapter 2 recapitulates the political reorientation of the Marxists and their decision to support the UN plan for the partition of Palestine. This story is relatively well known, and on many points I have relied on the work of others. My intention in retelling it is to draw a baseline defining the position common to the great majority of the Marxists in Egypt and Israel (and most of the Arab world) and to emphasize the general concordance of this position with the international consensus on the appropriate resolution to the Palestine question. This background permits us to appreciate the magnitude of the political and strategic realignments created by the 1948–49 Arab-Israeli war and the emergence of Israel; we can then examine how this new geopolitical fact decisively altered the terms of discourse about the conflict, enabling the Zionist consensus to establish its hegemony in Israel and the West while Arab opinion, which by the early 1950s was actually closer to the international consensus of 1947–48 than was the position of the Israeli government, was delegitimized and largely ignored.

The historical survey of the political economy of Egypt and Israel in Chapter 3 demonstrates how the ruling-class alliances in each country weakened the social base for Marxist politics, thus diminishing the capacity of the Marxist parties to advance their program for resolution of the Arab-Israeli conflict. In addition, the international orientation of the two countries was primarily a result of their internal social structures. Chapter 4 argues that from 1949 to 1955 the Marxists remained a viable political force and even increased their strength; moreover, while admittedly realistic chances to resolve the conflict during this period were remote, the Suez/Sinai War of 1956 was not the inevitable consequence of unmitigated Arab hostility to Israel. As Chapter 5 relates, Egyptian and Israeli Marxists were in contact with each other during these years, though the role of Henri Curiel and his comrades in this activity was the subject of much contention and recrimination among Egyptian communists.

Chapter 6 contends that only after the 1956 war were hegemonic nationalist discourses consolidated in both Egypt and Israel. Consequently, MAKI was isolated in Israel (though it maintained and even sharpened its opposition to prevailing government policies on the Arab-Israeli conflict), while MAPAM abandoned its effort to constitute a radical alternative to the activist politico-military conception. The Egyptian communists were crippled by their support for a regime that sharply controlled their freedom of action. Chapter 7 relates the denouement of Egyptian and Israeli communism in the final years before the dissolution of the Egyptian parties and the split in MAKI.

There are certain structural imbalances in the following narrative that result from the character of the political formations under consideration and their documentary legacy. Since MAPAM was not a Leninist party operating on the principles of democratic centralism, its leaders often publicly disagreed with each other. In addition, despite important lacunae, the Hashomer Hatzaʿir archive at Givʿat Haviva is rich in evidence relating to inner-party struggles. All political movements are defined by a tension among ideology, political strategy, and social practice. MAPAM's intimate links to a network of economic and social institutions—the kibbutzim—made disaggregation of these components much easier for MAPAM than for the communist parties, whose material resources and social base were much weaker. Moreover, the communist parties by their nature sought to obscure all public signs of internal disagreement. It seems, for instance, that any record of inner-party debate was removed or never included in the MAKI papers deposited at Yad Tabenkin, the Kibbutz Meʾuhad archive in Efal. Shmuʾel Mikunis's papers at the Lavon Institute for Labor Research in Tel Aviv do contain his personal record of the inner-party struggle in the highest bodies of MAKI, but only from 1961 on.

The documentary record of the Egyptian communist movement is sparse. The papers of Henri Curiel in Paris are the only collection of internal party records available, and their value is attenuated by distance from Egypt and the fact that only Curiel's letters to Egypt and no letters from Egypt to Paris are preserved. I have relied heavily on interviews with former leading members of the Egyptian communist movement to reconstruct its history, with the full knowledge that members of rival historic factions "remember" events and debates differently. Conflicting recollections were weighed and collated with written records when available, but the result is an account that is thinner and contains a somewhat greater margin of error than I hope is the case for the Israeli parties.

NARRATION AND POLITICS

Because of the salient role of the Palestinian/Arab–Israeli conflict in Western and especially American politics, all of us are to some extent aware of the hegemonic Zionist representation of its history. I am attempting to construct an alternative narrative, to retrieve a counterhegemonic history of the conflict as perceived by the Marxist left and to validate it by situating it within the revisionist historiography mentioned previously. In so doing I am engaging in a debate over what is important in the past and constructing a narrative with a significance different from that of the received version. Part of my purpose is to contribute to the revision of what I believe are widespread erroneous interpretations of the history of the Palestinian/Arab–Israeli conflict and the struggle of the Marxist left for its peaceful resolution. A broader goal is to reconceptualize the issues in the conflict to enable them to be resolved.

It is legitimate to ask whether focusing on political forces whose influence was limited does not unduly distort the historical record. Gramsci warned in his guidelines for writing the history of political parties: "The sectarian will become excited over petty internal matters, which will have an esoteric significance for him, and fill him with mystical enthusiasm. The historian ... will emphasize above all the real effectiveness of the party."[29] I endorse this maxim and do not intend to attribute more influence to the Marxists than they actually had. But I also believe that the approach to the Arab-Israeli conflict advanced by the Marxists has a significance beyond their incapacity to implement their vision during the period under review.

A utopian element is involved in emphasizing the historical role of actors whose principles may have been admirable but whose effectiveness was radically restricted by the circumstances in which they operated. Tony Judt has provocatively declared that we are living "at the tail end of the history of Marxism as a living idea."[30] While the historic potential of the specific political formations examined in this book was probably exhausted some time ago, this pithy comment correctly suggests that the history of Marxism as a living idea is not quite over. It is still very much alive in certain parts of the third world, including Egypt, where, although the Marxists are weak and organizationally dispersed, Marxism remains the foil against which all other political ideologies distinguish themselves. While in Israel the Communist Party continues to function, its political influence is due to its standing as the leading representative of the Palestinian Arab citizens of Israel. This function, unassailable on its own terms, is a very different project from that which MAKI envisioned for itself at the time of its establishment. MAPAM's independent organizational existence was marginal between 1969 and 1984, when it was the junior partner in the Alignment dominated by MAPAI's successor, the Labor Party. MAPAM left the Alignment in 1984, refusing to join the national unity government formed by Labor and the Likud, but by then it was an ideological and organizational shadow of its former self.

Although we may not be able to "learn the lessons" of the history of the Palestinian/Arab–Israeli conflict, studying what happened to those who struggled to uphold the principles of self-determination, mutual recognition, and peaceful coexistence offers another reward. These values remain relevant to the conflict today; indeed, they are steadily gaining recognition as essential components in the conflict's resolution.

Such an unabashedly presentist preoccupation poses the question of historical objectivity even more sharply than is usually the case. Of course, objectivity commonly means ideas that coincide with our previously held prejudices and preconceptions. Some proponents of objectivity in historical scholarship employ this standard to validate a comfortable consensus interpretation that affirms and reinforces the prevailing structure of power and knowledge. Yet historical study can also challenge these structures by demystifying ideologies and critically examining the myths on which they are based. I do not deny that my own precommitments have influenced the historical account presented in this book, but neither do I believe that this distinguishes me from other historians or that I have intentionally distorted the issues by choosing to frame the narrative in the terms of the discourse I am attempting to analyze.

Hayden White has insisted that the purpose of narrativizing is to moralize.[31] I hope that this narrative will be saved from becoming a morality play by its rejection of a demonological cold-war historiographical framework on the one hand and avoidance of Marxist teleology on the other. While this book does take the form of a narrative, it is an uncompleted narrative that breaks off at a moment of failure for internationalism, the triumph of uncompromising nationalism, and the continuation and intensification of the Palestinian/Arab–Israeli conflict. I do not believe that it is historically inevitable that this failure will be reversed; neither do I conceal my desire for this outcome.

CHAPTER II

The Creation of Israel: Zionism as Anti-Imperialism

Throughout the era of the British mandate in Palestine, the international communist movement regarded Zionism as a settler-colonial movement expropriating the rights of the indigenous population in alliance with British imperialism. Before October 1947, communists had argued that creating a Jewish state would permanently exacerbate relations between Arabs and Jews and provide the Western imperial powers with an excuse to continue to intervene in regional affairs. Hashomer Hatza'ir (The Young Guard), the largest component of the future MAPAM, although fully committed to Zionism, also considered that establishing a purely Jewish state in Palestine would perpetrate an unacceptable injustice against the Arab majority in Palestine; it therefore argued that a binational state was the only just way to realize the aims of Zionism.

In the very last months of the mandate, most Arab and Jewish Marxists in Palestine and Egypt accepted the Soviet Union's determination that the first priority for advancing the anti-imperialist struggle in the Middle East (a priority, of course, undistinguished from Soviet national interests) was to expel British imperialism from the region. This issue was decisive in defining their attitude toward the partition of Palestine and the establishment of a Jewish state. Thus, for a brief period, the Zionist movement became a powerful anti-imperialist force in the Middle East. MAPAM hoped that this development would promote a historic reconciliation between Zionism and communism. For the first time, Jewish communists in Palestine were able to overcome their isolation from their community and participate in its national project. Arab communists, even if they were unenthusiastic about the prospect of a Jewish state in Palestine, had to admit that the Zionist movement was stronger than the Arab anti-imperialist forces in Palestine, and the nationalist movements in the surrounding Arab countries, for their part, remained unable to replace their British-installed monarchies or the dependent postcolonial regimes in Lebanon and Syria.

The Soviet Union's determination that Zionism was the most reliable anti-British force in the Middle East, along with the pressing humanitarian need to find a haven for the Jewish survivors of Nazism and the expectation that their gratitude to the Soviet Union for its leading role in the victory over fascism would influence the policies of the Jewish state, led many Marxists to entertain unrealistic expectations about the future international orientation of the Zionist movement. Once Zionism was redefined as part of the anti-imperialist front, earlier questions about its nature were dropped from the agenda. Guided by tactical considerations and confident in the correct leadership of the Soviet Union, Middle Eastern Marxists did not carefully consider the regional impact of the creation of a Jewish state. Their vision was limited by the linear and teleological Marxism of the Comintern, which regarded anti-imperialist national liberation movements as inevitably allied to the progress of international socialism. Events in Palestine, however, were more complex than this model. The Marxist parties did not foresee that the creation of a Jewish state would remake the strategic contours of the Middle East because of its impact on Arab politics, or that the internal structure of a Zionist state would ultimately impel it toward a pro-Western international orientation despite the conflict with Great Britain immediately after World War II. Moreover, the communists never considered that the creation of a Jewish state would legitimize a Zionist political discourse, because their support for the creation of Israel was not motivated by Zionism. Nor did MAPAM consider that its oppositional current within Zionism would be fatally weakened once Ben-Gurion and MAPAI were able to deploy the power of a state against it.

THE UNIFICATION OF THE MARXIST-ZIONIST LEFT

MAPAM was founded in January 1948 by the union of three labor Zionist tendencies that had historically opposed MAPAI's dominance in the *yishuv* and Histadrut. Each of MAPAM's components—Ahdut Ha'avodah (Unity of Labor), Left Po'alei Tzion (Workers of Zion), and Hashomer Hatza'ir Workers' Party—brought a distinctive social base, ideological orientation, and political style to the united party. These differences were set aside to consolidate a left opposition to MAPAI on the eve of the establishment of the state of Israel.

Ahdut Ha'avodah originated as a left-wing faction in MAPAI in the late 1930s. In 1944 it was expelled and became a separate party. The underlying political cause of the split was Ahdut Ha'avodah's suspicion that Ben-Gurion was willing to partition Palestine in order to achieve a Jewish state immediately after World War II. Ahdut Ha'avodah was attracted to the Soviet Union during the war, but it opposed Leninist-style party organization: thus the immediate reason for the split with MAPAI was Ahdut Ha'avodah's rejection of the principle of majority rule and the prohibition of factions in MAPAI.

The Kibbutz Me'uhad (United Kibbutz) federation of kibbutzim was Ahdut Ha'avodah's social base; and it also had strong support in Tel Aviv, especially among construction workers. Kibbutz Me'uhad was instrumental in creating the labor Zionist military apparatus, the Haganah, and especially its elite unit, the Palmah. Many well-known military figures, including Yisra'el Galili and Yigal Allon, were Kibbutz Me'uhad members. As a consequence of its close association with the Zionist military establishment, Kibbutz Me'uhad was a leading proponent of politico-military activism even before it was adopted by the Ben-Gurion–Dayan–Peres faction in MAPAI.

Like the majority of labor Zionists, Ahdut Ha'avodah did not recognize the national rights of Palestinian Arabs. Instead it favored a socialist Jewish state in all of Palestine. Kibbutz Me'uhad's leader, Yitzhak Tabenkin, even advocated "transferring" the Palestinian Arabs out of the country. Ahdut Ha'avodah opposed admitting Arabs to the Histadrut, did not admit Arabs to its own ranks, and later opposed MAPAM's admission of Arab members.

Hashomer Hatza'ir Workers' Party claimed nearly ten thousand members when it was established in 1946. Two-thirds of these belonged to Kibbutz Artzi (National Kibbutz), the kibbutz federation founded in 1927 by members of the worldwide (but mainly Eastern European) Hashomer Hatza'ir youth movement; the rest were former members of Kibbutz Artzi's urban ally, the Socialist League. Hashomer Hatza'ir was the largest and most disciplined component of MAPAM. The intense emotional experiences of the youth movement, which many of its graduates cherished for the rest of their lives, and the all-encompassing collectivism of Kibbutz Artzi's kibbutzim gave Hashomer Hatza'ir a unique character. Far more than a political movement, it was a comprehensive way of life.

In the middle of World War II a left wing emerged in Hashomer Hatza'ir led by veteran kibbutz members Ya'akov Riftin, El'azar Peri (Prai), Mordehai Oren, and Aharon Cohen. Their outlook, which they termed "the orientation toward the forces of tomorrow," was very close to that of orthodox Soviet Marxism. Hashomer Hatza'ir's leaders, Me'ir Ya'ari and Ya'akov Hazan, were less eager than the left-wingers to harmonize their line with that of the international communist movement, and they were always aware that the economic health of the kibbutzim depended on maintaining good relations with the social democratic and bourgeois majority in the Zionist movement and the state of Israel. Nonetheless, through the early 1950s all of Hashomer Hatza'ir and MAPAM adopted a strongly pro-Soviet international orientation.

Hashomer Hatza'ir's most distinctive contribution to MAPAM was its active commitment to Arab-Jewish political cooperation. In 1940, Kibbutz Artzi organized an intensive Arabic course for selected cadres as a prelude to establishing an Arab Department whose task was to cultivate relations with progressive elements in the Palestinian Arab community. Under Aharon Cohen's leadership the Arab Department later became the organizational center of MAPAM's work among Palestinian Arabs. Hashomer Hatza'ir was the only Zionist party to recognize the national rights of Palestinian Arabs. Until 1941 this recognition was expressed in a vague call for a binational state in Palestine, one neither exclusively Jewish nor Arab.

When a conference of mainly American Zionists, urged on by Ben-Gurion, adopted the Biltmore Program in 1942 and officially stated for the first time that the goal of Zionism was to establish a Jewish commonwealth in Palestine at the end of the war, Hashomer Hatza'ir began to elaborate its own alternative. Many Zionists believed that immediate establishment of a Jewish state when Jews comprised less than one-third of the population of Palestine could be achieved only by partitioning the country. Like Ahdut Ha'avodah, Hashomer Hatza'ir opposed this course. Binationalism, it argued, would avert the need for partition and create conditions for achieving a Jewish majority in the country. The group sought to postpone a decision on the future of Palestine and transform the mandate into an international trusteeship, hoping that Soviet influence would have a chance to positively influence the future of the country.¹ For Hashomer Hatzaʻir, binationalism was both a means to realizing Zionism and an expression of its own internationalist and socialist commitments.

While no other Jewish political forces in Palestine formulated a binationalist position in quite the same terms, before the adoption of the UN partition plan Hashomer Hatzaʻir did have political partners, especially the Ihud (Unity) association, a small but prestigious circle of intellectuals led by Martin Buber, Judah Magnes, Haim Kalvarisky, and Ernst Simon. Ihud, Hashomer Hatzaʻir, independents, and individuals from other parties joined to promote their binationalist ideas in the League for Arab-Jewish Rapprochement and Cooperation. Although before 1948 binationalism and the values it embodied were minority positions in the Zionist movement, they were still considered legitimate. But neither Hashomer Hatzaʻir nor any of its allies had a strategy rooted in material conditions for achieving a binationalist state. Of all the Zionist leaders, only Ben-Gurion possessed the political genius to apply the combination of diplomatic stratagem and military force required to establish a Jewish state. Ben-Gurion was also unique in understanding that the existence of a Jewish state would dramatically alter the balance of power between the Zionists and the Arabs, not to mention within the Zionist movement as well. Thus, after 1948 the binational option and, more gradually, many of the political and ethical values it expressed were eliminated from the spectrum of reasonable opinion.

Hashomer Hatzaʻir's difficulty in keeping the binationalist idea on the political agenda lay in the historic tension between its commitment to revolutionary socialist internationalism on the one hand and Zionism on the other. The contradictory requirements of these two ideals had already led to periodic crises,² in every one of which the majority of Hashomer Hatzaʻir gave priority to the group's Zionist commitments. Still, an apparent contradiction between two component parts of a belief system does not mean that its adherents "really" believe in only one of those component parts. Hashomer Hatzaʻir's history should not be interpreted in a manner that either minimizes the contradiction or trivializes its commitments to both elements of its ideological synthesis.

Left Poʻalei Tzion's roots were in the Russian revolutionary movement, its "proletarian Zionism" inspired by a synthesis of Marxism and Zionism as elaborated by Ber Borochov. In 1920, the World Union of Poʻalei Tzion split over affiliation with the Comintern; some of the movement's members in Palestine went on to establish the Palestine Communist Party. Further splits and a purist approach to politics (until the late 1930s, for example, the party refused to participate in the World Zionist Organization, which it regarded as controlled by the Jewish bourgeoisie) made Left Poʻalei Tzion a small, marginal party based primarily among urban immigrants from Eastern Europe whose political vision was formed by the October Revolution.

Left Poʻalei Tzion opposed MAPAI's policy of excluding Arabs from the Histadrut and advocated joint organization of Palestinian Arab and Jewish workers—a unique position in the labor Zionist camp. The party actively supported Arab labor struggles and recruited a small group of perhaps twenty-five Palestinian Arab workers led by George Nassar of Jaffa directly into its ranks. They subsequently became the only Arabs to join MAPAM at its founding (although their status was highly problematic). Left Poʻalei Tzion believed that joint organization of Arab and Jewish workers would resolve the national question in Palestine; the party made little effort to analyze the particularities of the issue, preferring to stress the abstract ideological principle of proletarian internationalism.

In April 1946, Ahdut Haʻavodah and Left Poʻalei Tzion fused to form the Ahdut Haʻavodah–Poʻalei Tzion Party. Thereafter, the majority of former Left Poʻalei Tzion, led by Moshe Erem, closed ranks with Ahdut Haʻavodah. After the formation of MAPAM, the faction of former Left Poʻalei Tzion led by Yitzhak Yitzhaki became allied with Hashomer Hatzaʻir.

Hashomer Hatzaʻir knew when it initiated unity discussions with Ahdut Haʻavodah–Poʻalei Tzion in the summer of 1947 that abandoning binationalism was a prerequisite to the talks' successful outcome. Ahdut Haʻavodah not only refused to accept any reference to binationalism in the platform of the projected new party, but it also rejected Hashomer Hatzaʻir's alternative proposal of "political equality" for the two peoples in a future reunited Eretz Israel, a formulation that suggested binationalism.[3] The UN General Assembly's resolution of November 29, 1947, to partition Palestine into an Arab and a Jewish state and constitute Jerusalem and its environs as an international *corpus separatum* made binationalism a moot point. Nonetheless, some Hashomer Hatzaʻir veterans found it difficult to accept the compromises necessary for unity. When the party Center met to discuss the draft unity platform, Eliʻezer Beʾeri (Bauer), a member of the Arab Department of Kibbutz Artzi and not a leftist, argued that the proposed platform "went beyond the boundaries of concessions we can agree to" on the Arab question.⁴ After MAPAM's founding he warned that the party platform contained

> unclarity and blurring in points on which blurring is forbidden. The Jewish-Arab question is the decisive question. The form of its resolution will determine the fate of large-scale *aliyah* and our fate in its entirety. Hashomer Hatzaʿir carried on high the flag of the struggle for a Jewish-Arab agreement. It is doubtful if the united party will do so.⁵

The most outspoken critic of unity was Eliʿezer Hacohen, a veteran of Kibbutz Bet Alfa not regarded as a leftist, who praised the realism of the party Center for agreeing to work for passage of the UN partition plan while recognizing the tragic dangers it posed for the new state. But the Center, Hacohen insisted, had correctly declared "that binationalism remains the only way to realize maximalist Zionism," and he wanted to see this point included in MAPAM's platform. In the characteristic style of the youth movement, he posed the issue of unity as a moral-existential question:

> a to-be-or-not-to-be question for Hashomer Hatzaʿir as a carrier of principles at all. Each of us knows at all times and almost routinely how to praise this wonderful thing called Hashomer Hatzaʿir, which we have created over a generation and which has all the precious qualities we have clung to. From time to time we stand before the demand, knocking at our door, to sacrifice this creation on some altar. Until now we have resisted this demand, knowing that there is no altar we will not better serve by our continued existence.... Even those who are in favor admit that the principled minimum that has been achieved is a minimum under pressure insufficient to unify the hearts in a vision of the messianic future. Rather, there are those who believe that our principles have a greater chance to predominate inside the joint framework in the long run.⁶

Hashomer Hatzaʿir's left-wingers strongly believed that their principles had "a greater chance to predominate inside the joint framework in the long run," and Yaʿari and Hazan supported unity for the same reason. Because they were confident in the inevitable victory of Marxism and proletarian revolution, the left and the left-leaning center of Hashomer Hatzaʿir were less apprehensive about unity than some who valued the movement's distinctive character above all. Aharon Cohen accepted Eliʿezer Hacohen's grim analysis of the current situation and agreed that the proposed unity program had many shortcomings. Nonetheless, Cohen argued that unity would consolidate the opposition to MAPAI's reformism, and this was the primary task to consider.⁷

The founding of MAPAM represented an effort to consolidate a diverse left-wing Zionist maximalism based on principled opposition to the partition of Palestine. The radicals in Kibbutz Artzi, joined by some ex-Palmah members of Kibbutz Me'uhad as well as urban workers and intellectuals led by Moshe Sneh (who joined MAPAM at its founding), saw this consolidation as compatible with and even contingent on transforming MAPAM into a territorial Marxist-Leninist party. Although they never comprised more than 20 to 30 percent of MAPAM, the leftists were extremely influential and included many of its leading activists: Peri was the first editor of the party daily, *Al hamishmar* (The guardian); Cohen headed the Arab Affairs Department; Riftin was one of the two party secretaries; and Peri, Riftin, and Sneh served as members of the first Knesset.

While MAPAM looked forward to the eventual reunification of Eretz Israel, the platform adopted at the founding congress committed the party to "participate to the fullest extent—in spite of its rejection of the partition solution in principle—in the construction and defense of the Jewish state." The ideological planks of the platform clearly stated MAPAM's commitment to Zionism as the solution of the Jewish problem. The central tasks of the nation were ingathering of the exiles, mass *aliyah,* and settlement. The Jewish working class would be an ally of all social and national liberation struggles throughout the world; its historic task was to engage in a revolutionary class struggle to establish a workers' government, end capitalism, and establish a classless socialist society. MAPAM saw itself as an "inseparable part of the revolutionary workers' movement." The party would strive to integrate the class struggle and socialist creativity (i.e., Zionist construction) in the city and the countryside.[8]

The platform was intentionally vague on four critical points. (1) All agreed on the goal of restoring the unity of Eretz Israel, but the future regime of the country was not specified. Would it be a binational or a Jewish state? Would Palestinian Arab national (or only civil) rights be recognized? (2) Would MAPAM become a territorial party by allowing Arab citizens of the Jewish state to join its ranks? (3) MAPAM did not specifically adopt Marxism-Leninism, and its attitude toward the Soviet Union was not clearly stated. (4) MAPAM's relationship to MAKI was not specified.

MAPAM AND THE 1948–49 WAR

MAPAM's entire political orientation, and its Arab policy in particular, were tested as soon as the party was formed, because a civil war between the Jewish and Arab communities of Palestine erupted immediately upon adoption of the UN partition plan, followed by an invasion of Arab states after the promulgation of Israel's declaration of independence on May 15, 1948. As a Zionist party, there was little question about whether MAPAM would participate in the interim state council (*moʿetzet hamedinah*) organized in March 1948. But some members of the party Center (mainly left-wingers) opposed joining the narrower MAPAI-led provisional government coalition because Prime Minister–designate Ben-Gurion offered MAPAM only two minor ministries. Still, the overwhelming majority favored joining the provisional government; that done, Mordechai Bentov (of Kibbutz Artzi) became minister of labor and Aharon Tzizling (of Kibbutz Meʾuhad), minister of agriculture.[9] In addition, since most of the officers of the Palmah, Haganah, and subsequently the IDF were MAPAM members, MAPAM assumed both political and operational responsibility for conducting Israel's war of independence.

The opponents of participation in the government argued that its nonsocialist, pro-American, and incorrect Arab policies were already determined. In fact, as Avi Shlaim has demonstrated in great detail, Ben-Gurion and his leading Arab affairs advisors had already acted to prevent the emergence of a Palestinian Arab state by reaching a tacit understanding with Amir ʿAbd Allah of Transjordan permitting the latter to annex territories allotted to that state by the United Nations. Ben-Gurion hoped that Israel's borders could be expanded beyond the area specified in the partition plan, and for this reason they were not stipulated in the Israeli declaration of independence. Plan D, a classic example of activist military strategy whose objective was to assume the offensive, annex territory in the Galilee and the Jerusalem corridor allotted to the Arab state, and expel any Arabs who resisted, was adopted by the Haganah on March 10 (three days after the MAPAM Center empowered the Political Committee to negotiate terms for entering the provisional government).

By February 1948 many wealthy and middle-class Palestinians had left Haifa, Jaffa, and Jerusalem, and Ben-Gurion began to look forward to major demographic changes in the country.[10] In April and May the exodus became a mass flight. There is no evidence that Ben-Gurion planned to expel the Palestinian Arabs before hostilities began, but his activist military strategy encouraged their departure, which he saw as a good thing. Moreover, he tacitly approved actions of individuals close to him, especially Yosef Weitz, head of the Jewish National Fund Lands

Department, who did evict Palestinian civilians, raze their villages, seize their lands, and erect new Jewish settlements on those lands during and immediately after the war.[11]

An IDF Intelligence Branch report of June 30, 1948, determined that 391,000 refugees had fled by June 1: 55 percent in response to hostile Haganah/IDF military operations; 15 percent because of armed actions by Zionist dissidents (most notably the massacre of Deir Yasin on April 9 by forces of ETZEL and LEHI); 2 percent owing to direct expulsion; 2 percent in response to Zionist whispering campaigns aimed at frightening Arabs away; and 1 percent because of fear of retaliation after Arab attacks on Jews. Only 5 percent of the refugees left on orders from the Arab Higher Committee or the Transjordanian government; indeed, Arab authorities made every effort to stop the flight.

During the first cease-fire from June 11 to July 9, most of the inhabited territory allotted to the Jewish state by the UN partition plan was secured. When fighting resumed, expulsions as a percentage of the eventual total of about seven hundred thousand refugees increased as the IDF began to occupy territory designated for the Arab state. In the single largest incident of forced expulsion, which occurred on July 12 during the drive to implement Plan D, some fifty thousand inhabitants of Lydda and Ramle were driven out of their cities.[12]

MAPAM protested the army's treatment of the civilian Arab population: the destruction of villages that had neither participated in military action nor given refuge to the invading Arab armies, the eviction of peasants and expropriation of agricultural land, the looting of property, the acts of needless cruelty—all the commonplaces of war. No one in the party was more militant, persistent, and farsighted in opposing the government's treatment of the Palestinian Arabs than Aharon Cohen. His report to the Political Committee on May 10 opened a discussion that culminated in a resolution opposing "the tendency to expel the Arabs from the areas of the Jewish state," the destruction of villages without military necessity, and illegal expropriation and intentional destruction of the means of livelihood of those Arabs who remained or who were entitled to return at the conclusion of hostilities, and recommending severe punishment for looting, robbery, or attacks on civilians. The party urged the government to call on peace-loving Arabs to remain in their homes and places of work and accept the authority of the Jewish state. It upheld for all peace-loving Arabs who remained or would return to Israel the right to work, an independent community life, personal security, medical care, markets, and education. While the resolution did not endorse Cohen's proposal to urge the government to welcome all the refugees back, it was nonetheless a comprehensive criticism of the government's Arab policies.[13]

Ben-Gurion may have feared that MAPAM would leave the government if an explicit resolution to expel and expropriate Arabs were adopted. Although MAPAM's opposition may explain why the cabinet never formally took this step, it did little to alter the course of events. On June 16, a day after MAPAM adopted its resolution criticizing the government's Arab policy, the cabinet informally agreed to prevent the Palestinian refugees from returning. On August 18 this decision was confirmed at a meeting of leading MAPAI Arabists.[14] The actions criticized in MAPAM's resolution continued to occur with increasing frequency.

Following the debate in the Political Committee and the massive expulsions from Lydda and Ramle, MAPAM expressed its criticism of the government's Arab policy more openly. At the July 13 session of the interim state council, Tzvi Luria asked Ben-Gurion if he knew that the army was destroying nonbelligerent Arab villages whose residents had fled during hostilities, and demanded that the government stop this activity and announce a policy change within two days. But Luria never received a direct answer to his question, and the matter dragged on into August with no resolution.[15] On July 11, Aharon Cohen illicitly received a copy of the June 30 IDF Intelligence Branch report on the refugees.[16] While he apparently used the information it contained in his writings and lectures, he never quoted from the document or mentioned it at a party meeting. Explicit reference to an illegally obtained intelligence report would have opened MAPAM to charges of wartime treason. For Cohen, traversing this barrier was inconceivable.

The efficacy of MAPAM's opposition to the government's conduct of the war, as well as to the underlying political strategy of maximizing the territory of the Jewish state and preventing the emergence of the Palestinian state called for by the UN partition resolution, was limited by actions of its own members in uniform and its kibbutzim that were in direct contradiction to official party policy. MAPAM members commanded many of the operations that resulted in major expulsions: Yigal Allon in the western Galilee; Allon and Shimon Avidan in the northern Negev; Moshe Carmel in the upper Galilee; and Allon and Yitzhak Rabin in Lydda and Ramle.[17] In his May 10 report, Cohen complained that MAPAM's officer-members were developing a line different from that of the party and that a policy of transferring the Arab population from territory under Jewish control was being implemented. In the first issue of MAPAM's ideological journal he criticized both the government and MAPAM members in uniform, warning prophetically that "a state based on national enmity and the rule of one people over another will certainly breed chauvinism and reaction in its internal life; and a reactionary state will of necessity become subjugated, sooner or later, to imperialism and its reactionary and aggressive policies in the international arena." [18]

At a seminar on Arab-Jewish relations held for MAPAM draftees on July 7, Cohen unequivocally stated that "the overwhelming majority of the refugees must return." He linked the moral imperative to treat noncombatants humanely to the political goals of restoring the territorial unity of Eretz Israel and realizing maximalist Zionism. Cohen argued that the vast majority of Palestinians had not wanted the war, which had been forced on them by the agents of al-Hajj Amin al-Husayni and the Arab Higher Committee, and that the Arab states had invaded Palestine for self-serving reasons. Furthermore, as Israel had already won the war, it should not let the Arab states assume responsibility for the refugees; they would, he said, only incite the refugees against the Jewish state. Cohen sharply criticized plunder, robbery, destruction of property without a military purpose, and attacks on the aged, women, children, and other civilians, remarking pointedly, "Those who are sitting here know well what I mean and there is no need to give examples." He defended MAPAM's (in fact, Hashomer Hatza'ir's) Arab policy in response to party members who asked, "Why not prevent the refugees from returning? Why not conquer all of Eretz Israel by military force? Why not execute a population transfer? Isn't it too late for politics to determine the course of events?" [19]

That Cohen's views were published in official MAPAM organs indicated that they were still within the range of acceptable opinion in the party. The top party leaders, however, were usually more guarded in their criticism of the government. For example, at a meeting of party military activists, Hazan sharply criticized the destruction of villages and expulsions carried out by party members, but distinguished between the inhabitants of Lydda, who, he believed, were justly expelled because they resumed hostilities after surrendering, and the inhabitants of Ramle, who were unjustly expelled without cause.[20]

Inconsistencies in the stand of some MAPAM leaders opened the party to charges of hypocrisy. Yosef Weitz, a strong proponent of transferring the Palestinian Arabs out of the Jewish state, criticized Hazan for opposing the destruction of villages and the eviction of their inhabitants while agreeing to allocate funds of the Jewish National Fund to carry out the destruction. He was outraged at a speech by Ya'ari to the Zionist Executive condemning the evictions, "as if he does not know that all his friends in the kibbutzim are doing it with complete devotion."[21]

Weitz was correct to assume that the leaders of MAPAM's kibbutz movements knew that their members were actively engaged in expropriating Arab property. As early as May and June, MAPAM kibbutzim, along with other Jewish settlements, began harvesting the crops of abandoned Arab villages and redistributing the seized lands among themselves.[22] Cohen informed the MAPAM Secretariat that MAPAM kibbutzim in the Haifa area had used armed force to drive Arabs out and take over their lands.[23] At the Kibbutz Me'uhad council meeting of June 8–9, Yitzhak Tabenkin deplored the taking of spoils: "There are those who say that there is no kibbutz" that had not shared such deeds, he lamented.[24]

The exigencies of war and the overriding concern to secure the Jewish state and provide a haven for the remnants of the holocaust explain in large part the "flexibility" of MAPAM's Arab policy. To these easily understood motivations must be added the dream shared by all of MAPAM to "restore the unity of the land." After the Arab offensive was blocked in June, the most hawkish elements of Ahdut Ha'avodah, such as Galili and Allon, as well as some left-wingers like Riftin, Sneh, and Cohen, agreed that the military objective of the war should be to conquer all of Eretz Israel. The difference between the two groups was that Ahdut Ha'avodah wanted to open up the whole country to Jewish settlement, whereas the left-wingers wanted Israel to prevent 'Abd Allah from occupying any part of Palestine in order to establish an independent Palestinian Arab state. Some continued to look forward to restoring the political unity of the country in a binational state.[25] The goal of occupying all of mandate Palestine helped MAPAM to overlook or diminish the significance of the excesses on the way to the goal; once the entire country was occupied and the reactionary forces of 'Abd Allah and his British imperialist backers evicted, any injustices could be set right.

Were the MAPAM leaders hypocrites, as Weitz implied? Ahdut Ha'avodah had never been as concerned about Arab rights as Hashomer Hatza'ir; it therefore cannot be accused of hypocrisy. Except for Aharon Cohen, who saw matters with extraordinary prescience, the

MAPAM leftists were blinded by their belief that they were on the right side of history. The Soviet Union, leader of the forces of tomorrow, had endorsed the establishment of a Jewish state as a blow against British imperialism. Wouldn't a strong Jewish state be an asset to the anti-imperialist camp? Since most of the Arab states attacking Israel were pawns of British imperialism, wouldn't any attempt to diminish the borders of the Jewish state enhance the influence of imperialism in the Middle East? As Zionists, the leftists could not have considered that the existence of a Zionist state (as opposed to a state for the Jews of Palestine and unrepatriated European Jewish refugees—which was, in fact, what the Soviet Union supported) might be problematic. A combination of wishful thinking and the normal distortion of perception caused by war allowed concerned MAPAM members to imagine that the party uniformly pursued the Arab policy advocated by Aharon Cohen. In any event, this issue was not central to their evaluation of the situation.

Thus, by the fall of 1948 all the components of MAPAM proved unable to articulate an alternative to the emerging hegemonic Zionist consensus on Arab-Jewish relations in which all Arab resistance to Zionist activity—even to secure objectives beyond the limits of the UN partition plan—was declared illegitimate and reactionary. MAPAM agreed that Israel's conduct of the war was entirely within the boundaries of legitimate self-defense. Meanwhile, the political program of the Zionist consensus was derived from the activist attitude toward (Jewish) geopolitical facts: refusal to withdraw from territories occupied in the war, refusal to repatriate the Palestinian refugees, and refusal to accept the existence of a Palestinian Arab state.

A clear indication of the distance MAPAM traversed during the war may be seen in its response to the September 1948 proposals of UN mediator Count Bernadotte, namely, that Israel retain the western Galilee, which it already occupied but which was to have been part of the Arab state, in exchange for ceding the Negev, which it did not yet occupy but which had been allotted to the Jewish state. MAPAM opposed the Bernadotte proposals as contradicting the UN partition plan and responded by adopting a resolution on October 7 that advocated major alterations of the partition boundaries in Israel's favor. The party now favored Israeli annexation of the western Galilee, a land corridor to Jerusalem, fortified heights on the borders, and guarantees for the Hebrew character of Jerusalem—all in contravention of the terms of the partition plan. These demands were close to the actual cease-fire lines drawn in 1949, which were based on the military status quo at the end of hostilities but slightly altered in Israel's favor.

MAPAM's October 7 resolution advocated the return of "peace-seeking refugees who acknowledge the sovereignty of the state of Israel"—a formulation suggesting that only a limited number of refugees should be welcomed back. While employing the rhetoric of militant anti-imperialism, programmatically MAPAM was moving toward the emerging Zionist consensus, as shaped and articulated by MAPAI, on the refugee question:

> The imperialist plots and the bloody attack of the reactionary Arab leadership on the Arab community and the state of Israel were the principal factors in the uprooting of hundreds of thousands of Arabs from the country. The masses of refugees should learn the lesson of their disaster and struggle for a democratic leadership for their nation and for a real peace with the Jewish nation and the state of Israel.[26]

A November 14 editorial in *Al hamishmar* went even further, stating that the refugees had fled as an expression of opposition to the state of Israel. This contradicted MAPAM's earlier argument, as well as similar statements made by Ben-Gurion and Golda Meir early in 1948, that the majority of Palestinian Arabs did not want and did not participate in the war. No one in MAPAM knew better than Aharon Cohen that the newspaper's claim was not only untrue but also likely to exacerbate Arab-Jewish relations. He protested the editorial, but his letter to the editor was not printed.[27]

Many elements of Hashomer Hatza'ir were profoundly disturbed by the gap between theory and practice in MAPAM and made strenuous emotional and intellectual efforts to sort things out. In December 1948, at the first national conference of Kibbutz Artzi following MAPAM's establishment and in the confines of what was regarded as a family, representatives of over fifty kibbutzim frankly evaluated the movement's course since endorsing partition. Their discussion revealed confusion, loss of confidence, and a struggle to find a coherent direction. Ya'ari opened the meeting with comprehensive defense of Hashomer Hatza'ir's historic path in response to what he termed a liquidationist tendency within the movement. He argued extensively against the view that recent events proved MAPAM's positions to be untenable, recalling that MAPAI's spiritual leader, Berl Katznelson, had supported a binational state in 1936 and that in 1937 Ben-Gurion had opposed a Jewish state before the Peel Commission. Ya'ari attacked the pro-British and then pro-American orientation of MAPAI and its shortsightedness for not imagining that "salvation would come from the East." He upheld the need to establish an independent Arab state in Palestine while keeping 'Abd Allah out of the country and reaffirmed that MAPAM endorsed the partition plan "as a constructive compromise that leads to restoring the wholeness of the land through an international agreement."[28]

The meeting was defined by the dramatic tension of Ya'ari's defense of the movement's historic principles juxtaposed to the new realities. Kibbutz representatives responded to Ya'ari's abstractions with anguished accounts of contrary thoughts and actions widespread in their kibbutzim. Whereas some defended the seizure of Arab property, horrified veterans unconditionally denounced it. Some criticized Yitzhak Rabin as a commander of the operation expelling the residents of Lydda and Ramle; Riftin defended him. Leftists argued that the failure of party members to uphold its moral values and political line during the war was due to the fact that MAPAM was not a properly disciplined Leninist party. The problems, they said, could be resolved by cooperating more closely with MAKI and adopting a clear Marxist-Leninist line. Others replied that there was no consensus in the party for immediately adopting Marxism-Leninism. Hazan articulated the prevalent malaise of the gathering:

> Until now we lived in a quiet reality; the vision was far off. We argued, but we were not tested. Now we have reached a situation in which everything you say today will be tested tomorrow. . . . Our movement does not know how to fit our ideology to our circumstances, to strive for the same goal under new conditions.[29]

The colorful comments of Yish'ayahu Be'eri from Mishmar Ha'emek about the difference between "the official opinion and the one heard in the [collective] shower rooms [of the kibbutzim]," as well as Eli'ezer Be'eri's report that some members of Kibbutz Artzi favored military conquest of all of Eretz Israel without setting up an Arab state, were softened or omitted entirely from the published account of the meeting. Such self-censorship helped Hashomer Hatza'ir, and consequently the rest of MAPAM, to avoid confronting the difficult task of reexamining its ideological assumptions. The confessions and recriminations at this meeting clearly indicated that Hashomer Hatza'ir's age of innocence was over. But no conclusions were drawn, and MAPAM leaders continued to believe that because the war was still in progress and the ultimate resolution of the conflict far from certain, everything might still be put right with a little help from the Soviet Union.

THE PALESTINE COMMUNIST PARTY'S ROAD TO BINATIONALISM

As a Jewish-Arab organization, the PCP had experienced the difficulties of managing relations between the two communities both in the party and in the wider political arena. The party had opposed Zionism since the mid-1920s, but tactical differences over how to view the overwhelmingly pro-Zionist Jewish working class persisted. In May 1943 these differences led to a split along national lines when Jewish party members led by Shmu'el Mikunis revolted against what they considered the "ultranationalist" leadership of the general secretary, Radwan al-Hilu ("Musa").[30] Some Jewish party leaders, including Me'ir Vilner, Ester Vilenska, Me'ir Slonim, and Simha Tzabari, remained loyal to Musa's leadership for a short time; but Vilner and Vilenska soon joined with Mikunis to convene the Eighth Party Congress in May 1944, which declared itself the continuator of the PCP. Slonim and Tzabari went on to establish the Jewish-national Communist Educational Association (CEA). The Arab party members eventually abandoned the ideal of a joint organization with Jews and founded the National Liberation League in early 1944 as an entirely Arab organization. Thus, at the end of World War II there were three major communist formations in Palestine: the Jewish PCP and CEA and the Arab NLL. In principle, each organization remained committed to internationalism; in practice, their national character and political development reflected the radically different political environment in each community.

In September 1945, the Ninth Congress of the PCP determined that Palestine was a "country with a binational character" and called for establishing a "democratic and independent Arab-Jewish state."[31] Short of endorsing the Zionist program to establish a Jewish national home in Palestine, this formulation recognized the existence of a Jewish national community in Palestine with rights equal to those of the indigenous Arab national community. Vilner, editor of the party newspaper, *Kol ha'am* (The people's voice), elaborated on this position in a pamphlet issued by the Central Committee in preparation for the Tenth Party Congress in 1946:

> Two national communities live in Palestine. Any program for the resolution of the problem of the country must take into consideration this fact and guarantee both nations equal rights and possibilities for free national devel-

opment. The national question in Palestine is *sui generis*. Palestine is a binational country, but the Arabs and Jews do not live in separate territories.

Although he did not defend the PCP's vision of a binational state in the Zionist terms used by Hashomer Hatza'ir, Vilner stressed the need for cooperation between the PCP and Zionist parties that agreed with the communist stand on specific programmatic issues, specifying Hashomer Hatza'ir and the Ihud association as especially likely partners for joint activity.[32]

Once the PCP defined the *yishuv* as a national community, it could legitimately aspire to participate in its political life. Yet it won less than 2 percent of the vote in the 1944 elections to the Jewish elected assembly (*asefat hanivharim*), and the Histadrut Executive Committee barred it from participating in the elections of 1941 and 1944. The leading role of the Soviet Union in the defeat of Nazism partly mitigated the marginal status of the PCP in the *yishuv*; its work in the Victory League, too, enabled it to cooperate with Hashomer Hatza'ir, Ahdut Ha'avodah, and elements of MAPAI on the basis of shared enthusiasm for the Soviet Union.

THE COMMUNIST EDUCATIONAL ASSOCIATION

The CEA was established in April 1945, in conscious imitation of the example set by the Communist Party of the United States, recently renamed the Communist Political Association. The CEA's platform attempted to articulate a Jewish national communism. It recognized the Jewish people as a national entity and fully supported establishing a Jewish national home in Palestine, independence for the *yishuv*, and the right to unlimited Jewish immigration and settlement. After Earl Browder was criticized as a revisionist for dissolving the American party, the CEA changed its name, first to the Communist Union of Palestine and then, in June 1947, to the Hebrew Communist Party. Hashomer Hatza'ir welcomed the Hebrew Communists' Congress in October 1947 and invited them to join MAPAM now that they embraced the Jewish national liberation movement.[33] In fact, many Hebrew Communists did ultimately join MAPAM in 1949, after a short stay in MAKI. Although the Hebrew Communists numbered only five hundred, their emergence further signaled the growing acceptability of Marxism and pro-Soviet sentiment among those who defined their politics within the Zionist consensus.[34]

THE PALESTINIAN ARAB INTELLIGENTSIA AND THE NATIONAL LIBERATION LEAGUE

The main impetus for the split in the PCP on the Arab side came from younger intellectuals. Bulus Farah, who was expelled from the PCP in 1940, had gathered around himself a group of educated young Arabs in Haifa—both party and nonparty members.[35] Farah regarded Musa as an "illiterate" incapable of leading a communist movement and, thinking the party should appeal to educated Arab youth, aspired to lead it himself.[36] This personal rivalry, however, should not obscure the general significance of the emergence of the young urban intelligentsia as a social force in the Palestinian Arab communist movement.

During the struggle with Mikunis's group in May 1943, younger Arab intellectuals—ʿAbd Allah Bandak, Yaʿqub al-ʿArmani, and Emile Habibi, with help from Tawfiq Tubi and a member of Farah's group—pushed the PCP toward a split by publishing a leaflet signed by Bandak, ʿArmani, and Habibi declaring that the Communist Party "is an Arab national party in whose ranks there are Jews who accept its national program."[37] The leaflet welcomed the dissolution of the Comintern and looked toward the closer integration of the communist and Arab nationalist movements. Although Musa and the Central Committee repudiated the leaflet, it strained the fragile unity between Jews and Arabs in the PCP to the breaking point. Musa retired from leadership in November 1943; the Arab PCP members, Bulus Farah and his group, and other radical intellectuals and trade unionists went on to establish the National Liberation League.

The NLL was a social movement representing a self-conscious alliance between two social strata in formation who were marginal to the traditional Palestinian political system, in which land ownership and bureaucratic or religious office were the main roads to political power and influence: the young intelligentsia, particularly urban Christians who did not belong to powerful landed families, and the urban working class. The intellectuals were organized in the League of Arab Intellectuals, led by Bandak, Habibi, Tubi, and Emile Tuma, and in two local Haifa clubs, the People's Club, led by Habibi, and the Rays of Hope Society, led by Farah and Tuma. From 1941 on these intellectuals began to organize trade unions, and by the end of World War II they had become recognized as leaders of the Arab Workers' Congress (AWC), a trade union federation formed in 1945 by radicalized members of two earlier Palestinian Arab trade union formations. The NLL's weekly (later biweekly), *Al-ittihad* (Unity), edited by Emile Tuma, appeared as the organ of the AWC after September 1945. Fu'ad Nassar, head of the Nazareth AWC branch, and Khalil Shanir, a veteran of the PCP and head of the Jaffa AWC branch, became important national leaders in the NLL. The AWC claimed a membership of twenty thousand in 1945 (perhaps an exaggeration if only dues-paying members were counted) and was supported by an even larger number of workers. Certainly the most significant Arab trade union organization in Palestine, it challenged the historic dominance of the more conservative Histadrut-supported Palestine Labor League in the industrialized Haifa region, where it organized workers in the port, Iraq Petroleum Company, Shell Oil Refinery, Steel Brothers, and the Royal Chemical Company; it was also the dominant force in the Arab trade union movement in Jaffa, Gaza, Jerusalem, Nazareth, and several smaller towns.

The NLL presented itself as a radical, democratic, nationalist organization "open to every Arab citizen," "the conscious vanguard of the national movement," and the "organization of the Arab working class and progressive forces." The only explicitly communist ideological principle was that embodied in the democratic centralist organizational structure. The NLL called for a "democratic government guaranteeing the rights of all inhabitants [of Palestine] without distinction" and opposed Zionist immigration, settlement, and a Jewish state, while distinguishing between the Zionist movement and the Jewish inhabitants of Palestine.[38] Cooperation with any Zionist party, however, was precluded on grounds that the objective of establishing a Jewish state in Palestine was incompatible with Arab-Jewish understanding. Only the PCP was considered a potential ally, despite what the NLL regarded as its Jewish nationalist deviation.

TWO PATHS TO ENDORSING PARTITION OF PALESTINE

The NLL's willingness to grant full civil rights to the Jewish community resulted directly from the communist background of its leaders and differentiated it from the rest of the Palestinian Arab nationalist movement. The PCP and the NLL were united in their ideological opposition to Zionism and to the demand for a Jewish state in Palestine; both believed that only through anti-imperialist solidarity could Jews and Arabs in Palestine end British colonial rule, establish the political independence of Palestine, and secure Arab-Jewish coexistence. Yet whereas the NLL situated itself within the Palestinian Arab nationalist movement, the PCP remained outside the Zionist consensus. Communism was never more than a temporary tactical ally of Zionism, but it was possible to conceive of a strategic alliance between communism and Arab nationalism. Therefore, Jewish and Arab communists usually adopted distinctive rhetorical styles expressing this differential relationship to their respective national communities.

The two lines in Palestinian communism confronted each other in February and March 1947 at the Conference of Communist Parties of the British Empire in London, the first time the NLL openly identified with the international communist movement. Emile Tuma, in his "Report on Palestine," emphasized that the Zionist movement was a strategic prop of British rule in the Middle East; quoting (imperfectly) Sir Ronald Storrs's comment that the Balfour Declaration would allow Britain to create "a little [loyal] Jewish Ulster" in the Arab Middle East, Tuma minimized the extent to which the Jewish national economy and society in Palestine existed independently of British imperialism. He argued that the failure of the Palestinian national leadership to adopt a positive attitude toward the Jewish masses of Palestine was "mainly due to imperialist zionist intrigue and to the privileged status of the Jewish community." Tuma advanced the NLL's program: an independent democratic Palestine with neither partition nor parity arrangements between the two communities.[39]

Shmu'el Mikunis, representing the PCP, addressed the conference the day after Tuma. His report emphasized the intensification of British colonial oppression in Palestine directed against both Arabs and Jews, arguing that World War II had accelerated capitalist development, albeit unevenly, in the two communities. For Mikunis, "the central national problem in Palestine" was "how to liberate the inhabitants, both Arabs and Jews, from the imperialist yoke." He denounced Ben-Gurion and the head of the Arab Higher Committee, Jamal al-Husayni, as being incapable of bringing a democratic regime to Palestine. Mikunis presented the program adopted by the Tenth Congress of the PCP: abrogation of the British mandate and evacuation of the British military forces; an independent democratic state with equal national and civil rights for both peoples; neither an exclusively Arab nor an exclusively Jewish state; legislative guarantees for democratic liberties. He urged that the Palestine question be submitted to the UN Security Council for urgent resolution.[40]

The sister parties tried, but failed, to bring the two Palestinian organizations together. In a meeting of delegations to discuss the Palestine problem prior to the main conference, Mikunis strongly objected to

Tuma's report, contending that it failed to mention the alliance between Arab landlords and merchants and the British government in Palestine.[41] After the conference, at a meeting of delegations from the NLL, the PCP, and the Communist Party of Great Britain, Mikunis stated that Tuma not only had disregarded his criticisms but had also compounded the problem by minimizing the main enemy, imperialism, and attacking one of its agents, Zionism, while altogether ignoring Arab proimperialist forces.[42]

Although the PCP differed from the NLL by recognizing the *yishuv* as a national community, it was not prepared to grant its right to self-determination—that is, the right to establish a separate state (and certainly not the right of the worldwide Jewish people to exercise self-determination in Palestine)—even as the Soviet Union moved toward accepting the former concept. *Kol ha'am*'s editorial of May 16, 1947, commenting on Andrei Gromyko's May 14 speech on the Palestine question at the United Nations, did not mention that the Soviet delegate had suggested the possibility of partition into separate Arab and Jewish states even while expressing his preference for an "independent democratic Arab-Jewish state." Rather, *Kol ha'am* emphasized that Gromyko agreed with the PCP's position that two nations lived in Palestine and that an independent Palestinian state must guarantee equal national rights for both.

In July 1947, Mikunis testified before the UN Special Committee on Palestine (UNSCOP), stating:

> We emphatically reject the idea of partition, as it is contrary to the economic and political interests of the two peoples. We advocate the plan that Palestine should be constituted as an independent, democratic bi-unitarian state, which means a single state inhabited and governed by two peoples, Jews and Arabs, with equal rights.

Such a plan could work despite the existing conflict between the two national communities because, as Vilner argued before UNSCOP, "The problem of Palestine is not the Jewish-Arab antagonism.... Colonial rule is the main source of the national antagonism existing in our country."[43] That the national conflict in Palestine (and later Israel) was not "real," but was created by the British (or the Americans), was central to the communist (and left-wing MAPAM) representation of the situation.

The PCP opposed the UNSCOP majority proposal recommending partition of Palestine and attacked American support for partition as advocating "dismemberment" of the country.[44] *Kol ha'am*'s first response to Soviet UN delegate M. Semyon Tsarapkin's speech announcing his country's reluctant support for partition as a bad solution but the only possible one, was a neutral report that did not indicate the PCP's position.[45] Not until October 16, when Mikunis addressed the Central Committee and explained the overriding importance of achieving an immediate termination of the British mandate, did the party endorse the partition plan. Even then, Mikunis pointed out the negative aspects of the partition solution and portrayed it as transitional to a federal state "tomorrow."[46]

After accepting partition the PCP became the Communist Party of the Land of Israel (MAKEI), marking the first time Palestinian communists embraced the Hebrew name for the country used by the Zionist movement, Eretz Israel. This change signified a willingness to participate in, and hence legitimate, a political discourse shaped by aims that hitherto had been considered exclusively Zionist. MAKEI now proclaimed itself to be the "pioneer [*halutz*] of the struggle for national and social liberation in light of the principles of Marxism-Leninism." The term *pioneer* was borrowed from the Zionist lexicon and had rich connotations evoking rural Zionist settlement (as well as expropriation of Arab peasants, as the PCP had often noted). And although the leaflet announcing the party's name change emphasized the importance of Arab-Jewish cooperation, its concluding slogans included "Long live the independent democratic Jewish state!"—without a parallel call for a Palestinian Arab state.[47] This omission may have been unintentional, because the party clearly did support establishing an Arab state in Palestine alongside a Jewish state; nonetheless, failure to mention this support in a Hebrew leaflet shows how either carelessness or concern not to weaken the anti-imperialist front in a moment of crisis could act to legitimate and reinforce the power of the Zionist discourse.

The most unequivocal statement of MAKEI's identification with the Jewish national cause was its leaflet celebrating the first day of Israel's independence, which explained that the British mandate had been terminated thanks to the "war of liberation" (*milhemet hashihrur*) waged by the *yishuv* and the support of the progressive forces of the world. It argued that the allies of the emergent state were "the entire Jewish people" and "all the forces of progress." Thus, the Jewish national movement in its entirety was identified as an anti-imperialist force, with no differentiation made between classes and political currents within the Zionist movement—the same sin Mikunis had attributed to Tuma regarding the Palestinian Arab nationalist movement in London. While the leaflet proclaimed the party's willingness to pursue peaceful and cooperative relations with the surrounding Arab states and the Palestinian Arab inhabitants of Israel, all in the context of a joint struggle against the imperialist enemy, once again the call for an independent Palestinian Arab state was missing from the list of concluding slogans.[48] After the Arab invasion began, Mikunis reiterated that the struggle to establish a Jewish state was part of the worldwide anti-imperialist struggle; adopting an ultrapatriotic stand, he demanded that the government refuse to accept a UN proposal for a temporary cease-fire because relenting in the military struggle against ʿAbd Allah and the other pawns of imperialism who had attacked Israel would benefit only the imperialist powers.[49]

In the face of an imminent war, MAKEI expressed its position most clearly in its military policy, fully supporting the military effort to establish the Jewish state against Arab opposition. On November 15, 1947, the Central Committee sent a letter to party members advocating that they join the Haganah.[50] Strengthening the Haganah, they said, was the only way to defend partition without delaying the British departure from Palestine. Nonetheless, the directive to join an organization formerly denounced as an instrument of Zionist oppression illustrates how circumstances pushed the party toward practical acceptance of the Zionist consensus and concrete support for acts it would later condemn.

Jewish communists, with the full approval of the Zionist leadership, engaged in diplomatic efforts to secure military aid for the *yishuv*. In February 1948, Mikunis traveled to Eastern Europe to negotiate supply of weapons, immigration of Jews, and the formation of a military unit to fight in Palestine. These efforts (along with earlier work by MAPAM's Mordehai Oren) "were probably critically influential in Czechoslovakia's decision to aid the Haganah," according to a well-researched account of this story.[51] In December, Central Committee member Eliyahu Gojansky also visited Eastern Europe to seek military aid. He died in a plane crash on his way home. The party named its Tel Aviv headquarters (Bet Elyosha) after him, and his martyrdom for the cause of Israeli independence was frequently invoked to assert the patriotic credentials of the Israeli communists.

The NLL also opposed partition of Palestine until Tsarapkin announced the Soviet Union's unequivocal support. The initial reaction to Tsarapkin's speech in *Al-ittihad* argued that "notwithstanding our friendship for the USSR, we do not tie ourselves to its policy, but formulate our own from existing local conditions and the aims of our people."[52] After the Tsarapkin speech, the NLL Secretariat was split: Emile Tuma was against partition; Fuʾad Nassar, Emile Habibi, Tawfiq

Tubi, and Rushdi Shahin were in favor. Early in December the Central Committee met in Nazareth. A majority of the members, led by Tuma, Bulus Farah, Musa Dajani, Mukhlis ʿAmr, and Khalil Shanir, opposed partition. Tuma and other opponents of partition from Haifa and Acre boycotted a second expanded Central Committee meeting in Nazareth later in the month: consequently, at that meeting partition received majority support.[53]

The NLL did not have much opportunity to publicize its support for partition because in February 1948 *Al-ittihad* was closed by British censors, and it did not appear again until October. The organization fell into disarray, with both opponents and supporters of partition acting independently. Tuma and others joined the Arab National Committee of Haifa, which attempted to organize military resistance to the Haganah's occupation of that city. The National Liberation League–Northern District issued a proclamation in March 1948 opposing partition.[54] Members of the NLL in the Galilee participated in armed resistance against Israeli occupation of the central and western Galilee—areas allotted to the Arab state by the UN partition plan. In April, the AWC Central Committee, probably influenced by the Haifa group and Jaffa AWC leader Khalil Shanir, wrote a letter of condolence to al-Hajj Amin al-Husayni when his kinsman, ʿAbd al-Qadir, was killed while leading military operations near Jerusalem.[55] In Jerusalem, Mukhlis ʿAmr and other members of the League of Arab Intellectuals took up the struggle against partition.[56]

The NLL split over the question of partition cannot be separated from the broader process of the disintegration of Palestinian Arab society that began immediately after the UN partition plan was adopted. Before the war, Haifa, with over seventy thousand Arab residents, was one of the NLL's strongest bases of support; after the Haganah occupied the city at the end of April 1948, however, only some three thousand Arab inhabitants remained.[57] This catastrophic demographic upheaval in the midst of war made maintenance of a coherent political organization and orderly political debate impossible.

TOWARD THE COMMUNIST PARTY OF ISRAEL

Despite its support for the Jewish national movement during the war, MAKEI maintained contact with the NLL and continued to defend the rights of the Palestinian Arabs. A circular letter from the MAKEI Secretariat to party members in early February 1948 reported that political agreement was reached with the NLL on several points: to achieve full political independence through anti-imperialist war; to struggle against internal and external provocations of communal violence; to struggle for cooperation and peace between the two peoples; to struggle for the democratic unity of the two states; and to establish a "territorial organization of all the communists with no distinction as to their national origins, with one secretariat and regional organizations for the two states and the Jerusalem area."[58] The MAKEI Secretariat's overoptimistic and homogenized account of the NLL struggle over the partition plan related that the NLL Secretariat had reported to the Nazareth plenum (only one meeting was mentioned) that the Jewish community in Palestine was "a nation in formation" and supported partition and that these positions had been accepted despite the opposition of Tuma, Shanir, and some of the Haifa cadres.

The agreement between MAKEI and the NLL did not, however, endorse a permanent partition. As Mikunis had suggested to the PCP Central Committee on October 16, 1947, partition was seen as a temporary measure that could be overcome by joint struggle of progressive Jews and Arabs. Moreover, viewing partition as a temporary measure was not simply a reluctant concession to the NLL's unwillingness to endorse permanent partition. MAKEI positively emphasized its commitment to this concept of partition when *Kol ha'am* quoted an Egyptian communist weekly that also defended partition as a stage in the struggle for a united Arab-Jewish state:

> The goal of all democrats concerned with the question of Palestine is the establishment of a united Arab-Jewish independent state. This goal will not be realized except through cooperation between the Arab and Jewish masses. In light of the circumstances, peace-loving and anti-imperialist nations have accepted the partition as a basis for the independence of Palestine.[59]

After the first cease-fire, Israeli military dominance was decisively established and the magnitude of the Arab military collapse was becoming evident. The impending Arab defeat and the destruction of Palestinian Arab society emboldened NLL supporters of partition. During the ten days of fighting between the first and second cease-fires in mid-July, the NLL, aided by Eli'ezer Be'eri of MAPAM's Arab Affairs Department and various IDF officers (probably also MAPAM supporters), distributed leaflets calling on Egyptian and Jordanian soldiers to return home and struggle to overthrow their own rulers. *Kol ha'am* and *Al hamishmar* reported the distribution of these leaflets and published a translated text, which called for a federal state recognizing both peoples' right to self-determination and concluded with the slogan, "Long live Eretz Israel, united and democratic."⁶⁰ The technical device of translating *Palestine* as *Eretz Israel* in the Hebrew dailies, while formally correct, rhetorically obscured the transformation of a land with an Arab majority into one with a Jewish majority.

Fu'ad Nassar, 'Awda al-Ashhab, and others were arrested by Egyptian troops for distributing these leaflets near Bethlehem and imprisoned in Abu 'Agayla in the Sinai Peninsula, along with dozens of other NLL members from Jaffa, Gaza, and Jerusalem. The NLL also organized mass demonstrations in Nablus, Hebron, and Ramallah calling for evacuation of the foreign Arab troops from Palestine.⁶¹ Even while undertaking provocative acts against the Arab war effort, then, the NLL still looked forward to a unified Arab-Jewish state.

Despite its opposition to a permanent partition, the NLL was forced to accept the emerging politico-military status quo before resolving its internal debate. Only on this basis was continued political action possible. As early as May 1948 the NLL and MAKEI jointly protested the Haganah's treatment of Haifa's Arabs in a memorandum to the Israeli government. MAKEI accused the Haganah of taking spoils, plundering homes and commercial establishments, and committing unnecessary acts of cruelty against the civilian Arab population of Haifa in the two weeks *after* it had conquered the city. The party demanded that travel restrictions on Arabs be abolished; identity cards provided; labor exchanges opened to Arab workers; the supply of food, electricity, and water to the Arab neighborhoods organized; harsh action against looters taken; and the democratic rights of the Arab population, including participation in municipal administration, guaranteed. Attached to MAKEI's memorandum was an NLL proclamation declaring that the remaining Arabs in Haifa intended to struggle both for their right to stay and against all policies inimical to their interests.⁶² In short, this was a de facto recognition of Israeli sovereignty.

In July, since *Al-ittihad* was still banned, Haifa NLL members requested MAPAM to intervene on their behalf and convince the interim government to grant them a license to publish a new newspaper. In response, Dov Bar Nir appealed to the minister of police and minorities, offering MAPAM's guarantee of responsibility for the political line of the paper, an additional service probably not requested by the NLL.⁶³ The government's combination of responsibility for police and "minorities" (i.e., Arabs) in one ministry neatly expressed the emerging structure of discipline and knowledge of Palestinian Arabs. After the 1949 elections the Ministry of Minorities was abolished, and responsibility for Arab affairs was vested directly in the prime minister's office. This bureaucratic maneuver tightly controlled discussion about Israel's Arab population and minimized its place on the public agenda of government. The NLL undoubtedly asked MAPAM rather than MAKEI to intervene on its behalf because MAPAM was a member of the coalition government; in other words, this was a pragmatic step toward acceptance of the status quo. Bar Nir's offer to vouch for the NLL indicated that some MAPAM members regarded themselves as not very distant from the communists. The requested license was never granted, however, and Mikunis's interpellation asking the government to explain the nonapproval went unanswered.[64]

In mid-August the AWC held a meeting in Haifa attended by two hundred people to protest the high unemployment among the city's Arab population and the monopoly of the Histadrut-controlled Palestine Labor League on job opportunities for Arab workers. The meeting also demanded improvement of the food supply by organizing a cooperative to bring food from the surrounding villages.[65] Yet it was not possible for the Arab communists to address these basic needs of their people without recognizing and dealing with the Israeli authorities.

De facto recognition was soon followed by ideological reassessment. In late September, the NLL Central Committee adopted a comprehensive self-criticism of its historic path as a prelude to announcing its willingness to reunite with the Jewish communists in the Communist Party of Israel (MAKI). The NLL leadership accepted responsibility for the 1943 split in the Palestine Communist Party by announcing that it recognized the danger of organizing the communist movement on a national basis; its mononational character, they claimed, had prevented the NLL from correctly understanding the emergence of a new reality in the country: the formation of a Jewish nation in Palestine. Failure to take into consideration the revolutionary forces rising within this Jewish nation had caused the NLL to imagine that the Palestinian Arabs alone could liberate Palestine from British imperialism. Thus, it neglected to denounce the bourgeois and neofeudal leadership of the Palestinian Arab national movement.

The stand of the NLL Central Committee in favor of the partition plan and the actions against the invading Arab armies were praised. The NLL pledged to continue the struggle to implement partition and establish an Arab state in Palestine. The policies of the state of Israel toward the Arab population were denounced, and the right of the Arab refugees to return affirmed. Given the identity of the NLL and MAKI political lines, nothing now prevented reestablishment of the internationalist unity of the communist movement on a territorial basis. Therefore, the NLL Central Committee called on all its members *within the borders of the state of Israel* to join MAKI. Branches of the NLL in the territory designated as part of the Arab state by the UN partition plan, including those areas now occupied by Israel, such as Nazareth, would continue to function as part of the NLL.

The Central Committee of MAKI responded to this NLL self-criticism on October 6. MAKI characterized its line and that of the PCP and MAKEI as "internationalist in essence," despite their entirely Jewish composition after 1943, and recounted their repeated declarations in favor of restoring the internationalist unity of the communist movement. It welcomed the change in the NLL's line on the national question in Palestine, since the party's previous line had prevented communist unity. The NLL's proposal for unity was accepted. This would be implemented by expanding the MAKI Central Committee through the addition of members of the NLL Central Committee *residing in Israel* and accepting the branches and members of the NLL *in the state of Israel* into the ranks of MAKI. An expanded plenum of the Central Committee would be held in Haifa on October 22 to discuss the party's line, reestablish its internationalist unity, and set a date for the Eleventh Party Congress. The MAKI Central Committee also welcomed the NLL's decision to organize the party in the Arab part of Palestine on an internationalist basis and directed MAKI members living in the territories designated for the Palestinian Arab state to join the communist party in that state. (In fact, there were no Jewish communists in these territories.)

Both these documents were published in *Al-ittihad* on October 18 (the first issue to appear since the British closed the paper in February) under the headline "Restoration of a United Internationalist Communist Party in Each of the Two States." Hebrew versions, with no substantial differences, appeared in *Kol ha'am* and in a pamphlet containing the documents of the unity meeting. Clearly, then, both Arab and Jewish communists agreed to the creation of two binational parties in the two states that were to have been established according to the terms (including those on boundaries) of the UN partition plan. The boundary question was further emphasized by the fact that Emile Habibi, as leader of the NLL in Nazareth—a city occupied by Israel in the war but that was to have been included in the Arab state—addressed the Haifa unity meeting as a "member of the Central Committee of the NLL in the Arab part of Palestine." Munʿim Jarjura, secretary of the Nazareth AWC branch and so not considered a member of MAKI, attended the Haifa meeting as a guest member of the presidium.

The final step in the NLL's political realignment before the unification of MAKI occurred in early October when the Iraqi, Lebanese, and Syrian communist parties and the NLL issued a joint communiqué condemning the Arab invasion of Palestine and supporting partition. The Egyptian communists, owing both to organizational disunity and to the fact that most of them were incarcerated soon after the war began, did not sign the document; nonetheless, the overwhelming majority of them agreed with its political line. The communiqué declared:

> The Palestine war was a direct result of the fierce struggle between England and the United States, who caused the war in order to exploit it to settle accounts between them.... The Palestine war revealed finally and completely the betrayal of the reactionary rulers in the Arab states and their complete submission to foreign imperialism.[66]

The Arab communist parties hailed the leading role of communists and of the Soviet Union in advancing progress throughout the world. The Soviet Union and the democratic forces of the world had supported the Arab peoples' struggle for independence from foreign rule. Although the Soviet Union originally favored a united independent state in Palestine, as a result of the heritage of enmity that British imperialism, assisted by Arab reaction and Zionism, had bequeathed to the peoples of Palestine, it now supported the establishment of two independent states. The results of the war proved the correctness of this position.

The rhetorical structure of this document reveals the problematic character of the Arab communists' stand. Anglo-American imperialism and Arab reaction were deemed primarily responsible for the war; there was no substantive critique of Zionist ideology or practice or of Israel's conduct of the war. The state of Israel was not even mentioned. The refugees appeared only in the last programmatic paragraph, which called for their right to return, the withdrawal of all troops (Israeli and Arab) from the territory designated for the Arab state, and the establishment of an Arab state in Palestine. Partition was justified only in terms of support for the stand of the Soviet Union, the leader of the world forces of progress. There was no independent analysis of the local situation, no reference to an Israeli-Jewish nation or its right to self-determination, and no discussion of the failures of the Palestinian Arab national movement. The declaration conveyed a tone of defeat and resignation. The only hope for the future, it seemed, resided in the leadership of the Soviet Union, whose correctness was confirmed by the disastrous outcome of the Palestine war.

The themes of the joint declaration of Arab communist parties were reiterated at the Haifa unity meeting, whose overall perspective was that the imperialists alone had caused the frictions between Jews and Arabs in Palestine/Eretz Israel and that unity against imperialism and the reactionary Arab invaders based on the struggle to implement the partition plan was possible because no contradictions existed between the two peoples' "real" interests. Mikunis emphasized that the Palestinian Arabs had not participated actively in the war; he quoted Ben-Gurion's statement to the MAPAI Council on February 7, 1948, that only a few Palestinian Arab villages took part in the military effort to prevent the creation of a Jewish state, as well as Golda Meir's comment at a press conference in the third month of the war that "out of hundreds of Arab villages included in the area of the Jewish state, only five or six agreed to serve as a base for the Arab attackers. Most of the mercenary rioters came from Iraq and Syria."[67] Thus the Palestinian Arabs were exonerated in terms that could only be regarded as disgraceful by Arab nationalists: in essence, by their failure to participate fully in the effort to prevent the expropriation of their homeland. This account of the war was not entirely correct, of course. There was Palestinian Arab resistance in some areas, for example the guerrilla forces that operated in the approaches to Jerusalem led by ʿAbd al-Qadir al-Husayni.

By sanctioning this narrative, MAKI detached the Palestinian Arabs from their national political context, denied their right to resist the expropriation of their homeland, and accepted the Zionist view that any Palestinian Arab resistance to the creation of Israel was illegitimate. Israel's military dominance and the reactionary leadership of both the Palestinian Arab national movement and the Arab states probably insured that any attempt by the Palestinian Arabs to resist partition more actively would have compounded their national catastrophe. Recognition of this reality, along with sympathy for the remnants of Nazism and the undeniable Zionist success in expelling the British, led to unification of MAKI on terms reflecting a Jewish national tilt. Nonetheless, MAKI retained legitimacy in the Palestinian Arab community both because its argument that the party had averted an even greater disaster was plausible and because its militant and consistent defense of Arab political and civil rights offered the only viable and coherent program for future struggle.

At the Haifa meeting, Mikunis sharply attacked the interim government's conduct of the war: its policies of expelling Arabs, expropriating their property, and detaining political activists (including communists and other leftists who favored partition); and, most of all, its indifference (in fact, active opposition) to the creation of an independent Palestinian Arab state. He summarized his criticism of Israel's conduct of the war with the warning: "If matters continue in this way, then the war of liberation of the state of Israel may turn into an antidemocratic war of conquest."[68] With this he placed a question mark over the progressive content of the war and its outcome. Mikunis's posing of the question (like Aharon Cohen's prediction quoted earlier) reveals extraordinary political perspicacity. Yet MAKI never returned to examine this issue; and when matters did "continue in this way," MAKI could not resolve the new political issues that arose as a consequence. In the celebration of the anti-imperialist victory represented by the creation and successful defense of the state of Israel, the problem embodied in Mikunis's prophetic remark was perhaps intentionally overlooked.

THE PALESTINE QUESTION AND THE EGYPTIAN COMMUNISTS

The Palestine question became a major issue in Egyptian politics only after World War II, although the Muslim Brothers, Young Egypt, and some elements in the Wafd had promoted the Palestine cause since the revolt of 1936–39. The Marxist left, while anti-Zionist, did not actively engage this issue. The political orientation of the left overall, in common with the majority of politically aware Egyptians, was toward local nationalism, not pan-Arabism. Consequently, Palestine remained a secondary concern for Egypt until the mid-1950s.

Yusuf Darwish, a Karaite Jew, was among the small number of political activists in Egypt who did develop an exceptional interest in Palestine in the 1930s. Influenced by a book he read as a law student in Paris in 1933, he became a militant anti-Zionist. During the 1936–39 Arab revolt in Palestine, Darwish contacted one of its leaders and raised money to support the revolt.[69] In 1940, he and two Sephardic Jewish comrades, Raymond Douek and Ahmad Sadiq Sa'd, began educating and organizing workers. In 1945 they constituted an informal Marxist group known by the name of the journal, *Al-fajr al-jadid* (New dawn), that they began to publish in May. New Dawn developed a strong base in several Cairo-area trade unions, especially that of the militant textile workers in Shubra al-Khayma.

Darwish transmitted his engagement in the Palestine question to his comrades, and the three Jewish founders of New Dawn soon acquired a reputation for uncompromising anti-Zionism. They were the first Egyptian Marxists to make contact with their Palestinian counterparts. Early in 1945, Bulus Farah and Mukhlis ʿAmr, on behalf of the AWC, urged New Dawn to send a trade union delegation to the preparatory conference of the World Federation of Trade Unions that was to convene in February and at which the Palestinians wanted to enhance Arab representation in order to counteract the Histadrut's presence. No Egyptians attended the conference, but several, including veteran trade unionist and New Dawn member Yusuf al-Mudarrik, attended the founding congress of the World Federation of Trade Unions in September in Paris, where the Arab presence did reduce the Histadrut's influence in the world federation.

The social composition and political orientation of New Dawn and the NLL were similar, and the friendly relations between the two organizations were reflected in many articles in *Al-fajr al-jadid* and New Dawn's weekly workers' newspaper, *Al-damir* (The conscience), encouraging the Palestinian Arab struggle, warning of the dangers of Zionism, promoting the NLL, and quoting *Al-ittihad*. New Dawn supported the first mass anti-Zionist demonstrations in Egypt on November 2, 1945, but criticized the Muslim Brothers and Young Egypt for falling into racist attacks on Egyptian Jews and their property.[70]

In the spring of 1946, Ahmad Sadiq Saʿd, using material supplied by ʿAmr and Farah of the NLL, published a book on the Palestine question, one of the first to appear on the subject in Egypt. His somewhat apologetic introduction admitted that "it might seem strange to the reader" to discuss Palestine during the upsurge of Egypt's own national movement. Saʿd adopted the line of argument presented a year later by Emile Tuma to the Conference of the Communist Parties of the British Empire, posing the issue solely as an Arab anticolonial struggle: "The question of Palestine is not that of Jewish immigration to the country, but rather the question of the national democratic demands of the Arab popular movement in Palestine."[71] Partition of Palestine was, therefore, completely rejected.

In contrast to New Dawn's focus on organizing workers, the Iskra

TABLE 1   SOCIAL COMPOSITION OF EMNL, ISKRA, AND DMNL MEMBERSHIP

	EMNL		Iskra		DMNL	
	No.	%	No.	%	No.	%
Workers	250	50	140	16	390	28
Students	80	16	200	22	280	20
Youth	90	18	—	—	90	6
Intellectuals	—	—	200	22	200	14
Foreigners	—	—	360	40	360	26
Army	25	5	—	—	25	2
Azharists	25	5	—	—	25	2
Sudanese	30	6	—	—	30	2
TOTAL	500		900		1,400	

SOURCE: Henri Curiel, "Les principales étapes de la lutte intérieure qui est déroulée autour du MDLN durant l'année: Mai 1947–Juin 1948 dite l'année de l'unité" (late 1955), appendix to *Pages autobiographiques* (typescript, 1977), p. 5.

NOTE: Curiel was trying to prove that the EMNL was more Egyptianized and more working class than Iskra. There were intellectuals and foreign citizens in the EMNL, though they were not organized separately, as they were in Iskra. Nonetheless, the point that Iskra had many more intellectuals and foreigners and far fewer workers is correct. Curiel also maintained that Iskra inflated the number of its members before unity, and that the DMNL actually had about a thousand members when it was formed.

organization, founded in 1942 and led by Hillel Schwartz, concentrated on recruiting intellectuals and training them in Marxist theory. A large number of foreign and Europeanized Jews belonged to Iskra (see Table 1); and several of the group's non-Jewish intellectuals became leading advocates of pan-Arabism in the communist movement during the 1950s and 1960s, among them Shuhdi ʿAtiyya al-Shafiʿi, Anouar Abdel-Malek, Latifa al-Zayyat, Michel Kamil, and Mohamed Sid-Ahmed. These activists received their training in Marxism in the 1940s from the Jewish and cosmopolitan leaders of Iskra, with whom they then shared a local Egyptian patriotic orientation.

The non-Jewish intellectuals of Iskra were often less militantly anti-Zionist than the Jews, who saw Zionism as a threat to their status as Egyptians. In late 1946 or early 1947 several of the Jews, led by Ezra Harari, formed the Jewish Anti-Zionist League, which campaigned aggressively among the Jews of Cairo. When it attempted to take over leadership of the Zionist Maccabee Club in the Dahir district, a physical clash ensued in April 1947 in which the police sided with the Zionists, and in June the government proscribed the league.[72] By contrast, al-Shafi'i, the first Egyptian Muslim to join the Iskra leadership, coauthored a comprehensive exposition of Egypt's national goals in which he briefly addressed the Palestine question, stating merely that "the persistence of imperialism in any part of the Arab world is a continuing threat to Egyptian independence." To combat this threat he called simply for a united front of Jews and Arabs in Palestine against imperialism and its Zionist tool.[73]

The Egyptian Movement for National Liberation was founded in 1943 by the legendary Henri Curiel, a Jew from a wealthy family and originally an Italian citizen who exercised a profound charismatic influence over many indigenous Egyptians despite his French education and broken Arabic. Curiel was a master of tactical maneuvering. His articulation of the principal task of Egyptian communists as building a multiclass national front (hence the name EMNL) to struggle for full national independence—"the line of popular democratic forces"—shaped the political debate in the communist movement of the 1940s.

Curiel brought the Palestine question to the attention of the EMNL in a long and detailed report composed in October 1945 at the height of the anti-Zionist press campaign in Egypt, which culminated in the mass demonstration and anti-Jewish riots of November 2.[74] In contrast to the Arab-centered analysis of Sadiq Sa'd and New Dawn, Curiel emphasized the economic, social, and political development of the *yishuv* and the growing antagonism between the Zionists and the British. The report included a detailed study of the Histadrut and its cooperatives, while sharply attacking Left Po'alei Tzion, Hashomer Hatza'ir, and the Communist Union and deploring the split in the Palestinian communist movement. Curiel criticized both the PCP for joining the Histadrut and opposing the British White Paper of 1939 and the NLL for failing to recognize the national character of the *yishuv;* however, he unequivocally opposed partition of Palestine. Calling for the reunification of the communist camp, Curiel appeared to reproach both groups evenhandedly; yet his criticism of the PCP was over tactical matters, whereas that of the NLL involved a basic question of principle. His characterization of Palestine as a "country with a binational character" (in the context of criticizing Left Po'alei Tzion's call for a "Jewish socialist state"), too, meant that Curiel was closer in position to the PCP than to the NLL.

The Palestine question became an immediate issue in Egypt in the spring of 1947, just as the EMNL and Iskra fused to form the Democratic Movement for National Liberation. The DMNL was by far the largest Egyptian communist organization, its influence amplified by a legal weekly, *Al-jamahir* (The masses), whose circulation averaged seven to eight thousand but occasionally reached as high as fifteen thousand.[75] The DMNL participated in demonstrations demanding British evacuation from Palestine, while trying to insure that these demonstrations did not assume an anti-Semitic character. On one occasion when anti-Zionist demonstrators attacked a store owned by an Egyptian Jew in al-Mansura, the DMNL's local members all stood in front of the store to protect it.[76] This differentiation of Jews and Zionists characterized the Arab communists and divided them from the rest of the Arab national movement, which did not make this distinction.

While there can be no legitimate doubt that Curiel and the EMNL ideologically rejected Zionism, Curiel freely admitted that he and his group had violently opposed the Jewish Anti-Zionist League, regarding its political line as a "grave error" that had led to "provocative scenes" with the middle-class Jews of Dahir. He believed Iskra's decision to accept the government's dissolution of the League on the eve of unification with the EMNL was a tacit admission of the bankruptcy of Iskra's entire political approach.[77] Curiel apparently thought that by refraining from attacking Zionist ideology directly (just as the DMNL did not criticize Islamic belief and observances) he could more easily convince Egyptian Jews not to identify with Zionism. His unwavering confidence in his political credo often led him to engage confirmed opponents in dialogue, and many times he did win them over. Yet Curiel's rivals regarded his personalistic political style and excessive tactical flexibility as opportunism, which not only opened him to accusations of being a Zionist but also undermined the status of Egyptian Jews in both the communist movement and the country at large.[78] More "provocative scenes" like the one in Dahir, which was favorably noted in the nationalist Egyptian press, might have persuaded more Egyptian nationalists that Egyptian Jews were generally not Zionists.

Al-jamahir defended the Soviet position on Palestine against attacks by conservative Arab political leaders but avoided mentioning Gromyko's suggestion that partition might be a necessary solution.[79] The DMNL saw the Palestine question as subordinate to Egypt's struggle for independence and the evacuation of all British troops and argued that the issue was being used by reactionaries to divert the Egyptian people from their own national struggle. *Al-jamahir*'s editorialist, sarcastically commenting on the advance of Egyptian troops to El Arish, asked if they hadn't seen the British troops occupying the Canal Zone on their way to the Palestine border.⁸⁰

Like the Palestinian communists, *Al-jamahir* endorsed the UN partition plan only after Tsarapkin declared the Soviet Union's support. It defended partition as necessary to expel the British and achieve independence following the failure of Arab-Jewish cooperation, but it did not argue that there was a Jewish national community in Palestine with political rights, as Curiel had noted in 1945 and Gromyko had argued before the UN on May 14, 1947. This latter analysis appeared only in the DMNL's internal theoretical bulletin, where it was necessary to demonstrate that partition was a valid Marxist solution to the Palestine problem.⁸¹ Instead *Al-jamahir* presented partition as a tactical step that would lead to a united state in the (indeterminate but presumably not too distant) future.⁸² Curiel recalled the attitude of the DMNL leadership: "I do not believe that, at first, we understood the partition decision or its reasons completely; but the entire international revolutionary movement was moving in the direction of supporting this decision. We hesitated at first, then we decided to support partition." ⁸³

Curiel thus suggested that the DMNL's decision to accept the UN partition plan was ultimately determined by its acceptance of the leading role of the Soviet Union in the international communist movement. Apparently this consideration was strong enough that no disagreement arose between Jewish and non-Jewish members of the organization's top leadership when the original decision was taken. Yusuf Hazan recalled that the Political Committee decided to accept the UN decisions by consensus in light of the Soviet stand;⁸⁴ and Mustafa Tiba portrayed the decision as the result of "extremism in internationalist commitment." He recalled that "the minority that rejected this stand was described as deviating from internationalism and breaking with Marxist teachings" and emphasized that Jews and non-Jews, as such, had no differences on this or any other question.⁸⁵ Tiba's testimony is especially weighty because, after serving as leader of the DMNL in 1948, he subsequently became a staunch opponent of Curiel within the communist movement; hence, he might have wished to attribute responsibility for the Egyptian communists' acceptance of partition to the influence of Curiel and other Jews in the DMNL.

In late 1947 and early 1948, the DMNL's position was close to that of MAKEI. The parties had been exchanging information since September 1947, when the editor of *Al-jamahir* wrote to *Kol ha'am* asking that it serve as *Al-jamahir*'s Palestine correspondent and offered to exchange publications.[86] On January 18, 1948, *Al-jamahir* approvingly quoted *Kol ha'am*'s condemnation of Begin's ETZEL for bombing the Arab-owned Semiramis Hotel and nearby houses in the Katamon district of Jerusalem. As previously noted, *Kol ha'am* returned the compliment later in the week by quoting *Al-jamahir*'s support for partition as a temporary measure that would lead to a united Palestine in the future.

Shortly after endorsing the UN partition plan, the DMNL was shattered by a succession of splits centered on criticism of Curiel's leadership and his national united-front strategy. Curiel and other Jewish DMNL members have consistently denied that Palestine was an issue in this debate. Raymond Stambouli and Yusuf Hazan, for example, recalled that the issues of *Al-jamahir* criticizing Egypt's plan to invade Palestine were extremely popular, especially in working-class districts.[87] Curiel regarded the struggle against him as an expression of national chauvinism:

> The merger brought some very brilliant intellectuals [from Iskra] into the movement. On the one hand, as intellectuals they were a little chauvinist and saw no reason why Egyptianization should not be completed by the elimination of Yunis [Curiel's nom de guerre]. On the other hand, if the role of foreigners was to be reduced to zero, they had a tendency to underestimate the stage of proletarianization: for them the essential was to be Egyptian.[88]

By contrast, according to Mohamed Sid-Ahmed, the first group to split from the DMNL—the Revolutionary Bloc, led by Shuhdi 'Atiyya al-Shafi'i and Anouar Abdel-Malek—vehemently objected when, after the DMNL endorsed the partition plan, communism was attacked as Zionism. Sid-Ahmed characterized this group's criticisms of Curiel and the other Jewish leaders as possibly "anti-Semitic a bit ... a violent reaction against the feeling that the whole movement was held and perhaps manipulated by Jews and that their commitment to Marxism was colored by things that might be alien to an authentic Egyptian Marxism."[89] This statement corroborates Curiel's view that the young indigenous intellectuals sought to Egyptianize the communist movement completely—in which case it would be difficult to believe that the Palestine question was not an issue. Nonetheless, it is extraordinary that on the eve of the 1948–49 war Jews sold copies of *Al-jamahir* in working-class neighborhoods without being physically assaulted (even if the number of copies sold may have been less than the "hundreds" Stambouli and Hazan remembered). The disparities in the recollections of Curiel, Yusuf Hazan, Mustafa Tiba, and Mohamed Sid-Ahmed concerning the existence of a debate on the Palestine question may be a question of timing. Perhaps the DMNL remained united on this question in late 1947 and early 1948, but once the magnitude of the Arab defeat in the Palestine war became apparent some members of the organization reconsidered their positions and drew far-reaching conclusions.

In late March 1948, *Al-jamahir* was banned. Martial law was declared days before Egypt invaded Palestine on May 15. Curiel and many other communists were incarcerated with Zionists—including the wealthy businessman with Zionist sympathies Ovadia Salim—and other opposition political activists in Huckstep, a former British army camp, where the debate over partition and the struggle within the DMNL continued. Rif'at al-Sa'id, then a young DMNL member, recalled that Salim was permitted to conduct his business affairs from the office of the camp commandant, directing his secretaries on the telephone and leaving the camp daily in his private car. This evidence taught him "who is with whom and against whom" and convinced him that the DMNL had been correct to oppose the Egyptian invasion of Palestine, as a diversion of the people's attention from the struggle against British imperialism and its Egyptian allies.[90]

Until the political prisoners were released in late 1949 and early 1950, the DMNL, now split into half a dozen factions, was in complete disarray and saw little activity. It did manage to circulate a statement on July 29, 1948, condemning Egypt's invasion of Palestine as an "unjust racist war directed by imperialism and traitors against Arab interests." It accused British and American imperialism of inciting a "religious war" and turning a national anti-imperialist struggle into an "anti-Jewish racial struggle" in order to stabilize their control of the Middle East.[91]

In contrast to the DMNL, New Dawn, reorganized in September 1946 as the Popular Vanguard for Liberation, opposed the prevailing opinion in the international communist movement on the Palestine question. As the organization's expert on Palestine, Ahmad Sadiq Sa'd was the greatest influence in shaping the group's official line. In the Popular Vanguard's internal bulletin, *Al-hadaf* (The goal), he echoed *Al-ittihad*'s argument that the Soviet Union's support for partition was not a question of principle but a tactical matter connected to Soviet state interests and therefore ought not to obligate Egyptian communists. When they were interviewed nearly forty years later, some former leaders of the organization maintained that under pressure to conform to the international communist line they subsequently retracted this stand and supported partition while they were jailed in 1948; others, however, said that no clear stand was ever adopted.[92]

The Jewish leaders of the Popular Vanguard for Liberation bitterly attacked the DMNL's stand on Palestine. They rejected the idea (which they attributed to Curiel) that Israel was a progressive democratic state and were scandalized when, in the detention camp at Huckstep, they overheard Curiel tell Jewish communists not proficient in Arabic that they should emigrate to Israel and join the struggle there because the Israeli working class was more developed and the revolution would occur there first.[93] The Popular Vanguard had little impact on public perception of the communists' stand, though, for even after fusing with the Popular Liberation Movement led by Mustafa Sadiq and Raoul Makarius and changing its name to Popular Democracy in 1949, the organization remained very small, with only about 160 members.[94] Its influence was further limited because it had no public organ after *Al-fajr al-jadid* and *Al-damir* were closed during the government's anti-communist campaign of July 1946, in response to which it conducted most of its activity in the framework of the Wafdist Vanguard, therefore submerging its independent outlook. Still, its criticisms of Curiel became widely shared by other communists.

THE MARXIST LEFT AFTER PARTITION

The struggle against Curiel and his political line (or distorted versions of it), the role of Jews in the DMNL, the split in the organization, and the question of Palestine were all linked and became part of the accepted explanation for the failures of the Egyptian communist movement for communists and noncommunists alike. In fact, there is little evidence that the Egyptian communists suffered a dramatic loss of popularity because of the DMNL's stand on Palestine; but the outbreak of war in 1948 gave the government an excuse to declare martial law and break the momentum of the rising tide of the nationalist movement, in which the communists were playing an important role. Thus the left, after failing to ride the crest of the nationalist wave of 1945–46 to victory, lost yet another opportunity to bring an end to the old regime.

The creation of the state of Israel embodied a double Arab failure. For both Egyptian and Palestinian communists, the decision to support partition was necessary because of Arab failures in the struggle against Zionism. But then the Arab Marxists proved incapable of insuring implementation of the terms of the UN resolution, despite support from the Soviet Union and Israeli Marxists. The Soviet Union endorsed the partition of Palestine mainly because this seemed the quickest and surest way to expel the British from the Middle East—a logic that was accepted both by Jewish and Arab communists and by MAPAM. As a consequence, the Zionist movement emerged by default as the leading anti-imperialist force in the Middle East.

However, the creation of a Zionist state and the war required to defend that state had a logic of their own. In Israel, these developments led to the institutionalization of Ben-Gurion's activist politico-military strategy and structured the hegemonic Zionist discourse on the significance of the Jewish state and its relationship to the Palestinian Arabs. The principle issues in the Palestinian-Israeli conflict—the refugee question, the location of Israel's borders, the creation of a Palestinian state, the character of Israeli democracy—became defined by a mythologized account that demonized Palestinian opposition to Zionism and denied realities experienced and criticized by many Zionists themselves.

In contrast, the Marxist narrative focused on the imperialist plot to destroy Jewish-Arab unity, at the same time indirectly delegitimizing Palestinian opposition to Zionism because this was expressed as opposition to partition. Marxism had no theoretical category for a national or intercommunal struggle in which the leadership of both sides was not particularly anti-imperialist. Thus, the Marxists adopted positions that the Arab world considered "objectively" Zionist. Their support for partition was assimilated to the hegemonic Zionist discourse; for not only did they lack the strength to compel creation of a Palestinian state, but Ben-Gurion and MAPAI were able, with the assistance of ʿAbd Allah, Britain, and the United States, to prevent this from happening as well.

MAKI's support for Israel's violation of the partition plan through annexation of Jerusalem;[95] MAPAM's October 7, 1948, resolution on boundary modifications, its new formulation of the refugee question, and the behavior of its kibbutzim and members in uniform during the war; the demands of both MAPAM and MAKI that the Israeli government reject the UN-sponsored cease-fires and Count Bernadotte's proposed territorial compromise—all these stands were justified in the name of anti-imperialist struggle, and their adoption contributed to consolidating the hegemonic Zionist discourse. Curiel and the DMNL were accused, probably with justification, of the same abandonment of critical consciousness, although most of the Egyptian communists were equally guilty.

The magnitude of the regional political realignment created by the establishment of the state of Israel was appreciated neither by the regional Marxist left nor, it seems, by the Soviet Union. Potential Arab Marxist perspectives were blocked by the temporary dispersion of the Egyptian communist movement, the absorption of the NLL into MAKI, and the October 1948 declaration of the Arab communist parties. The communists and the left wing of MAPAM imagined that Israel was going to be simply a normal state in which the class struggle would go on. They did not understand the internal, regional, and international implications of Israel's settler-colonial heritage and the ways in which this heritage would be extended into the statehood period.

CHAPTER III

The Political Economy of Hegemony

The Soviet Union and Czechoslovakia provided critical military and diplomatic support for the establishment of the state of Israel. The United States, in contrast, though it quickly recognized Israel, actually attempted in the spring of 1948 to delay the Jewish state's declaration of independence, supported proposals for resolving the Arab-Israeli conflict that were perceived to be inimical to Israeli interests (such as those of Count Bernadotte), and, during the 1949 Lausanne conference, pressured Israel to agree to repatriate one hundred thousand Palestinian refugees. Based on the 1947–49 diplomatic record of the two great powers, MAKI and MAPAM hoped that the state of Israel would look to the Soviet Union for international support, a possibility that continuing British paramountcy in Egypt, Transjordan, and Iraq and close American ties with Saudi Arabia appeared to enhance.

Why were the hopes of MAKI and MAPAM, which seem almost ridiculous in retrospect, unfulfilled? The most fundamental reason is that Zionism and Nasserist Arab nationalism were based on dissimilar class alliances, with opposite implications for the international orientation of the two movements. Egyptian-Israeli relations in the 1950s and 1960s must be situated in the context of their differential relationship to Western imperialism—meaning not only Western political domination of the Middle East, but also, and more fundamentally, the role of Western capital in the internal social structures and economies of the various Middle Eastern states. The international orientations of Egypt and Israel and their approach to the Arab-Israeli conflict were not simply independent expressions of the preferences of particular ruling groups; rather, they were rooted in the specific social character of these two countries' national projects.

With the eclipse of independent Palestinian political action after 1948, the Arab-Israeli conflict was transformed from a communal civil war into an international dispute whose resolution was perceived primarily as a problem of foreign policy. The Marxist parties themselves, adopting a rather un-Marxist line of thought, tended to regard foreign policy and international orientation as independent variables, more as commitments that could influence the internal character of a regime than as expressions of its prevailing balance of social forces. Thus, for the communists, Soviet support for the creation of Israel superseded their historic objections to Zionism; similarly, Soviet diplomatic and military support for Egypt after 1955 was believed to be a force that could mitigate or overcome Egypt's undemocratic domestic policies. As a consequence, overcoming certain illusions about Israel was accompanied by embracing illusions about Nasserist Egypt. The differential rate at which this occurred, along with the natural tendency for Israeli Jews to be more sensitive to illusory thinking about Egypt than about their own country, and vice versa, explains both the growing political divergence of the Egyptian and Israeli communists and the structural cleavage underlying the eventual split in MAKI. For MAPAM, in contrast, the fact that the state of Israel was a fulfillment of Zionism prevented the party from undertaking a fundamental analysis of its social character; hence, despite the party's consistent disapproval of Israel's international orientation even after the Suez/Sinai War, most Jews in the party were unable to appreciate the positive aspects of the Nasserist regime because they regarded it primarily as a threat to Israel.

LABOR AND CAPITAL IN THE ZIONIST MOVEMENT

The working class established its hegemony over the Zionist movement in the early 1930s. Organizationally this was expressed by the formation and emergence of MAPAI as the dominant party within the *yishuv* and the World Zionist Organization, MAPAI's control of a commanding majority within the Histadrut, and the election of MAPAI leader David Ben-Gurion as chairman of the Jewish Agency. This hegemony was maintained, although the relations among the component elements of the alliance of social forces on which it was based shifted over time, until the victory of the Likud in the 1977 Knesset elections. The leading role of the working class was necessary for the realization of the Zionist project, for it alone was capable of undertaking the tasks of construction, settlement, and development of an armed force that were necessary for the *yishuv* to establish itself in an already inhabited, politically hostile country. The labor Zionist slogans "Jewish labor" (*Avodah 'ivrit*), "Conquest of the land" (*Kibush hakarka'*), and "Jewish products" (*Totzeret ha'aretz*) expressed the class interests of urban and rural Jewish workers seeking to exclude cheaper Arab labor from the market, expand access to agricultural land, and secure a market for their products, as well as the national goal of building a Jewish society in Palestine. The Histadrut became the preeminent institution in the *yishuv* largely because it was not primarily a trade union. Though of course this was one of its functions, it also established a health service, an insurance fund, a sports federation, a theater, a daily newspaper, a bank, an army (the Palmah and Haganah), and a large number of cooperative and corporate enterprises that dominated the transportation, construction, and mixed farming sectors of the Jewish economy.

Official efforts at encouraging entrepreneurial capital investment in the Zionist project in Palestine met with only limited success owing to the insecure conditions there. The Zionist institutions, the Histadrut, and later the state of Israel therefore recruited capital from abroad in the form of donations and concessionary loans, resources that can be defined as collective capital. Although these funds were invested and managed according to the norms of the capitalist market, with the intention of yielding a profit, profitability was often subordinated to the national-political goals of Zionist settlement and construction. As the dominant party in the Zionist institutions, MAPAI used highly political criteria in managing and allocating this imported capital. The Histadrut's enterprises—major recipients of imported capital—were also managed mainly by political appointees of the MAPAI majority.

Despite the leading political role of the working class in Zionist settlement, construction, and armed defense, labor was ultimately dependent on capital imported from the West to finance the Zionist project. The protective umbrella of the British mandatory regime was also an essential component of Zionist progress. Therefore, MAPAI's political strategy was to form an alliance between collective and private capital and to maintain good relations with Great Britain so as to ensure maximum support for the establishment of the Jewish state, as well as to safeguard the interests of the Jewish workers whose particular interests it represented. Private capital in the *yishuv* was protected and encouraged. Periodic clashes occurred between Jewish labor and capital over such issues as wages and employers' desire to hire cheaper Arab labor, but MAPAI sought to restrain the class struggle within the Jewish community in the interest of national construction; in exchange, the entire Zionist movement accepted the leading role of labor and its MAPAI-led institutions in the *yishuv*. MAPAI's moderate social-democratic outlook was firmly anticommunist and Western-oriented. The party opposed launching an armed struggle to expel the British from Palestine (except briefly in 1945–46), and when it did begin forcefully to resist British policies, Ben-Gurion had already reoriented the Zionist movement toward the United States, a shift symbolized by the 1942 Biltmore Conference in New York.

The settler-colonial component of the Zionist project had a continuing influence on the economy, ideology, and diplomacy of the statehood period. Appropriating the property of the Palestinian refugees constituted a form of primitive capital accumulation that helped to expand the Jewish economy, especially the agricultural sector. Israel's Jewish population more than doubled between May 15, 1948, and the end of 1951. The 684,000 newcomers—some 250,000 of whom lived in houses formerly owned by Arabs—knew nothing of the Palestinian Arab society that had existed before 1948. By 1954 over one-third of Israel's Jewish population lived on absentee Arab property. During and after 1948 over 350 Arab villages that had existed during the mandate period were demolished and replaced by new Jewish settlements;[1] 350 of 370 new settlements established between 1948 and 1953 were on absentee Arab property. The Orwellian language of the Absentee Property Law of 1950 defined nearly half of the Palestinian Arabs legally residing in Israel as "present-absentees" because they had only temporarily (or so they imagined) left their villages during the 1948–49 war. This definition allowed the Custodian of Absentee Property to confiscate nearly 40 percent of their lands (about one million dunams, or one-quarter of a million acres, of cultivable land). The Land Acquisitions Law of 1953 regularized the process of expropriation for other categories of Arab land. All together, approximately 4.5 million dunams of cultivable land were confiscated from absent, present, and "present-absentee" Arabs, increasing the area available to Jewish farmers by 250 percent. The UN Refugee Office estimated the value of abandoned Arab movable and real property at nearly £120 million (greater than Israel's total domestic capital formation from 1949 to 1953).[2]

The continuing expropriation, expulsion, and domination of the Palestinian Arab minority in Israel was enforced by the military government, which controlled most Arab-inhabited areas from 1948 to 1966 employing segmentation, cooptation, and coercion to keep Arabs powerless and dependent. The military authorities marginalized the social presence of Arab citizens by elaborating both a technology of repression and a body of "knowledge" about them that confined and defined them in categories like "fifth column," "security risk," "terrorists," and "non-Jewish minorities." Arabs were required to obtain travel passes to leave the vicinity of their villages and towns. Military officials often distributed travel passes and other favors to clan heads in exchange for their families' electoral support of MAPAI; in contrast, access to Arab villagers by organizers and activists of other parties, especially MAKI, was restricted.

By making it difficult for those seeking employment in the cities to travel to work, travel passes regulated the access of Arabs to the wage labor market. Arabs were also denied membership in the trade unions of the Histadrut until 1952, and even after that date many Arabs who asked to join were not admitted. Lack of union membership was used to justify excluding Arabs from jobs or driving them out of jobs they already held. In 1959, the Histadrut permitted Arabs to become full members of the organization; this right, however, was not effectively implemented until the 1965 Histadrut elections. Arab agriculture was disadvantaged by a shortage of land due to extensive confiscations and lack of access to the technical and financial support of the Zionist institutions. In sum, Arabs were denied equal opportunity with Jews in all sectors of the economy.

Despite the relative weakness of the industrial sector and the continued reticence of private capital to invest in industry, Israel was able to live at a standard far higher than its real productive capacity would have permitted and to undertake a program of rapid economic development because of an extraordinary influx of imported capital. The net rate of domestic saving was about zero from 1949 to 1965; hence, Israel's economic development was financed by over $6 billion in capital imports, which amounted to approximately 25 percent of the GNP during this period. Over two-thirds of this imported capital consisted of unilateral transfers requiring no return of dividends or interest: donations from world Jewry, reparations from the West German government, and grants from the U.S. government.[3]

Although it is not immediately evident from Table 2, the United

TABLE 2   CAPITAL IMPORTS TO ISRAEL, 1949-65
(in millions of U.S. dollars)

	World Jewry	W. Germany	U.S. Govt.	Total
Unilateral transfers	2,152.7	1,736.7	313.9	4,203.3
Long-term capital	1,405.7	—	418.6	1,824.3
TOTAL	3,558.4	1,736.7	732.5	6,027.6

SOURCE: Nadav Halevi and Ruth Klinov-Malul, *The Economic Development of Israel* (New York, 1968), p. 298.

States was the most important source of capital imports in this era, as it is today. While generally supporting Israel, the U.S. government was critical of Ben-Gurion's activist military policies and maintained a diplomatic distance from the Jewish state in the 1950s, seeking to preserve friendly relations with the Arab states. U.S. grants to Israel were therefore a minuscule percentage of the current level and until 1965 made up only a small share of total unilateral transfers, 7.5 percent. World Jewry provided 51 percent of unilateral transfers, with American Jews accounting for the overwhelming majority of these funds. The U.S. government also supplied 23 percent of the long-term capital imports on which repayment was required; together with privately invested capital and loans from American Jews, these loans constituted 62 percent of Israel's repayable long-term capital imports during 1950–55 and 30 percent during 1956–60.[4]

Israel's heavy dependence on capital from the United States and West Germany tied it firmly to the Western bloc, and this link was reinforced at all levels of the economy. Over 25 percent of the total receipts of the Israeli government came from abroad during 1949–61;[5] in the 1950s, some 70 percent of Israel's foreign trade was with the United States and Western Europe.[6] Tourists, an important source of foreign exchange, also came overwhelmingly from the West, Americans generally being the largest spenders.

MAPAI-controlled institutions managed the distribution of most of the imported capital in the statehood era, just as they had during the mandate. The government alone disbursed about two-thirds of all capital invested in Israel in the 1950s, and over two-fifths in the next decade.[7] The Histadrut employed 20–25 percent of the labor force in the 1950s; that figure for the government and the Histadrut together stood at over 40 percent. Half of all Histadrut members depended to some extent on the organization for their livelihood during these years.[8] Employment in the state or Histadrut sector often meant having the right connections in MAPAI. As major employers, the Histadrut and the state had an interest in restraining working-class militancy, and since they were controlled by the same party, they generally cooperated to do so.

As the dominant Israeli party, MAPAI also managed the immigrant absorption apparatus. Settlers from Asia and Africa—the majority of those who arrived during the 1950s—were subjected to systematic discrimination and scornful dismissal of their cultural heritage. They were disproportionately concentrated at the lowest rungs of the employment ladder, in agriculture, construction, and unskilled industrial jobs.[9] With this rapid influx of cheap, unskilled Oriental labor, many veteran Ashkenazi workers who had participated in the post-Stalingrad wave of radicalization were promoted into the ranks of management or moved into the rapidly expanding service and professional sectors of the economy, becoming part of the "state-made middle class."[10] The remade, largely Oriental, Jewish working class of the 1950s lacked trade union experience and was unfamiliar with the ground rules of Israeli politics. Culturally differentiated from the veteran settlers, these newcomers were disoriented by the requirements of adapting to a new environment that had little in common with Jewish life as they had lived it in their countries of origin. Thus, despite the low wages and inadequate housing, education, and social services that were the common condition of many Oriental immigrants, they were easily disciplined by their dependency on MAPAI for housing, health care, and employment, in a decade when the unemployment rate hovered around 7–9 percent.[11] Ethnic stratification of the labor force, the replacement of veteran workers by new immigrants in many blue-collar jobs, and the social control exercised by MAPAI through both the Histadrut and the immigration absorbtion bureaucracy successfully deradicalized the working class.

The benefits of the economic development funded by imported capital were, of course, unevenly distributed. Orthodox Israeli economists maintain that real wages rose steadily during the early 1950s. Yet as a brilliant maverick, Shimshon Bichler, has demonstrated, this view is unsupportable, for no reliable Israeli national statistics exist before 1953.[12] The share of wages in the national economy almost certainly declined as the gap between the rich and the poor widened significantly, reinforced by the concentration of Oriental immigrants in the poorest Jewish population sectors. Real wages may even have fallen during the austerity period (*tzena'*) of 1949–51 because food and other commodities were rationed and prices skyrocketed on the vigorous black market. Meanwhile, taxes rose to cover the high costs of building a military establishment and absorbing new immigrants. There is no dispute that the devaluation of the Israeli pound and the removal of some price controls—the salient features of the New Economic Policy of February 1952—sharply reduced nominal wages as well.

MAPAM and MAKI opposed the New Economic Policy, and workers frequently demonstrated to demand wage increases—sometimes backed by the Histadrut, more often organized by MAKI or MAPAM separately or (occasionally) jointly, both before and after the introduction of the policy. These economic struggles caused leaders of both MAKI and MAPAM to believe that intensification of class struggle driven by the failures of the Israeli economy would enable the Marxist left to win the working class away from MAPAI. But even given the difficulty of statistical measurement for the early 1950s, there is little doubt (frequent assertions by MAKI and MAPAM to the contrary notwithstanding) that the standard of living of Israeli workers rose steadily after the early 1950s, especially upon the arrival of reparations payments from West Germany, which stimulated a period of rapid economic development beginning in 1954–55.

Because of the difficult economic conditions of the early part of the decade, the number of strikes and strikers among Jewish workers increased in the 1950s in comparison with the mandate period, which MAKI and MAPAM regarded as evidence that class struggle was intensifying. But strikes were more routine, shorter, and more narrowly focused on wages than before. The social and ideological character of the labor movement continued to weaken as trade unions and other workers' institutions underwent increasing bureaucratization by the Histadrut leadership.[13] Three major exceptions to this tendency may be noted: the seamen's strike, the academicians' strike, and the Ata textile mill strike. Still, in the end these exceptions only serve to demonstrate the inability of Jewish workers to break the grip of MAPAI's hegemony.

THE SEAMEN'S STRIKE AND ISRAEL'S INTERNATIONAL ORIENTATION

The forty-three-day seamen's strike of November–December 1951 began over the narrow issue of what proportion of seamen's wages would be paid in foreign currency. As it developed, the question broadened into one of trade union autonomy from the control of the Haifa Labor Council, the center of MAPAI's powerful political machine in the city, and the central bodies of the Histadrut. Ultimately, the strike came to symbolize the comprehensive confrontation between the worldviews of MAPAI and MAPAM/MAKI.[14] The dissident leaders of the seamen's union were supported by MAPAM and MAKI against the national seamen's federation, the Haifa Labor Council, and the central bodies of the Histadrut, which refused to sanction the strike. Ben-Gurion insisted that the strike was not about economic issues at all, but a political plot:

> an attempt by the enemies of the state to paralyze the Hebrew fleet which has found partners in certain factions who are primarily motivated by the possibility of sabotaging the state.... The community of workers [i.e., the central bodies of the Histadrut] determines if this is a strike, and not the Yevsektzia [the Jewish Communist Party, which existed briefly in the post-revolutionary Soviet Union—often used as a derisory name for MAKI] and its agents and partners in other factions.[15]

As the strike broke out, an intense debate over Israel's foreign policy orientation, including the question of whether Israel should join a Western-sponsored Middle East military alliance, which MAPAM and MAKI opposed, was occurring in the Knesset. Ya'akov Hazan, Yisra'el Galili, Yitzhak Sadeh, Moshe Sneh, Shmu'el Mikunis, and Me'ir Vilner had just shared the platform at a celebration of the anniversary of the Bolshevik revolution sponsored by the Israel-USSR Friendship League. Kibbutz Me'uhad was in the midst of a bitter split between MAPAM and MAPAI supporters over the question of support for the Soviet Union. In May 1950, the Histadrut had left the World Federation of Trade Unions, and on July 2, 1950, the Knesset voted to support American intervention in Korea—both decisions strongly opposed by MAPAM and MAKI.[16]

In this context, Ben-Gurion chose to represent the seamen's strike as a battle over Israel's international orientation and the divergent paths thereby implied for its national development. Having thus defined the stakes, Ben-Gurion and the government had no alternative but to smash the strike, which they did following a violent clash between strikers and police on December 14. MAKI obliged Ben-Gurion by accepting his challenge. Mikunis agreed that the strike was a struggle over global issues, a

> more comprehensive confrontation between the reactionary triad—imperialism, the government, and the MAPAI leadership—and the advance companies of the forces of independence, peace, and democracy of those who are faithful to the day-to-day and historic interests of the masses of the working people.[17]

Mikunis linked his criticism of the government's handling of the strike to its anti-Soviet foreign policy. Some of the strikers and their supporters radicalized through the protest also adopted this view of the issue. Nimrod Eshel, leader of the strike, was a MAPAM left-winger. After the seamen's defeat he toured the MAPAM kibbutzim, where his militant class-struggle orientation impressed some of those who eventually left MAPAM with Moshe Sneh and joined MAKI,[18] as did Eshel and another strike leader, Akiva Orr—a rare instance when MAKI did gain new members through the class struggles of the early 1950s.

The unusual intensity of the seamen's strike derived from its representation as a battle over Israel's international orientation. Because MAPAI and its coalition partners understood the historic dependence of the Zionist movement on political support from the West and the continuing need for massive capital imports, Ben-Gurion's insistence on maintaining a Western international orientation won general acceptance. Israel signaled its preference for a pro-American orientation by accepting a $100 million loan from the Export-Import Bank in March 1949, endorsing the U.S. intervention in Korea (Ben-Gurion favored dispatching Israeli troops to Korea), rejecting feelers from the People's Republic of China for establishing diplomatic relations, and repeatedly offering to conclude a military alliance with the United States. But the Eisenhower administration, concerned about American relations with the Arab states, rebuffed Israel's advances. Therefore, from the early 1950s to 1967 Israel's principal international allies were France and West Germany, its present American orientation having been consolidated only in the 1967–70 period.

Israel's alliance with France led it to oppose independence for Tunisia, Morocco, and Algeria and Egypt's nationalization of the Suez Canal and to collude with France and Britain in the Suez/Sinai War, actions that increased Arab hostility to Israel and expanded the conflict with the Palestinians into a regional confrontation with the Arab world. The widening of the conflict merely confirmed the activist interpretation of Israel's experiences with its Arab neighbors; the effects of the French alliance, then, were accepted as a function of Israel's existential condition. For most Jews, Arab hostility unquestionably justified Israel's quest for military ties to the West (though some could not accept the alliance with West Germany).

This foreign policy orientation prevailed despite the consistent opposition of MAKI and MAPAM, significant neutralist sentiment within MAPAI's ranks, broad sympathy for the Soviet Union in the late 1940s and early 1950s, and the critical contribution of the Soviet Union to the creation of the state of Israel. After all, the capital and political protection necessary to construct the Jewish state as envisaged by Ben-Gurion and MAPAI could come only from the West. Neither the Soviet Union nor its Jewish citizens could possibly have provided enough capital to maintain a European standard of living for Israel's Ashkenazi Jews; there was no possibility that American Jewry would be replaced as Israel's main source of economic support. Restrictions on the immigration of Jews from the Eastern European countries, Soviet reactions against Israel's attempts to speak directly to and for the Jews of the Soviet Union, and the appearance of official anti-Semitism in the Soviet-bloc countries consolidated and justified MAPAI's preexisting foreign policy inclinations. The defeat of the seamen's strike signaled that the Jewish working class, despite its combativeness on economic issues, had neither the strength nor the independent political vision to establish an alternative to MAPAI: MAKI and MAPAM had failed to marshal the material and political resources needed to effect the international reorientation they sought.

CONFIRMATION OF MAPAI HEGEMONY

The two other major strikes of the 1950s also illustrate how MAPAI's control of the Histadrut kept the labor movement subservient to the overall goal of building the state and its hegemonic party while, despite MAPAI's nominally socialist ideology, creating favorable conditions for the development of capital. The thirteen-day academician's strike of February 1956, although it successfully defeated the government's effort to cut wages, established the principle of a large wage differential between blue- and white-collar workers. The white-collar workers who benefited from this policy counterbalanced MAPAI's eroding support among blue-collar workers and helped the party to remain in power until 1977, when disaffected Oriental blue-collar workers provided the mass base for the electoral victory of Begin's Likud.[19] The votes of Arab citizens, induced by the "persuasive" techniques of military government officials to support MAPAI, also compensated for the loss of blue-collar working-class support.

In May 1957, the 1,680 workers of the Ata textile mill began a three-month strike over management's decision to dismiss workers in order to increase plant efficiency. Ata was then the largest industrial enterprise in Israel. Its location near "red Haifa," the traditional center of the labor movement, favored a workers' victory in the strike. The MAPAI leaders of the Histadrut, however, ended the walkout with no conclusive result. In retaliation, the workers deprived MAPAI of its majority on the Ata workers' committee in the 1958 elections and installed a new coalition of MAPAM and Ahdut Ha'avodah (which split from MAPAM in 1954) representatives. Yet by 1958 their opposition was qualitatively different than in the early 1950s and no longer represented a potential for a radically different course, especially in such a localized arena. MAKI received 33 percent more votes than in the previous election, but this was still insufficient to win a seat on the committee.[20]

The long-term radicalization of even a small number of workers that accompanied the seamen's strike was atypical. More characteristic of the political trajectory of the Jewish working class was the fate of the joint MAKI/Left Socialist Party (LSP) list in the June 1953 elections for the Tel Aviv metal workers' union—a key sector of the industrial proletariat. In the 1945 election, the future component elements of MAPAM had defeated MAPAI and won a majority of the seats on the union executive committee, an expression of the postwar turn to the left within the *yishuv*. In 1953, despite concerted efforts by MAKI/LSP proponents to make the election a demonstration of worker support for a consistent, militant, united left, MAPAI regained its majority. MAPAM and MAKI/LSP won 24 percent and 6 percent of the vote, respectively.[21]

By 1959, MAKI's participation in a trade union struggle was the exception to the rule. When party members joined a demonstration of 1,500 metal workers demanding higher wages in Tel Aviv on February 2, 1959, the Central Committee reported: "This was the first time that our members came to a demonstration together with workers from their workplaces."[22] MAKI's decision to concentrate its attention on the working class after the 1959 election debacle did not stop the steady erosion of the party's support among Jewish workers. During the early 1950s, MAKI had workers' cells in several major Haifa-area enterprises, including the Ata textile mill, the oil refinery, the port, and the Deshanim fertilizer plant;[23] by the early 1960s these cells no longer existed.

The left was even weaker in the national labor movement. MAKI won 4.5 percent of the vote in the 1955 elections to the Histadrut Congress, a significant increase over the 2.6 percent it received in 1949. But the combined vote for MAKI, MAPAM, and Ahdut Ha'avodah declined from 37.1 percent to 32.5 percent during those same years. In 1959 MAPAI and Ahdut Ha'avodah together won the same number of congress delegates they had in 1955, as did MAPAM and MAKI. The elections for the Tenth Congress of the Histadrut took place after the 1965 split in MAKI. The MAKI slate, led by Mikunis and Sneh, received 1.6 percent of the vote, a fair indication of communist strength in the Jewish working class. The RAKAH list, headed by Vilner and Tubi, received 1.3 percent of the vote, mostly from Arabs voting in Histadrut elections for the first time. MAPAM received 14.5 percent of the vote, and the newly formed Alignment of MAPAI and Ahdut Ha'avodah garnered a bare majority of 50.9 percent. These electoral results confirm the secular course of the Jewish working class toward the right—a trend consistent with the structure of Israel's political economy.

Ben-Gurion and MAPAI built a political economy that integrated expropriation of Arab property, limits on Arab access to desirable jobs through a nationally segmented and stratified labor market, discipline of the working class by the Histadrut, pursuit of capital imports from the West, a rising standard of living, and total and constant confrontation with "the Arabs." Consequently, the positions of MAKI and MAPAM on the Arab-Israeli conflict became thoroughly repellent to the great majority of Jewish workers. With MAPAI able to satisfy the material needs of Jewish workers and their political allies and provide a coherent interpretive framework for explaining the causes and character of the Arab-Israeli conflict that resonated with the Jewish experiences of genocide in Europe and of insecure minority status in the Arab world (greatly exacerbated by the conflict in Palestine), MAKI's strength among Jewish workers declined in the second half of the 1950s. Despite the party's consistent and militant defense of labor's economic interests, workers rejected the party's stand on the Arab-Israeli conflict and embraced the hegemonic Zionist political discourse as articulated by MAPAI. Most of those who did not eventually found their way to the Likud. MAPAM lost support among urban workers for the same reason, as well as because of its primary orientation toward the kibbutz movement; however, since no one denied that MAPAM was a Zionist party, and since by the late 1950s it had abandoned many of its original positions on the Palestinian/Arab–Israeli conflict, it was somewhat less affected by the deradicalization of the Jewish working class.

DERADICALIZATION AND DEPOLITICIZATION OF THE KIBBUTZIM

The kibbutz movements were the core of MAPAM and provided a high proportion of its ideologues, functionaries, and activists. Contrary to the theory of Hashomer Hatza'ir, which regarded the kibbutzim as the vanguard of the socialist revolution in Israel, the material requirements for the survival of the kibbutzim as economic units in a capitalist society were in contradiction to the political role Kibbutz Artzi envisaged for itself and led to the deradicalization and depoliticization of most of its members. A small minority of kibbutz members were attracted to the left, but more often the kibbutzim were a force for conservatism within MAPAM. This fact was reflected in the division of labor in kibbutz leadership between those who devoted themselves to economic tasks and those who fulfilled political tasks. Individuals responsible for managing the economy of the kibbutzim and the kibbutz federations typically did not participate actively in the political life of MAPAM, and none were identified with the party's left wing.

Because most of the capital of the kibbutzim was supplied by the Jewish Agency—in the form of grants until 1930, and as low-interest loans thereafter—it was necessary to preserve good relations with the bourgeois and social democratic majority in the Jewish Agency and the World Zionist Organization. Even the leftists in Hashomer Hatza'ir appreciated this need, as one of them wrote in a movement journal:

> The party faces this problem: What is our stand regarding the Zionist movement, since it serves as a tool of Anglo-American imperialism? It is clear that this problem is very severe. But at the same time, it is very delicate, because any attack we might make on the Zionist movement is liable to cause cessation of the economic support which MAPAM's kibbutzim receive.[24]

Younger kibbutzim depended most heavily on the kibbutz federations, the Zionist institutions, and the state for economic support. Over one hundred kibbutzim established after 1948 would have gone bankrupt were it not for the assistance they received from the Jewish Agency. Until the mid-1960s, most kibbutzim operated at a loss. As late as 1963, 122 of a total of 228 kibbutzim (from all the kibbutz federations) relied on financial subsidies from the Jewish Agency for their survival.[25]

The kibbutzim were sustained by the Jewish Agency and the government not because they represented the vanguard of the socialist revolution, but because they played a vital role in establishing a Jewish presence in formerly Arab areas of the country and defending the borders.

These tasks made the kibbutzim essential national institutions; but the consciousness shaped by their national role eventually undermined whatever revolutionary socialist commitments kibbutz members may have had, except among a small minority.

The material interests of the kibbutzim often clashed with the economic and national demands of the Palestinian Arabs. As Yossi Amitay has noted, the settlement of kibbutzim on Arab lands was the sharpest contradiction between theory and practice in MAPAM's stand on Arab-Israeli relations.[26] Until 1948, the kibbutzim had suffered from a land shortage: in 1947 they cultivated 30.9 dunams of land per family; by 1952 the figure had risen to 88 dunams.[27] Most of this increase came about because many kibbutzim, including veteran kibbutzim whose members had received extensive ideological training, augmented their land holdings by seizing abandoned Palestinian lands or occupying lands confiscated from Arabs who remained in the state of Israel, while new kibbutzim were frequently located entirely on such lands.[28]

The kibbutzim were also an important force behind MAPAM's acceptance of the post-1949 territorial status quo. In 1947, nine kibbutzim of Kibbutz Artzi (one-quarter of the total) were in territory allotted to the Arab state by the UN partition plan. Nine of the fourteen kibbutzim established in 1948–49 were also outside the partition plan borders, as were nine more established in the early 1950s. Thus, by 1955 two-fifths of the kibbutzim of Kibbutz Artzi were located on lands outside the Jewish state as defined in the partition plan.

The experiences of many young kibbutzim settled after 1948 impelled them not toward the left but toward depoliticization. Border kibbutzim were often isolated from the political and cultural life of the country. They clashed regularly with Palestinian infiltrators or argued with their Arab neighbors over boundaries and grazing rights. Physical conditions were sometimes so difficult that few members had time or energy for political concerns. The impact of such circumstances on the political consciousness of kibbutz members is exemplified by the experiences of two kibbutzim established in the early poststatehood period at opposite ends of the country: Sasa on the Lebanese border, and Lahav on the "green line" southwest of Hebron—both situated on lands outside the borders of the Jewish state according to the UN partition plan. These kibbutzim, located in remote and difficult spots, epitomized Hashomer Hatza'ir's pioneering socialist-Zionism; their experiences reveal the contradictions between the material requirements of kibbutz life and MAPAM's expressed political ideals.

On February 15, 1948, the Palmah attacked the village of Sasa (population 1,130), located in solidly Arab territory twelve miles from the nearest Jewish settlement. The attack, in which twenty homes were dynamited, was one of the first operations in the Palmah's new strategy of active retaliation against Arabs, even those who had not attacked Jews, "to impress and intimidate the Arab villagers."[29] In late October 1948, Saʿsa was conquered during Operation Hiram. Yisraʾel Galili reported to MAPAM's Political Committee that the IDF had murdered civilians who raised white flags and expelled the entire village; similar atrocities occurred in several neighboring villages during the IDF sweep through the upper Galilee.[30] On January 13, 1949, about fifty members of Hashomer Hatzaʿir from the United States and Canada (joined by thirty more the next month and several more later in the year) settled on the cold, isolated, but strategically located spot, where they lived in the remaining Arab houses. They had little knowledge of the country and its conditions. As one settler expressed it, they thought it was "strange to see Yehoshua [Dayan, the agricultural advisor from Kibbutz Ein Hashofet] chatting away with an Arab or two in our dining hall, in Arabic of course. Most of us still feel very strange in the company of our neighbors."[31]

Shortly after the settlers arrived, the IDF, which maintained a large presence in the kibbutz through the 1970s, blew up the village mosque. Some members opposed this act, but according to the kibbutz diary, most agreed that

> it had to be done. It would have been useless to preserve this symbol of a population which showed itself to be, when one views the thing factually and unsentimentally, our hardened enemies whom we have no intention of permitting to return. The whole appearance of the village has undergone a transformation. It's now a mass of ruins, and yet most of us agree it's better this way. The hovels, the filth, the medieval atmosphere—it's gone now for the most part. Bring on the bulldozers and let's plant trees.[32]

An undoubtedly deep and sincere belief in the justice and progressive content of the Zionist constructive project rendered the diarist entirely unselfconscious about the fact that its realization entailed literally razing to the ground a previously existing society. The kibbutz paid homage to this previous existence by hiring Arab workers to construct all its buildings out of stone in Arab architectural style.

The physical difficulties of settling on a remote hilltop without running water, heat, or motorized transport absorbed all the energies of Americans unused to such conditions and left most of them little time for political subtleties. Sasa's military commander, Yak Matek, had no qualms about blowing up the mosque. Since it was impossible to build a kibbutz with a mosque in the middle, he believed

> the whole discussion was pointless. . . . Were we going to leave Sasa before we really started building our own settlement and try to solve the problem of the Jewish-Arab conflict with all its injustices on both sides leaving the building of the settlement to wait?
>
> It was nothing new to us that we had been living in what was previously an Arab village . . . so why the hesitation now? In many discussions of this sort where we forget about the practical and people get carried away into ideological trends . . . nothing is concluded in the end.[33]

Others were more sensitive to the moral dilemma of founding their community on the ruins of a previously existing society and made at least a rhetorical effort to resolve it. On the very first day of settlement one kibbutz member wrote home:

> I am thinking of the deserted village of Sasa, which we entered so proudly and energetically this morning, and the lives of the Arabs, who lived here. I wandered through some of the hovels, looked at the overturned jugs, grains, books, baby shoes, and smelled the smell of destruction, musty and rotten, with which many of us became familiar in France and Germany. Are we also destroying, pillaging, being cruel in this ancient land, we Kibbutz Hei [the fifth kibbutz of Hashomer Hatza'ir in North America], from thousands of miles away, with our ideals and our refusals to stoop to the world's rottenness? Perhaps. We have moved into Sasa; it is ours; we are responsible for our acts, even though we are bound under the direction and discipline of the national agencies and those of our movement. But do we have an alternative, can we step aside, refuse to be morally sullied by Sasa and demand some other section of our Homeland on which to build our homes? I do not think so. We are not responsible for this cruel and forced contradiction; we would prefer to disown it if we could; we bear no hatred towards the Arab workers and peasants. But we have been forced into a position where we must fight for our lives and the lives of our people, and today life is determined largely by frontiers, and frontiers must be defended no matter what the price. We do not have the right to shunt this physical and moral responsibility off on others. The kibbutz that we build at Sasa will be dedicated not only to the renaissance of our own people but to mankind and the future of mankind. As far as I and most, if not all of us are concerned, this includes our Arab neighbors.[34]

Practical concerns soon tempered such idealism. When two Arabs from the neighboring village of Jish stopped by after the 1949 elections to discuss MAPAM's political program, the kibbutz diarist noted: "They look like intelligent chaps, but it's been very difficult for us to be genuinely interested in politics these past few days." [35] By mid-February the most valuable abandoned property of the former inhabitants of Sasa, the tobacco crop, was packed up by Arab workers and taken to a government warehouse. The presence of these workers taught the kibbutz diarist to appreciate "the infernal complicatedness of the Arab question . . . right on our doorstep." [36]

Lahav has a radically different social profile from that of Sasa. It was settled on August 4, 1952, by *sabra* veterans of Hashomer Hatza'ir from Kiryat Haim, Rehovot, and Petah Tikvah and a Rumanian youth group educated in Kibbutz Kfar Menahem who knew the country and its conditions well.[37] But the physical conditions were analogous and may explain the political similarity between the two kibbutzim. Lahav is situated on a vast tract of marginal agricultural land in the northern Negev. Lack of sufficient water for irrigation kept the kibbutz constantly in debt; it was supported by the Jewish Agency into the 1970s.

At Sasa many of the first settlers left soon after arriving because they had the option of returning to America. But Lahav's settlers had nowhere else to go until urban jobs became more readily available in Israel. An unusually high proportion of the original settlers—about 70 percent—remained in the kibbutz until 1957, when enhanced opportunities in the city induced many of them to leave the hardships of semi-desert life. For those who remained, economic deprivation, social demoralization, distance from Tel Aviv, and a provincial background shaped a minimalist cultural and political life.

Lahav's lands were formerly occupied by the villages of Umm Ramamim and Zag and the semisedentarized Laqiya al-Asad bedouin. Many of the villagers fled after the IDF conquered Beersheba in late October 1948; the rest were "transferred" across the border after the conclusion of the armistice agreement with Transjordan in March 1949. Two bedouin were employed by the kibbutz as agricultural wage laborers on lands formerly occupied by one of their clans. Despite their training in Hashomer Hatza'ir's principles of "brotherhood of peoples," some kibbutz members avoided sharing a table with these workers in the communal dining room at lunchtime. At best, most residents of Lahav were indifferent to their Arab neighbors. One of the few who did show an interest in them became a military intelligence officer. Another worked to create the museum of bedouin culture established near the kibbutz in 1980. Nothing in the museum acknowledges that Lahav was previously inhabited by the very bedouin whose culture it celebrates and reduces to artifacts; most of the exhibits display materials gathered during the Israeli occupation of the Sinai—a relocation of cultural property dimly evoking the transfer of ancient Egyptian treasures to the British Museum and the Louvre.

Both Lahav and Sasa were unusual among kibbutzim of their age cohort because their members displayed little support for the Kibbutz Artzi left. The weakness of the left at Lahav is especially remarkable given the large number of leftists with a similar social background (veterans of Hashomer Hatza'ir from Tel Aviv) at nearby Shuval. Still, the degree of depoliticization at Sasa and Lahav, though exceptional, is significant, as these were exemplary cases of "pioneering" that commanded the admiration and support of the rest of Hashomer Hatza'ir and MAPAM. Their experiences illustrate the difficulty of sustaining a dual commitment to the Zionist settlement project and socialist internationalism.

In the discussions leading to the unification of MAPAM and during the 1948–49 war, Kibbutz Artzi Arabists Aharon Cohen and Eli'ezer Be'eri shared the insight that Arab-Israeli relations would determine the future of the Jewish state. The realities of kibbutz life and the importance of the kibbutzim in MAPAM explain why the intraparty debate of the early 1950s could not unfold around this issue.

THE OLD REGIME AND THE EGYPTIAN NATIONAL MOVEMENT

The Egyptian monarchy rested on a social foundation composed of the twelve thousand owners of fifty feddans or more (0.4 percent of all landowners) who controlled 35 percent of agricultural land.[38] King Faruq sat atop this heap of landed privilege, and the royal family was among the largest landholders. These landowners were the primary collaborators in European, and particularly British, domination of the Egyptian economy, their cotton crop—Egypt's major export commodity and the leading factor in the national economy—being marketed in Europe through a network controlled by resident Europeans, semiforeigners (*mutamassirun*), and local minorities (though beginning in the 1930s local textile mills, both foreign- and indigenously owned, began to absorb an increasing proportion of the cotton). The monocrop export regime, the pivotal role of foreigners in the economy, the monarchy's reliance on the large cotton growers, and ultimately the garrison of British troops kept Egypt subservient to British interests despite the nominal independence attained in 1922.

Even though certain precapitalist social relations persisted in the countryside, the agricultural economy was essentially capitalist. Because of their social conservatism and opposition to land reform, the large landowners were widely perceived as "feudalists" who impeded national independence and retarded industrial development; yet a minority had invested in industry as early as 1920, through financing of Bank Misr. The Wafd, a Congress-type umbrella party, emerged during the 1919 nationalist uprising and carried the flag of secular nationalism and liberal democracy throughout the era of the monarchy. By the mid-1930s, however, the increasing influence of large landowners in the party leadership became an obstacle to the Wafd's capacity to advance its proclaimed program.

The Western-educated, urban middle strata (the *effendiyya*) were the activists of all the political parties and movements during the monarchy. Disappointment with the Wafd's failure to end the British occupation and its increasing conservatism, lack of employment opportunities for high school and university graduates, and the influence of both fascist and communist ideologies that challenged the power of the British Empire worldwide caused the young *effendiyya* to become radicalized in the late 1930s, and out of this political milieu emerged the post–World War II communist movement.[39] Young radicalized students and graduates sought to ally with the emerging workers' movement, seize leadership of the nationalist movement from the Wafd, and infuse it with a progressive social program. The potential power of the alliance of radicalized students and militant trade unionists was first manifested in the establishment of the National Committee of Workers and Students, formed in the heat of the nationalist upsurge of August 1945–July 1946 and led by communists and young left Wafdists organized in the Wafdist Vanguard.

After recovering from the government's July 1946 repression campaign, the left-wing nationalist alliance reasserted itself in the form of a strike wave and student protests from September 1947 to May 1948. The Egyptian government's decision to "come to the aid" of the Palestinian Arabs by launching an unplanned invasion, accompanied by the declaration of martial law and the arrest of the political opposition, allowed the monarchy to defeat this second postwar nationalist upsurge. This was the immediate local context for the Egyptian communists' resolution to support the partition of Palestine; moreover, the inept military campaign and the revelation that malfunctioning weapons were supplied to the army by friends of King Faruq unmasked the monarchy's corruption and incapacity to rule. Nonetheless, the regime was still able to check all opposition: the communists were imprisoned as Zionists; the radical Islamist Society of Muslim Brothers was dissolved and many of its members jailed; and the Wafd was kept out of power by rigged elections in 1944 and the connivance of the British occupiers.

The monarchy remained in power, despite its inability to resolve Egypt's pressing economic problems and achieve an evacuation of British forces, because the social base of the opposition was diverse and unable to unite. The political loyalties of the *effendiyya* were spread across the entire political spectrum. The working class was small and the workers' movement lacked the political experience to lead the entire national movement, as even the communists recognized. Poor peasants, sharecroppers, and rural wage workers, who had the greatest grievances against the prevailing social order, were largely unorganized; practically speaking, politics was a Cairo-centered activity. While the Wafd had a substantial network of rural support, mobilization of the poor and landless would have threatened the interests of the rich peasants—the source of the party's rural power—as well as the large landowners in the party hierarchy. When the Wafd returned to power for the last time in 1950, the contradiction between the social conservatism of its propertied leaders and the radical democratic impulses of the Wafdist Vanguard rendered it impotent. Unable to carry out significant reforms or save the monarchy, it was swept away by the third wave of the postwar mass nationalist movement, which lasted from October 1951 to January 1952.

THE COUP OF JULY 23, 1952

The legitimacy of the regime established by the military coup of July 23, 1952, had a simple basis. When all the civilian political forces proved incapable of decisive action, the army successfully accomplished tasks widely recognized as necessary by the lower and middle classes as well as by the small class of Egyptian industrialists: ending political corruption and power abuses by the monarchy; curbing the economic and social power of large landowners and the foreign and semiforeign business class; promoting industrial development; and, by an agreement signed in October 1954, ending the British occupation. Accomplishing these tasks required a radical reduction of European influence at all levels of Egyptian society.

The U.S. embassy and the CIA encouraged Gamal Abdel Nasser and the Free Officers in their movement to overthrow the monarchy, recognizing the need for social reform and hoping to succeed the British as the paramount power in Egypt.[40] Abdel Nasser could not, however, accede to American requests that Egypt join a regional military alliance that would permit foreign troops on Egyptian soil, without risking his claim to political legitimacy. Even the last Wafd government of the monarchy had refused to participate in a proposed Middle East Defense Organization, recognizing that such affiliation would never be accepted by an Egyptian public mobilized under slogans like "Immediate evacuation," "Complete independence," and "Egypt for the Egyptians."

Although the Free Officers embraced the social demands of the nationalist movement in a vague, general way, their early economic program was limited and ambiguously defined as opposing "feudalism" and establishing "social justice." From 1952 to 1956 the ruling Revolutionary Command Council (RCC) encouraged private capital to develop the national economy. It did not envisage the policies of nationalization and economic planning adopted after the Suez/Sinai War.

The land reform of September 9, 1952, was the only structural economic reform adopted before the 1956 war. In retrospect, many inadequacies in the land reform are apparent, but it had great symbolic importance and convinced many Egyptians that the new regime was committed to reform and equity. Inspired not by socialist collectivism but by the liberal goal of promoting small peasant proprietors, the land reform was designed to coax the landed magnates to shift their capital to industry; confiscation of property, exaction of revolutionary retribution, and smashing of all remnants of the old ruling class were not a part of the program. Only lands of the former royal family were seized outright; other large landowners were permitted to sell or redivide their property before the law took effect. Those who failed to reduce their holdings to the limit of two hundred feddans plus one hundred feddans for dependent children, received government bonds bearing 3 percent interest as compensation for their lands. The government hoped that these bonds would become negotiable instruments and that the proceeds from their sale would be invested in industry. It also expected the land reform to expand the market for Egyptian industrial products because peasants who increased their production through land acquisitions would have more income to spend on consumer goods.[41] While the redistributed lands were insufficient to provide a viable plot (generally considered to be five feddans) for all who wished to farm, the land reform and the banning of all the old-regime political parties in January 1953 did break the political power of the large landowners.

This economic program was not in contradiction with U.S. support for the RCC, and aspects of it drew on American advice. Egypt also turned to the United States to purchase arms to rebuild its army. Arms acquisition was considered an urgent national security issue following the ignominious defeat by Israel; it was also a requisite for maintaining the loyalty of the officer corps in the first years of the new, and not wholly stable, regime. Secretary of State John Foster Dulles refused to believe, despite the expressed opinion of many career diplomats and CIA officers, that an Egyptian regime that rejected joining a Western military alliance and advocated that other Arab states do the same was acting out of indigenously generated nationalist motives. Hence, when the United States linked arms sales and foreign aid to conditions Abdel Nasser regarded as infringements on Egyptian sovereignty, the RCC was forced to abandon its American orientation and turn instead to the nonaligned movement and the Soviet bloc.

THE REVOLUTIONARY COMMAND COUNCIL AND THE WORKING CLASS

The turn toward the Soviet Union was not immediately reflected in the social policies of the regime. The RCC faced the same dilemma confronted by many state-building regimes: how to mobilize the nation while maintaining social peace and discipline. Its response was to discourage all forms of collective action not initiated by the government or its series of single parties—the Liberation Rally, the National Union, and the Arab Socialist Union. The government now regarded the same demands, demonstrations, and strikes applauded by many nationalists before the military coup as provocations and threats to social peace that might destabilize the new nationalist regime and disrupt Egypt's economic development. Students and workers—the primary social base of the left following the war—were closely supervised, though the majority of both groups supported the regime because of its nationalist appeal, despite its undemocratic character and their doubts about the efficacy of the Anglo-Egyptian evacuation agreement.

In order to avoid any disruption of production and maintain an attractive climate for private capital investment, the RCC unleashed extensive repression against the left-wingers in the labor movement.[42] Explicitly rejecting the view that there was or ought to be a struggle between classes in Egyptian society, it sought to isolate and eliminate militant trade union leaders, especially communists and those prepared to ally with them, and replace them with elements loyal to and to a certain extent dependent on the RCC. Those who were not jailed or removed from their positions must certainly have been intimidated seeing what happened to those who stepped beyond the acceptable boundaries as defined by the regime. The repression of the trade union movement's left wing was an essential component of the RCC's labor strategy and preceded any of the labor reform measures it eventually undertook.

The sharpest example of this repression may be seen in the RCC's response to the strike and riot at the Misr Fine Spinning and Weaving Company in Kafr al-Dawwar on August 12, 1952. Although the striking workers clearly supported the new regime, expecting that it would grant their economic demands, the army intervened and a violent clash ensued. A hastily convened military tribunal tried and condemned two workers, Mustafa Khamis and Muhammad al-Baqri, to death. Their execution became a rallying cry for workers who opposed the regime, and it is no accident that this textile mill became a center of communist influence in the mid-1950s.

The military intervention at Kafr al-Dawwar came about because of the conviction of some RCC members that in order to encourage private capital investment in industry by both Egyptians and foreigners, the labor militancy that had been a prominent feature of the social crisis of the last years of the monarchy had to be quashed. Unsubstantiated fears that communists had instigated the strike at Kafr al-Dawwar motivated the decision to execute Khamis and al-Baqri. ʿAbd al-Munʿim Amin, who presided at the military tribunal that found them guilty, was known to have close relations to the American embassy and to favor encouraging foreign capital investment in Egypt.

The new regime's commitment to industrial development motivated the state to seek a new relationship with the working class. Labor policy reforms were required to control industrial conflict, increase the purchasing power of workers, and encourage greater productivity. Laws 317, 318, and 319 of December 1952 granted many long-standing demands of the trade union movement. In March 1953, as the RCC and the cabinet considered a law to encourage foreign capital investment, all except Khalid Muhyi al-Din agreed that to encourage such investment it would be necessary to amend the Law of Individual Contracts to give employers more freedom to dismiss workers arbitrarily—that is, to dismiss workers not for misbehavior on the job but solely because of production cutbacks or other market considerations.[43] Muhyi al-Din, who was close to the DMNL, submitted a letter of resignation over this issue. Abdel Nasser intervened, however, and the crisis was resolved by an agreement to prohibit employers from dismissing workers for trade union activity—though in practice this prohibition was loosely enforced. Pro–labor reform forces succeeded through subsequent regulations and legislation in further restricting employers' ability to close factories and lay off or dismiss workers.[44]

The improvements in labor legislation and the special attention the RCC gave to cultivating good relations with trade union leaders explain why Abdel Nasser received general union support in his struggle for power against Muhammad Naguib during the crisis of March 1954.[45] On the whole, the organized labor movement now saw the state as a reliable ally—a dramatic change from the era of the monarchy. But the state's commitment to workers' interests was limited by its goal of industrial development and by its unwillingness to permit the labor movement to exercise even the limited civil autonomy it had enjoyed under the monarchy. Although the regime's new labor legislation provided job security, wage increases, and encouragement for trade unions, enforcement of this legislation was completely out of the hands of workers themselves. The most critical indication of the RCC's intention to restrict working-class collective action was its decision to declare strikes illegal; thus, workers had no means to insure that the new legislation was applied. An unspoken bargain was struck: no strikes, in exchange for no dismissals without cause. Yet without the credible threat of a strike, employers often found ways to circumvent the law.

Although the formation of individual trade unions was encouraged, the RCC refused to allow the formation of a national trade union federation in the fall of 1952, despite its promises to the contrary, because it feared the influence the left might have in such an organization. Instead the council sanctioned the Permanent Conference of Egyptian Trade Unions as a controlled forum that would allow trade unionists to engage in a dialogue with the regime. Some of the participants in this body resigned in protest over Major Ahmad ʿAbd Allah Tuʿayma's efforts to interfere in trade union affairs. (As director of trade union affairs for the Liberation Rally, Tuʿayma was charged with winning the support of the trade unions for the new regime.) The formation of the General Federation of Egyptian Trade Unions (GFETU) was delayed until January 30, 1957, and even then the government took no chances on the political composition of the federation leadership. The government merely submitted its candidates for the executive board of the GFETU to the founding conference; there were no nominations from the floor, and no election was held. The government continued to appoint the GFETU executive board for several more terms of office.[46]

Ahmad Fahim, GFETU vice president and representative of the textile workers' unions, was the only member of the executive board associated with the left in the workers' movement, although he was a pragmatist and never a communist. In 1942 he had helped form a separate union for textile foremen in the Cairo suburb of Shubra al-Khayma that had weakened both worker unity and the communists' influence. In the spring of 1955, the RCC pressured several unions to withdraw their legal business from the office of Yusuf Darwish, who since becoming legal counsel for the Shubra al-Khayma textile workers' union in 1942 had been a key figure in establishing New Dawn's influence among trade unionists. Fahim agreed to transfer the business of the Cairo Textile Workers' Union, of which he was then president, to a new attorney.[47] His appointment to the GFETU executive may have been a concession to the left's continuing strength in the textile industry, but the regime clearly sought to use Fahim to contain labor militancy and bring the left under the government's control.

Despite RCC repression of the working-class left, the institution of a corporatist regime of labor control and real improvements in the job security and standard of living of organized industrial workers won the regime the support of most trade union leaders. The communists, of course, criticized the regime's labor policies, but such criticism had a diminishing impact as most of the movement's base of support in the working class was eroded by the combination of repression and reform. Moreover, when the communists began to reassess their attitude toward the regime in 1955, the impetus lay primarily in the government's anti-imperialist foreign policy. Therefore, the economic struggle of the working class and other social questions became largely subordinated to the task of uniting with the regime against the imperialist enemy.

THE WORKERS' MOVEMENT AND THE 1956 WAR

During the Suez crisis and the 1956 war, trade unions mobilized support for the nationalization of the Suez Canal and actively participated in the national defense. Trade union leaders called a general strike on August 16, 1956, to coincide with the London conference as a demonstration of support for the canal's nationalization. Many unions collected financial contributions from their members to aid the war effort. The textile federation urged its unions to set aside labor disputes during the war, and production in some mills was increased. The Trade Union Committee for Popular Resistance organized workers to support the national defense; together, trade union leaders and rank-and-file workers established over fifty local committees, some with hundreds of members.

Although it welcomed most of the trade union actions around the Suez crisis, the government felt threatened by activities that might change the balance of forces within the regime. For example, it regarded the establishment of the Trade Union Committee for Popular Resistance with suspicion because of the prominence of communists and other leftists in the organization. For the left in the labor movement, the image of the armed working class defending the homeland had positive associations that opened new political horizons. But the government could not accept the prospect of armed workers led by communists, even if the purpose of arming workers was to defend the national soil of Egypt. On November 26, 1956, it closed the law office of Yusuf Darwish, a leading organizer of the committee, though it was reopened on December 6, following protests by workers and others.[48] After the war the popular resistance committees were quickly disbanded.

During and after the war the left tried to emphasize the role that workers had played *as workers* in the Suez crisis, a political theme that appeared frequently in the pages of *Al-masa'* (The evening).[49] Four well-known trade unionists—Fathi Kamil, Ahmad Fahim, Sayyid 'Abd al-Wahhab Nada, and Nur Sulayman Jasr—published a book describing the contribution of the working class to the war effort. They recounted workers' enthusiastic expressions of support for the anti-imperialist and nationalist stands of the government, arguing that workers had "played the most important role in the defeat of imperialism."[50] This phrase, however, which was intended to establish a legitimate nationalist basis for granting workers' economic and political demands, claimed for the working class a political role far exceeding what the government was prepared to accept.

This book was also noteworthy because it was published by the Dar al-Fikr (House of Thought) publishing house operated by the Unified Egyptian Communist Party (UECP), successor to the DMNL. Nada and Jasr were members of the UECP, while Fahim and Kamil had a history of cooperation with the communists. Publication of this volume therefore represented an attempt to reconstruct the progressive coalition whose efforts to organize a general federation of trade unions in 1951 and 1952 had been blocked by both the monarchy and the RCC. The committees of popular resistance and the proclamations about the leading role of the working class in the anti-imperialist struggle were intended to articulate and implement a more radical version of Nasserism than the government itself embraced. The communists and their allies who advocated this perspective envisioned the working class as the vanguard of the national united front against imperialism; the government, in contrast, viewed the working class as only one element in a coalition of popular forces that was, in fact, led by the army. Even as Abdel Nasser proceeded to implement new economic policies enthusiastically embraced by the communists, he never considered loosening the bonds of social control over the working class.

GUIDED CAPITALISM

In 1957, the government embarked on a new economic policy aptly described by Patrick O'Brien as "guided capitalism." In January, a National Planning Commission was organized; that same month the Economic Organization was established to manage the foreign assets sequestered after the Suez/Sinai War of 1956 and all other publicly owned industrial and commercial enterprises. Since the Egyptian bourgeoisie and private foreign capital had failed to invest in basic industrial projects on their own initiative, the state now took the opportunity provided by the seizure of a substantial amount of foreign capital to become more closely involved in directing the economy. Before the end of 1957 Abdel Nasser announced that the path for Egypt's economic development was to be "democratic cooperative socialism." "National" capital was still encouraged to play a role in developing production, but it was not to be permitted to exercise decisive power over the government. These policies reversed the relative importance of private and public capital in Egypt. In 1952–53, 72 percent of gross capital formation took place in the private sector; by 1959–60 the state was responsible for 74 percent of gross capital formation.[51]

Contrary to the expectations of many communists, however, the shift in the balance of private and public capital did not automatically imply a dramatic change in the social relations between labor and capital. Powerful forces within the government itself adopted a conservative interpretation of the new economic policy. Minister of Finance and Economy ʿAbd al-Munʿim al-Qaysuni, an influential technocrat and strong supporter of foreign investment and private enterprise, asserted that the government had established the Economic Organization not to compete with private enterprise, but to stimulate investment.[52] Minister of Agriculture and Agrarian Reform Sayyid Mar'i, a former large landowner, argued that the right to form trade unions should not be extended to agricultural laborers, a very substantial fraction of the wage labor force.[53] In February 1959, a ministerial decision classified the employees of the Transport Authority as state employees and therefore ineligible to join a trade union, whereupon their trade union was dissolved retroactively and its funds transferred to the Ministry of Social Affairs and Labor.[54] By 1959 the call for democratic cooperative socialism had receded from prominence, while the speeches of Abdel Nasser repeatedly encouraged and reassured private capital.[55] The government seemed to be turning away from an officially sympathetic stand toward workers and trade unions.

The debates within the highest councils of the state and between the state and radical workers over the operative content of democratic cooperative socialism were accompanied by an intensification of industrial conflict.[56] The labor columns of *Al-masa'* regularly reported labor disputes whose causes and circumstances do not differ substantially from those of the old regime. Workers continued to complain of low wages, unemployment, and dismissal from work due to production cutbacks or the introduction of mechanization. Many enterprises continued to enforce labor discipline by deducting fines from workers' pay. Contract labor was still the normal mode in certain industries, notably construction and longshore work. Some categories of workers remained outside the scope of the Law of Individual Contracts. Collective contracts, though permitted by law, were rare. Trade union activists were subject to many pressures from employers, including frequent dismissals from their jobs. Employers continued to abuse the six-month probationary period by dismissing workers just before they completed probation, perhaps then immediately to rehire them for a second probationary period; this practice allowed employers to avoid paying the minimum wage as well as to evade the restrictions on dismissing fully qualified workers. They were also able thereby to eliminate militant workers and prevent them from gaining permanent jobs. Abuse of the probationary period was especially widespread in the textile industry, where the workers' federation vigorously demanded a reduction in the length of the probationary period, a limit of one probationary period per worker with the same employer, and transfer of probation time from one employer to another if the same work was to be performed.[57]

Chronic unemployment in the textile industry and a preponderance of textile workers in the industrial labor force made that industry the most visible arena for labor-management disputes over arbitrary dismissals, but such disputes were by no means limited to textile manufacturing. In 1958, Salman ʿAli, president of the Safaga Phosphate Company Workers' Union, reported that all the workers had been dismissed and replaced by new employees (presumably receiving lower wages or diminished benefits) with no prior notice. ʿAli expressed his surprise that this action had been taken after the formerly British-owned company was Egyptianized.[58] Many workers expected that a reforming nationalist government would resolve *both* their national and their class grievances. Clearly, this was not necessarily so.

After July 23, 1952, the public perception and social status of "the worker" underwent a dramatic transformation. Under the old regime, workers were a despised underclass who, at best, commanded public attention only because the wave of post–World War II industrial conflict forced "the workers' question" onto the social and political agenda. In contrast, the new regime hailed the virtues of industrialization, and as part of the campaign to win public approval for its economic policies it promoted a positive view of industrial workers as playing a vital role in the development of the Egyptian national economy.

A striking advertisement in *Al-masaʾ* announcing the sale of shares in the Egyptian Iron and Steel Company (at £E2 each, guaranteed by the government to return at least 4 percent) graphically conveyed the approved new image of the working class. Under the title "Yesterday," the ad portrays a traditionally clad fellah with a hoe standing in a field; under the title "Today," a worker in modern clothing in front of an industrial plant wields a sledgehammer. The caption under the pictures proclaims: "Yesterday we depended on agriculture alone. Today we build our industrial glory with iron and steel."[59] The government promoted this positive image of workers to stimulate industrial employment and productivity, encourage public concern about the welfare of workers, and foster respect and recognition for the role that workers were playing in the construction of a modern and independent Egypt. Yet all the government's improvements in the social and material status of the working class were contained within a fixed framework: corporatist integration into a bureaucratic-authoritarian regime in which workers had neither autonomy nor legitimate independent power.

The government's concern for productivity and economic development limited workers' freedom to express their own vision of their role in the new industrial Egypt. By effectively banning the public use of certain words, the government established the terms of political discourse and marginalized those whose vision exceeded what the government was prepared to grant. Thus, Sayyid ʿAli Rustum, a member of the executive board of the Cairo Textile Workers' Union, argued that trade union rights could not be protected unless workers had the right to strike. But he did not use the word *strike* (*idrab*); instead he used (or *Al-masaʾ* printed) "peaceful stoppage of work" (*al-tawaqquf al-silmi ʿan al-ʿamal*).[60] Similarly, when *Al-masaʾ* reported on the January 1958 conference of the textile union federation, the account noted that a call had been made for abolishing compulsory arbitration and "establishing the right to refrain from work" (*tanzim haqq al-imtinaʿ ʿan al-ʿamal*).[61] The word *strike* simply disappeared from the public political vocabulary. Strikes could be referred to by elliptical phrases, but they could not be openly and directly advocated. Once this restriction on language became internalized by workers and political activists, it tended to become a fact of life that could not be seriously questioned. The limits of permitted language thus became the limits of politics.

Because of such restrictions on explicitly political discourse, literary forms were, as they always had been, an important vehicle of expression for workers. The workers' column of *Al-masaʾ*, especially under the editorship of Lufti al-Khuli, encouraged workers to submit poetry and short stories for publication. One of the most popular forms of workers' literary expression was colloquial poetry (*zajal*). After the Suez/Sinai War it took weeks for all the poems submitted to be printed. Most of the poetry reflected a nationalist consciousness shared by workers and other supporters of the Nasserist regime and the participation and support of organized workers in its anti-imperialist campaigns.

Only a few workers' poems of this period reveal a specifically working-class consciousness rooted in the experiences of work. One Tahir al-ʿAmiri, a worker at the Filature Nationale spinning mill in Alexandria, published a poem entitled "I the Worker" in the bulletin of the federation of textile unions.[62] Its refrain, "I the worker built this glory with my arms," repeats a theme first popularized in "The Egyptian Worker" ("*Al-ʿamil al-misri*") by Bayram al-Tunisi, a popular poet of the 1919 revolution.[63] The title of al-ʿAmiri's poem is "borrowed" from the title poem of a collection published in 1946 by an earlier textile worker–poet, Fathi al-Maghribi. Situated in this tradition of populist and workers' poetry, the poem offers compelling evidence that some Egyptian workers continued to view the working class as a unique and vanguard constructive element in Egyptian society. This formulation was one of the principal political and cultural images associated with the radical tradition in the workers' movement.

Although it was severely diminished and confined primarily to a narrow sector of the textile industry where workers had been most influenced by Marxism, the spirit of working-class radicalism nourished by the communists in the 1940s and early 1950s survived into the period of Abdel Nasser's ascendancy. Working-class opposition to the regime increased after 1954, especially during the period of guided capitalism, when the regime's efforts to ally with the "national bourgeoisie" led to a diminished rate of growth in real wages and a drive to raise productivity that sometimes led to worker dismissals. However, even this limited workers' opposition was constrained by the need to maintain the sporadic national united front between the communists and the regime.

THE COMMUNIST INTELLIGENTSIA'S ACCOMMODATION WITH NASSERISM

After the 1956 war all the communists were united in enthusiastic support for Abdel Nasser's anti-imperialist foreign policy. During the era of guided capitalism, well before the "socialist transformation" of 1961, communist intellectuals began to perceive economic planning and the nationalization of significant sectors of the economy as a prelude to socialism. This view was legitimated by Soviet and Eastern European theorists who espoused the concept of the "noncapitalist road of development."[64] Inspired by this theoretical innovation, or by the more traditional notion of the need for the proletariat to ally with the national bourgeoisie in the national liberation struggle, Egyptian communists minimized the significance of the continuing struggle between labor and capital and of the state's attack on labor movement autonomy by absorbing the trade unions into the state apparatus and repressing workers who refused to accept state tutelage. The communist intelligentsia, in its zeal to unite with the Nasserist state in the anti-imperialist struggle, played its own small role in limiting the extent to which an autonomous workers' voice could be raised.

This situation is illustrated by the critical response of Anouar Abdel-Malek, a former DMNL member and a prominent figure in the editorial committee of *Al-masa'*, to a poem by Darwish Muhammad al-Mihi entitled "The Story of May First."⁶⁵ The poem plainly retold the story of the 1886 Chicago Haymarket affair, which gave birth to the May First international workers' holiday. The poet expressed solidarity with the American workers and called on all workers to celebrate May Day. While acknowledging the poem as an expression of international working-class solidarity, Abdel-Malek objected that the poem made no reference to imperialism. It was not proper, he wrote, to speak about the events in the poem without linking them to current events and mentioning American imperialism. This criticism suggests a political-cultural class struggle within the communist movement: the worker-poet articulated his unadorned class sentiment, while the intellectual-critic argued against expressing class consciousness independent of the anti-imperialist national struggle.

This response to a rather simple poem advocating international working-class solidarity, a sentiment that in principle Marxists should have applauded without reservation, indicates the difficulty of sustaining an independent working-class vision outside the limits of Nasserist political discourse. As long as the communists subordinated articulation of this goal to support for Nasserist anti-imperialism, the small number of workers who did actively attempt to preserve such a vision had to face virtually insurmountable opposition by a much strengthened Egyptian state. When the Nasserist-communist alliance dissolved in 1959 and all known communists were arrested, the organized, politically conscious, working-class opposition was eliminated in Egypt, not to reappear until after the 1967 war—most notably in the wave of strikes and protests responding to the "open door" economic policy introduced by Anwar al-Sadat in 1974.

The communist intelligentsia's accommodation with Nasserism was facilitated by the regime's removal of many of the social grievances that had contributed to radicalization of the intelligentsia in the 1930s and 1940s. Educational opportunities expanded very rapidly after 1952: from 1953–54 to 1965–66, average student enrollment for all educational levels combined increased by 132 percent. Tuition fees were reduced in 1956 and 1961 and abolished entirely in 1962, making university education available to the children of the lower middle class.⁶⁶ Because the increasing number of university graduates was larger than the economy could absorb, the government removed the potential pressure of an unemployed intelligentsia by guaranteeing all graduates who could not find private employment a position in the state bureaucracy. Some of these state employees were dissatisfied by the lack of meaningful work to perform, but at least their incomes were sufficient to sustain them until the period of rapid inflation released by the open door economic policy.

ARAB SOCIALISM

Nationalization of the banks and large commercial and industrial enterprises initiated the era of Arab socialism in 1960–61. The limit on land holdings was further reduced to one hundred feddans. New consumptionist policies further increased the standard of living, although the principal beneficiaries were skilled and white-collar workers and owners of agricultural plots of twenty to fifty feddans. Real wages increased at a faster rate between 1961 and 1964 than they had in the period of guided capitalism, and there was a modest redistribution of national income as rents, profits, interest, and dividends declined relative to wages and salaries.[67] Despite these advances, rural villages and agricultural cooperatives were often dominated by the same families that had been local powers under the old regime.[68] Trade unions remained under the control of the government. In 1962, Anwar Salama resigned the presidency of the GFETU and became minister of labor, the first worker to serve in an Egyptian cabinet. From 1969 to the late 1980s the presidency of the GFETU and the Ministry of Labor (now the Ministry of Manpower and Training) were occupied by the same individual, a corporeal expression of the integration of the trade unions into the state apparatus.

The international orientation of Arab socialism was pan-Arab and pro-Soviet. Pan-Arabism had been advocated by some elements of Egyptian society as early as the 1930s. Bank Misr, for example, had long viewed the broader Arab world as a market for Egypt's industrial exports and a natural hinterland for the bank's activity. In 1954, the Nasserist regime began to embrace pan-Arabism as an instrument for asserting Egyptian leadership of the Arab world. The Arab world's support of Egypt in its decision to nationalize the Suez Canal and in the Suez/Sinai War consolidated the regime's pan-Arab outlook. As a result of Israel's attack on Egypt and the harsher stand toward the Palestinian/Arab–Israeli conflict implicit in pan-Arabism, Abdel Nasser's rhetorical stance toward Israel became more aggressive than it had been before the 1956 war. Yet in practice he continued to exercise caution and restraint.

Pan-Arabism did not necessarily imply an anti-Western orientation. In the 1940s the British had promoted such an outlook to buttress their influence in the Arab world—which is why the communists first opposed it. As for the United States, since it had demanded the evacuation of British, French, and Israeli troops from Egyptian territory after the 1956 war just as strongly as the Soviet Union did, it was well positioned to expand its influence in the Arab world. However, announcement of the Eisenhower doctrine in January 1957 quickly dissipated any Egyptian appreciation for America's stand, which Abdel Nasser correctly perceived as directed against his growing influence in the Arab world. Covert American actions in Syria and Jordan in 1957 and the invasion of Lebanon in 1958 confirmed his suspicions.

American inability to accommodate Egypt's assertion of independence, combined with the continued failure of both Egyptian and foreign private capital to invest in industrial projects, ultimately drove Abdel Nasser toward the Soviet Union and its economic model. Although the industrial development of countries like Brazil and South Korea in the 1970s has demonstrated that metropolitan capital does not necessarily block third world industrialization, in the 1960s Marxists generally believed this to be the case. Abdel Nasser, too, gradually accepted this view, along with the necessity of economic planning and a large public sector. The nationalization of the commanding heights of the economy created an affinity between the economies of Egypt and the Soviet bloc. An uncritical view of the Soviet Union and the similarities between Egyptian and Soviet modes of planning and bureaucratic control allowed the Egyptian communists and many Soviet economists to believe that Egypt was on the "noncapitalist road of development." As a consequence, the communists endorsed the policies of Arab socialism from their prison cells.

Ironically, just as the communists were released from jail in 1964, the Arab socialist system entered a general crisis, as increased consumption and investment were not simultaneously sustainable. The rate of investment and real wages began to decline. The fact that wages as a share of the national income peaked in 1963–64 indicated that the more egalitarian distribution of the national income was only a temporary phenomenon.[69] The communists did not call on the regime to account for these failures because by then their parties were in the process of dissolution; in any case, the scope of the crisis was not yet widely recognized. Moreover, because the onset of the crisis was shortly followed by the 1967 Arab-Israeli war, the economic shortcomings of Arab socialism were attributed to the war and its aftermath, which did indeed exacerbate Egypt's economic problems. The government was thus absolved of responsibility for its economic failures, and most of the political energy that these problems might have generated became focused on the conflict with Israel.

CHAPTER IV

A Window of Opportunity? 1949–1955

With the benefit of hindsight it is easy to judge that even in the uncertain situation of late 1948 and early 1949 the intractability of the Palestinian/Arab–Israeli conflict and the limited capacity of the Marxist left to struggle for its resolution on the basis of mutual recognition and self-determination were immanent. Yet such a judgment obscures the processes that have formed the present situation. By examining these processes we may appreciate the historical construction of the categories and conceptions in which we now frame our understanding of the conflict. My purpose here is not to argue that there was a realistic chance to resolve the conflict peacefully during the period 1949–55. However, during this period the Marxist left, in alliance or in coincidence with other efforts, was able to sustain an alternative conception of the conflict that opposed emerging hegemonic nationalist political discourses in both Israel and Egypt.

Until 1954, the main concern of all the political forces in Egypt was to expel the British troops from the Suez Canal Zone. The communists continued to advocate a peaceful settlement of the conflict with Israel, just as in 1947–48, while the RCC was busy stabilizing its own rule. The conflict with Israel was not a salient issue in Egypt. The ascendancy of the activist outlook precluded Israeli recognition of the possibilities for peaceful resolution of the conflict at this moment and also made consideration of the sort of concessions that would have been necessary to maximize this potential inconceivable. By late 1954 Abdel Nasser had begun to conceptualize the conflict in much broader terms. The

Lavon affair (see Chapter 1) and the first expressions of Egypt's emergent pan-Arab orientation now made any accommodation with Israel much more problematic for both the regime and the communist movement. Nonetheless, until 1956 Abdel Nasser agreed to participate in diplomatic efforts to resolve or moderate the conflict, albeit on the basis of conditions far beyond what Israel was prepared to accept. At this point, Egypt's differences with Israel were not usually represented as an existential battle of destiny, as after the 1956 war they came to be.

In Israel, MAPAM emerged as the second largest bloc in the Knesset after the 1949 elections, and MAKI continued to grow, reaching the peak of its strength in the 1955 Knesset elections. Therefore, there was a significant Israeli constituency for a peaceful settlement of the conflict based on the principle—if not the precise boundaries—of the UN partition plan. Despite the Jewish tilt in the line of unified MAKI, the party consistently defended the rights of the Palestinian Arabs, including their right to an independent state and the right of all refugees to return or receive compensation, and relentlessly opposed Israeli government policy on the conflict. Although MAPAM eventually capitulated to the hegemonic Zionist discourse and abandoned radical opposition to MAPAI's positions on the Palestinian/Arab–Israeli conflict, sections of the party continued to move toward the left until the Slansky trial in Czechoslovakia in November 1952; some elements of MAPAM continued their trajectory toward the left even afterward.

MAPAM and MAKI, however, unlike Ben-Gurion, did not appreciate that the establishment of a state would reorder the Zionist discourse and eliminate binationalism and Palestinian Arab national rights—ideas that had been respectable despite their minority status in the prestate Zionist movement—from the political agenda. The Marxist left was transformed by its need to accommodate to the hegemonic discourse in order to participate in national politics. This necessity ultimately diminished the left's oppositional capacity, not only on this issue but on others as well. After 1956, the conflict assumed a static and permanent character; its peaceful resolution on the basis of the partition plan principles was eliminated from the political agenda in both countries.

THE JEWISH QUESTION IN EGYPTIAN COMMUNISM

Many Egyptian communists attributed their incarceration as Zionists during the 1948–49 war and their failure to lead the post–World War II upsurges in the nationalist movement in expelling the British to the "opportunism" of the DMNL: its lack of a written program and internal regulations; its tactical flexibility; its members' lack of theoretical training; its lax recruitment standards; its loose structure, combining aspects of a front and a party; its national united front strategy; and its overattention to nonproletarian social forces—in sum, to the failure to build an orthodox Bolshevik organization. Variations of these criticisms were common to all the groups that split from the DMNL in 1947–50.

Yet as Curiel and Mohamed Sid-Ahmed indicated, there was a subtext to this criticism. The individual most responsible for shaping the line of the DMNL was Curiel; and Curiel was a cosmopolitan Jew, as were many others at all levels of the DMNL. In a country dominated economically by Europeans and suffering a British military occupation, it was more than a little unusual for a French-educated, cosmopolitan, petty bourgeois and bourgeois minority, detached from the fabric of popular life, to become so prominent in a movement claiming to represent the disenfranchised masses. In the post-1948 atmosphere of defeat, Curiel's leadership and the Jewish presence in the movement became focal points of communist self-criticism as well as of the regime's continuing attacks on the movement. The style and tone of these criticisms, as much as their content, ultimately affected the communists' stand on the Palestine question.

Of all the major communist groups, Iskra had the highest proportion of educated, upper-class foreigners and francophone Jews; its Marxism was characterized by bookish theoretical discussion, liberation of women, and Jews reaching beyond the boundaries of their community. Many Jews and their schoolmates from elite Egyptian families were recruited into Iskra from Cairo's French lycée through combined social and political activities. The first women in the communist movement were mainly from Iskra.[1] Young men and women mixed easily at Iskra's public events, scandalizing their conservative contemporaries. Leaders encouraged premarital sex as part of the assault on Egyptian bourgeois ideology in the same spirit that they provocatively promoted atheism. Mixed couples were formed, with several marriages resulting, usually between Jewish women and Muslim or Coptic men. Mohamed Sid-Ahmed, a former Iskra member and schoolmate of several Jewish members, summarized the effects of the social style of Iskra (and its successors) thus: "We imported things that do not fit in the cultural setting.... We tried not to see them.... Then we paid the price."[2]

Egyptian literary representations of the communist movement have focused on sexual libertinism, a good indication of the prominence of this theme in the public perception. The inevitable personal and political tensions in Iskra's ambience were vividly depicted in Yusuf Idris's semiautobiographical novel *Al-bayda'* (The fair one), about a young Muslim doctor drawn into work on a communist newspaper through a love affair with a Greek woman. The Egyptian émigré Waguih Ghali used the same trope—a love affair between a wealthy Jewish communist woman and a European-educated Copt—in *Beer in the Snooker Club*, a refreshingly unrestrained satire of the political dilettantism, cultural alienation, and self-indulgence of the upper-class left.

Curiel opposed Iskra's social style, criticizing its "sexual scandals" and its method of recruiting through "*haflat* [parties] ... in which dancing and flirting came to the aid of political discussion."[3] He also disparaged Iskra's lack of workers. The Jewish presence in the united DMNL was smaller than in Iskra. The first Central Committee included, out of ten members, two Jews (Curiel and Schwartz); several other Jews occupied secondary leadership posts. After several splits in the organization, in April 1948 the women's section organizer, Aimée Setton, became the third Jew in a Central Committee of seventeen.[4] Jews formed a larger proportion of the leadership of two DMNL splinter groups: Voice of the Opposition, which formed in mid-1948 and in December fused with Toward a Bolshevik Organization to become the Egyptian Communist Organization (MISHMISH, al-Munazzama al-Shuyu'iyya al-Misriyya); and Toward an Egyptian Communist Party (NAHSHAM, Nahwa Hizb Shuyu'i Misri).

Nonetheless, Iskra's reputation became part of the identity of the DMNL and was associated with the role of Jews in the movement. When three DMNL members—two Muslim men and a Jewish woman—were arrested, the U.S. ambassador took the occasion to report that "the popularity of communism with Egyptian students [was widely believed to be] due to the fact that 'cooperative' young girls belong to every cell."[5] Several veteran communists cited discomfort with their perception of the DMNL's social norms as one factor that repelled them from the organization.[6] Fu'ad Mursi spoke more bitterly than others of what he considered the

> very bad experience with Jews in the Egyptian communist movement. It was a symbol of dissolution: sexual dissolution, moral dissolution. This might be justified as liberation of thought. But the Egyptian people did not accept this or regard it as anything other than dissolution.[7]

Disapproval of Curiel and the DMNL led Mursi and Isma'il Sabri 'Abd Allah, graduate students in economics who had joined the Communist Party of France while living in Paris, to establish a new organization, the Communist Party of Egypt, in late 1949, when Mursi returned to Egypt after obtaining his doctorate. (This group was commonly known as al-Raya [The Flag] after its underground newspaper, *Rayat al-shaʿb* [People's flag]; I shall use this designation here to avoid confusion with the united Communist Party of Egypt formed in 1958.) Al-Raya's leaders were convinced that Jews and sexual libertinism had been responsible for the errors of the DMNL; as a consequence, Jews and women were excluded from membership. Al-Raya later admitted women (at first only wives and sisters whose activity could be "supervised" by their male relations), but Jews were never accepted.[8]

Al-Raya was founded during a period of reorganization in the communist movement, after martial law was lifted and detainees were released from prison. By 1951–52, though beset by continuing factionalism, the DMNL absorbed some of those who had split in 1947–48 and reemerged as the largest and most active organization, with about two thousand members.[9] Popular Democracy continued to work within the Wafd, having no more than three hundred members and no independent public presence. Al-Raya was the smallest of the major organizations, with less than one hundred members, mostly intellectuals, carrying on only underground activity.[10] In the first stage of reorganization Jews remained an important, though diminished, component of the communist movement despite internal criticism of their role and the government's efforts to equate communism with Zionism. Curiel was still the leader of the DMNL; Hillel Schwartz was at the head of NAHSHAM; Odette and Sidney Solomon were the dominant figures in MISHMISH; Yusuf Darwish, Ahmad Sadiq Saʿd, and Raymond Douek continued in leading positions in Popular Democracy.

In 1950–51, however, large numbers of Jews were arrested for a second time when the Wafd government launched a new anticommunist campaign in a futile attempt to preserve the embattled monarchy. Arrest reports provide rough statistical evidence of the extent of Jewish participation in the Egyptian communist movement during the 1950s. As Table 3 indicates, 17.4 percent of those arrested as communists in 1949–50 were Jews, a far greater percentage than their share of the total population (less than 0.05 percent). Among the detainees were many leaders, including Curiel and Schwartz, who were expelled from Egypt in the summer of 1950. Curiel was deported as a foreigner even though he had renounced his Italian citizenship and become an Egyptian citizen on reaching his majority fifteen years earlier. Many other

Jewish communists reluctantly accepted the Egyptian government's definition of their status as foreigners and left the country.

After arriving in Paris, Curiel organized the Egyptian-Jewish communist émigrés into a DMNL branch in exile, which became known as the "Rome group." They provided financial support to the DMNL, translated its documents and publications into French, and circulated them in Europe. This activity was viewed by the DMNL's opponents, both inside and outside the communist movement, as "proof" that the organization was controlled by Jews. Although Curiel remained a member of the Central Committee, sending advice (often ignored) on theoretical matters, he was not in touch with the DMNL's day-to-day activity. In May 1953 he complained that he had not been consulted by the leadership for two and a half years.[11] After 1950, except for Curiel, there were no Jewish members of the DMNL Central Committee.

The DMNL, in accord with Curiel's strategic conception, supported the coup of July 23, 1952, as an expression of the "national democratic movement."[12] All the other communist organizations opposed the new regime, especially after the repression of the strike at Kafr al-Dawwar and the execution of two workers accused of leading it. Despite these events and the arrest of other communists, especially trade unionists, the DMNL continued to support the new regime. Even after the RCC banned all political parties but its own Liberation Rally and closed the DMNL's legal press in January 1953, the DMNL refrained from open opposition until August, when, with encouragement from the American embassy in Cairo, the RCC launched a campaign to suppress communist activity.

In 1953–54, as the American embassy reported, "the overwhelming majority" of those arrested were Muslims,[13] whereas the percentage of Jews convicted of communist activity (9.6 percent) declined to almost half that in 1949–50 (Table 3). Moreover, none of the Jews arrested after 1950 were leaders. In the two most important cases—those of September 1 and December 31, 1954—only four of sixty-nine defendants were Jews (5.8 percent), three of whom later left Egypt. In the two cases with the largest numbers of Jewish defendants, most were not actually members of communist groups, and in one of these most of the defendants were acquitted. The case of October 4, 1954, was significant, however, in that Joyce Blau, who had served as a courier between Curiel and the DMNL leadership, was among the accused. Following her arrest, communication between Paris and Egypt was even less frequent. After 1954 the number of Jews arrested became inconsequential.

TABLE 3   ARRESTS FOR COMMUNIST ACTIVITY IN EGYPT, 1949–58

	Total No. Arrested	Jews Arrested	Comments
Apr. 1949	3, 21, 5, 3	2, 4, 0, 0	4 separate arrests
early 1949	3, 3	0, 0	Second arrest was of Revolutionary Bloc leaders
spring 1950	2	0	MISHMISH Alexandria
	35	3	8 separate arrests, including NAHSHAM leadership: Hillel Schwartz, Marie Rosenthal, Robert Setton
Aug. 1950	5	4	MISHMISH Cairo leaders: Sidney and Odette Solomon, Aslan and Mirayy Cohen, Mohamed Sid-Ahmed
Sept. 1950	3, 3,	1, 1	
Nov. 1950	2, 4	0, 1	Second arrest was of Yusuf Darwish and other Popular Democracy leaders
Total 1949–50	92	16	
Oct. 1953	4	0	
Nov. 1953	16, 8	0, 8	First figure includes 3 al-Raya cases; in fourth arrest, only 2 were convicted, and most were not communists
Dec. 1953	2	0	
Jan. 1954	3, 26	0, 0	In first arrest 7 others were taken in as well; identity uncertain, probably not Jews; second arrest was an al-Raya case

Sept. 1954	25	3	Major DMNL case; Naomi Canel, Marie Rosenthal, Albert Arie
Oct. 1954	7	7	falsely accused of DMNL membership
Feb. 1954–Dec. 1954	44	1	National Democratic Front case; Clement Lebovitch
Total 1953–54	135	13 (19 if unconvicted Jews are included)	
Feb. 1955	21	0	
June 1955–June 1956	69	0	al-Raya case; 29 acquitted, including Isma'il Sabri 'Abd Allah
Aug. 1957	18	1	al-Raya case; includes a Jew mistakenly admitted
Feb. 1958	8	0	
Total 1955–58	116	1	

SOURCES: *Akhir lahza*, Apr. 27, 1949; *Al-asas*, Apr. 28, May 3, June 24, 1949; *Al-misri*, July 14, 1949; USNA RG 84, Cairo Embassy General Records, 1950–52, 231/350.21; 1954, 258/350.21; U.S. State Department Central Files, Egypt 1950–54, 774.001/9-454; *Nouvelles d'Égypte*, nos. 6 (Oct. 7, 1953), 10 (Dec. 31, 1953), 11 (Jan. 15, 1954), 24 (Feb. 1955); *L'humanité*, June 29, 1956; *Al-ahram*, Feb. 1, Sept. 2, Dec. 31, 1954; Feb. 6, 1955; Aug. 30, 1957; Feb. 18, 1958.

NOTE: This table was compiled from the press archives of *Al-akhbar* and *Al-ahram*, American diplomatic reports, and reports of the DMNL's "Rome group" in Paris. There are no press archives or diplomatic reports for 1948, when a very large number of Jews were arrested and charged with communism, and they are incomplete for subsequent years. Thus, the sample is neither complete nor random, but large enough to be roughly representative.

False allegations about the Jewish role in the communist movement persisted, even though it diminished sharply after 1950. The press highlighted every arrest of Jews to "prove" that communism and Zionism were synonymous. Jews were almost always designated "Israelites" (*isra'iliyun*, as opposed to *yahud*, "Jews") to suggest an identity between communist Jews and the state of Israel. An intercepted letter from Curiel to the DMNL leadership urging the conclusion of an Egyptian-Israeli peace agreement was publicized to demonstrate the communists' treason; the Egyptian communists, moreover, were said to be led by Jews residing in France, Italy, and Israel.[14] Since the press gave such extraordinary publicity to arrests of Jews, the sample of reported arrests in Table 3 may actually exaggerate the percentages of Jewish communists.

THE RISE OF THE INDIGENOUS INTELLIGENTSIA

The declining role of Jews in the communist movement was inversely related to the influx of young indigenous intellectuals and their rise to leadership positions. The formation of a new generation of communist leaders began with the Revolutionary Bloc's 1947 revolt against Curiel's leadership of the DMNL. Al-Raya, primarily an organization of the indigenous intelligentsia, expressed its aspirations for leadership and nationalist orientation most explicitly by excluding Jews from its ranks. This trend gained strength as more university students joined the movement in the mid-1950s. One student, Mahmud Amin al-ʿAlim, became a leader of a DMNL splinter group, Nucleus of the Egyptian Communist Party (Nawat al-Hizb al-Shuyuʿi al-Misri), an organization with few or no Jewish members. He described its goal during this period as unification of the communist movement and exclusion of foreigners, because "it was not possible to have someone named Schwartz or Curiel at the head of the communist movement."[15] Philip Gallab, a student leader of al-Raya at Ibrahim Pasha (later ʿAyn Shams) University in 1953–56, said that many leftist students suspected that the DMNL "was a foreign tendency with Zionist inclinations," an impression that had influenced his decision about which organization to join.[16]

The proportion of students and graduates in the communist movement grew and that of workers declined as the RCC detached the communists from the working-class support they had won in the 1940s, except for isolated strongholds in the textile centers of Shubra al-Khayma and Kafr al-Dawwar. Students joined the communist ranks because they opposed the military dictatorship and feared that the Anglo-Egyptian negotiations would betray the nationalist demand for total and unconditional evacuation of British troops from the Suez Canal Zone. Consequently, the universities became the main arena of struggle between communists (and other opposition forces) and the regime.

The framework for left opposition politics on the campuses was the National Democratic Front, an alliance of communists, the Wafd, and other opposition forces. Students boldly confronted the regime even as opposition was smashed or neutralized among workers and other social strata. During the student union election campaign of 1953, the DMNL's Communist Student League (Rabitat al-Talaba al-Shuyu'iyin) and supporters of the National Democratic Front barricaded Abdel Nasser, then visiting the Cairo University campus, into the dean's office. When a Wafdist student member of the Front was killed in jail, his colleagues at Ibrahim Pasha University distributed a provocative leaflet entitled "Down with Naguib, Killer of 'Isam." The author of the leaflet, Communist Student League member Rif'at al-Sa'id, was rebuked by the DMNL leadership for "leftism" because the DMNL had not yet adopted a stand of total opposition to the regime. After the mass arrest of DMNL leaders in August, the students assumed greater responsibility for managing the organization and, as repression increased, continued to challenge the regime.

Al-Raya was very active among students and began to grow in this period. Students were attracted by its uncompromised opposition to the "fascist dictatorship," its emphasis on mastering Marxist theory, and its purely Egyptian character. Several of Egypt's future leading economists joined al-Raya as students in the mid-1950s. One of them, 'Amr Muhyi al-Din, led a coalition of communists and Muslim Brothers at Ibrahim Pasha University in a lengthy sit-in during June–July 1954 to protest the Anglo-Egyptian evacuation agreement.[18]

The ethos of the communist intelligentsia of the mid-1950s was articulated by Fu'ad Mursi, then a professor at Alexandria University. His 1954 pamphlet entitled "Who Are the Egyptian Communists and What Do They Want?" explained: "Because we are nationalist Egyptians, we have become communists." This orientation was common to many students in the communist movement beyond the ranks of al-Raya.[19] Assigning priority to the nationalist struggle was not an innovation of Mursi and al-Raya; it was first articulated by Curiel in the 1940s and concretized in the practice of the DMNL, including its support of the

Free Officers in 1952. New Dawn, too, despite tactical differences with the DMNL, shared this strategic perspective, which it implemented by working within the Wafd. In the mid-1950s, though, a new element began to influence the nationalist outlook of the communist intelligentsia: pan-Arabism. While Jews and non-Jews found a common language in the local Egyptian patriotic (*watani*) orientation of the communist movement of the 1940s, the injection of pan-Arab nationalist (*qawmi*) themes strained this unity to the breaking point.

A book of literary studies by Mahmud Amin al-ʿAlim and ʿAbd al-ʿAzim Anis, *On Egyptian Culture,* initiated the trajectory toward pan-Arabism.[20] The central essays, in which the young Marxists, calling for a literature of realism, social engagement, and renewal, assaulted the doyens of Egyptian letters Taha Husayn and ʿAbbas Mahmud al-ʿAqqad, first appeared in February–March 1954. By successfully executing the first sustained work of Marxist cultural criticism in Egypt and engaging leading figures of contemporary literature in debate, the authors showed that Marxism could be Arabized. Moreover, by attacking Taha Husayn's *The Future of Culture in Egypt*[21]—a programmatic assertion of Egypt's historical Mediterranean identity—al-ʿAlim and Anis implicitly asserted an Arabist alternative. They argued that culture was the product not of eternal essences but of social reality and that the dominant social reality in Egypt was the struggle against imperialism. By extension, Taha Husayn's cultural orientation emphasizing Egypt's shared heritage with Mediterranean Europe was untenable; Egypt could feel a common bond only with other Arab societies engaged in the same struggle.

When *On Egyptian Culture* appeared, Anis was working in Beirut after having been expelled from his university in Egypt. Publication of the book in Beirut was facilitated by Anis's Syrian and Lebanese communist comrades, whose pan-Arab orientation was more developed than that of the Egyptians. In his preface to the book, the Lebanese communist Husayn Muruwwa apologized for its exclusively Egyptian focus but claimed that it might just as well have been entitled "On Arab Culture" because the Egyptian examples "reflect various aspects of the proximity between Arab culture in Egypt and other parts of the Arab world."[22] Anis's pan-Arabism became even more pronounced when he completed his doctoral studies in mathematics in England and returned to Egypt after the 1956 war. As foreign editor of *Al-masaʿ*, his lively reporting on Syria and Lebanon brought an awareness of the wider Arab world to his readers.

Other early expressions of an emerging pan-Arab nationalist orientation in the communist movement are difficult to discern because between 1953 and 1955 the organizations were in disarray and absorbed in fruitless factional contention. Some elements in the movement, however, did adopt a more conciliatory stance toward the regime as a result of its new foreign policy orientation, in which pan-Arabism was becoming an important element. In March 1954, on the eve of the confrontation between Naguib and Abdel Nasser, a group of imprisoned members of the DMNL Central Committee issued a "military prison manifesto" supporting the regime.[23] The active leadership that remained at liberty repudiated this statement, and the ensuing internal debate paralyzed the DMNL during the March 1954 crisis. Within the communist ranks the rising tide of pan-Arabism was reflected by efforts to unify the various tendencies. Yet before unity could be achieved, "the question of Yunis" (Curiel's nom de guerre) had to be resolved.

"THE QUESTION OF YUNIS"

On November 21, 1952, when the DMNL still supported the RCC, *L'humanité* published an exposé of the "factional activity of the comrades Marty-Tillon" in the Communist Party of France.[24] Among the crimes attributed to Marty was his connection to a "dubious Egyptian couple whom he met while passing through Cairo in 1943" who were related to a Trotskyist accused of being an informer during the war. The couple was Henri and Rosette Curiel, and they had indeed hosted Marty in Cairo when he stopped there briefly on his way from Moscow to Algiers to join the French National Liberation Committee. Why did the leadership of the French party unnecessarily implicate Curiel in an internal dispute to which he had no connection? Elie Mignot, head of the party's Colonial Bureau, may have been influenced by Egyptian émigrés opposed to Curiel. Moreover, the French were always partial to al-Raya because its two principal leaders, Fu'ad Mursi and Isma'il Sabri 'Abd Allah, had been trained in their party and were loyal to its orthodox style. Gilles Perrault's admiring biography of Curiel suggests that the attack was motivated by the DMNL's support for the coup of July 23, 1952, in opposition to both Moscow and the French party.[25] In the era of ascendant Stalinism, this deviation may well have been considered sufficient cause.

Although the Communist Party of France provided no evidence that Curiel had acted improperly, the aspersions cast upon him by the "big brother party" were a political death sentence for him in Egypt. People who had known and worked with Curiel for years refused to have anything to do with him until his name was cleared.[26] Other organizations declined to consider uniting with the DMNL until "the question of Yunis" was settled. When the DMNL's rivals saw their accusations of Curiel's opportunism vindicated, another question mark was placed over the Jewish role in the movement.

In February 1955, six splinter organizations reunited with the DMNL to form the Unified Egyptian Communist Party (al-Hizb al-Shuyuʿi al-Misri al-Muwwahad). Curiel and the Rome group were so out of touch with their Egyptian comrades that they learned of this decision—which they enthusiastically endorsed—from the Sudanese communists.[27] Suspension of Curiel's membership, though, was one condition of unity imposed by the other organizations, with the article in *L'humanité* serving as the formal basis for this demand. The DMNL's leader on the eve of unity, Kamal ʿAbd al-Halim, a close associate of Curiel and the husband of a Jewish DMNL member, Naomi Canel, was also suspended from the UECP—the official reason probably being his "rightism" (he was the DMNL leader most sympathetic to the Nasserist regime) and not his relations with Curiel or his Jewish wife. Curiel, ʿAbd al-Halim, and four other suspended members were readmitted to the UECP in July 1956; Curiel's place on the Central Committee, however, was taken by a worker. Although it considered Curiel's demotion "submission to bourgeois nationalism," the Rome group loyally accepted the decision.[28] Curiel rejoined the Central Committee after the 1956 war.[29]

WAS THERE A "ZIONIST DEVIATION" IN THE DMNL?

The leadership of the indigenous intelligentsia was established through struggle against the older Jewish and cosmopolitan leaders, and there was always a danger that this struggle would affect the communists' stand on the Palestinian/Arab–Israeli conflict. The Revolutionary Bloc's criticism of the DMNL leadership had raised, at least in some DMNL members' minds, the suspicion that Curiel and the other Jewish leaders might be too sympathetic to Zionism. The leaders of Popular Democracy certainly thought so. With Curiel's reputation beclouded by the Marty affair, rumors about his Zionist sympathies spread, particularly among younger student members of the movement who had not known Curiel or other Jewish communists personally.

Is there any evidence to sustain the charge of Zionism that was directed against Curiel and the DMNL? Since no complete collection of Egyptian communist documents exists (with the possible exception of the files of the Egyptian police, who have not shared their resources with researchers), the answer to this question must remain tentative. Yet I have seen nothing to substantiate the allegation. Individual opinions expressed verbally may have differed from the DMNL's official stand; this could be expected in an organization with loose discipline.[30] It is also likely that because their French education posed the Jewish question as a problem in *European* history, the Jewish and upper-class members of the DMNL used a rhetorical style in discussing Palestine and the Arab-Israeli conflict that differed from the style of Egyptians educated in Arabic.

Voice of the Opposition/MISHMISH was the only organization whose analysis of the Palestine question contained what might be regarded as Zionist deviations. It condemned Egypt's invasion of Palestine as a "racist war" incited by imperialism—though all the communists did this. In addition, however, MISHMISH analyzed the 1948 war as a war of the Arab bourgeoisies against their proletariats designed to divert the latter from the class struggle. Since Zionism was losing its grip over an increasingly radicalized Jewish working class, Israel might become a socialist state. Therefore, the Arab bourgeoisies had attacked the Jewish proletariat in particular. MISHMISH defended the Jewish community's right to self-determination in Palestine, asserting that the Jews had become "a democratic people"; Arab rule would "destroy this island of democracy which might constitute a good influence on the Arab part of Palestine and play a positive role in the Middle East."[31]

The MISHMISH leaders were all Jewish and upper-class former Iskra members; few workers belonged to the organization despite its "100 percent proletarian" line. Its misunderstanding of the Arab-Israeli conflict and the nature of Israel flowed from its narrowly workerist orientation and its dismissal of the national struggle as an appropriate communist issue. Although MISHMISH was one of the larger DMNL splinters, with several hundred members in 1949, most adherents were soon arrested because they employed adventurist tactics like sending "young Jewish girls from the center of Cairo . . . to [organize and sell newspapers to workers in] Shubra al-Khayma under martial law and without any experience."[32] The organization became inactive after the arrest of the leadership in August 1950 and dissolved in 1954 when its Jewish leaders, Odette and Sidney Solomon, left Egypt.

The communists devoted little effort to analyzing the Arab-Israeli conflict after the 1948–49 war because local Egyptian national issues became increasingly more pressing: the tottering monarchy; the coup of July 23, 1952; and the negotiations to end British occupation of the Canal Zone. The DMNL's successive legal weeklies from 1950 to 1952—*Al-bashir* (The herald), *Al-malayin* (The millions), and *Al-wajib* (The duty)—for example, devoted less space to Arab-Israeli matters than had their predecessor, *Al-jamahir*. Only in late 1953 did increased tension on the Arab-Israeli borders, particularly following the Israeli raids on al-Burayj and Qibya, once again bring the conflict to the fore.

The DMNL, concerned that cross-border raids would threaten the uneasy truce in the Middle East, called for a "just and democratic peace" between Egypt and Israel.[33] It regarded the imperialist powers as responsible for the tension between Israel and the Arab states, just as it had in 1948. It reiterated this analysis in its July 1954 solidarity message to the conference of communist parties in the sphere of influence of British imperialism, which also saluted MAKI for leading the way in the struggle for peace between Israel and the Arab states and for defending the rights of the Arab refugees, the rights of the Arab minority in Israel, and the struggle against "Zionism, agent of American imperialism, and its territorial expansion plans in the Middle East."[34]

The hostility of al-Raya's leaders toward the historic role of Jews in the communist movement was not expressed as disapproval of the DMNL or UECP stand on the Palestine question. In the final three pages of a tract developing al-Raya's analysis of Egyptian society and politics, Mursi argued that Egypt's feudalists and bourgeoisie invaded Palestine because of the feudalist-imperialist struggle between Egypt's King Faruq and Jordan's King ʿAbd Allah and in order to distract the Egyptian people from their true problems. The booklet concluded with a call to end the state of war between Israel and Egypt and create an "independent democratic Arab state in the part of Palestine that the UN allotted to the Arabs."[35]

Reflecting the local Egyptian political orientation of the communist movement in the early 1950s, al-Raya attacked the "fascist militarists" of the RCC for promoting a campaign to collect contributions for the Palestinian refugees in the Gaza Strip because it placed a burden on the Egyptian people; the real solution to the refugee problem, in contrast, lay in "creating a democratic independent Palestinian Arab state through withdrawal of the foreign armies occupying our lands and refraining from inciting racist hatred against the Jews."[36] In response to the clashes on the Egyptian-Israeli border in late 1953, al-Raya called for "peace with Israel on the basis of the Arab refugees' right to form their independent state."[37]

Al-Raya attacked the UECP as being simply a reincarnation of the DMNL. In late 1955 it presented a comprehensive history of the lines of the two organizations, which denounced the opportunism of the DMNL/UECP for its positions on the coup of July 23, 1952; the military dictatorship; the Anglo-Egyptian evacuation agreement; Egyptian foreign policy; and the Czech arms deal. Unlike the UECP, al-Raya remained strongly opposed to the ruling regime. In a twenty-two-page document, only one and one-half pages were devoted to the Palestine question; in this short section, moreover—and in contrast to the thrust of the rest of the document—the DMNL/UECP's position on the Arab-Israeli conflict received no criticism. Al-Raya supported the creation of a Palestinian Arab state within the borders allotted by the UN partition plan, on territory to be relinquished by Israel, Jordan, and Egypt.[38]

Therefore, at least until shortly before the Suez/Sinai War there was no substantive difference between the stands of the DMNL/UECP and of al-Raya on the Palestinian/Arab-Israeli conflict, even though the latter was uninfluenced by the presence of Jewish members, whether past or present. Nonetheless, al-Raya continued to attack the DMNL and the UECP as though they were still directed by Curiel. This sustained criticism encouraged suspicions that the DMNL and UECP might be subject to Zionist influence, since Curiel was still under a cloud because of the Matty affair. Subsequently, the apprehension of several Egyptian Jewish saboteurs dispatched by Israel in August 1954 undermined the security of the entire Egyptian Jewish community and raised further doubts about Jews' reliability in the communist movement.[39] Logical demonstration that Curiel and the Jewish communists were not Zionists was less powerful than the dynamic development of the conflict with Israel. The social friction between Jews and non-Jews in the movement, whose origins lay far away in the 1940s, became sharper as the Arab-Israeli conflict intensified, the Nasser regime gained legitimacy through nationalist success, and the social character of the communist movement changed.

A MAPAM—MAKI UNITED FRONT?

In the rapidly polarizing world of the cold war, MAPAM and MAKI both regarded support for the Soviet Union and the international path of the October revolution to be the most fundamental political question. On this foundation, it was not difficult to imagine a high level of cooperation between MAPAM and MAKI. Despite MAPAM's major concessions to the Zionist consensus even before the end of 1948, it continued to consider itself and to be considered by others as a revolutionary Marxist party. Although the leaders of MAKI were critical of MAPAM's inconsistencies on Arab-Israeli issues, they continued to view MAPAM as a potential ally. Moreover, since the Soviet Union still regarded Israel as the leading anti-imperialist force in the Middle East, the MAPAM leftists believed it would eventually be possible to steer the international communist movement away from its historic opposition to Zionism both by demonstrating unwavering loyalty to the Soviet Union and by building the Zionist left in Israel. They, too, looked forward to good relations between MAKI and MAPAM.

In early June 1948, MAKI's Central Committee urgently requested that the MAPAM leadership enter consultations to explore joint mobilization for Israel's war of independence and other areas of "great national importance."[40] Later that month, MAKI distributed a leaflet to MAPAM's first national conference proposing the formation of a united front based on a common program: mobilization of all national and international forces for the war effort and the sovereignty of the state of Israel; full independence of Israel, no foreign bases, and no cession of territory to ʿAbd Allah; unlimited *aliyah;* opposition to Bernadotte's proposals; economic development; equal rights for all Israel's citizens; a pact of friendship with the Soviet Union and the peoples' democracies; a democratic policy toward the Arab minority in Israel; defense of the interests of the working class; and struggle against the danger of fascism in the *yishuv*. While the leaflet acknowledged ideological differences between the two parties, it did not discuss these, nor did it explicitly address the question of Zionism. MAKI's proposed program also omitted establishment of a Palestinian Arab state, although this goal was implied in the item opposing territorial annexations by ʿAbd Allah. MAPAM and MAKI certainly agreed on this point, and it was included in the draft program MAKI proposed in late August as the basis for a joint list in Israel's first parliamentary elections.[41]

MAKI's proposals for a front and a joint electoral list with MAPAM exceeded the limited cooperation with Zionist parties envisioned by the PCP as early as 1946. Since MAPAM was by far the larger party, MAKI would have been the junior partner in a front. Thus, MAPAM would have given the front its mass base, while MAKI's participation would have secured the imprimatur of the international communist movement, a valuable consideration for many MAPAM members. To build such a front MAKI was prepared to replace the distinction between Zionists and non-Zionists with one between the "peace-seeking camp of progress linked to the progressive workers' movement, friends of the Soviet Union, and the popular democracies" on the one hand and the "camp of proimperialist reaction" on the other.

Ahdut Ha'avodah opposed any form of cooperation that drew MAPAM and MAKI together. While the urban left, led by Sneh, Berman, and Tubin, and scattered individuals in Kibbutz Artzi favored a comprehensive front with MAKI, Riftin, Peri, and most of the Kibbutz Artzi left favored joint action on issues where there was agreement but rejected a comprehensive front, believing that the creation of the Jewish state was only "the beginning of the realization of Zionism."[42] For them, unreserved identification with "the world of revolution" was the way both to realize maximalist Zionism and to make Zionism acceptable to the international communist movement; therefore, MAPAM should "do everything so that MAKI will be extraneous," there being "no need for two communist parties in one country."[43]

This strategy required drawing a sharp line between MAKI and MAPAM—despite the high degree of programmatic unity between them—and especially between MAKI and the left of MAPAM. During the fall of 1948 many MAPAM leaders polemicized against MAKI in order to sharpen the distinction between communism and Zionism. Nahum Nir and Me'ir Talmi, representing MAPAM's right and center, respectively, and left-winger El'azar Peri all repudiated Ilya Ehrenburg's widely publicized *Pravda* article that supported establishment of the state of Israel but at the same time advocated assimilation for Jews in the Soviet Union. Peri was even more adamant than Nir and Talmi in insisting that Zionism was a condition for a united front, because

> the very fact of our existence in this country is Zionism. Therefore, it is impossible for a public body or political list to be a-Zionist.... MAPAM cannot permit itself to appear in such an unusual manner. MAPAM is not a sect. It sees itself as responsible for the affairs of the entire nation, and it seeks to win the trust of the democratic majority in this nation. An a-Zionist united front will not win the nation; it will repel it.[44]

The majority of MAPAM agreed that in Israel Zionism was the fundamental political line of demarcation; it therefore rejected MAKI's proposals for a front and a joint electoral list, though it did offer to maintain permanent contact and coordination.

ELECTIONS TO THE CONSTITUENT ASSEMBLY (FIRST KNESSET)

On January 25, 1949, Israel held elections for its Constituent Assembly. The war had ended, but armistice agreements between Israel and the invading Arab states were not yet signed; the creation of a Palestinian state in the near future thus did not seem impossible. MAPAM's electoral propaganda emphasized the importance of its members in the Palmah and its contributions to *aliyah*, settlement, and defense. Its maximum program advocated

> a socialist state, a free workers' society without exploitation and oppression in all of Eretz Israel, which will concentrate in its borders the vast majority of the Jewish people from all its exiles and dispersions and maintain relations of peace and brotherhood with the masses of the Arab people living in Palestine.

Unification of Eretz Israel would be achieved by peaceful means. After the Arab invaders were expelled from the country and the remaining peace-seeking Arabs established their state, the economic union envisioned by the UN partition plan would be implemented. Friendship built on mutually beneficial economic relations would lay the basis for "one free state of the Jewish people returning to its homeland and settling there and [of] the masses of the Arab people residing there." To preserve the possibility of achieving this goal MAPAM opposed any peace agreement with ʿAbd Allah or annexations by any Arab state.[45]

This platform did not win much support among Palestinian Arabs, not only because MAPAM, in accordance with its resolution of October 7, 1948, advocated Israeli annexation of territory occupied by the IDF beyond the UN partition boundaries, but also because the envisioned united state would undoubtedly have a Jewish majority; in addition, owing to opposition by former Ahdut Haʿavodah members, MAPAM did not declare that Arabs would enjoy national rights in this state. Also in deference to Ahdut Haʿavodah, MAPAM accepted no Arab members; rather, Arabs were encouraged to vote for an all-Arab electoral list—the Popular Arab Bloc—which MAPAM established only three weeks before the elections. As head of the Arab Affairs Department, Aharon Cohen directed MAPAM's electoral work among Arabs; he instructed that

> in the event of questions about the Communists it should be explained that regarding basic principles and program there is almost no difference between

our list and [that of] the Communists in matters relating to the Arabs, but the Arab voter should know that the Communist Party is very weak among the Jewish public and is unpopular because for many years it opposed the national aspirations of the Jews.[46]

This was Cohen's personal stand; however, there were indeed significant differences between the two parties' approach to the Arabs, as Cohen explained in internal bulletins and memoranda to MAPAM's leading bodies. After the elections and throughout 1949 he energetically campaigned for a more sustained commitment to political work in the Arab community, immediate admission of Arabs to MAPAM, and a change in the party's policy against admitting Arabs to the Histadrut.[47] The MAPAM left supported these proposals; Ahdut Ha'avodah opposed them.

As a Jewish-Arab party after October 22, 1948, MAKI faced fewer obstacles to presenting a unified appeal to both Jewish and Arab voters, based on its unequivocal support for the UN partition plan. Nonetheless, outside Haifa MAKI remained overwhelmingly Jewish. Many of its Arab members remained incarcerated, despite their willingness to recognize Israel, when the IDF captured the camp where the Egyptian army had interned Palestinian Arab communists. During the IDF conquest of the Galilee, too, Arab communists were arrested for resisting the entry of Israeli forces into territory designated by the UN for the Arab state. Communist activity in the Arab community gradually resumed during the months following the October unity meeting as branches of MAKI and the AWC and distribution of *Al-ittihad* were reorganized. MAKI's electoral campaign in the Arab community was impeded when the military government prohibited campaigning in Arab areas under its control, a decision that was reversed only after January 10. The government also originally planned to print ballot cards in Hebrew alone and supplied Arabic ballots only after protests by MAKI and MAPAM.[48] MAKI's consolidation as a Jewish-Arab party was delayed as well: in the territories designated by the UN for inclusion in the Palestinian Arab state, the NLL remained the sole communist party; thus, the election campaign in the occupied territories was conducted in the name of the NLL, not of MAKI. In Acre, for example, Hanna Naqqara addressed a meeting called by the NLL and urged Arabs to vote for MAKI because it was the only Jewish-Arab party in Israel and fought equally for the rights of both peoples. Naqqara announced that, although he was not a party member, he would vote for MAKI, and he invited those who supported establishment of a Palestinian state in the Arab areas (including Acre), freedom for the Arab prisoners, return of the refugees, and an end to national oppression to do likewise.[49]

MAKI's electoral propaganda was based on an internationalist appeal for establishment of a Palestinian Arab state in accordance with the UN partition plan of November 29, 1947; safeguarding of the independence of Israel; peace between Israel and the neighboring Arab states; complete equality between Arabs and Jews within Israel; return of the Palestinian refugees; release of all the Palestinian prisoners; an end to the military government; jobs for all Palestinians who sought work; equal wages for Jews and Arabs; equal rights for women; free and equal education for Jews and Arabs; freedom of religion. MAKI stressed that it was the only Jewish-Arab party in the country.[50] Tawfiq Tubi and Emile Habibi occupied the second and fifth places on MAKI's list, positions high enough to guarantee Arab representation in the party's Knesset bloc.

The election results indicated the existence of a viable Israeli Jewish left.[51] Two-thirds of MAKI's voters and over 95 percent of MAPAM's were Jews. MAKI received nearly twice as many Arab votes as MAPAM, but since Arabs made up only about 5.5 percent of the electorate, their electoral significance was minor. MAKI won four Knesset seats, although it lost one of them when the former Hebrew Communists left MAKI and joined MAPAM. With MAPAI's forty-six Knesset seats and MAPAM's nineteen, a strong labor Zionist coalition government of the two largest parties could have been established. But Ben-Gurion had no interest in a left–social democratic government and refused to make significant programmatic concessions to MAPAM. Ahdut Ha'avodah generally favored participation in MAPAI-led governments, but, outraged by Ben-Gurion's arrogance and his decision to disband the Palmah, it joined the overwhelming majority at MAPAM's Second Council in rejecting government participation on Ben-Gurion's terms.[52] MAPAM and MAKI thus became the left opposition to the government. MAPAM appeared to be upholding its commitments as a revolutionary socialist party, and it seemed that there was substantial support for this policy among Jewish workers.

MARXISM ENGAGED IN A JEWISH PROBLEMATIC

Despite MAPAM's rejection of MAKI's proposal for a joint electoral list and the natural exacerbation of differences between the two parties during the election campaign, MAKI maintained its orientation toward establishing a front with MAPAM. It proposed a joint MAKI-MAPAM electoral list in the elections for the Seventh Congress of the Histadrut in May 1949, and in nearly every subsequent national, local, and Histadrut election—though by the mid-1950s such proposals were merely a formality. While no front was established, MAKI and MAPAM did cooperate in several arenas during 1949: opposing the Histadrut's affiliation with the International Confederation of Free Trade Unions; founding the Israel Peace Council; founding and leading the Israel–Soviet Union Friendship League; calling joint May Day demonstrations in Lydda and Ramle attended by Jews and Arabs. The two parties also appeared to share the same approach to the Palestine question. On April 4, 1949, they voted against Knesset ratification of the armistice agreement with Transjordan on the grounds that it recognized ʿAbd Allah's annexation of the West Bank, blocked the establishment of a Palestinian Arab state, and accepted the existence of British bases in Eretz Israel (that is, on the West Bank).[53]

MAKI's pursuit of a front with MAPAM was part of its orientation around a Jewish problematic that placed the questions of Israel's security, *aliyah,* and the fate of European Jewry at the center of political debate and relegated the "Arab question" to a secondary status. Despite MAKI's clear ideological rejection of Zionism, it shared with MAPAM and the Zionist left a common definition of the principal political issues facing Israel in 1948–49. MAKI adopted an Israeli patriotic stance in opposing creation of a neutral no-man's-land between Egypt and Israel, the Mixed Armistice Commissions established at the 1949 Israeli-Arab armistice talks, and the internationalization of Jerusalem, as stipulated by the UN partition plan, arguing that these measures might enhance the imperialist military presence in the Middle East and diminished Israel's independence.[54] MAKI and MAPAM were both very suspicious of American pressure on Israel to repatriate some of the Palestinian refugees.[55] For the first time in its history, MAKI expressed concern about absorption of *aliyah:* a congress of communist IDF soldiers complained that foreign volunteers, many of them from the people's democracies of Eastern Europe, were being treated unequally, a fact that might cause them to leave Israel.[56]

By the end of 1948, Rumania, Hungary, and Poland had begun to restrict Jewish immigration and put Jews on trial for Zionist activity. *Al hamishmar* opposed these measures as contrary to "the Stalinist conception of national liberation" and attacked MAKI for its uncritical support of the people's democracies despite their restriction of *aliyah*.[57] MAKI's Eleventh Congress convened in October 1949 as polemics with

MAPAM over the question of *aliyah* intensified. Vilner reported to the congress that "the difference between Marxism and Zionism is not support for the state, *aliyah* and *hityashvut* [settlement]. Marxists not only 'favor *aliyah*,' but fight for an economic program of jobs and housing which will permit absorbing a large *aliyah* and prevent the great suffering of the *olim* [immigrants]."[58] General Secretary Mikunis, in his closing speech to the congress, confirmed Vilner's endorsement of *aliyah*, stating: "*Aliyah* to Israel is not Zionism. Zionism is viewing *aliyah* as the solution to the 'Jewish problem.'"[59] While embracing the Zionist program of *aliyah*, Vilner stressed the importance of intensifying the ideological struggle against Zionism. MAKI had neglected this task in the recent past, he argued, because of its desire to establish a united front with MAPAM. Vilner classified all Zionism, including MAPAM's socialist-Zionism, as "bourgeois nationalism" and denounced the "ingathering of the exiles" as a utopian and reactionary slogan.

The reports and speeches of MAKI's Jewish leaders at the Eleventh Congress reflected the party's concessions to the Zionist discourse. The term *aliyah*, for example, was an innovation in the MAKI lexicon: the speakers at the Tenth Congress had employed for "immigration" the more neutral term *hagirah*, which did not have the spiritual connotation of the word appropriated by the Zionist movement. *Hityashvut* (settlement), too, was a term with labor Zionist connotations; it was usually employed in connection with agricultural settlement, which MAKI regarded as a utopian and backward-looking development in opposition to the vanguard role of the urban working class. Moreover, by focusing on ideological rather than programmatic differences between Marxism and Zionism, Vilner and Mikunis avoided direct confrontation with the settler-colonial aspect of the Zionist project: settling Jewish immigrants on formerly Arab land.

Of course, MAKI opposed all forms of discrimination and oppression against Palestinian Arabs. The Central Committee's report to the congress firmly supported the Palestinian Arabs' right to self-determination and their right to establish a state as an expression of their just national aspirations. But rather than specify that the borders between Israel and the Palestinian Arab state should be those of the UN partition plan, the report stipulated that they would be decided by "the two states in friendly negotiations in light of the interests of the workers, independence and freedom of the two peoples, and the success of the struggle against imperialism and its satellites."[60]

The first step in the retreat from the partition borders as the territorial basis for Palestinian self-determination had already been taken in late April 1949, when references to the NLL disappeared from *Al-ittihad* and *Kol ha'am* without explanation. According to Emile Habibi, MAKI abandoned its commitment to maintain the NLL as a separate organization in the Palestinian territories occupied by Israel during the war, the better to fight against the expulsion of Arabs and for their civil rights. The only means of accomplishing these ends was by insisting that Israeli law be applied to these territories.[61] As the Arab community was in desperate circumstances, immediate measures to improve its condition were urgently required. Yet abandoning the separate existence of the NLL also constituted de facto acceptance of the territorial status quo and recognition that a Palestinian Arab state would not be established in the near future. The disappearance of the NLL, even if by early 1949 in places like Acre and Nazareth it existed only as a verbal construction, suggested MAKI's acceptance that Zionist military successes would define the political agenda. No other communist party in the Middle East made this adjustment to the new status quo.

Although MAKI's concessions to the Zionist consensus were far less substantial than MAPAM's, they were justified in the same discursive terms. The creation of Israel was a victory for the anti-imperialist forces in the Middle East; strengthening that state was considered a legitimate progressive goal. The regional Arab left was weak and disorganized, and there was no reason to defend the territorial ambitions of the reactionary Arab rulers allied to Great Britain, who were actively suppressing popular aspirations at home. The Arab members of MAKI did not exert much influence on the party's direction for several years owing to the social and political disorganization of the Palestinian Arab community after 1948 and the constant repression directed against it by the Israeli authorities. Moreover, concern for the Jewish victims of Nazism was natural and appropriate for a movement that placed the struggle against fascism and war at the center of its international political agenda. MAKI was certainly unconscious of the extent to which its post-1948 orientation contributed to legitimating the Zionist project, and despite its concessions to the Zionist political discourse, no political force in Israel struggled harder or more consistently to defend the rights of Israel's Arab minority while upholding the principle of the Palestinian Arabs' right to self-determination.

THE RISE AND DECLINE OF THE LEFT IN MAPAM

The MAKI-MAPAM polemics in the fall of 1948 did not arise only because of Eastern European policies toward Jewish immigration; the

MAPAM leadership, and especially its Kibbutz Artzi component, also felt threatened because MAKI's more consistent Marxism appealed to some MAPAM members and undermined the ideological authority of MAPAM's socialist-Zionist synthesis. As long as MAPAM considered itself a revolutionary socialist party in the pro-Soviet camp, MAKI could win members from MAPAM by pointing to the inconsistencies between MAPAM's theory and its practice. Of MAPAM adherents, younger members of Kibbutz Artzi and city workers particularly were attracted to MAKI. For example, in the 1949 elections three members of the newly settled Kibbutz Barkai had voted for MAKI. One of them, an elected officer, was subsequently expelled from the kibbutz by a vote of eight to three for violating ideological collectivism (Kibbutz Artzi's version of democratic centralism)—but seventy-five kibbutz members abstained from the vote, a dangerous sign in a commune that placed a high value on social and political conformity.[62] In June, twenty-eight young members of Kibbutz Zikim, among them former leading members of Hashomer Hatza'ir in Rumania, joined MAKI; they too were expelled at the insistence of Kibbutz Artzi's secretariat—but over the objections of nearly forty members of Zikim who voted against their expulsion.[63] Also notable is the fact that "a group of MAPAM members" sent greetings to MAKI's Eleventh Congress and called for cooperation and a left front between the two parties.[64] These incidents, and the sharp response to them by the leaders of MAPAM and Kibbutz Artzi, indicate that despite the determination by the MAPAM leadership that Zionism marked an inviolable boundary between MAKI and MAPAM, that line was in fact permeable, and often to MAPAM's disadvantage.

Although MAPAM's left wing made up a minority of 20–30 percent of the party's forty-seven thousand members in 1950–52, it dominated the party's public image.[65] Nonetheless, the MAPAM left was itself divided. Sneh and his mainly urban followers were motivated by orthodox Marxist appeals to class sentiment and, above all, by Soviet loyalism. Sneh rarely used the symbols and slogans of the Zionist lexicon. In contrast, Riftin, Peri, and their followers in Kibbutz Artzi, while they argued that the difference between MAPAM and the international communist movement was restricted to the Jewish national question, were primarily motivated by Zionist sentiment. As Peri explained, "For us, the national struggle—Zionism, ingathering of the exiles—is not only a struggle for national liberation, it is the way to carry out the socialist revolution."[66] Full unity with the international communist movement could be achieved only after MAPAM's socialist-Zionist synthesis was recognized as the Jewish road to revolution.

Because the kibbutz left insisted on the importance of the Zionist tasks of the Jewish working class, it opposed cooperation with MAKI on Jewish-national issues. Despite many shared positions on the Arab-Israeli dispute, cooperation on this issue was virtually nil, although MAPAM and MAKI did vote together against the Absentee Property Law of 1950. Conversely, on global political issues where MAPAM's actions had little practical influence—opposition to arming West Germany and its inclusion in NATO, opposition to accepting U.S. aid, opposition to American intervention in Korea—MAPAM and MAKI voted together in the Knesset, and their members demonstrated together in the streets.[67]

The left, by not placing Arab-Israeli issues at the center of the intra-party struggle in MAPAM, allowed itself to become increasingly marginalized in this arena. Aharon Cohen repeatedly complained that the party's activity in the Arab community was insufficient before the 1949 elections, inconsistent because of understaffing and underfunding afterward, and impeded by failure to accept Arabs as full party members when several dozen were willing to join.[68] Twenty-five Arabs submitted a petition to MAPAM's Third Council in November 1949 asking to join the party.[69] In response, the council established a separate Arab Section whose members would still not be full party members. Four Arabs were added to the eleven Jewish members of the Arab Affairs Department, which served as the leadership of the Arab Section and the coordinating body between it and the party. Nevertheless, MAPAM kept a tight rein on Arab Section activity. Throughout the 1950s, for example, Yosef Vashitz edited its Arabic newspaper, *Al-mirsad* (The watchtower). Even after Arabs became full members of MAPAM following the split of Ahdut Ha'avodah in 1954, Jews directed the Arab Affairs Department until 1961, and at least 50 percent of the department's members were Jews.

In November 1950, Aharon Cohen resigned as head of the Arab Affairs Department. His personal papers do not mention the reason for his departure—an omission in the otherwise extensive record of his activity reflecting his unwavering party loyalty—but it is clear that by this time his positions on "the Arab question" were considered too radical by the majority of MAPAM and Kibbutz Artzi. Rustum Bastuni, a leading member of the Arab Section who served as secretary for Arab affairs of MAPAM's parliamentary faction, respected Cohen and regarded his departure as a blow to the Arab Section and to MAPAM's development toward internationalism; Cohen, he felt, was the only one in the party who insisted on accepting Arab members immediately. Cohen's successors, Yosef Vashitz and Eliʿezer Beʾeri, got along badly with Bastuni. Bastuni, criticizing Vashitz's "dictatorial" style of work, demanded that Cohen be returned to his position and threatened that leading Arab Section members would resign if the Arab Affairs Department did not heed their opinions.[70] Whatever the personal issues in this dispute may have been, Cohen's departure from the Arab Affairs Department and his subsequent virtual retirement from leadership in MAPAM was a decisive defeat for the left on Arab-Israeli questions. Cohen was the only MAPAM leftist with sufficient knowledge, commitment, and stature in the Arab community to make Arab-Israeli relations a central component of the left's program.

Well before MAPAM's Second Party Congress in June 1951, its three tendencies had crystallized into factionally organized sections. Hashomer Hatzaʿir joined with Sneh and his followers, the former Hebrew Communists and the Yitzhaki faction of Left Poʿalei Tzion, to form the Party Unity Front, which, led by Meʾir Yaʿari, Yaʿakov Hazan, and Yitzhak Yitzhaki, controlled 60 percent of the votes at the congress. Ahdut Haʿavodah controlled 35 percent of the votes, and its ally, the Erem group of Left Poʿalei Tzion, had 5 percent. Ahdut Haʿavodah and the Erem group agreed on all matters except admission of Arabs to the party and the Histadrut. The main business of the congress was adopting a party program, for which all three sections presented drafts. The main issues of contention between the Unity Front and Ahdut Haʿavodah/Erem involved (1) adopting Marxism-Leninism or Borochovism as the party ideology, (2) integrating into the international communist camp by stating clearly that recognition of Zionism was the only difference between that movement and MAPAM, (3) allowing Arab membership in the party, and (4) maintaining the sectional organization of the party or imposing majority rule.[71] In addition, most of Ahdut Haʿavodah wanted to accept MAPAI's conditions for joining the government, while the Unity Front preferred an opposition stance unless MAPAM received some programmatic concessions from MAPAI.

The Arab Section held its own congress in April 1951, where it adopted a manifesto advocating reunifying the country—including both banks of the Jordan, thus increasing the number of Arabs in the united state—with the right of both nations to self-determination and the unequivocal right of all refugees to return. On other matters—

Marxism-Leninism, abolition of party sections, and, of course, Arab membership in the party—the Arab Section shared the positions of the Unity Front.[72]

All of MAPAM continued to look forward to the country's reunification, although Hashomer Hatzaʻir (as opposed to Ahdut Haʻavodah) insisted that this process must occur peacefully. The Unity Front proposed recognizing the Palestinian Arabs' right to self-determination and independence in those parts of the country outside the state of Israel, in the framework of an economic union that would permit Jews and Arabs to settle anywhere in the territory of former mandate Palestine (in effect, endorsing fully Israel's territorial acquisitions in the 1948–49 war while opposing ʻAbd Allah's annexation of the West Bank).[73] The formulations of the new party program (known as the Haifa program), while less clear, were in basic accord with the Unity Front proposals. Although Ahdut Haʻavodah attacked the Unity Front for advocating the return of *all* the Palestinian refugees,[74] the Haifa program's positions on the refugee question were so close to those of the Unity Front as to prove this claim untrue. The Haifa program advocated that Israel "participate in solving the problem of the peace-seeking refugees in the context of a comprehensive peace settlement including the Arab states and in accordance with Israel's development plans."[75] It also advocated comprehensive civil rights for the Arab minority in Israel: abolition of the military government, municipal elections in Arab localities, equal pay for equal work, membership in the Histadrut, the right to work, equal prices for agricultural produce, and so forth. Thus compromise formulations were found between the positions of the Unity Front and Ahdut Haʻavodah that reflected the Front's leading role in the party and the strong left-wing influence in the Unity Front on aspects of the Arab-Israeli dispute whose resolution lay in the indeterminate future.

On the issues that would have meant an immediate change, however—accepting Arab members into the party and replacing factional parity with majority rule—the Haifa program declared only MAPAM's intention to develop into a territorial party of the entire working class. The Arab Section had demanded opening the doors of the party to Arabs immediately, and the left—Sneh as well as Simha Flapan and Mordechai Bentov of Kibbutz Artzi—spoke forthrightly about the need to take concrete steps toward realizing this objective.[76] Ahdut Haʻavodah threatened a split if the congress majority decided to admit Arabs or liquidate the sections, and the Unity Front (including the left) conceded to this ultimatum.

On ideological, organizational, and Arab-Israeli issues the MAPAM left (together with the center, led by Ya'ari and Hazan) was willing to compromise or concede to Ahdut Ha'avodah in order to preserve party unity. As the cold war intensified and the Israeli government actively pursued an alliance with the West, the "orientation toward the forces of tomorrow" and identification with the "world of revolution" led by the Soviet Union became the central issue defining the left within MAPAM. Yet the resurgence of anti-Semitism in Eastern Europe, in addition to earlier restraints on Jewish immigration, made pro-Soviet orthodoxy increasingly difficult to defend within the framework of a Zionist discourse. The MAPAM left was tested over its international orientation, but it could not withstand the challenge to this, the weakest of its characteristic positions.

In November 1952, the government of Czechoslovakia announced that Mordehai Oren, who had traveled to Europe to attend a meeting of the World Federation of Trade Unions, had been arrested in connection with charges made against Rudolf Slansky and other mostly Jewish Czech Communist Party leaders—among other things, that they were Jewish bourgeois nationalists and Zionist agents responsible for encouraging the emigration of Czech Jews to Israel and aiding Israel in the 1948–49 war. The Slansky trial was a frame-up that employed blatant anti-Semitism to curry favor with the non-Jewish masses and so secure absolute supremacy of the Soviet Union in Eastern Europe and eliminate any independent Titoist tendencies. Oren was charged with espionage, to "prove" that the defendants had links to Israel and the Zionist movement. MAPAM was shaken to its foundations by seeing a leader of the Kibbutz Artzi left caught up in such virulent anti-Semitism and accused of heinous anticommunist crimes despite his fervent loyalty to the Soviet Union and close relations with many East European communist leaders.

An editorial in *Al hamishmar* declared that MAPAM was confident of Oren's innocence and denounced the Prague trial.[77] The left opposed this stand. Riftin put the matter squarely before the Political Committee: "It is impossible to be an inseparable part [of the world of revolution] without being for Prague." Sneh said the trial posed a "choice between national solidarity and international solidarity" and that "in this matter there ought to have been international solidarity." Ya'ari, the author of the *Al hamishmar* editorial, voiced the opposite opinion:

> We were presented with the problem of losing our Zionist world or losing our socialist world.... I believe we must struggle to defend Zionism, not only the Zionism of MAPAM, but the liberation of the entire nation of

Israel. . . . I will not stand behind an anti-Zionist trial, and this is clearly an anti-Zionist trial.[78]

At the end of the Political Committee discussion, the vote was twenty-six to seven in favor of endorsing *Al hamishmar*'s editorial.

In early December 1952, the Unity Front leadership attempted to reconcile the differences within its ranks by adopting a resolution on the Prague trial proposed by Ya'ari and amended by Riftin, Peri, and Sneh. The resolution was presented to the MAPAM Council on December 24, but Ahdut Ha'avodah and the Erem group rejected it as insufficiently critical of the Czech regime (and by extension of the Soviet Union). Ya'ari and Hazan then engineered a compromise with Ahdut Ha'avodah/Erem on a new resolution, which Riftin, Peri, and Sneh, however, opposed because it broadened the criticism of the Prague trial into an anti-Soviet line. Ya'ari and Hazan invoked the discipline of the Unity Front to insure passage of the compromise resolution, despite opposition from both the kibbutz and urban left; this the council approved by a vote of 232 in favor to 48 against, with 18 abstentions and 104 absent. Despite this overwhelming vote, Galili and other Ahdut Ha'avodah leaders were unsatisfied and wanted to expel from MAPAM those who opposed the resolution and justified the Prague trial. Riftin defended Sneh, while others in Kibbutz Artzi nervously tried to stop the debate, fearing a split in their own ranks.[79]

As a result of the vote in the MAPAM Council, on January 13, 1953, Knesset members (MKs) Moshe Sneh and Adolph Berman and Tel Aviv city councillor Pinhas Tubin announced that they were leaving the Unity Front and organizing a Left Section within MAPAM. The Left Section issued a manifesto proclaiming loyalty to the Haifa program and calling for (1) abrogation of the council's resolution on the Prague trial, (2) return of those who voted against the resolution, including Political Secretary Riftin, to their leadership positions, (3) ideological and organizational resistance to the right in the party, (4) departure from the Zionist Executive and the World Jewish Congress Executive, (5) enhanced unity between kibbutz and city workers, (6) a united front with MAKI, (7) immediate admission of Arab members to the party, and (8) elections for a new party congress.[80] A majority of the secretariat of the Arab Section voted to support the Left Section's positions, and Bastuni joined Sneh, Berman, and Tubin in the provisional leadership of the Left Section. The Arab leaders supported the left because they believed it was the only faction that fought consistently for admitting Arabs as full members of MAPAM.[81]

MAPAM's Central Committee demanded that the Left Section dissolve by January 25 and that its leaders deposit their resignations from the Knesset and the Tel Aviv city council with the Unity Front and relinquish their positions on the Central Committee, the editorial board of *Al hamishmar,* the Israel Peace Council, and the Israel-USSR Friendship League.[82] The Left Section rejected this ultimatum, and on January 28 the MAPAM Council voted to expel the Left Section from the party, ignoring all protests that nothing in the section's manifesto contradicted the Haifa program or represented an opinion that had not been voiced previously in MAPAM.[83] The Ya'ari-Hazan forces voted with Ahdut Ha'avodah for expulsion, despite opposition from within the Unity Front led by Riftin, Peri, Preminger (of the former Hebrew Communists), and others.

The division within the ranks of the Unity Front and Kibbutz Artzi forced Ya'ari and Hazan to clarify MAPAM's ideological stand. They rejected decisively the Left Section's drive to replace MAPAM's socialist-Zionist synthesis with primary loyalty to Marxism and internationalism. At the critical moment of confrontation, the priority of the Zionist component of their worldview translated into a strategic preference for unity of the "pioneering Zionist forces" (Hashomer Hatza'ir and Ahdut Ha'avodah) over unity of the left (Hashomer Hatza'ir and Sneh), despite the former alliance of the latter. Following the clash with Sneh, those who had opposed expelling the Left Section were removed from the Unity Front leadership.[84] The Executive Committee of Kibbutz Artzi also purged those who had voted against the Prague resolution at the MAPAM Council or opposed expelling the Left Section for violating ideological collectivism.[85]

The leaders of Kibbutz Artzi considered this issue so fundamental that they accepted help from the General Security Services in ferreting out Sneh's supporters in the kibbutzim.[86] Each kibbutz administered a referendum/loyalty oath to its members requiring them to vote on a resolution expressing (1) support for the resolution of the MAPAM Council on the Prague trial; (2) the "absolute obligation" of all members of Kibbutz Artzi to support the positions of the Unity Front and the party, accept the principle of ideological collectivism, and submit to the discipline of the movement, the Front, and the party; and (3) condemnation of factional activity (i.e., sympathy for the Left Section) within the kibbutz, Kibbutz Artzi, and the Unity Front.[87] Over 20 percent of Kibbutz Artzi members abstained or voted against the first clause of the resolution, a statement of political sympathy with Sneh and/or Riftin and Peri.[88] Opposition was especially strong at Ein Shemer (Riftin's kibbutz), Mesilot, Har El, Lehavot Habashan, Karmiah, Zikim, and Shuval. Over two hundred kibbutz members were expelled for their political opposition, including large groups from Ein Shemer and Shuval. A smaller number of Kibbutz Meʾuhad members were also expelled, including a group from Yaron and the majority of the members of Yad Hanah, who nevertheless remained on the kibbutz despite efforts to dislodge them. Reprisals were also taken against leftists who remained in the kibbutzim; Aharon Cohen, for example, was removed from his teaching position in the high school of his kibbutz.

By early 1954 the ranks of Kibbutz Artzi were purified. The kibbutz and city leaders who had voted against the resolution on the Prague trial at the December 1952 MAPAM Council but who remained in the party were invited to rejoin the leadership of the Unity Front.[89] Peri, Riftin, Cohen, and Flapan rejoined Kibbutz Artzi's Executive Committee. To unite Kibbutz Artzi around the expulsion of the left and its political implications, Yaʿari submitted his ideological summation of the struggle against Sneh for adoption by the Executive Committee.[90] Peri tried to refute Yaʿari's theses by upholding a monistic Marxist worldview in which Borochovism was simply "a Marxist formulation of the Jewish question" and not an independent synthesis; to demonstrate that his rejection of the socialist-Zionist synthesis differed from Sneh's (which liquidated Zionism), however, Peri announced that he would vote for Yaʿari's theses—though in fact he and five others abstained.[91]

At the Eighth Council of Kibbutz Artzi, which convened in April 1954 to ratify his theses, Yaʿari attacked Peri and Riftin personally and threatened to expel them from the movement if they did not undertake a self-criticism and disband their faction.[92] Peri passionately defended his position, however. At this late date, when the battle was already lost, he identified the "Arab question" as the core of the argument: "There was one issue that always served as the identifying mark of Hashomer Hatzaʿir, that characterized its public appearance—that is the Arab question."[93] Flapan earlier struck the same note at the Kibbutz Artzi Executive Committee, where he complained that "the response of all the important kibbutzim in Kibbutz Artzi" to the Qibya raid (see Chapter 1) "was not in accord with the line of Hashomer Hatzaʿir."[94] In the end, though, Peri, Riftin, and the rest of the Kibbutz Artzi left declared their loyalty to the unity of Hashomer Hatzaʿir and ended the struggle against Yaʿari's theses.

Riftin and Peri were now defeated within Kibbutz Artzi, but still relations between the Unity Front and Ahdut Ha'avodah continued to deteriorate; in August 1954 this process culminated in a split in MAPAM and the reformation of Ahdut Ha'avodah as a separate party. MAPAM, in which Hashomer Hatza'ir was now the overwhelmingly preponderant force, proceeded to admit Arabs to its ranks and even underwent a nominal reradicalization. Nonetheless, the MAPAM left was smashed and with it any chance that MAPAM would constitute either a counterhegemonic alternative to the prevailing Zionist discourse on Arab-Israeli questions or even a consistent voice of opposition within it.

THE LEFT SOCIALIST PARTY

Kibbutz Artzi became a prominent arena for the struggle against the left in MAPAM because Ya'ari and Hazan, by invoking the principle of ideological collectivism, could be sure of winning a decisive victory there. But the MAPAM left was primarily an urban, not a kibbutz, phenomenon, and its leaders—Sneh, Berman, and Tubin—were not kibbutz members. The kibbutz left, for its part, was fragmented and diverse and had little chance of surviving in the kibbutzim. It was relatively stronger in younger kibbutzim (Shuval, Har El, Zikim, Karmiah) and among younger members of older kibbutzim (Ein Shemer, Lehavot Habashan, Mesilot), which suggests a residual enthusiasm for the training in Marxism received by members of Hashomer Hatza'ir not yet tempered by the pragmatic requirements of kibbutz life. A small group of veteran kibbutz members (Peri, Riftin, Oren, Cohen) who continued to take their Marxism seriously legitimized and encouraged the youthful kibbutz left, but these men never contemplated breaking with Hashomer Hatza'ir. At Ein Shemer, Riftin exercised a strong personal influence over a group of young Egyptians new to the kibbutz. Twenty-one of them took their Marxism a step beyond where Riftin himself was willing to go and were expelled for supporting Sneh.[95] Still, the presence of the left was weak among kibbutz youth compared to MAPAM youth in the cities. Its strength in some older kibbutzim may have been due to the intense ideological training of the original settlers in Hashomer Hatza'ir. In kibbutzim where the veteran settlers also had some higher education or urban culture, political élan was sometimes sustained by an exceptionally high level of cultural and political activity. As small gemeinschaft communities, kibbutzim were easily influenced by outstanding individuals: thus, the presence of a committed leftist leader had a great impact in a few kibbutzim, whereas the absence of such a figure usually meant that the influence on the left was minimal.

The economic dependence of the younger kibbutzim was used as a club to bring them into line. Riftin tried to convince members of Har El not to follow Sneh out of MAPAM, telling them: "In three months you will be bankrupt." Another MAPAM leader asked them, "Do you believe it is possible to maintain a kibbutz without depending on the Zionist institutions?"[96] Only a few members left Har El following the Prague trial, but the kibbutz continued to look to Riftin for leadership regarding opposition to Ya'ari and Hazan. Kibbutz leaders believed that because of their political stand Har El was subjected to economic retaliation by Kibbutz Artzi and the Zionist institutions;[97] in 1955, most of the founders left the kibbutz, and it had to be reorganized.

Although kibbutz members were a minority of the left in MAPAM, many of those expelled from kibbutzim following the Prague trial were among the most dedicated cadres of the Left Socialist Party, an organization formed by Sneh's followers in May 1953 and in which former kibbutz members constituted about a third of the active cadres.[98] The LSP was an entirely Jewish group, and it was motivated by a Jewish problematic. Although Rustum Bastuni had joined the Left Section, he was wooed back to MAPAM before the LSP was established;[99] only one Arab attended the founding congress of the LSP. Emblematic of the LSP's Jewish character was the first joint activity between its youth section (named after the first commander of the Palmah, Yitzhak Sadeh) and the Young Communist League of Israel (BANKI): a demonstration on April 11, 1953, the anniversary of the Warsaw Ghetto revolt. Over a third of the party's draft program was devoted to "the Jewish national problem." While supporting the right of the Palestinian people to establish an independent state (without specifying its borders), the right of the refugees to return, and full equality for the Arab minority in Israel, the majority of those who formed the LSP regarded themselves as Zionists and advocated the territorial concentration of the Jewish people in Israel.

Several former kibbutz members who joined the LSP agreed that Arab-Israeli relations were never mentioned in the discussions that led to their expulsion and were not a motive force for the left.[100] The decisive line dividing the left from the rest of MAPAM, therefore, was not Arab-Israeli relations, but rather Marxism-Leninism, loyalty to the Soviet Union, the "orientation toward the forces of tomorrow," and the building of a revolutionary party. Conducting the debate in these terms avoided the need directly to confront the Zionist discourse and the contradictions at the heart of the colonial project, of which the kibbutzim were a leading expression. The left in MAPAM, the LSP, and MAKI all opposed the Zionist consensus on Arab-Israeli relations but were unable to center the national political debate in Israel on this question. This capacity to structure public discussion was the most fundamental expression of the hegemonic status of the Zionist discourse.

When the debate in MAPAM over the Slansky trial erupted, it revolved around an evaluation of the international situation. Was a third world war inevitable? If so, was it not necessary to support the Soviet Union without reservation? How could a revolutionary Marxist party participate in a coalition government led by MAPAI, with its pro-Western orientation? The Prague trial itself was not the issue; indeed, many MAPAM leftists would have preferred to avoid it, recognizing (even if only in their innermost souls) its problematic character. But once the struggle was joined, it was necessary to defend the socialist legality of the trial as a symbol for the whole complex of issues involved in viewing the Soviet Union as the leader of the forces of progress in the world. These were the questions that occupied the kibbutz members who abstained or voted no in the Kibbutz Artzi referendum.[101] Sneh's advantage in this debate was his polemical brilliance and the clarity and consistency of his logic; but he could only appeal to the limited number of people who were motivated by these issues.

The ideological discussions that led to the formation of the LSP also centered on these questions. The point of departure of the party program was the bipolar international situation: "Our period is characterized by the extraordinary intensification of the class struggle on an international scale."[102] Such circumstances required allying unequivocally with the forces of progress. As Adolph Berman wrote in the first issue of the party weekly, "Any disassociation from the Soviet Union and the popular democracies drags MAPAM to the other side of the divide, to undoing the last link to the world of the future."[103] He compared the Slansky trial to earlier tests of proletarian internationalism—the Moscow trials, the Hitler-Stalin pact, the Finland war, the struggle against Tito. While this comparison was appropriate, Berman failed to grasp the ultimate irony in this analogy.

MAKI fully endorsed this perspective, welcoming the formation of the LSP and polemicizing against MAPAM: "In circumstances of the formation of two camps in the world, on the one hand the camp of peace and democracy, and on the other the camp of war and imperialism, all political bodies must decide on which side they stand."[104]

Shmu'el Amir, Sneh's personal secretary and a leader among those expelled from Kibbutz Artzi, followed Sneh's lead in promoting the ideological consolidation of the LSP. His lectures to party branches included such titles as "What is Imperialism?" "Labor and Capital," "The Leninist Foundations of the Party," "The Revolutionary Party," "The 1905 Revolution," and "Struggles of Lenin Against Economist and Menshevik Opportunism." Not one lecture was on the Arab-Israeli conflict, and only a small minority were about Israeli questions at all.[105] Amir was born in Germany and had graduated high school in Palestine; he thought Israeli conditions played little role in the formation of the LSP and was personally propelled to the left by international considerations. "I am a leftist because of fascism in Germany," he said.[106]

At the end of World War II, Sneh had concluded that the Soviet Union and the historic forces it embodied represented the future. He believed that a Jewish state could be secured only if it was allied with these forces, and his political trajectory was founded on that belief.[107] Until MAPAM's denunciation of the Slansky trial, Sneh had hoped that MAPAM could lead Israel in this direction. Thereafter he thought the LSP might replace MAPAM as a mass party of the radical left.[108] But although the founders of the LSP considered themselves Zionists, their views lay far outside the Zionist consensus. Despite the intense activity of its cadres, the LSP never had more than a thousand members.[109]

The one ideological difference between MAKI and the LSP rested in the LSP's support for territorial concentration of the Jewish people in Israel. When the LSP showed no signs of becoming a mass party, Sneh decided there was no sense in emphasizing this difference, and in January 1954 he began to look toward the unity of the two parties.[110] The ideological disparity was eliminated by Sneh's book *On the National Question: Conclusions in the Light of Marxism-Leninism*, which the LSP Central Committee endorsed.[111] This book's ideological refutation of Zionism and the concept of a worldwide Jewish nation paved the way for LSP members to join MAKI in October 1954.

DEFENSE OF THE RIGHTS OF THE ARAB MINORITY

The LSP and MAKI fused just as MAKI was becoming the leading political force in the Arab community, a position based on its tireless defense of the Arab minority in Israel and support for the right of the Palestinian people to self-determination and of the refugees to return to their homes. This activity is chronicled in hundreds of Arabic leaflets and many Hebrew ones as well, in numerous *Al-ittihad* articles, and in the less voluminous, but regular, coverage of *Kol ha'am*.[112] Nearly every Arabic leaflet, especially those issued by the Central Committee, included among its concluding slogans "Long live Jewish-Arab brotherhood," or a variant of that theme. MAKI was not embarrassed or reticent about appealing to the Arab community in this way, though such an approach might have proved a liability among militant nationalists. Internationalist working-class solidarity, however, was not the only basis for communist action in defense of Arab rights; this struggle always had a multiclass character. Within the Arab community, MAKI acted both as the party of the working class and as the tribune of the Palestinian people. For example, in 1949 the communists led a strike of Arab agricultural workers in the Galilee olive orchards against the Arab owners. The next year the same orchard owners turned to a communist, the lawyer Hanna Naqqara, to represent them against the Israeli authorities who sequestered their harvest and forced them to sell it at low prices.[113]

In principle, MAKI viewed the Palestine question as primarily a matter of securing Palestinian Arab national rights, Jewish national rights having already been secured through the establishment of Israel. In practice, MAKI focused on defending Arab civil rights in Israel: primarily the rights to remain on the land, to remain in the country, and to enjoy equal protection under the law. MAKI organized dozens of local struggles against expropriation of Arab lands, especially in connection with the construction of the Israeli national water carrier through the Galilee. It protested the expulsion of nearly two thousand Palestinians from Majdal in August 1950, as well as smaller-scale expulsions from Shafa 'Amr, Nahf, and other villages.[114]

In the early 1950s MAKI tried to enlist MAPAM's cooperation to defend Arab rights, but MAPAM usually refused to work with MAKI on this issue, as it was related to the Jewish national question. MAKI and MAPAM both opposed the Absentee Property Law of 1950; MAPAM was absent from the vote on the Land Acquisition Law of 1953, but MAKI voted against it. In April 1954, to campaign against these laws, MAKI initiated the Committee to Defend the Rights of the Arab Minority. That October the committee organized a large Jewish-Arab protest conference. Emile Tuma and Hanna Naqqara appealed to Simha Flapan and MAPAM MK Yusuf Khamis for cooperation in this campaign; MAPAM, however, refused.[115]

MAKI also agitated for local elections in Arab towns and villages. When the government began to permit such elections in 1954, MAKI used them to build its strength in the villages of the Galilee. It sought to form popular-front lists to demand abolition of the military government and the travel permit system, restoration of confiscated land, abolition of the head tax used to fund education, higher prices for agricultural produce, an improved water supply, jobs for workers, and admission of Arab workers to the Histadrut. MAKI and its allies won significant victories in several Arab localities, particularly Nazareth, where MAKI gained 38 percent of the vote and six of fifteen seats in the municipal council—twice as many as the next largest list. Nonetheless, the MAPAI-sponsored lists excluded MAKI from participation in the governing coalition.[116]

MAKI devoted particular attention to organizing the Arab working class. On April 9–11, 1949, eighty-four delegates representing five thousand workers in Israel and the occupied territories convened the Fourth Congress of the AWC in Nazareth.[117] In an effort to prevent MAKI from becoming a force among Arab workers, the state and the Histadrut broke various strikes of the AWC and restricted its activity.

On September 10, 1949, thirty-six AWC members struck against the Arab-owned Nazareth Cigarette Company. The AWC had been negotiating with the management for a new contract, and the deputy military governor of Nazareth had participated in the talks. Days before the strike, nine AWC members at the cigarette factory had secretly joined the Histadrut-sponsored Palestine Labor League. The ostensible cause of the strike was the company's refusal to pay a share equal to 10 percent of wages into the workers' health and unemployment insurance fund, as demanded by the AWC, for the two months between the expiration of the old contract and the start of the new one. The real issue, though, was the AWC's effort to maintain its leadership of the workers, which the Histadrut and the military government were secretly subverting.

MAPAM's Aharon Cohen actively cooperated with the military government and the Haifa Labor Office to undermine the AWC and defeat the strike.[118] Meanwhile, MAKI organized solidarity and material support from both Arab and Jewish workers; it sought to build binational working-class unity by praising the small contributions of Jewish workers as a "sharp blow against the propagandists of national separatism."[119] After nearly two months the strike was defeated; in the end, the workers were not strong enough to withstand the combined efforts of the military government, the Histadrut, and MAPAM. The failure of this strike seriously weakened the AWC, which afterward MAPAM continued to attack. Several AWC members employed in MAPAM kibbutzim were either fired or pressured to join the Palestine Labor League, soon renamed the Israel Labor League.[120]

The military government refused to permit the AWC to hold its Fifth Congress in September 1950 but finally allowed it in April 1951.[121] In addition to reconfirming the call for peace between Israel and its neighbors, for creation of a Palestinian state, and for the return of the refugees, the AWC congress demanded that the Histadrut open its ranks to Arab workers, integrate its labor exchanges, and abandon segregation of Jews and Arabs. At the same time, the Israel Labor League was criticized for not advancing these demands.

In January 1952, the AWC initiated a campaign in which seventy thousand signatures of Arab and Jewish workers were collected on a petition demanding admission of Arab workers to the Histadrut and integration of labor exchanges. In July, a National Public Committee for a Unified Histadrut for All the Workers in Israel was established. Over the objections of Flapan and other leftists, MAPAM rejected MAKI's request for joint action in this effort. Instead, MAPAM's Arab Affairs Department conducted its own petition campaign; however, in this case no signatures of Jewish workers were enlisted, because MAPAM feared that fewer Jewish workers would sign the petition than had voted for MAPAM in the previous election.[122] The MAPAM leadership clearly understood that its Jewish working-class supporters were not all internationalists.

In September 1952, the Histadrut agreed to accept Arabs into its trade union department (though not as full members) and to integrate the labor exchanges; this decision was not, however, fully implemented. In December 1955, the MAKI-organized National Committee for the Entry of the Arab Worker to the Histadrut submitted a memorandum to the Eighth Congress of the Histadrut claiming that only thirty-five hundred Arabs had been admitted to trade unions out of eleven thousand who applied, that most labor exchanges still refused to admit Arab workers, and that the Histadrut had not established medical clinics (a major membership benefit) in most Arab areas. There were also reports that MAPAI leaders had organized the expulsion of Arab workers from their jobs under the pretext that they were not union members.[123]

On October 13, 1952, the AWC called a strike of the Nazareth municipality workers that lasted until the end of November. The military governor ordered the strikers dismissed on the first day of the strike and then hired strikebreakers through his office. The strike leaders were arrested, and on November 21 they declared a hunger strike. Yet despite the workers' militancy, the strike failed.[124] Because the military government had intervened to defeat two major AWC strikes in Nazareth and the Histadrut had just agreed in principle to admit Arab workers to its trade unions, MAKI decided to disband the AWC. This decision was consistent with the principle of organizing workers of all nationalities in one trade union federation, a goal of communists since the 1920s. But because the Histadrut moved very slowly to admit Arab workers, many Arab workers were deprived of effective trade union protection for most of the 1950s, while one more Palestinian Arab institution with a link to pre-1948 political life ceased to exist.

The struggle against the military government was central to MAKI's work in the Arab community, with complaints about government abuses appearing regularly in party literature. In late 1955, owing to suspicions that MAPAI was using military governors to control the Arab population for its own benefit, the Knesset formed a commission of investigation. MAKI seized the opportunity to intensify its activity against both the military apparatus and the system of travel permits. In January 1956, its Knesset faction submitted a memorandum urging abolition of the military government, with details given of how MAKI-sponsored activity in the Arab areas and the movement of MAKI activists had been constrained. Large Jewish-Arab protest meetings were organized in Nazareth on February 11, 1956, and in Haifa on June 23, 1956. MAPAM MK Yusuf Khamis at first endorsed the Nazareth meeting but later withdrew (most likely because of pressure from Jewish party members) and restricted his participation to the sending of greetings that were read by his father, who did attend the gathering.[125] Although MAPAM opposed the military government, it was too frightened of being associated with MAKI to cooperate with the party that had the broadest base in the Arab community. MAKI persevered in its dissent, however, joined by many nonparty activists in the Arab community and a small number of Jews. After 1961 MAPAM and many other Jewish political forces intensified their opposition to the military government, activity that resulted in the government's abolition in 1966.

As a result of its diligent defense of Arab rights, MAKI was by 1955 the preeminent political force in the Arab community, as even its rivals admitted.[126] MAKI based its work in the Arab community on consistent calls for internationalist solidarity between Jews and Arabs and pride in its status (until October 1954) as the only Jewish-Arab party in Israel. Following the 1949 Knesset elections, *Al-ittihad* articulated the strategic perspective of the Palestinian Arab communists toward the Jewish public; they were willing to recognize Israel and accept it as a framework for political action in return for Jewish working-class support of the Palestinian Arabs' right to self-determination and an independent state:

> When we communists repeat that it is our duty to struggle for establishing an Arab state in Palestine, we don't do so simply because we wish to represent the desire of the Arab masses, but because we believe that such a struggle, if it is also centered around the forces of the Jewish working class, can be successful.[127]

In other words, the Arab leaders of MAKI committed themselves to internationalism and to joint Jewish-Arab struggle because they believed these to be the best means of defending the rights of the Palestinian people.

Yet the Jewish working class proved incapable of delivering its part of the bargain. Moreover, even though MAKI unwaveringly recognized Israel as a Jewish state, it was excluded from participation in the political game and regarded as a pariah by most Jewish political forces. The communists were under constant pressure to accommodate to the hegemonic Zionist discourse lest they become isolated from the Jewish working class. Thus, the program adopted at the Twelfth MAKI Congress in May 1952 advocated "peace with the neighboring countries on the basis of mutual respect for national sovereignty, abrogation of territorial annexations, and recognition of the right of the Palestinian Arab people to establish its independent democratic state [and] the right of the Arab refugees to return to their country"—which could be interpreted as a demand that Israel, Jordan, and Egypt evacuate the territories allotted to the Arab state by the UN partition plan. The program also stated, though, that "the interest of the anti-imperialist struggle for peace and national liberation requires opposing any attempt to raise the question of borders today and opposing attempts to rectify the borders and conquer territory by large or 'small' military means."[128]

It would have been reckless for Israel's Arab citizens to launch a revolt for secession, nor could the left have supported a war by the reactionary Arab states to regain Palestinian Arab territory. These real constraints justified the tactical stand of not raising the question of borders "today." Over time, the balance between the tactical requirements of the day and the principle of upholding the territorial basis for Palestinian Arab self-determination established by the UN partition plan shifted. What began as tactical necessity became the limit of political vision. MAKI ultimately acceded to the Zionist consensus, which held that the results of the war had established new minimum borders for Israel. This meant that MAKI's line differed from that of the Arab communist parties, who continued to uphold the UN partition plan boundaries as the basis for a peaceful settlement of the Arab-Israeli conflict.

MAKI did not regard its concessions as involving questions of principle. Still, abandoning the claim that territory occupied by Israel in excess of the partition plan was "occupied Arab territory" tended to delegitimize the national demands of Palestinian Arab citizens of Israel, even as it perhaps improved those citizens' capacity to win certain civil rights struggles, like abolition of the military government. In the Jewish community, MAKI's concessions to the Zionist discourse enabled the party to avoid total isolation, though they were far from sufficient to gain the party broad legitimacy.

CHAPTER V

Internationalism in Practice: Relations Between the Egyptian and Israeli Marxists

The first contacts between Israeli and Arab communists after the 1948 war were based on a shared misperception of Israel's regional role similar to that articulated by Voice of the Opposition/MISHMISH. Some Arab communists hoped that Israel would be an ally in their struggle against reactionary forces in the Arab world. Thus, in May 1949 Khalid Bakdash, leader of the Communist Party of Syria, came to Haifa and met with Palestinian Arab communists and Israeli officials to discuss the communists' role in the struggle against King 'Abd Allah. Although these contacts aroused some concern in American diplomatic circles, they had no apparent results.[1]

After the armistice with Egypt and the demarcation of the boundary between Israel and the Egyptian-held Gaza Strip, NLL members living in Gaza crossed secretly into Israel to meet with Mikunis and Tubi. The Egyptian press reported that fourteen such meetings occurred at Be'erot Yitzhak between April and July 1949 with the knowledge of Israeli authorities; they ceased after the Egyptian government broke up the remnants of the NLL in Gaza with the arrest of thirty-three communists on July 20.[2] Thereafter the communists of Gaza were constantly repressed by the Egyptian authorities, and despite repeated attempts to reorganize, they never established a stable organization or maintained regular contacts with either their Israeli or their Egyptian comrades.[3]

After these initial inconclusive meetings in Israel, direct contacts between Arab and Israeli Marxists became sporadic for a time. The disunity of the Egyptian communist movement and its continued repression made maintenance of any international relations difficult. Direct contact with Israelis was especially problematic because of the history of the Jewish question in the Egyptian movement and suspicions about Curiel. In the early 1950s, occasional meetings between Israeli Marxists and their Arab counterparts resumed, most commonly at international conferences organized by the nonparty organizations of the communist movement: the World Peace Council, the World Federation of Democratic Youth, the World Federation of Democratic Women, and the International Association of Democratic Jurists. In the first of these encounters, Mohamed Sid-Ahmed, then a member of MISHMISH, met Tawfiq Tubi in Paris at the inaugural Congress of the Partisans of Peace in October 1949; this meeting was unofficial, however, because Sid-Ahmed, who had been sent abroad by his family to distance him from radical politics, had no authority to speak for the Egyptian movement.[4] Subsequent meetings of the World Peace Council provided an especially conducive framework for an important series of contacts and peace initiatives inspired by the Rome group of the DMNL/UECP.

THE INTERNATIONAL PEACE MOVEMENT

When the DMNL began to reorganize in early 1950, it made the international campaign in support of Frédéric Joliot-Curie's Stockholm appeal for world peace the center of its effort to build a broad national united front. Some twelve thousand signatures supporting the Stockholm appeal were collected, with an even greater number gathered on additional peace appeals in 1951. In January 1951, the DMNL initiated the Preparatory Committee for the Egyptian Partisans of Peace together with many noncommunist intellectuals and political personalities: former Egyptian ambassador to the Soviet Union Kamil al-Bindari ("the red Pasha"); feminist activist Saiza Nabrawi; leaders of the Wafdist Vanguard ʿAziz Fahmi and Muhammad Mandur; former minister and member of the Liberal Constitutionalist Party Hifni Mahmud Pasha; former member of parliament Ibrahim Talʿat; editor of *Ruz al-yusuf* Ihsan ʿAbd al-Quddus; progressive Islamic scholar Khalid Muhammad Khalid; and shaykh Jabir al-Tamimi of the Muslim Brothers. Yusuf Hilmi, a lawyer and member of the Nationalist Party, served as secretary-general of the movement and editor of its weekly magazine, *Al-katib* (The Scribe), which achieved a circulation of ten to twelve thousand. Popular Democracy participated in the Partisans of Peace, although not without friction with the DMNL, and was represented on the preparatory committee by the veteran trade unionist Yusuf al-Mudarrik. Al-Raya did not join in this effort.

By assiduously reading the Arabic press, Aharon Cohen followed the progress of the left in the Arab world and wrote regular and fairly accurate reports in *Al hamishmar*, especially on developments that he considered conducive to promoting Arab-Israeli peace.[6] He reported on the activity of the Egyptian Partisans of Peace, enthusiastically arguing that they demonstrated the Egyptian people's desire for peace with Israel, and he quoted statements by the Egyptian Fabian writer Salama Musa calling for an end to the "cold war between Israel and the Arab states." Cohen also analyzed the strike wave in Egypt in 1951, led by communist trade unionists in the textile industry, as a development that would strengthen the forces favoring a peaceful settlement of the conflict with Israel.

In contrast, MAKI in the early 1950s seemed to have little interest in the Egyptian communist movement. Perhaps MAKI was cautious about reporting activity involving communists lest it appear to promote the "wrong" faction. An article in *Al-ittihad* on the Egyptian workers' movement, for example—a subject on which communists could be expected to have independent sources of information—was based entirely on information drawn from an article by the former U.S. labor attaché in Cairo.[7]

MAKI and MAPAM cooperated in establishing the Israeli Peace Council, and its activities were, for a time, quite successful. Its efforts resulted in some 40 percent of all adult Israelis endorsing the Stockholm peace appeal. In September 1951, Cohen, Menahem Dorman (of MAPAM's Ahdut Ha'avodah faction), and Emile Habibi represented the Israeli Peace Council at a preparatory meeting for a regional Middle East peace conference in Rome attended by delegations from Egypt, Syria, Lebanon, Iraq, Algeria, Morocco, Tunisia, and Iran. According to Dorman, the Israelis proposed that the conference issue a call for Arab-Israeli peace without preconditions or foreign mediators. The Lebanese delegation replied that it would only support a call for a "just peace" based on the November 29, 1947, UN resolution, but the Israelis rejected these terms for peace.

Yusuf Hilmi, the head of the Egyptian delegation, was a pivotal figure at the meeting, at which there were extensive Egyptian-Israeli contacts, both formal and informal. At first he expressed his apprehension that the Israeli presence would be used to discredit the peace movement in Egypt. Cohen, however, won Hilmi's confidence with his response, which he delivered in Arabic. As a result, in a long public speech one afternoon Hilmi studiously avoided denouncing Zionism. Hilmi, Cohen, and Dorman also held several private discussions, and Cohen included excerpts from a recent *Al-katib* article by Hilmi in his report of the meeting for *Al hamishmar*.[8]

The main question debated at the meetings was, What is the main problem facing the peoples of the Middle East—the danger of a third world war or the anti-imperialist struggle for national liberation?[9] By deciding that the possible outbreak of a new world war was the greater problem and focusing on the conflicts in Korea and Vietnam, the conference avoided taking a position on Arab-Israeli issues.

An Israeli delegation including MAKI and MAPAM members attended the World Peace Congress in Vienna in November 1951. As the meeting was held shortly after Egypt abrogated the Anglo-Egyptian treaty of 1936, Kamil al-Bindari's statement for the Egyptian delegation was devoted entirely to Egypt's request for support of its efforts to expel the British occupiers; no mention was made of the Arab-Israeli conflict.[10] Tawfiq Tubi spoke for the Israeli delegation at one session on the problem of peace between Israel and the Arab countries and proposed that the campaign against Western efforts to construct a Middle East regional alliance (which eventually culminated in the Baghdad Pact) should include a call for Israel-Arab peace based on rejection of military blocs and respect for the independence and sovereignty of all states in the region. Saiza Nabrawi responded that if only Israel did justice to the Palestinian refugees, this would be a great step for peace.[11] The Israeli and Arab delegates undoubtedly held informal discussions, but there is no record of them. The resolutions of the Vienna Congress regarding the Middle East did not address the Arab-Israeli conflict, and there was apparently no effort between the Israeli and Arab delegations to reach an agreement on this issue.

In early 1952, meetings between Israelis and Egyptian and other Arab leftists were again interrupted. The Rome preparatory meeting had decided to convene a conference in Cairo in January 1952, to be attended by Israelis as well. This gathering never convened, however, because the Egyptian government declared martial law after the Cairo fire on January 26. Yusuf Hilmi and other leaders of the peace movement were arrested and the Partisans of Peace proscribed.

THE ROME GROUP AND DMNL-MAKI CONTACTS

Thereafter, at international meetings of the nonparty organizations of the communist movement, Egypt was often represented by the émigré Egyptian-Jewish communists in Paris led by Henri Curiel and known within the DMNL as the Rome group. This group was more anxious than most DMNL members residing in Egypt to pursue contacts with progressive Israelis and consistently saw such meetings as important facilitators in the struggle for a peaceful settlement of the Arab-Israeli conflict. At the congress of the World Federation of Democratic Youth in Bucharest in July 1953, members of the Rome group arranged meetings between the Israeli delegation, led by the head of BANKI, Uzi Burstein, and delegations from Egypt and Iraq.[12] Yusuf Hazan and Emile Habibi met in Vienna in November 1953 at a gathering of the World Peace Council, where Habibi criticized DMNL support for the Egyptian coup of July 23, 1952.[13] MAKI did not respond enthusiastically to the Rome group's efforts to initiate such meetings, probably because continuing factionalism in the Egyptian communist movement made identification of *the* communist party difficult to determine. The DMNL was under suspicion because of its support for the military coup, in opposition to the rest of the international communist movement, and allegations of Curiel's involvement in the Marty affair. In accord with the prevailing protocols of the communist movement, then, MAKI adopted a conservative attitude toward the Egyptian communists.

During the summer of 1953 the DMNL sent a letter to MAKI, the first formal contact between the two parties in several years. Curiel may have proposed this initiative and was apparently the intermediary who transmitted the letter. At the least he knew of its contents, because in a report he sent back to Egypt on Arab-Israeli relations he criticized the DMNL leadership for addressing only general issues of peace and democracy in this letter and failing to mention the conflict. Curiel was encouraged by the meeting in Bucharest and wanted the DMNL to give higher priority to contacts with progressive Israelis. He argued that the democratic forces in Israel led by MAKI were "struggling for the same objectives as we" and praised the struggles of MAKI and the LSP against Zionist ideology. To prove his point he quoted Mikunis from an article in MAKI's theoretical journal: "Zionism was and remains a reactionary bourgeois trend, connected with imperialism for all the years of its existence, allied with it and loyally serving it."[14] Curiel urged the DMNL leadership to popularize the struggles of "our powerful allies,"

MAKI and the Israeli democratic forces, in defense of the rights of the Arabs of Israel, in defense of the interests of the refugees, and against the provocations of the Israeli government (which were no less than those of the Arab states).

The thrust of Curiel's report was to reiterate the correctness of DMNL support for the UN partition plan of 1947; moreover, it confirmed that Soviet support for partition had been the primary motivation for the DMNL's stand. He praised the DMNL for resisting the anti-Jewish sentiment that had overtaken Egypt and the Arab world in 1948. Curiel believed that the DMNL comrades had a better attitude than other Arab communists on this issue: they had confidence in MAKI and the Israeli people and were not chauvinists. However, he also maintained that after 1948 the DMNL did not defend its positions with the same clarity as before, only mentioning the issue in a few imprecise articles in *Al-katib* and in a paragraph in the organization's draft program.[15] Curiel wanted the DMNL to pay more attention to the Arab-Israeli conflict, although now it would no longer be possible simply to follow the lead of the Soviet Union as in 1948 or of the other Arab communist parties or Egyptian communists. In Curiel's opinion, the refugees and the borders of the Palestinian Arab state were the principle problems to be dealt with; yet he offered no specific solutions. In fact, his programmatic suggestions demanded Jordanian and Egyptian withdrawal from the West Bank and the Gaza Strip and the creation of democratic Palestinian administrations, but did not mention Israeli withdrawal from the territories occupied in 1948–49.[16] This vagueness about borders suggests that Curiel's views were closer to those of MAKI (as stated in its 1952 program) than to those of the Egyptian and other Arab communists, who explicitly insisted on the UN partition plan boundaries. Curiel's stand could be interpreted as prefiguring the post-1967 proposal to establish a Palestinian Arab state in the West Bank and the Gaza Strip.

International meetings with Israelis assumed much greater importance for Curiel and the Rome group than for communists living in Egypt, for this was the only activity open to the Paris émigrés that allowed them to feel like an organic part of the Egyptian movement. The communists in Egypt, in contrast, could not travel abroad and experience the exhilaration of meeting strangers who shared the same commitments and world outlook. They were of necessity oriented toward Egyptian national issues. For them, as for all currents of Egyptian political opinion, the main question had to do with securing the evacuation of British troops from the Suez Canal Zone; Palestine was a secondary problem. At this time, moreover, the DMNL was engaged in a major internal struggle, which ultimately led to a split and the formation of the DMNL–Revolutionary Current. And meanwhile, the RCC was intensifying its attacks on all the communists. These were unpropitious circumstances in which to pursue risky international contacts.

Curiel was not one to be deterred by such details, and the Rome group continued to seek international relations, inspired by his conception and sense of priorities. When Yusuf Hilmi was released from prison in March 1954 along with other leaders of the Partisans of Peace, he made his way to Paris. There Curiel introduced him to Amos Kenan, a mercurial, bohemian Israeli journalist.[17] These three, continuing the contacts between Egyptians and Israelis initiated at Bucharest, began to meet with Gila Cohen, a member of MAKI temporarily living in Paris while studying art; Haya Harari, an Israeli actress; ʿAdnan Abu Sinayna of the Sudanese Communist Party; members of the Iraqi Communist Party; representatives of the Rome group; and possibly the Egyptian filmmaker ʿAbd al-Qadir al-Tlimsani. Later they were joined by Eli Lobel, who had been expelled from Kibbutz Nirim and joined the LSP in 1953.[18] (Had he remained in Israel Lobel would likely have joined MAKI, but Charles Bettelheim invited him to Paris in 1954 to work on problems of economic development in India. Through this work Lobel met Samir Amin, who had been close to al-Raya before coming to Paris to study economics.) The group which met during 1954–55, was known as the Arab-Israeli Committee for Peace. While no MAPAM members participated regularly, in the spring of 1956 Yusuf Hilmi met with MAPAM's Yisraʾel Barzilai, then the Israeli minister of health, and Yaʿakov Mayus, secretary of MAPAM's Israeli Peace Committee, and other such meetings may have occurred.[19] After the 1956 war only the members of the Rome group and Israelis living in Paris remained active, and the committee became the Egyptian-Israeli Committee for Peace. In this form it issued a French bulletin for a short while, of which only Curiel's introduction to the first issue has survived.[20]

These activities were not formally sanctioned by MAKI or the DMNL. Indeed, the existence of the Rome group embarrassed the DMNL leadership. Publicizing these meetings with Israelis in Paris would only have confirmed DMNL critics' worst suspicions, so the Paris discussions were played down. MAKI not only failed to publicize these contacts, but it continued to avoid mentioning the activities of the

Egyptian communist movement as well, even after the meeting in Bucharest and the letter from the DMNL. MAKI did, however, publicize the activities of the Communist Party of Iraq, which had not changed its stand in favor of the partition of Palestine since 1948. MAKI even intervened in a factional struggle within the Iraqi party by translating a polemic published by the party's central newspaper against the Workers' Flag group.[21] The Egyptians were also omitted from a pamphlet published by MAKI's Central Committee on the struggle for peace in the Arab countries, though statements of the Iraqi and Jordanian Communist parties were reprinted.[22] The presence of many former members of the Communist Party of Iraq in MAKI's ranks (they arrived in Israel with the rest of the Iraqi Jewish community in 1950–51) and the historic ties to the leaders of the Jordanian party, who had belonged to the NLL and were personally known by many Arab members of MAKI, probably made MAKI feel closer to those parties than to the Egyptian movement and more confident that it correctly understood the significance of their published views.

Despite the lack of official Israeli party approval, the meetings in Paris were important for bringing Israelis (even anticommunists like Amos Kenan) into contact with Egyptians and other Arabs who sought a peaceful solution to the Palestinian/Arab–Israeli conflict based on the right of self-determination of the Israeli and Palestinian peoples and the partition of Palestine. The impact on Egypt was more limited because Yusuf Hilmi was the only Egyptian regularly involved in these meetings who returned to live in Egypt.

Although the 1956 war made talk of peace increasingly difficult in both Egypt and Israel, the seeds planted in the course of these contacts began to grow several years later. In 1957, Amos Kenan introduced Henri Curiel to Uri Avnery, editor of the iconoclastic Israeli weekly *Haʿolam hazeh* (This world), whom Curiel then introduced to members of the Algerian National Liberation Front.[23] Encouraged by Curiel and the Algerians, Avnery joined with Natan Yalin-Mor, Maxime Ghilan, Shalom Cohen, and Amos Kenan—Avnery's comrades in the Semitic Action organization—to establish the Israeli Committee for a Free Algeria, which opposed official Israeli policy by supporting Algeria's struggle for independence from France and encouraged Algerian Jews not to join the French *colons* in opposing independence. Many of those involved in the Israeli Committee for a Free Algeria became outspoken opponents of the Israeli occupation of the West Bank and the Gaza Strip after 1967: Natan Yalin-Mor was a leading member of the Israeli Committee for Israel-Palestine Peace until his death; Maxime Ghilan became editor of the Paris monthly *Israel & Palestine;* and Amos Kenan has regularly criticized Israel's policies toward Palestinian Arabs both in his weekly columns in the mass-circulation daily *Yediʿot aharonot* and in his dystopian novel *The Road to Ein Harod.*

An indirect product of the 1950s Paris meetings was Ahmad El Kodsy (pseudonym of Samir Amin) and Eli Lobel's *The Arab World and Israel.*[24] Their effort to develop an analysis of nationalism and class struggle in the Arab world and of the nature of the Arab-Israeli conflict—an analysis critical of both Israeli and Arab state policies—was influential in presenting Middle Eastern issues to French- and English-speaking progressive circles in the wake of the 1967 war.

After that war, Khalid Muhyi al-Din, Yusuf Hilmi's successor as head of the Egyptian Peace Council, and Uri Avnery met in Bulgaria. Muhyi al-Din subsequently proposed an international conference on the problem of peace in the Middle East, which was held in Bologna, Italy, in 1971. Although the conference was a disappointment for many of those involved in its planning, some of whom did not even attend, nonetheless as the first open meeting between Arabs and Israelis since the 1967 war it established a precedent for the many nongovernmental Palestinian/Arab–Israeli encounters that began in the mid-1970s and have continued to the present. Among these were the first meetings between Israelis and representatives of the PLO, which Curiel was instrumental in arranging.[25] Influenced by Curiel, many of the prominent Israelis who have advocated mutual recognition and peaceful coexistence of a Palestinian Arab state alongside Israel—Uri Avnery, Matti Peled, Yaʿakov Arnon, Meʾir Paʾil, Lova Eliav, Yossi Amitay, Simha Flapan, Eliʿezer Feiler—became directly or indirectly involved in these and further such meetings.

After Curiel was assassinated by unidentified assailants in 1978 he became much better known in Israel thanks to the efforts of people inspired by his struggle for a just peace between Israel and the Palestinian Arabs. In 1982 the Mifras publishing house, which is operated by independent Israeli radicals, released a Hebrew edition of *For a Just Peace in the Middle East,* a collection of Curiel's writings on the Arab-Israeli conflict originally published by his Parisian friends after his death.[26] Two years later Shimon Balas, the husband of Gila Cohen and also a former member of MAKI, portrayed Curiel's last year in a thinly veiled biographical novel, *The Last Winter.*[27] Although Curiel's political activities in Paris discomforted some of his comrades in Egypt and some have criticized his political style as undisciplined, eccentric, and theoretically uninformed, his unflagging dedication to the cause of peace and his relentless efforts to forge a link between Arabs and Israelis seeking peaceful coexistence must be acknowledged.

YUSUF HILMI'S PEACE INITIATIVE

Yusuf Hilmi's arrival in Paris in 1954 enhanced the significance of the Egyptian-Israeli contacts already under way there. As the official leader of the Egyptian peace movement and a member of the World Peace Council, he was able to obtain an international audience for his views. In Paris, Hilmi worked closely with the Rome group and, through them, asked to join the DMNL. Although this request was transmitted to Egypt, it is unclear whether he was accepted by the leadership there. In any case, the Rome group considered him a member of their organization and enthusiastically endorsed his 1955 initiatives promoting the peaceful settlement of the Arab-Israeli conflict. Many party members in Egypt, however, were less than pleased with Hilmi's activities in Paris.[28]

The framework for Hilmi's initiative was the resolution on the Arab-Israeli conflict adopted by the Bandung conference of Asian and African countries in April 1955, which stated: "In view of the existing tension in the Middle East caused by the situation in Palestine and of the danger of that tension to world peace, the Asian-African Conference declared its support for the rights of the Arab people of Palestine and called for the implementation of the United Nations resolutions on Palestine and of the peaceful settlement of the Palestine question."[29] This resolution was formulated by Gamal Abdel Nasser, who emerged as a major proponent of positive neutralism at the conference. It was, therefore, an indirect statement of Egyptian government policy, and Abdel Nasser made several statements confirming his commitment to its terms after his return from Bandung. The Egyptian interpretation of the resolution was that it directed Israel to return to the UN partition boundaries and to repatriate all the Palestinian refugees; in return, Egypt would recognize Israel, since it was established by a UN resolution, and embrace the principle of a peaceful resolution to the conflict.

The Israeli government bitterly resented having been excluded from the conference at the insistence of the Arab states. It regarded the resolution as a hostile message, not as an opportunity for a diplomatic breakthrough. Most Israelis saw themselves as the sole victims of the conflict and were unwilling to consider either cession of territory or repatriation of the refugees. Premier Sharett's belligerent comment to a *Newsweek* interviewer who, a week after the Bandung conference, asked what Israel would be willing to concede to obtain peace with its Arab neighbors was, "Why should Israel offer anything at all?"[30] If this was the response of someone considered a moderate in Israeli terms, what could Egypt expect from the activist elements loyal to Ben-Gurion, who was then in temporary semiretirement at his Negev kibbutz? Abdel Nasser's comments in a companion interview were more conciliatory: while he was sharply critical of Israel, he insisted that Egypt had no aggressive intentions and confirmed his support for the Bandung resolution.

Yusuf Hilmi used the Bandung resolution to promote the concept of an Arab-Israeli peace settlement as consistent with the declared policy of the Egyptian government. He wrote to Abdel Nasser urging him to prove his intention to redeem the verbal commitments made in Bandung by allowing an Egyptian delegation to attend the June 1955 World Assembly of Peace in Helsinki.[31] Such a delegation undoubtedly would have included communist sympathizers, however, and Abdel Nasser refused. Consequently, Hilmi was the sole Egyptian delegate at Helsinki. Perhaps because he had no opportunity to consult with his colleagues from Egypt and wanted to avoid isolating himself further, Hilmi did not address the meeting publicly but submitted only a written statement.

The statement argued that the Bandung resolution was the first formal declaration approved by the Arab states that envisioned a peaceful resolution of the conflict and that it merited a reciprocal step from the "Israeli government" and the "Israeli nation." Use of these terms, which unequivocally recognized Israel's national sovereignty, indicated that Hilmi's thinking was in fact more advanced than that of Abdel Nasser, who preferred the oblique terms of the Bandung text. Hilmi also advocated taking positive steps toward peace and urged the defenders of peace in Israel and the Arab states to establish jointly the general principles for a just solution and peaceful coexistence. Hilmi's statements were enthusiastically reprinted by MAKI and widely circulated.[32] Their impact in Israel was diminished, however, by Egypt's announcement on September 27 of an arms purchase agreement with Czechoslovakia, which Prime Minister–designate Ben-Gurion used to inflame anxieties about Egypt's aggressive intentions toward Israel.

Even more dramatic were Hilmi's letter to Abdel Nasser and his "Appeal to the Israeli People," both dated November 10, 1955.[33] In addressing Abdel Nasser, Hilmi characterized himself as a loyal Egyptian citizen who supported the Bandung conference and its resolution on the Palestine question. He regretted that Egypt had not taken concrete steps to implement the resolution in the face of imperialist opposition to achieving a just peace between Israel and Egypt. He directly criticized the "imbeciles, or spies if you like, or, if you prefer, agents of imperialism" among Abdel Nasser's advisors who raised the slogan, "Let's throw Israel into the sea." Hilmi insisted on distinguishing between the government of Israel and provocative elements, on the one hand, and the masses of people living in Israel who bore the burden of war, on the other. He advised Abdel Nasser to adopt the stance of the Soviet Union and take initiatives for peace, criticized him for not having responded to Ben-Gurion's invitation (perhaps a reference to Ben-Gurion's Knesset speech welcoming the new Egyptian regime after the coup of July 23, 1952), and urged him to make a clear statement recognizing the Israeli people's right to a state. Finally, he called for an international conference similar to the Geneva conference on Vietnam and enclosed a copy of his appeal to the Israeli people that would be published in the Israeli press.

Addressing the Israeli people, Hilmi identified himself as a patriotic Egyptian and veteran of the peace movement. He recalled that he had written in *Al-katib* that the Israeli people were no less peace-loving than Egyptians, noting their response to the Stockholm appeal. He acknowledged as well that MAPAM publications had quoted his articles in *Al-katib* and that some of the Israeli press had quoted his statement at Helsinki in June. Hilmi reassured the Israeli people that the Egyptian government did not want and was not preparing for a war with Israel and that the arms being purchased from Czechoslovakia were not so intended. He urged the Israeli people to appreciate the new attitude of the Arab states as reflected in the Bandung resolution. Reviewing the history of the conflict, Hilmi reiterated the Egyptian communists' analysis that the British had instigated the 1948–49 war to distract the Egyptian people from the struggle against the British occupation. He reaffirmed that democratic Egyptians, who accepted Israel's right to exist alongside a Palestinian Arab state, had opposed that war. Once again, Hilmi called for an international conference to find a peaceful resolution of the Arab-Israeli conflict based on recognition of the right of the Israeli people and the Palestinian Arab people to independent democratic states.

What was the status and significance of Yusuf Hilmi's exceptionally bold initiative? Certainly the urgent sincerity of these messages cannot be doubted. There was no reason for him to act as he did unless he was motivated by the deepest conviction. The Rome group and MAKI fully supported Hilmi's actions. UECP members in Egypt were less enthusiastic. Although they upheld the same programmatic positions as Hilmi—resolution of the conflict based on implementation of the UN partition plan, repatriation of the refugees, and establishment of a Palestinian Arab state—there was a striking difference between the rhetorical framework of Hilmi's statements and that of communists living in Egypt.[34]

Hilmi adopted a patriotic stance supporting Abdel Nasser's new foreign policy orientation (the Bandung conference, positive neutralism, the Czech arms purchase) and criticized Israeli government policy mercilessly, as the UECP in Egypt did. But he also criticized Abdel Nasser sharply for not pursuing peace more consistently, used expressions like "the Israeli people," and repeatedly and without qualification endorsed their right to an independent state. By acknowledging that the Arab states had invaded Israel unjustly in 1948, Hilmi avoided identifying Israel as the sole aggressor in the conflict. In contrast, by 1955 the UECP no longer criticized the Egyptian government for attacking Israel in 1948 but instead emphasized at great length (and incorrectly) that Israeli aggressiveness toward Egypt, Syria, and Jordan was directed by American imperialism, on which the new state was economically dependent. Because it supported the new anti-imperialist policies of the Egyptian regime, the UECP did not explicitly condemn Abdel Nasser for failing to follow up the Bandung resolution with an active peace initiative, as Hilmi did. Although the UECP referred repeatedly to Israel and to the possibility of peaceful coexistence, slogans like "Long live Arab Palestine, independent and democratic," and "Long live the struggle of the Arab peoples against American imperialism" were not reassuring to an Israeli Jewish audience, as Hilmi tried to be.

The rhetorical contrast between Hilmi's declarations and those of the UECP in Egypt, which displayed little substantive difference, illustrates clearly the effect of the emergent Nasserist Arab-nationalist political discourse on the Egyptian communists. In the context of the UECP's decision to back Abdel Nasser's refusal to join the Baghdad Pact, the Bandung conference and its political slogan of positive neutralism, the Czech arms deal, and Abdel Nasser's increasingly militant anti-imperialism, it was counterproductive for the party to distance itself from the Egyptian national consensus by recalling its opposition to the

1948 invasion of Palestine and criticizing Egypt and the Arab states for perpetuating the Arab-Israeli conflict. In contrast, because the Rome group and Yusuf Hilmi were unconstrained by the emergent Arab-nationalist political discourse, Hilmi was free to articulate what was unspeakable in Egypt; this difference also exacerbated relations between communists in Paris and Cairo. Publication of Hilmi's Helsinki statement, his letters to Abdel Nasser, and his appeal to the Israeli people prompted some members of the UECP to demand dissolution of the Rome group.[35]

The Rome group must have understood that Hilmi was treading on the edge of permissible political discourse in his mode of expression. The Arabic version of his letter to Abdel Nasser (probably the authentic original text), which was printed in *Kifah shuʿub al-sharq al-awsat*, contained the sentence "Israel has existed and will continue to exist and it is impossible to throw it into the sea"; but this statement was omitted from the French version, printed in *Nouvelles d'Égypte*. Such a phrase could have been maliciously interpreted as Israeli jingoism or a challenge to Egyptian national honor. At the very least, its uncompromising realism was jarring to those accustomed to the common Arab-world representation of Israel. Perhaps by excising this sentence the Rome group hoped to avoid being held responsible for Hilmi's statement (though in Egypt, the Arabic text was more likely to arouse a negative response than the French).

The difference between the enthusiastic reception of Hilmi's message by MAKI and the Rome group and the lukewarm to critical response in Egypt highlights the importance of the discursive context for political action. In Paris, surrounded and supported by Egyptian Jewish émigrés, Hilmi could articulate his ideas uninhibited by an Egyptian political arena defined by mounting nationalist sentiment, increasing mass support for Abdel Nasser, and an emerging rapprochement between the regime and all currents in the communist movement. In Egypt, any positive reference to Israel following the trial of the Jewish saboteurs and the Israeli raid on Gaza, in which Israel was regarded as the unprovoked aggressor, would have been attacked as utterly unpatriotic. For Egyptians in Egypt, these incidents only reconfirmed Israel's aggressive intentions; criticism of Abdel Nasser for failing to take peace initiatives would have seemed out of touch with reality.

In fact, Abdel Nasser did respond positively to efforts of the American Friends Service Committee and an emissary of President Eisenhower to mediate a diplomatic settlement between Egypt and Israel in

1955 and 1956. The failure of these attempts confirmed that Israel was unprepared to consider anything like the terms of the Bandung resolution, while Abdel Nasser's insistence that these negotiations remain secret indicated his lack of confidence that he could win the full support of the RCC for a peace agreement. In the end, the very fact that these talks were secret meant that the spectrum of permissible political discourse in Egypt or Israel remained unchanged.

The response to Hilmi's efforts was modest in Israel too. The overwhelming majority of Jewish Israelis, including MAPAM and Ahdut Ha'avodah, could not imagine a peace based on the partition boundaries and repatriation of the refugees. Menahem Dorman of Ahdut Ha'avodah unequivocally rejected Hilmi's proposals in the party daily; he criticized Hilmi harshly for failing to denounce other Arab delegates at Helsinki who called for the destruction of Israel, and he condemned Hilmi for refusing to meet with him at that important conference.[36] Displaying no appreciation for Egyptian political realities, Dorman saw Hilmi's proposals as a ruse to effect a reconciliation with Abdel Nasser.

Al hamishmar published Hilmi's "Appeal to the Israeli People" with two responses. An anonymous commentator (perhaps Ya'akov Mayus), representing the right wing in MAPAM, began by attacking MAKI and then argued that Hilmi's efforts did "not serve the cause of peace as they abet the plots of Sir Anthony Eden and the Baghdad Pact" because they were based on the UN partition plan.[37] Ongoing contention between MAPAM and MAKI in the Israeli Peace Committee, which had split since Sneh's expulsion from MAPAM, may have been a factor shaping this response.

Speaking for the MAPAM left was El'azar Peri, who welcomed Hilmi's call for peace but rejected all his assumptions. Peri both objected to Hilmi's assertion that the Egyptian government did not want war with Israel and refused the characterization of Israel as an aggressor, stating that the Arab states had rejected the UN partition plan and now allowed armed attacks from their territory against Israel by fedayeen. Peri did not regard the Bandung resolution as an indication of peaceful intentions and argued that peace was not possible on the basis of the partition plan borders: "Since years have passed since then, since facts on the ground have been created in the course of time, since a democratic [Palestinian] Arab state did not arise, the 1947 UN decisions cannot be implemented literally regarding the borders."[38]

In contrast to the Zionist left, MAKI did publicize and support Hilmi's statements. Motivated by publication of Hilmi's letters, the Central

Committee decided to intensify the campaign for peace at its meeting of December 14–16, 1955.[39] Nonetheless, the speeches of the party leaders in this campaign mentioned neither Hilmi nor the Egyptian communists.

From 1955 to 1959, MAKI irregularly received the publications of the Rome group, but it did not attach much importance to or seek to develop this contact, despite having relatively greater freedom to do so than its Egyptian counterparts.[40] MAKI apparently did not respond to the letter from the DMNL in 1953 either, or to another letter sent by the UECP in 1956 offering to establish relations.[41] In the final analysis, the Israeli communists were too inhibited by the conventions of orthodoxy to seek formal contact with organizations so problematic as the Rome group or the UECP.

Yusuf Hilmi was freed from the confines of Egyptian political discourse by being resident in Paris. His meetings with Israelis and émigré Egyptian Jews created new parameters of permissible political expression, and the contacts between Israelis and Egyptians opened for them possibilities unimaginable at home. Yet this liberation of political conceptualization and expression put the participants on the margins of national politics in their own countries. Yusuf Hilmi, for example, did not resume his position as secretary-general of the Partisans of Peace after he returned to Egypt; his place was taken by Khalid Muhyi al-Din. The Rome group continued to promote peaceful settlement of the Arab-Israeli conflict, but it became increasingly marginal to the communist movement in Egypt. Uri Avnery and other noncommunist Israelis connected with the Rome group in the 1950s were even less influential in Jewish circles than MAKI (though this situation changed in the late 1960s). But as the idea of peace based on recognition of both Palestinian and Israeli national rights began to gain legitimacy after the 1973 war, Israelis, and to a lesser extent Egyptians, took a renewed interest in the activities of Yusuf Hilmi, Henri Curiel, and the Rome group.

CHAPTER VI

The Consolidation of Nationalist Politics: 1955–1958

By the end of 1954 public enthusiasm in Egypt for the new regime had ebbed, and, despite his triumph over Naguib in the crisis of March 1954, Abdel Nasser's personal popularity was at a low point and the new regime's stability was in doubt. In October an Anglo-Egyptian agreement on the total evacuation by June 1956 of British troops from the military base in the Suez Canal Zone was signed—though it allowed the British base to be reactivated in the event of an attack against Turkey, Egypt, or any other Arab country. This clause and the amicable negotiations that produced the agreement (which contravened the traditional militant nationalist demand that negotiations for revised Anglo-Egyptian relations follow full British military withdrawal) prompted all the political opposition forces—the Muslim Brothers, the Wafd, and the communists—to oppose the treaty as a fraud that fell short of guaranteeing full independence and sovereignty. The Muslim Brothers even attempted to assassinate Abdel Nasser. When the plot failed, the Brothers were proscribed in Egypt for the second time in five years.

In order to secure its power the RCC continued its antidemocratic suppression of the opposition forces. Al-Raya's harsh denunciation of Abdel Nasser as a pro-Western military dictator seemed well supported. But this assessment had to be radically revised during 1955, when Abdel Nasser led the campaign against Arab adherence to the Baghdad Pact, emerged as a leader of the nonaligned nations at the Bandung conference of Asian and African states, and concluded an agreement to purchase arms from Czechoslovakia. Nationalization of the Suez Canal on July 23, 1956, and the tripartite attack on Egypt in October of that year further confirmed not only Abdel Nasser's emergence as an antiimperialist hero on a world scale but also an alliance between the communists and the Egyptian regime.

The summer of 1955 was the high-water mark for the Marxist left in Israel. In the July Knesset elections, MAKI received 4.5 percent of the votes and six parliamentary seats.[1] Its work in the Arab community had increased MAKI's share of the Arab vote to 34.9 percent of the urban and 15.6 percent of the rural and bedouin voters. Yet MAKI remained an overwhelmingly Jewish party with a 69 percent Jewish electorate. In addition, MAKI's success appeared to be part of a general radicalization of the Jewish working class. Despite the split in MAPAM the previous year, the combined total of nineteen seats for MAPAM and Ahdut Ha'avodah (7.3 and 8.1 percent of the votes, and nine and ten seats, respectively) was greater than the fifteen seats won by united MAPAM in the 1951 elections. MAPAI, though it remained the dominant party, declined in strength, losing five Knesset seats for a total of forty. Ben-Gurion replaced Sharett as the leader of MAPAI and head of a new coalition government that included, for the first time, MAPAM and Ahdut Ha'avodah. Many in these two parties considered Sharett's more conciliatory attitude toward the Arab-Israeli conflict to be a function of his greater subservience to the United States and did not overly regret his departure; they hoped that a coalition of the three labor Zionist parties would have a more leftist outlook than Israel's previous governments.

Ben-Gurion, however, never intended to abandon his activist approach to the Arab-Israeli conflict. Even before the election campaign, Ben-Gurion and the activists in MAPAI, supported by Ahdut Ha'avodah and Herut, used the Egyptian response to Israel's February 1955 raid on Gaza to incite militarist sentiments; the new hardened line on Arab-Israeli issues persisted up to and after the Suez/Sinai War. By encouraging hysteria about the increase in cross-border raids from Egypt following Israel's attack on Gaza and about the military threat from Egypt because of the Czech arms deal, Ben-Gurion established "security" as the overriding political issue in Israel. Any possibility that the new government might have pursued a radically prolabor social policy was eliminated as public attention was directed toward the impending confrontation with Egypt.

Thus, 1955 was a turning point in the Middle East, with Egypt becoming a leading force in the anti-imperialist movement of the nonaligned nations of Asia and Africa and Israel committing itself unalterably to a pro-Western orientation—which culminated in the Anglo-French-Israeli attack on Egypt in 1956. Both Western observers and Egyptian and Israeli Marxists focused their attention on these dramatic changes. As I argued above, the two countries' international orientations were integrally linked to their political economies, the social composition of their nationalist movements, and the overall logic of the military conflict (once the Israeli activists seized the initiative in determining its development). These elements jointly constituted a nationalist political discourse in Egypt and Israel in which fundamentally conflicting visions of the requirements of national independence came to be perceived as mutually exclusive.

In this environment, after the Suez/Sinai War the Marxists, because of their internationalist commitments, found themselves excluded from effective participation in the national political arena. This happened sooner in Israel than in Egypt, since even before the war MAPAI dominance of Israel's political economy was institutionally secured; the activists then gradually established their control over the military tempo of the conflict through the creation of Unit 101 in 1953, Dayan's appointment as IDF chief-of-staff in 1954, Ben-Gurion's return to the cabinet as minister of defense in February and accession to the premiership in November 1955, and Sharett's ouster from the cabinet in June 1956. In Egypt, although Abdel Nasser's political standing was greatly enhanced by the events of 1955 and 1956, the state began to assert its control over the economy only after the 1956 war, at which time pan-Arab nationalism became the sole legitimate political orientation. Pan-Arabism's more consistently and intractably hostile attitude to Israel, relative to the view characteristic of local Egyptian patriotism, seemed fully justified by Israel's aggression. Egypt's increasingly close ties to the Soviet Union also strengthened the Nasserist state and enhanced its ability to suppress the communists when Abdel Nasser felt it was necessary to do so.

THE ILLUSION OF SUCCESS

MAKI's relative success in 1955 was the result of temporary, local, and incidental factors. Since the elections of 1951 the party ranks had been augmented by about 250 new Jewish members—former members of

MAPAM and the LSP led by Moshe Sneh.[2] Several of Sneh's followers enrolled in the Hebrew University of Jerusalem in the mid-1950s, where they organized an active and successful MAKI student cell that was especially strong in the medical school. As a result, in May 1955 MAKI won 10.6 percent of the vote in the student union elections.[3] The vigorous organizational work of former LSP members dramatically increased MAKI's 1955 Knesset vote in such localities as the Tel Aviv suburb of Bat Yam, where MAKI received 6.1 percent of the vote (as opposed to 2.6 and 1 percent in 1951 and 1949, respectively). The election results in Bat Yam were also due to the large number of new Bulgarian immigrants, supporters of the Communist Party in Bulgaria who gave their support to MAKI in Israel. Bulgarians were also prominent among MAKI's supporters in Yehud, Ramle, and Jaffa[4]—localities where MAKI's vote was higher than its national average. New Iraqi immigrants who had been supporters and members of the Communist Party of Iraq also added significantly to MAKI's vote in 1955—for example, in the immigrant camps (*ma'abarot*) of Ramat Hasharon, where MAKI received 9.5 percent of the vote, and Kiryat Ono, where it received 6.5 percent. During 1951-55, MAKI published several irregular Arabic newspapers in new immigrant camps with large numbers of Arabic speakers.[5] These publications emphasized demands for adequate housing, health care, schools, and jobs and criticized MAPAI's management of the camps. Nonetheless MAKI never won a significant following among Oriental Jews other than the Iraqis.

These modest successes were undermined, however, by the steady rightward shift of the entire framework of Israeli politics as Ben-Gurion and his activist followers recast the Zionist political discourse, glorifying the state (a state dominated by MAPAI, of course) and particularly its military arm as the central institutions and supreme values of the new Jew.[6] The preeminence of the Histadrut during the mandate period was replaced by that of the state and the IDF. Since it was controlled by the same political party, the Histadrut eventually conceded to Ben-Gurion's statist policies in most arenas.

Emblematic of the Histadrut's loss of status was the abolition of the labor trend in the public school system in 1953.[7] This trend, which was autonomously directed in accord with the Histadrut's outlook, educated 43.4 percent of all students in 1952–53. It was opposed, however, by bourgeois and religious political parties as an obstacle to their winning the souls of new immigrants. The existence of three educational trends in the public schools—labor, general, and religious—brought down the government in 1951 and precipitated a cabinet crisis in 1952. With the dismantling of the labor trend, symbols like the red flag and the celebration of May Day disappeared from the public schools and eventually from public consciousness.

As the Histadrut's leading role in Jewish society was assumed by the state, the political leadership of the Jewish working class, though formally still embracing variants of socialist ideology, began to adopt increasingly class-accommodationist positions. Ben-Gurion himself stopped speaking of socialism. Despite workers' frequent economic struggles over wages, prices, and taxes, the political trajectory of the Jewish working class was now away from the Marxist left, while MAPAI embraced an ever milder version of social democracy in order to encourage and protect private capital investment. The expanding hegemony of MAPAI over the working class, and thereby over all of Israeli society and the Zionist movement, meant that the apparent advances of the Marxist left were transitory and illusory. Although the Marxist left was still a viable political force among Jewish workers in 1955, the secular trend was toward the right, regardless of contemporary perceptions to the contrary.

BANDUNG AND THE CZECH ARMS DEAL

While Ben-Gurion and MAPAI were aggressively undermining the institutions and ideological structures that might have supported a policy of nonalignment and actively pursuing military alliances with the West, the logic of decolonization propelled Egypt in the opposite direction. In the early years of his rule Abdel Nasser possessed neither the direct control over the national economy nor the institutional and cultural apparatus (except for his control over the army) that sustained MAPAI hegemony in Israel. But his persistent commitment to Egyptian national independence (as expressed by his refusal to permit Western military bases in Egypt), his opposition to Egyptian (and Arab) membership in the Baghdad Pact, his attendance at the Bandung conference of Asian and African states, his leading role in the movement for nonalignment and positive neutralism, and his strengthening of the Egyptian army through the purchase of weapons from Czechoslovakia eventually paralyzed the internal opposition and established Nasserist pan-Arabism as the hegemonic discourse in Egyptian politics.

During the months between the Bandung conference and the announcement of the sale of Czech arms to Egypt, the communist organizations began to reassess their attitude toward Abdel Nasser. Popular Democracy was the first to call for support of the regime's new foreign policy, based on its rejection of the Baghdad Pact and its participation in the Bandung conference.[8] In February 1955 the UECP was formed, uniting several splinters of the DMNL, on the basis of rejecting the DMNL's originally positive attitude toward the coup of July 23, 1952. But by the end of the year the party began to reassess its attitude. Al-Raya was the most reluctant of the three major communist tendencies to revise its stand. It attacked Abdel Nasser's trip to Bandung with a headline in *Rayat al-sha'b* proclaiming, "Egypt's bankrupt fascist seeks glory in Bandung."[9] While al-Raya remained skeptical about the regime's intentions for another year and attacked the UECP for being too enthusiastic in its support of the new foreign policy, it hailed the Egyptian-Czech arms accord as "a step forward on the road to the independence of our country" and one in a series of developments that "could result in a profound change" in Egypt's international orientation.[10] Finally, in the spring of 1956 al-Raya issued a statement endorsing the regime's foreign policy and urging support for the new constitution in the referendum of June 23, 1956.[11]

That Egypt's acquisition of arms from the Soviet bloc might constitute a threat to Israel's security was simply not a consideration for Egypt's communists, much less a reason to hesitate in endorsing the sale. Even Yusuf Hilmi believed that the agreement confirmed the peaceful intentions of the Egyptian government: after all, Czechoslovakia, as a member of the international peace camp, would not supply arms for aggressive purposes; its only aim was to defend Egypt's independence.[12]

Thus, by mid-1956 all three communist groups had accepted that Abdel Nasser's anti-imperialist foreign policy required them to support the regime. Criticisms about the lack of democracy in Egypt, police interference in trade unions, the prohibition of strikes, the ban on political parties other than the Liberation Rally, and the continued imprisonment of communists were subordinated to the task of building a national united front against imperialism. This realignment was consolidated by enthusiastic communist support for Egypt's nationalization of the Suez Canal on July 23, 1956.

Even as Bandung and the Czech arms deal established the terms for a rapprochement between the Egyptian communists and Abdel Nasser (though communists continued to be arrested and jailed), these same events complicated MAKI's position in Israel. MAKI was reluctant to express any support for the Egyptian regime. On March 28, 1955, shortly before Abdel Nasser's departure for Bandung, Me'ir Vilner addressed the Knesset and, in the context of condemning the Israeli raid on Gaza the previous month, castigated Ben-Gurion for his Knesset speech of August 18, 1952, in which the prime minister had welcomed the new Egyptian regime and expressed the hope that it would seek peace with Israel. According to Vilner, this attitude demonstrated Ben-Gurion's willingness "to join the Egyptian military clique in an anti-Soviet military pact under the patronage of the United States."[13] MAKI, although it criticized the Bandung conferees for not inviting Israel to the meeting (because of Arab opposition), endorsed the political outcome of the conference, including its resolution on settling the Arab-Israeli conflict. Sneh, for his part, attacked MAPAM for opposing the conference and its resolution on the conflict.[14] But even after Abdel Nasser returned from Bandung and made several statements rejecting the Baghdad Pact and Iraq's adherence to it, MAKI still criticized the Egyptian regime. For example, *Al-ittihad* reported that 750 communists were imprisoned in Cairo prison, including 68 from Gaza, among them the poet Mu'in Basisu; and the seventeen-day hunger strike of inmates of the Barrages prison and a hunger strike of women prisoners, including Naomi Canel (identified only as the wife of Kamal 'Abd al-Halim), to improve conditions were covered in detail.[15] In contrast to such critical reports about Egyptian antidemocratic repression, except for al-Raya the Egyptian communists now made every effort to broaden the basis for an alliance with the regime.

Such reports in *Al-ittihad* suggest that the Arab leaders of MAKI remained critical of Abdel Nasser and were not influenced by emergent pan-Arab nationalism to adopt the stand of most Egyptian communists toward the Nasserist regime. Emile Habibi's polemic against Jewish chauvinism in MAPAM published during the 1955 Knesset campaign, "Proletarian Internationalism Against Social Chauvinism," provided additional evidence that the Arabs and Jews of MAKI remained united on an internationalist basis. As MAKI's leading spokesperson on Palestinian Arab rights, Habibi would have been one of the first to reflect any nationalist sentiment prevalent among MAKI's Arab cadres; but this pamphlet, although it severely criticized Israel's oppression of the Palestinian Arab national minority, revealed no such tilt.[16]

The reorientation of Egyptian foreign policy symbolized by Abdel Nasser's prominent role at Bandung began to widen the gap between MAKI and the Egyptian communists vis-à-vis the Arab-Israeli conflict.

The divergent pressures operating on the two movements were clearly expressed in MAKI's response to news of the Czech arms agreement. On September 22, 1955, the *Kol haʿam* headline announced, "The Soviet Union has not sent and is not about to send arms to the Arab countries," and the editorial denounced as anti-Soviet lies reports in other Israeli dailies that such shipments were imminent. On September 27, *Kol haʿam* again denied that the Soviet Union was about to supply arms to Egypt; it also attacked the American offer to sell Egypt $10 million worth of arms saying such a step would only increase tensions in the Middle East, exacerbate relations between Egypt and Israel, and encourage an arms race between the two countries. The same day, however, Abdel Nasser announced that a Czech-Egyptian arms sale agreement had been concluded.

After maintaining silence for several days, on October 2 *Kol haʿam* reported on both Radio Prague's announcement of the arms agreement and a *London Times* interview with Abdel Nasser in which he said that the only reason for Egypt's acquisition of arms was fear of Israeli expansionism. On October 2 and 4, *Kol haʿam* published translations of articles by Soviet Middle East experts Y. Primakov and N. Vatolina on the new conditions in Egypt and the Arab world. Moshe Sneh assumed major responsibility for adjusting MAKI's line to these new conditions. In an October 4 article in *Kol haʿam* he defended the arms sale, arguing that it was "not directed against Israel" but was intended to "defend [Egypt] from imperialist pressure" to join the Baghdad Pact. While this consideration undoubtedly played a part in the revision of Soviet policy toward Egypt, Sneh ignored Abdel Nasser's own statement quoted in *Kol haʿam* two days earlier that Egypt was acquiring arms to defend itself against a potential threat from Israel. Instead he maintained that Czech arms would encourage Egypt to pursue a policy of nonalignment and increase the chances for Arab-Israeli peace, at the same time that he criticized Egypt for inconsistency regarding peace with Israel. Earlier, on September 30, *Al-ittihad* had endorsed the arms sale in the same terms as Sneh used in *Kol haʿam*. On October 5, *Kol haʿam* "balanced" its report of the sale by reprinting an article dated September 30, 1948, stating that Czechoslovakia would not give in to American pressure and would continue to supply arms to Israel.

Kol haʿam's obvious discomfort with the Czech-Egyptian arms deal indicated that MAKI was still embedded in a Jewish problematic in which identification with the Soviet Union was justified because of its role in the victory against Nazism and its support for the establishment of a Jewish state. Sneh argued that the Soviet Union would be willing to provide aid to Israel too, if only Israel refused to join an anti-Soviet military alliance and "if it would just preserve its national independence."[17] By contrast, the Egyptian and other Arab communists welcomed the shift in Soviet policy and had no trouble explaining it: as a natural consequence of the Zionist project's very nature, the Israeli government had consistently pursued a pro-Western foreign policy. Ben-Gurion's activist military policies and the continued denial of the Palestinian people's right to self-determination had exacerbated tensions between Egypt and Israel, creating a threat to the stability of the Egyptian regime. In light of Israel's fundamental character and international orientation and, on the other side, Egypt's prominent role in forming an anti-imperialist bloc of the former colonial and semicolonial countries, the Soviet Union had begun to "lean" toward Egypt, though it did not retreat from its commitment to recognize Israel and the UN partition plan. Even if he fully believed this explanation of Soviet policy as advanced by the Arab communists—and there is much evidence that he did not—Sneh could not present this argument to an Israeli Jewish audience. It would only have intensified MAKI's isolation by increasing the dissonance between the party's line and the terms of political discourse in Israel.

Of course, MAKI continued to endorse the policies of the Soviet Union, even after Nikita Khrushchev, in a speech to the Supreme Soviet on December 29, 1955, declared: "The state of Israel, ever since it came into being, has been threatening its neighbors and pursuing a policy hostile to them"[18]—an assertion that strictly speaking was incorrect, since the Arab states attacked Israel in 1948. The Arab invasion had always been an important component of MAKI's (and the Egyptian communists') explanation of the origins and significance of the war. The Khrushchev speech was widely perceived in Israel as a turn in Soviet policy. Many MAPAM members with an emotional attachment to the Soviet Union were especially upset by what they regarded as the Soviet Union's new "anti-Israel" stand, and it is likely that many Jewish members of MAKI were also distressed by Khrushchev's statement. MAPAM had already made clear that its commitment to Zionism preceded its loyalty to the Soviet Union; its leaders therefore did not hesitate to criticize what they saw as the revision in Soviet policy. MAKI, in turn, attacked MAPAM for criticizing the Czech-Egyptian arms sale and the Khrushchev speech.[19]

MAKI's response to the emerging relationship between Egypt and the Soviet Union was to launch an intensified peace campaign.[20] In January 1956, the party organized mass peace rallies in the major cities. Emile Habibi spoke in the Arab slum district of Wadi Nisnas in Haifa, linking the protest against mounting war fever in Israel to the struggle against the national oppression of the Arab minority. He reminded the crowd of the communists' stand in 1948:

> We communists who opposed the Arab rulers' invasion of our country in 1948, we who defended the right of the Jews and the Arabs to establish their independent states and who regarded that invasion as an imperialist plot against both the Jews and the Arabs—with the same strength, courage, and loyalty to our people we also oppose today the policy of military raids that Ben-Gurion organizes on the borders of the Arab states.[21]

These remarks appeared in *Kol ha'am* but were not quoted in *Al-ittihad*'s report of the rally. *Al-ittihad* did, however, quote Mikunis's speech to a rally in Tel Aviv's Moghrabi Square, in which he said that "all Israeli patriots, and the Communist Party first among them, will do all in their power . . . to preserve peace and oppose the preparations for war and to work for a change in the policies of the Israeli government and the establishment of a government of peace and national independence."[22] It is unlikely that many Arabs attended the Tel Aviv rally, and perhaps for that reason the issue of oppression of the Palestinian Arab national minority was not prominently mentioned there, as it was in Haifa.

Al-ittihad's failure to report the above quote from Habibi's speech and the Tel Aviv demonstration's failure to raise oppression of the Arabs as an issue show that MAKI's propaganda appeal emphasized different themes to Jewish and Arab audiences. Yet this does not mean that by the end of 1955 changes in Soviet foreign policy had produced a conflictual situation between Jewish and Arab party members, as Alain Greilsammer has argued.[23] On the contrary, Habibi went out of his way to remind a mainly Arab audience that the communists had supported the creation of the state of Israel, and *Al-ittihad* chose to quote an excerpt from Mikunis's speech in which the struggle for peace was framed entirely in patriotic Israeli terms. These choices indicate an effort to maintain internationalist unity in the party based on the line that had guided MAKI since its formation. As Greilsammer admits, the political content of *Al-ittihad* and *Kol ha'am* was virtually the same during this period.[24] The peace campaign was not conducted under the influence of an Arab tilt. MAKI's criticism of Abdel Nasser after Bandung, its hesitation over the Czech arms sale, and party leaders' unequivocal expressions of internationalism refute Greilsammer's claim that the party had entered an "Arab period" as early as 1954 and had begun to present itself as the party of Arab nationalism.[25] The party certainly defended the national and civil rights of the Palestinian Arab minority in Israel, a theme that Arab leaders like Habibi emphasized when addressing Arab audiences, but MAKI portrayed itself still as "the party of Israeli patriotism and proletarian internationalism." Greilsammer's argument reflects not so much a change in MAKI's policy as the hegemonic Zionist discourse that has always represented support for Palestinian Arab rights and fundamental criticism of military activism as "extremist," "anti-Israel," and "pro-Arab."

Although MAKI had not shifted from a Jewish to an Arab problematic before Bandung and the Czech-Egyptian arms deal, these developments did force the communists to begin reconceptualizing the Arab-Israeli conflict. When border tensions escalated in the second half of 1953, MAKI repeatedly argued that the incidents, for which it blamed the Israeli and Arab governments equally, were "organized by the American and British imperialists."[26] This was also the stand of the DMNL in 1953 and 1954.

By December 1955, although the UECP still viewed American imperialism as the motive force in the conflict, Israel was identified as the principal agent of imperialism in the Middle East: "American imperialism . . . has made Israel its spearhead in its Middle Eastern policy directed against Egypt, Syria, Lebanon, Jordan, and Saudi Arabia—a springboard for extending its influence and domination over the economy and politics of the Arab countries."[27] Thus, even before the 1956 war, in the eyes of Egyptian communists Israel had become the aggressor. This shift allowed them to participate in the national campaign to defend their government's anti-imperialist policies without needing to pay much attention to whether Abdel Nasser was pursuing peace as actively as he might have.

By contrast, Curiel continued personally to uphold the DMNL's earlier position, even after the 1956 war. In a letter to a UECP member in Egypt he noted that "placing the stress on imperialist responsibility in the Arab-Israeli conflict is not only accurate but facilitates to a certain degree the solution by making Israel's responsibility lighter."[28] Curiel had met with Mikunis and Sneh when they passed through Paris on their way back to Israel from Moscow, and he apparently agreed with them that the forces of peace in Israel would be strengthened if progressives in the Arab world adopted this analysis.[29] Communists in

Egypt, however, found this perspective much less convincing. Yusuf Hilmi's suggestions, supported by Curiel and the Rome group, that the Egyptian government was inconsistent and insufficiently energetic in its pursuit of peace were submerged by the tide of nationalist euphoria created by the nationalization of the Suez Canal.

In Israel, it was difficult enough to convince a Jewish audience that the Arab and Israeli governments were equally responsible for the conflict and that its continuation served only the cause of imperialism; to argue that Israel was the aggressor and the willing servant of imperialist interests, while Egypt and the other Arab states merely sought peace (as demonstrated by the Bandung resolution and Egypt's improved relations with the international peace camp headed by the Soviet Union), was beyond the limit of legitimate political discourse. The elementary facts that might have supported such an argument—the activities of Unit 101 and its successors, Israel's responsibility for the Egyptian Jewish sabotage ring of July 1954, the failure of a series of mediation attempts, and Ben-Gurion's efforts since early 1955 to convince the cabinet to launch a preemptive war against Egypt—were unknown in Israel. For most of the Jewish public they were also unknowable. When UN observers criticized Israeli retaliation raids, or the Egyptian government executed Egyptian Jews as spies and saboteurs, or the Arab states offered, in effect, to accept the terms of the UN partition plan eight years after they rejected it, these acts were represented in the hegemonic Zionist discourse as virulent anti-Semitic threats against the security of the Jewish state.

Following the Egyptian-Czech arms accord, Sneh tried to demonstrate that Israel in fact was becoming the aggressor in the conflict.[30] He did so, though, by emphasizing Israel's pursuit of a military alliance with the United States, which would of necessity have been directed against the Soviet Union. This approach to the issue missed the main point. Sneh was, of course, correct in saying that Israel desired a military alliance with the United States. But Israel had no wish to confront the Soviet Union; it wanted only to strengthen its position against its Arab neighbors. The United States, for its part, rejected Israel's advances because it hoped to include the Arab states in an anti-Soviet pact and was unwilling to enroll Israel unless its conflict with these potential allies was resolved, or at least moderated.

Moreover, Egypt's motive for seeking Soviet-bloc weapons was not to confront American imperialism. As Abdel Nasser stated repeatedly, it was Israel's raid on Gaza on February 28, 1955, that convinced him that the Egyptian army had to have new weapons.[31] After the raid he reversed Egypt's previous policy of restraining Palestinian infiltration and authorized the organization of fedayeen squads to commit acts of sabotage in Israel.[32] Intensified hostilities on the Egyptian-Israeli border in August then led him to accept the Soviet/Czech offer after he had tried and failed to obtain arms from the United States.

Thus, for both Israel and Egypt the national conflict was an independent and sufficient motive for seeking a military relationship with a great power. Ben-Gurion and MAPAI had long before decided that Israel would seek alliances only with the West; Abdel Nasser would have been prepared to pursue a Western orientation if only the West had agreed to respect his vision of Egyptian independence. In the era of the cold war, analyses giving priority to local factors were out of favor in both camps. Consequently, MAKI did not fully understand the dynamics that led to the 1956 war, even while it energetically opposed Israel's preparations for it.

THE SUEZ/SINAI WAR AND MAPAM'S CAPITULATION

In a seminal article written during the 1955 Knesset election campaign, Me'ir Ya'ari announced that after the voting MAPAM was prepared to join a coalition government that would include MAPAI and Ahdut Ha'avodah.[33] Although Ya'ari stated that such a coalition would have to be based on programmatic compromises, he did not specify MAPAM's minimum demands in joining a MAPAI-led government. During the campaign, however, MAPAM repeatedly proposed a coalition government of the "pioneering and labor parties." Given the defeat of the left within MAPAM and the split with Ahdut Ha'avodah, Ya'ari's article and MAPAM's electoral strategy indicated that the party was growing weary of opposition politics, that it was prepared to abandon the project of articulating a historic alternative and accept Ahdut Ha'avodah's historic stand that the role of the labor Zionist left was to be merely a corrective to MAPAI.

A central issue in the campaign was how Israel should respond to the intensified violations of its border and acts of sabotage and terror. The activists in MAPAI, Ahdut Ha'avodah, and Herut argued that Israel was already in a state of war and outbid each other in demanding a strong military response. On July 9, Ben-Gurion and Sharett both promised to open the port of Eilat and the Straits of Tiran, closed by the Egyptian blockade—by force if necessary. While MAPAM rejected activism in principle, its opposition had always been inconsistent and ineffectual. The pride it took in its contribution to the Zionist military establishment (especially during the period of unity with Ahdut Ha'avodah) had often prevented the party from forthrightly denouncing specific acts of the activists. Even leaders of the left, like Riftin, were loathe to criticize the army directly;[34] and editorials in *Al hamishmar* had supported the retaliation raids of Tel Mutila, Qibya, Nahalin, and Gaza.[35]

During the election campaign, Ahdut Ha'avodah accused MAPAM of lacking military vigilance, echoing the polemics that had led up to the split the previous year. MAPAM countered by promoting the military role of its kibbutzim to demonstrate their national political legitimacy. For example, *Al hamishmar* published a front-page map of the Gaza border area, with twelve of the twenty-seven kibbutzim located there identified as belonging to Kibbutz Artzi; the caption read, "Who is the Guardian of the Borders?"[36] Responding to activist criticism in this way and offering only restrained criticism of the political vision and military actions that had provoked the recent acts of terror, however, only served to legitimate the mounting national hysteria.

Although MAPAM interpreted the election results as a chance to augment the influence of the Zionist left, they were also a victory for activism: Herut increased its representation from eight to fifteen Knesset seats, and Ahdut Ha'avodah, which had been a minority in united MAPAM, now had ten seats to MAPAM's nine. MAPAI's loss of five seats was interpreted as a repudiation of Sharett's diplomatic approach to resolving the Arab-Israeli conflict. Ben-Gurion lost no time in heating up the border, ending a period of relative calm that had prevailed since early June. A large Israeli raid on Khan Yunis on August 31 climaxed ten days of fighting around the border of the Gaza Strip; and on September 21 Israel occupied the al-'Awja demilitarized zone. These clashes finalized Abdel Nasser's decision to acquire Czech arms. The commander of the UN Mixed Armistice Commission, General Burns, commented: "No Israeli ever so much as suggested that it was the tough Ben-Gurion–Dayan policy that practically forced Nasser to accept the Russo-Czech arms proposals. What other enemy threatened Egypt?"[37] Instead, after the announcement of the arms deal, while coalition negotiations were still in progress, Ahdut Ha'avodah, the activists in MAPAI, and Herut began to demand a preemptive war against Egypt. On October 22, before the Knesset voted its confidence in the new government, Ben-Gurion ordered Dayan to prepare a plan to capture

Sharm al-Shaykh and the Straits of Tiran in order to open the Gulf of Aqaba to Israeli shipping.[38] The cabinet refused to authorize implementing this plan in December, but with Ahdut Ha'avodah in the coalition and Ben-Gurion returning to the premiership, the activist faction in the government was considerably strengthened, and it was only a matter of time before it prevailed.

MAPAM joined the coalition despite the new government's activist character and MAPAI's refusal to make any significant policy concessions to MAPAM. Richard Weintraub explained MAPAM's decision in an editorial in Kibbutz Artzi's ideological journal.[39] He began by attacking MAKI's support of Abdel Nasser and then argued that the current emergency (the Egyptian acquisition of Czech weapons) justified MAPAM's entering the government. He believed that because of the presence of MAPAM and Ahdut Ha'avodah the new government would be socially progressive, though he failed to mention that MAPAI had rejected MAPAM's demand for an end to the wage freeze, which was achieved only by the academicians' strike in early 1956. Weintraub's final argument for MAPAM's participation in the coalition was that it would prevent Israel from signing a military pact with the United States. He could not, however, cite a single programmatic concession achieved by MAPAM.

By justifying MAPAM's action in terms of a security emergency, Weintraub acceded to the representation of Egypt's arms acquisition as a threat to Israel and embraced the principle that Egypt was forbidden to do what was permitted to Israel. Israel, after all, had been secretly acquiring arms from France since July 1954, yet no one in MAPAM denounced this as a threat to Egypt's security. Weintraub probably did not know that the activists had already decided on a military confrontation with Egypt; nonetheless, his acceptance of the terms of the hegemonic discourse made it impossible for him to understand whatever evidence was available on the matter. The notion that MAPAM's presence in the government would prevent a military alliance with the United States was a formalistic attempt to maintain ideological consistency by injecting a false issue into the debate, since it was well known that the Eisenhower administration consistently opposed such an alliance. Had Ben-Gurion been able to overcome this opposition he would not have hesitated for a moment to bring down the government over the issue, with full confidence that MAPAM's objections would be repudiated at the polls. Weintraub, like Sneh, could not disentangle a pro-Western international orientation from the autonomous objectives of the activists, though he did note that despite American opposition to Israeli activism, Ben-Gurion continued to pursue U.S. support.

MAPAM's critique of Israeli foreign policy emphasized its own demand for neutralism, which MAPAI consistently rejected. MAPAM also failed to challenge the hegemonic representation of Israel's attacks on Egypt as legitimate acts of self-defense. A resolution of the party Center responding to the Egyptian-Czech arms deal and Khrushchev's speech to the Supreme Soviet expressed

> great sorrow that arms from a socialist country are flowing into a state that refuses to enter into negotiations on peace with Israel, weapons that are given without conditions to a dictator who declares his plans to destroy Israel.
> Although MAPAM is vigorously opposed to the pro-Western policy line of the Israeli government in recent years, the Center declares that there is no basis for the claim that Israel "has threatened its neighbors since the first days of its existence." The state of Israel has not threatened and does not threaten the borders of its neighbors.[40]

While this resolution was being debated and adopted, U.S. presidential emissary Robert B. Anderson was shuttling between Cairo and Tel Aviv attempting to mediate the Egyptian-Israeli conflict.[41] At least some of MAPAM's leaders must have known about these contacts, since MAPAM was now a coalition partner, although they may have been less informed about the numerous other meetings held when the party had been in opposition. Although Abdel Nasser insisted that these contacts be kept secret, it was not true that Egypt refused to negotiate with Israel. Indeed, shortly after the new Israeli government was formed Abdel Nasser had agreed to talks on the basis of British prime minister Anthony Eden's November 9 proposal for an Arab-Israeli peace based on a territorial compromise between the partition borders and the armistice lines of 1949. Israel, however, rejected the initiative, insisting that the precondition for any talks was acceptance of the territorial status quo.[42] Thus, while MAPAM was correct to point out the historical inaccuracy in Khrushchev's speech, the determination that Israel did not threaten its neighbors' borders ignored the entire history of activist military exploits since al-Burayj and Qibya.

MAPAM's uncritical repetition of the false axiom that Israel always sought peace while the Arab states refused to negotiate only undermined its campaign against a preemptive war and strengthened the activists' hand. For if this axiom were correct, it was reasonable to argue that a moment would come when a preemptive strike by Israel would be justified. The political debate could only be about what circumstances were severe enough to justify such a step. Once the scope of discussion was narrowed to that issue, it did not seem a dramatic abandonment of principle to participate in a war once it began, even if MAPAM preferred to wait a little longer to try to resolve the conflict by other means.

Crippled by its acceptance of the terms of the hegemonic discourse on the conflict, MAPAM did not begin an intensive campaign against activism and the calls for a preemptive war until after Israel attacked the Jordanian police station in Qalqilya on October 10, 1956—the largest military action since the 1948–49 war. Even then *Al hamishmar*, while demanding that all possible measures be taken to prevent war, did not explicitly condemn the raid itself;. it did, however, rebuke the Western powers for voicing such a criticism.[43]

By this time Ben-Gurion had already decided to attack Egypt. When the war began on October 29, MAPAM announced that it would fulfill its responsibilities as a member of the coalition:

> The storm that we said was possible to prevent has occurred. We are in a supreme test. The army and the nation will withstand it. We will not now return to the question of whether it was necessary for events to unfold along this path. We are in battle ... therefore we will stand with bravery and heroism and with firm resolution to ensure the peace of Israel and its future.[44]

After Israel won the war and occupied the Gaza Strip and the Sinai Peninsula, MAPAM's Political Committee adopted a resolution calling on Israel to annex the Gaza Strip, even as it continued to criticize the activist thinking that had resulted in the war.[45] MAPAM energetically supported the government's resistance to demands by the United Nations and the United States that Israel evacuate all the territories occupied during the war and joined the other coalition parties in sponsoring nationwide demonstrations calling for annexation of Sharm al-Shaykh and the Gaza Strip.[46] Hazan dramatically proclaimed in the Knesset, "The political battle threatens us with liquidation of the just results of the glorious military battle."[47]

When Israel finally submitted to international pressure to withdraw from Sharm al-Shaykh and the Gaza Strip, MAPAM, despite its opposition to this decision by the government majority, elected to remain in the coalition.[48] As in 1948, then, MAPAM deployed the rhetoric of militant anti-imperialism to justify annexing territory beyond what the international community considered to be a legitimate part of Israel, whereas MAPAI pragmatically concluded that Israel could not stand alone against international opinion, especially since the United States demanded an Israeli withdrawal no less adamantly than the Soviet Union. But just as MAPAM's resolution of October 7, 1948, justified the results of Israel's first war, despite the party's severe criticism of the manner in which it was conducted and its effects on the Palestinian Arab civilian population, so the demand to annex Gaza retroactively justified the 1956 war and legitimized the logic of activism.

The two moments, however, differed fundamentally regardless of the structural similarity and historical continuity between them. By 1957 MAPAM was a much smaller party, its left wing decimated; it had already failed to struggle consistently on Arab-Israeli issues for nearly a decade; further, it had joined the government without receiving any significant programmatic concessions and failed to leave when that government launched a war that MAPAM opposed. Neither personal dishonesty nor a series of unfortunate accidents brought MAPAM to the end of its path as a radical opposition force in Israel. Critics of the party have often explained its history, including the failure to uphold its own ideals on the Arab-Israeli conflict, as simply the inevitable consequence of its commitment to Zionism, or at least to giving Zionism precedence over internationalism. While this must be an element of the explanation, I have emphasized the material conditions, historical processes, and discursive logic that led to MAPAM's capitulation in 1956–57, not to justify or rationalize, but to demonstrate the extent to which their effects permeated all of Israeli society.

THE NASSERIST-COMMUNIST ALLIANCE

By mid-1956 the three major currents in the Egyptian communist movement were united in supporting the government on the basis of its anti-imperialist foreign policy. The logic of this new stand was expressed in a report adopted by the UECP in April 1956 entitled "Imperialism Is the Principal Enemy." The report declared: "We support the Nasser government . . . in its peace and independence policies . . . and protect it from any imperialist maneuvers."[49] Although it criticized the lack of democratic freedoms in Egypt and called on the government to mobilize the masses, free political prisoners, abolish censorship, and cease police intervention in trade union, peasant union, student union, and professional syndicate elections, the UECP subordinated these democratic demands to building anti-imperialist unity. Thus, even before the nationalization of the Suez Canal on July 23, 1956, the communist movement, proceeding from the premise that the anti-imperialist struggle for national liberation was the most urgent item on Egypt's political agenda, now accepted the leading role of the Nasserist state in the anti-imperialist struggle and abandoned its previous strategy of constructing an alternative anti-imperialist front opposed to the regime.

In light of their political weakness, the communists could only be junior partners in a national front and participate on terms set by Abdel Nasser. In return for their support, Abdel Nasser began to release many (but not all) communists from prison and unofficially permitted them a limited degree of public activity.[50] In early 1956, the Dar al-Fikr publishing house, run by members of the UECP, was opened. Among its first publications were poems by party leader Kamal ʿAbd al-Halim and a translation of Mao Zedong's *On Art and Literature*. Several other communist-run publishing houses were opened, and communists and other leftists began to write in the daily newspapers *Al-shaʿb* (The people) and *Al-jumhuriyya* (The republic) and to appear on the radio's second program. In February the government authorized establishment of a progressive film society, Aflam al-Nur (Films of Light); its founders included ʿAbd al-Qadir al-Tlimsani, who had been in contact with the Rome group and may have met with Israelis in Paris. Inji Aflatun, a member of al-Raya and the National Council of the Partisans of Peace whose husband was still imprisoned, was allowed to organize an exhibit of her paintings. On October 6, the first issue of *Al-masaʾ*, staffed by numerous communists and communist sympathizers, appeared.

The nationalization of the Suez Canal on July 23, 1956, consolidated communist support for the Egyptian regime. Former opponents of the regime were forced to concede that Abdel Nasser and the army were advancing the cause of Egypt's national independence more boldly than they had ever imagined possible. Enthusiastic Arab support for nationalization of the canal established Abdel Nasser as the preeminent political leader in the Arab world and consolidated pan-Arab nationalism as the hegemonic political discourse in Egypt. Communists active in culture and the media adopted Arab nationalist terms of reference. Elliptical efforts to project a distinct communist voice were lost on all but the most sophisticated political sensibilities. Gradually the communists' rapprochement with the regime led to a reformulation of their view of the Arab-Israeli conflict. While continuing to support the UN partition plan as the basis for peaceful resolution of the dispute, their statements now began to incorporate the more extreme anti-Zionist rhetoric of the pan-Arab nationalist movement.

In December 1955 the UECP's underground organ, *Kifah al-shaʿb*, possibly in response to the statements of Yusuf Hilmi and the Rome group, offered a new comprehensive analysis of "the Israeli question":

> Since the creation of the state of Israel in 1948 the Israeli question has fundamentally changed. . . . All the factors that gave birth to the Palestine question have disappeared. It is very clear that American imperialism has used those factors as a pretext to make Israel the spearhead of its policies in the Middle East.[51]

Clearly, the UECP incorrectly believed that the United States encouraged Israel to refuse all peaceful solutions to the conflict.

Despite this harsh evaluation of Israel, the UECP reconfirmed its support for the positions adopted by the overwhelming majority of Egyptian communists in 1947: implementation of the 1947 UN partition resolution; return of the Palestinian refugees, with reparations for property losses suffered; and establishment of an independent democratic Palestinian state. The UECP still looked forward to a peaceful resolution to the conflict, arguing that it would be "easy to find a peaceful settlement with Israel once it extricated itself from the influence of imperialism and the Arab states installed representative governments."[52] This conception of the path to peace seems influenced by the more militantly anti-Israeli stand of the Communist Party of Syria, which maintained that peace with Israel was impossible until it was free of imperialist influence.[53] Thus, the UECP's stand on the Arab-Israeli conflict at the beginning of its alliance with the regime displayed both continuity with its historic position and the new rhetoric of Arab nationalism.

This same tension was reflected in "Imperialism Is the Principal Enemy." Among the manifestations of imperialist pressure on Egypt and the Arab world that it described was the threat of an Israeli attack. Quoting *Newsweek*, the report suggested that Israel's objectives in such an event would be annexation of the West Bank and the Gaza Strip—objectives that the UECP incorrectly believed had been approved by both the United States and Britain. The concluding slogans of the report included "Down with Zionism!" "Long live the front of Arab peoples against imperialism, military pacts, and Zionism!" and "Long live the national culture, the Egyptian Arab culture, the culture of peace, and national independence!"—thus accentuating the anti-Zionist theme in

UECP propaganda, which had been restrained from 1948 to mid-1955. The rhetorical framework of this document was enthusiastic identification with pan-Arabism as the leading anti-imperialist force in the Middle East. In this context, when Israel did pose a serious military threat to Egypt, calls for a peaceful resolution to the Arab-Israeli conflict were subordinated to the call for militant national unity against Zionism and imperialism. For example, a joint May Day leaflet of the UECP and Workers' Vanguard called only for "reconstitution of the Palestinian Arab nation and opposing any other solution to the refugee problem, including settling them in the Arab countries or Sinai"; no mention was made of the possibility of a peaceful settlement.[54]

The Soviet Union still exercised a disciplining influence on the Egyptian communists. On April 17, 1956, the Soviet Foreign Ministry issued a statement calling for the peaceful resolution of the Arab-Israeli conflict. Writing in the influential political weekly, *Ruz al-yusuf*, Mahmud Amin al-ʿAlim, a leader of the anti-Curiel group in the UECP, supported the Soviet call for an international peace conference, in which Israel would participate "since it is a side in the dispute." He also asserted Egypt's right "to insist that the Palestinian Arab people be represented at such a conference by a popular delegation or committee."[55]

When *Al-masaʾ* first appeared, its editorial manifesto devoted only minor attention to the Palestine question, with defense of the Palestinian people included together with support for the people of Cyprus and Algeria in a general statement low down on the list of causes to be championed.[56] But as Israel prepared to attack Egypt, the newspaper's tone changed. Responding to Israel's attack on the Jordanian police station in Qalqilya, Khalid Muhyi al-Din presented a partial (and partly erroneous) chronology of Israeli retaliation raids designed to demonstrate that major Israeli attacks against Egypt and Jordan had occurred only *after* both countries had declined to join the Baghdad pact, Egypt had obtained Czech arms, and Jordan had supported Egypt's nationalization of the Suez Canal. The conclusion was that the primary beneficiary of Israeli actions was Western imperialism and that the aim of the attacks was to "break the Arab front and turn the attention of the Arabs from the direct battle with imperialism to an indirect battle with its stepdaughter [*rabiba*], Israel."[57]

This analysis combined the traditional communist view that the Arab-Israeli conflict was not the essential problem with the implication that Israel was not a sovereign independent state but merely an imperialist dependency. Egypt's decision to send military aid to Jordan following Israel's attack on Qalqilya, Muhyi al-Din concluded, showed that "all the Arabs today are united against imperialism and against Israel." The characterization of Israel as an imperialist pawn, as seen earlier in the *Kifah al sha'b* article on "the Israeli question" and in "Imperialism Is the Principal Enemy," eventually developed into the view that since Israel was merely "the stepdaughter of imperialism," it was not a legitimate expression of the Israeli people's right to self-determination; thus, its existence had no justification.

Yusuf Hilmi and the Rome group saw this analysis as a potential danger to peaceful resolution of the conflict with Israel and tried to address it in their propaganda work. The Rome group formed a Committee to Defend the Nationalization of the Suez Canal, which supplied the European press with documents and manifestos prepared by the UECP justifying Egypt's action.[58] Hilmi sent, via MAKI, a new appeal to the Israeli people defending nationalization of the canal, explaining that it was not a hostile act directed against Israel but rather a step in Egypt's liberation from imperialism and noting that neither France nor England had defended Israel's right to pass through the canal when it was under foreign control. He urged the Israeli people to support Egypt's right to the canal and reject calls for a preventive war against Egypt, because recent events had demonstrated that "Abdel Nasser was perhaps the only one among the Arab politicians who saw the necessity of putting an end to the continuing dispute between the Arab states and Israel by a peaceful agreement."[59] Hilmi recalled that Abdel Nasser had recently told French foreign minister Christian Pineau, "Egypt will never attack Israel. I am among those who support establishing peaceful relations with her [Israel]."[60] Israelis should, he said, overcome their apprehensions and fears, which were being nourished by imperialist propaganda, because these fears "have isolated you to a certain extent from participating in the causes of the Arab peoples, although they are the causes of all peoples, including yourselves." He hoped that the Israeli people would join all the other peoples of the world in demanding "Hands off Egypt" and reject the opportunist current in Israel, which sought to use the nationalization crisis solely to secure Israel's right to navigation through the canal. Hilmi reiterated his support for a complete solution to the Palestinian problem and a permanent peace with Israel based on friendship, understanding, and fruitful cooperation, closing his appeal with the admonition: "The honor of the Israeli people is in the balance."[61] Although Hilmi's entreaty was more conciliatory than the calls of communists residing in Egypt, its assumptions were still too far outside the framework of the hegemonic discourse in Israel to generate a significant response.

During the Anglo-French-Israeli attack, the communists participated fully in the national defense of Egypt. Prisoners in Kharga asked to be released so that they could join in the battle.[62] The communists were especially active in organizing resistance to the Anglo-French occupation of Port Said, sending journalists and political organizers into the city to publish an underground newspaper, conduct mass demonstrations, and, in cooperation with the Egyptian army, launch armed resistance against the European occupiers. In the rear, the communists organized committees of popular resistance to support the struggle in Port Said.[63] At this time all the communists subordinated their criticisms of the government to the cause of the national defense.

The fragmentary report by *Al-masa'* of the government's closure of the law offices of two Jewish communists, Yusuf Darwish and Shihata Harun, reflected its general strategy of minimizing expressions of opposition to the regime. But the paper obliquely signaled its commitment to protecting the rights of Egyptian Jews by headlining the minister of interior's promise that, contrary to prevailing rumors, the government would not expel Jews or confiscate their property.[64] The government did not, however, honor this promise; the property of Jews with foreign citizenship was expropriated after the war. *Al-masa'* also reported the refusal of one Joseph Baruch, a Jewish resident of Port Said with Iranian citizenship, to cooperate with the European occupiers—an affirmation of the patriotism of Egyptian Jews that ran counter to the general expectations of the government and people of Egypt.[65] It also gave front-page coverage to a Tass dispatch reporting the contents of an article by Shmu'el Mikunis on the negative results of Israel's aggression against Egypt.[66]

Yusuf Hilmi's appeal, while it proffered the hand of recognition and friendship to the Israeli people, nevertheless suggested that Israel's stand on Egypt's confrontation with Western imerialism was a test. If Israel failed the test, it was likely to lose the opportunity for a peaceful resolution of the conflict as represented by Abdel Nasser's stated policy since Bandung. And Israel did fail, thus contributing to removing the barriers that had prevented Egyptian progressives from calling for its outright destruction. During the war, *Al-masa'* ran a cartoon captioned, "Arab unity will erase Israel," and an article the same day proclaimed that "Israel is carrying out today the task for which it was created [by Britain]."[67] In other words, the establishment of a Jewish state was not, as the Egyptian and Israeli communists had represented it in 1948, a component of the anti-imperialist struggle against Great Britain, but instead an imperialist maneuver against the Arabs.

Al-masa' operated under constraints that prevented it from reporting the views of Egyptian communists as such. It conveyed the communists' analysis of the political significance of the war by reporting the views of the leader of the Communist Party of Syria, Khalid Bakdash. In a lengthy interview in which he emphasized that all Arab communists stood with the Arab national anti-imperialist front and regarded the struggle for national liberation as the highest priority, Bakdash declared:

> The communists in Syria and Lebanon have always opposed and exposed Israel's claim to be a democratic and peace-loving country and said that Israel is an imperialist base and a tool against the Arab liberation movement and for oppression against the Arab countries. We have always found complete understanding on this subject in the Soviet Union and the People's Republic of China and the other socialist countries.[68]

The Communist Party of Syria was distinguished among the Arab communist parties by its opposition to the partition of Palestine, and this statement reflected the Syrian communists' historically more severe attitude toward Israel. It was, of course, incorrect that the Soviet Union had "always" endorsed this analysis. However, Bakdash was the senior leader among Arab communists; his opinions therefore carried great weight and were a license for Egyptian communists to revise their views in light of the new situation.

After the 1956 war, the UECP undertook an internal debate on Israel's right to statehood and the possibility of achieving peace with the aggressor. In letters and reports during 1957 Curiel insisted that despite Israel's aggression there was no change in the international communist movement's position regarding its right to existence and that the Soviet statement of April 17, 1956, calling for a peaceful resolution of the conflict remained valid.[69] Hence peaceful settlement should, he said, continue to be a central element of the UECP's propaganda. Party leaders in Egypt, however, evidently had doubts about the validity of this approach in light of the war. The precise terms of the debate are unclear because the reports of Hamido (Muhammad Shatta) and 'Aziz (Sharif Hatata), to which Curiel was apparently responding, are unavailable. In any case, Curiel referred to these reports as "courageous,"[70] and since Shatta and Hatata were personally very close to Curiel, their positions were probably similar to his. Curiel supported Hatata's assessment that MAPAM and Aḥdut Ha'avodah, along with MAKI, were to be counted among the peace forces in Israel and should be supported—a position that seems not to have taken into account Aḥdut Ha'avodah's attack on Yusuf Hilmi's peace initiative in 1955. He also quoted *L'humanité*'s favorable report of MAKI's Thirteenth Congress, noting its strong stand against Israel's aggression, and urged the UECP to publicize the congress resolutions, which he considered to provide a basis for peaceful resolution of the conflict (see below). No documents are available to indicate the views of the other Egyptian communist organizations. According to Fu'ad Mursi, al-Raya continued to uphold the UN partition plan; because of Israel's close association with British and French imperialism in the 1956 war, though, questions arose concerning the legitimacy of the partition, and members of the party began to say that Israel's "existence as a state is fragile." [71]

Al-masa', too, upheld the partition plan. One day after it published an Indian journalist's interview with Abdel Nasser in which the president refused to affirm (but did not directly deny) that resolution of the dispute with Israel was still possible on the terms set by the UN resolutions of 1947 and 1948, *Al-masa'* editorialized: "The peaceful resolution of the Palestine problem should be on the basis of implementing the UN resolutions of 1947–1948, especially returning the refugees to their homes and compensating them for the money and property they have lost." [72] This was as sharp an expression of disagreement with Abdel Nasser as *Al-masa'* ever permitted itself. Public and official opinion in Israel had long regarded Arab willingness to settle the conflict based on the partition boundaries as an expression of hostility. But in the context of the pan-Arab nationalist discourse now dominant in Egypt, *Al-masa'*'s call for peace just days after Israel's evacuation of the Gaza Strip was certainly a courageous statement of principle.

After the evacuation, the Arab-Israeli dispute receded into the background and was mentioned only infrequently in *Al-masa'*. Yet when the history of the Palestine conflict was rehearsed on the anniversary of Israel's establishment, American imperialism was portrayed as the sole sponsor of the Jewish state. Soviet support for the partition of Palestine and the role of Czech arms in assuring Israel's survival were not mentioned, even by communist or former-communist reporters.[73] This was another significant departure from the historic analysis of the Egyptian communists; the contrast with MAKI's propaganda line, which never missed an opportunity to recall these facts, could not have been sharper.

UNIFICATION OF THE EGYPTIAN COMMUNIST MOVEMENT

Unity discussions among the three major communist tendencies began in late 1956 with the participation of Velio Spano of the Communist Party of Italy and 'Amr 'Abd Allah of the Communist Party of Iraq, who had been delegated by the international communist movement in this cause. In March 1957, Popular Democracy convened a congress and became the Workers' and Peasants' Communist Party (WPCP)—marking the first time it openly identified itself as a communist organization. Reversing its historically cautious organizational policies, the party adopted a strategy of rapid recruitment. During the July 1957 parliamentary election campaign it enrolled many workers and others who had been on the periphery of the group and so quickly became the largest of the three major communist organizations, with about a thousand members.[74] Of the three organizations, the WPCP was the most resistant to unity: its leaders detested Curiel and his followers and considered Kamal 'Abd al-Halim and the Dar al-Fikr group to be unreliable rightists.[75]

The WPCP was also the only organization with Jews among its leaders. Yet as a condition of unity al-Raya demanded that Jews be excluded from the leadership of the party and that the Rome group be dissolved. Leaders of the UECP who were close to Curiel (like Kamal 'Abd al-Halim) opposed these conditions, whereas those not originally affiliated with the DMNL (like Mahmud Amin al-'Alim) were more willing to accede to al-Raya's demand. This explains why, in a report they submitted on Arab unity, al-'Alim and 'Abd al-'Azim Anis, the leading theoreticians of pan-Arab nationalism within the communist movement, advocated excluding Jews from the Central Committee.[76] They defended this position in letters to the communists imprisoned at Kharga—where Muhammad Shatta and Zaki Murad, supporters of Curiel, probably opposed it.

In June 1957 the UECP accepted al-Raya's conditions, and the two parties fused to form the United Egyptian Communist Party (al-Muttahid). In October, the Political Bureau of the new party informed the Rome group that it was dissolved, though because of the continuing unity discussions with the WPCP the decision was not finalized until March 1958.[77]

Accepting al-Raya's demands had little practical effect, of course, because the UECP had no Jewish leaders and the Rome group had long since lost touch with the changed conditions of Egyptian politics and the ongoing activity of the party. Nonetheless, these organizational changes, according to Fu'ad Mursi, signaled a comprehensive political reorientation toward pan-Arab nationalism that also involved a revision of the Egyptian communists' position on the partition of Palestine.[78]

DMNL partisan Rif'at al-Sa'id wrote that the Rome group

> persevered in a series of particular positions on the Middle East crisis [i.e., the Arab-Israeli conflict], which, though they appeared theoretically correct, were difficult to defend in practice. Therefore, it is possible to say that the dissolution of the Rome group was not simply the fruit of the alliance of the WPCP and al-Raya and certain external pressures [clearly not, since it was dissolved before the WPCP agreed to unity]. It is also possible to say that some of those in the other camp [i.e., the DMNL/UECP] were also pleased with this decision, even though they did not wish to undertake it.[79]

The Rome group regarded the party's decision to order its dissolution as a submission to racism. Its objections were detailed in a letter of protest whose contents confirm that the group's continuing advocacy of peace between Israel and the Arab states had in part motivated the demand for its dissolution.[80] The group argued that its line coincided with that of MAKI, the international communist movement, and the Soviet Union; at the same time, it insisted that it had never represented this as the line of the UECP and that it had loyally upheld the party's decisions even when it had believed them to be incorrect.

Curiel's letters to Egypt during late 1956 and early 1957 indicate that, in addition to differences of opinion on the Arab-Israeli conflict, he disagreed with other elements of UECP's line.[81] He displayed increasing impatience with the party's uncritical support of the Egyptian government and objected to defending Abdel Nasser personally or his internal regime. Although Curiel had consistently supported the Egyptian regime since July 23, 1952, and considered the DMNL's period of opposition an error, he also regarded Abdel Nasser as a nationalist and nothing more. He believed that the UECP had exaggerated the threat posed to Egypt by the Suez Canal crisis, and mocked the party's characterization of the popular resistance in Port Said as a "new Stalingrad."

The WPCP condemned as racist al-Raya's demand that Jews be excluded from the united party's leadership. Its worker members were strongly attached to Yusuf Darwish, and they opposed unity unless he joined the new Central Committee. As former WPCP leader Hilmi Yasin recalled, "The workers said, 'Yusuf Darwish is our Lord.'"[82] Darwish had actually converted to Islam ten years earlier in order to marry a rabbinic Jew (Jewish religious authorities would not approve a marriage between a Karaite and a rabbinic Jew, whereas Muslim law authorized marriages between a Muslim man and a Jewish woman); Ahmad Sadiq Saʿd and Raymond Douek likewise had converted during 1957 to remove this issue as an obstacle to unity. But al-Raya still considered them all Jews and demanded their exclusion from the leadership.[83] Fuʾad Mursi, Ismaʿil Sabri ʿAbd Allah, and Saʿd Zahran were especially persistent on this point.

Velio Spano insisted that communist unity be achieved immediately and that discussion of all ideological differences be deferred until after unity. Spano spoke with great authority as a leading figure in the international movement (he had just visited Mao Zedong); this demand therefore put heavy pressure on the WPCP to agree to unite.[84] In his report on the talks' progress, Spano noted the "cosmopolitanism" and foreign origins of the Egyptian communist leadership as well as the "bookish" and "Talmudic" character of the movement; he also sharply criticized Henri Curiel for failing to join the Communist Party of France and continuing to work in the Egyptian movement while residing in Europe.[85] These observations could be interpreted as signifying agreement with al-Raya's historic stand on the negative Jewish role in the communist movement. Spano also reproached the Egyptian communists for their early opposition to Abdel Nasser, but he gave no credit to Curiel and the DMNL for defending the coup of July 23, 1952, nor did he note that the stand of al-Raya, the WPCP, and the communist parties of Europe opposing the Free Officers' regime, in addition to Abdel Nasser's unremitting attacks on the communists, had in fact forced the DMNL to retract its support for the new regime in 1953. Although Spano criticized al-Raya for sectarianism into early 1956, he characterized it as the organization with the most serious cadres and the highest level of ideological training.

Anointed with the oil of internationally recognized orthodoxy, al-Raya's refusal to concede on the Jewish issue seemed insurmountable. As a consequence, this and all other political differences were put aside. The WPCP capitulated, and on January 8, 1958, the united Communist Party of Egypt (CPE) was established with about twenty-four hundred members. The new party was headed by a Permanent Committee composed of one representative of each of its three constituent tendencies:

Abu Sayf Yusuf (general secretary, formerly of the WPCP), Fu'ad Mursi (formerly of al-Raya), and Kamal 'Abd al-Halim (formerly of the UECP). The Political Bureau also maintained parity between the three former groups, each having five representatives. The Central Committee was the highest body, in which the division of seats reflected the relative numerical strength of the three currents—WPCP, fourteen; UECP, eleven; al-Raya, nine.[86]

The surrender of the Egyptian communists to al-Raya's demand came about because of external pressure, Israel's recent aggression against Egypt, and the communists' desire to integrate with the rising tide of anti-imperialist pan-Arab nationalism led by Abdel Nasser. Since al-Raya had always excluded Jews from its ranks, the demand did not represent a new idea within the movement. Its success did, however, as Fu'ad Mursi suggested, indicate a broad political realignment: it symbolized the victory of al-Raya's historic perspective despite the faction's numerical weakness in the CPE. Because al-Raya had never had a significant working-class or Jewish membership, it represented, more so than the other communist groups, the aspirations of the indigenous Egyptian radical intelligentsia. And ultimately, no fundamental antagonism divided the perspective of this intelligentsia from that of the Nasserist regime.

The general line of communist unity was based on a pan-Arab nationalist orientation that had been developing in the ranks of al-Raya and the non-DMNL components of the UECP since 1954–55. This orientation treated the Palestinian/Arab–Israeli conflict as part of the struggle for Arab unity and regarded Israel primarily as an obstacle to this unity implanted by the imperialist powers in the heart of the Arab world. Thus, when al-Muttahid, in response to a letter from the WPCP, summarized its party program, it noted that the party

> affirmed the necessity of achieving full Arab unity on a firm [pan-Arab] national basis and obligated itself to struggle for achieving federal unity with Syria as a departure point for full unity and also to reject peace [sulh] with Israel on an imperialist basis and to adhere to the UN General Assembly partition resolution of 1947 as a minimum basis for resolving the Palestine question. We have also affirmed that the decisive ultimate resolution of this question will not be realized except by the final liquidation of imperialism in the Arab East.[87]

This formulation combined the Egyptian communists' historic support for the partition of Palestine with the Syrian communists' more militant notion that there could be no resolution of the Arab-Israeli conflict until imperialism was defeated. Al-Muttahid's support for partition was reluctant and partial. Partition was not defended as a just solution for a difficult question that insured the national rights of the two peoples living in historic Palestine; rather, it was grudgingly accepted as the largest obstacle that could be permitted to impede Arab unity, and then only temporarily.

The general CPE line was developed in the discussion bulletin of the unity bureau established by al-Muttahid and the WPCP. The first point of the proposed program announced: "We support without hesitation the government of President Abdel Nasser in its policies of independence and peace, and we struggle with all our might to solidify the unity between the people and the government." As before, the communists would continue to promote world peace; yet the conflict with Israel was not mentioned here—as in the al-Muttahid program, it was treated briefly in the section declaring support for pan-Arab unity and a federal union of Egypt and Syria:

> We struggle for the Arab countries to form a protective screen and oppose a united front to Zionist expansionism sanctioned by world imperialism. We struggle for the rights of the Arab refugees to return to their lands and be compensated, and we reject any peace with Israel that imperialism wishes to impose on the Arab countries.[88]

No mention was made of what, if any, peace with Israel would be acceptable.

The CPE gave nearly uncritical support to the Nasserist regime; support for the government's foreign policies became its first political priority. It fully endorsed the formation of the United Arab Republic (UAR) and suppressed its reservations about Abdel Nasser's demand that all Syrian political parties (including the Communist Party) be dissolved and replaced by the National Union and about establishing a unitary as opposed to a federal form of government. In the context of such great enthusiasm for Nasserist pan-Arabism and exaggerated evaluations of Arab nationalism's anti-imperialist potential, the CPE's position on Palestine became nearly indistinguishable from that of the pan-Arab nationalists. A statement of the CPE Political Bureau endorsing establishment of the UAR referred to Israel only in passing by noting that unity of Egypt and Syria would be directed "against imperialism and against Israel, the willing tool of imperialism, and against Zionism."[89]

All of the tendencies demonstrated by the communists to abandon their earlier perspective on peaceful resolution of the Arab-Israeli dispute were crystallized in the title of ʿAbd al-Munʿim al-Ghazzali's book published by Dar al-Fikr in 1958: *Israel Is an Imperialist Base and Not a Nation.*[90] Using false historical arguments that overemphasized the extent of American support for Israel and the significance of U.S. and French policy differences in the Middle East, al-Ghazzali claimed that Israel's existence was due solely to imperialist (primarily American) financial and military support. (He of course did not mention that the Soviet Union had supported the partition of Palestine or that Czechoslovakia had supplied arms to Israel during the 1948–49 war.) He then demanded the dismantling of the state of Israel and all the Zionist institutions, abrogation of the UN partition plan, and establishment of an Arab state in all of Palestine. The precise status of al-Ghazzali's book within the CPE is uncertain because it was published after the beginnings of a split in the party. However, Dar al-Fikr was managed by former DMNL members close to Curiel; their willingness to publish the book indicated a sharp departure from their historic views and signified an end to the Egyptian communists' effort to articulate an alternative perspective to that of the Nasserist regime on the resolution of the Arab-Israeli conflict.

THE TWENTIETH CONGRESS OF THE COMMUNIST PARTY OF THE SOVIET UNION AND NATIONAL COMMUNISM

Nikita Khrushchev's revelation of Stalin's crimes in February 1956, at the Twentieth Congress of the Communist Party of the Soviet Union, did not cause massive defections from the communist parties of the Middle East as it did in parts of Western Europe and North America. In both Egypt and Israel, the most important effect of the congress, when its impact was absorbed, was to loosen discipline within the communist movement and legitimate and encourage the development of "national communism"—a trend that ultimately widened the gap between MAKI and the Egyptian communists on the Palestine question and the Arab-Israeli conflict.

In Egypt, the Twentieth Congress seems to have made little immediate impression, perhaps because it was overshadowed by the struggle over the Suez Canal nationalization, the Suez/Sinai War, and the movement to unify the communist organizations. The "lessons of the Twentieth Party Congress" began to be articulated only in the fall of 1957, when the Egyptian communist movement was unifying around a line of support for pan-Arabism and the Nasserist regime and developing a theoretical rationale for this orientation. In an article published in al-Muttahid's internal organ entitled "Marxism: The Living Theory," Fu'ad Mursi explained the significance of the congress thus: "Each communist party today must consider its own country." Egyptian communists therefore had to apply Marxism to Egyptian conditions and "invent solutions for our country rooted in our specific cultural heritage and develop them in our struggle." Mursi's own application of Marxism produced a doctrine of Egyptian exceptionalism grounded in an early elaboration of the theory of the noncapitalist road of development. He characterized the Egyptian bourgeoisie as an entirely new type without historical parallel. In the era of late-capitalist crisis, it was a permanently national and progressive force because it would be unable to transform itself into a monopoly bourgeoisie; it was influenced by socialist ideas and linked to the world socialist camp because only this camp supported its aspirations for economic development. Its historic path was toward neither capitalism nor socialism but toward state capitalism. The current working-class–bourgeois alliance was a new form of class struggle in which the working class would seek to "educate" the bourgeoisie in the correct understanding of the Egyptian national revolution. Working-class leadership of the national front would be established peacefully and gradually, thus creating the conditions for the transition to socialism.[91]

'Abd al-'Azim Anis, writing in *Al-masa'* (where he could not say that his analysis was based on the lessons of the Twentieth Party Congress), developed the same perspective in an article on the new state party, the National Union. According to Anis, Egyptian society was "one of the new forms of transition to socialism by peaceful means without passage through the full stage of capitalism as Western Europe historically knew it." Anis therefore supported the establishment of the National Union, which he portrayed as a more democratic organization than it actually was—a combination of wishful thinking and gentle prodding of the government.[92]

For the Egyptian communists, the theory of noncapitalist development justified abandoning the struggle for a fundamental alternative to the Nasserist regime, since the Nasserist path would lead to socialism in any case. Peace with Israel was no longer an item on the political agenda. The UN observer troops stationed on the Egyptian side of the Arab-Israeli frontier after the 1956 war (Israel refused to allow UN forces on its side of the line) had nearly eliminated border incidents, and the Palestinians were subdued as an independent political force. Since the conflict seemed to be both perpetual and benign, the CPE saw no purpose in raising an issue that would impede Arab unity and perhaps isolate the party politically. In light of Israel's aggression and alliance with Anglo-French imperialism, many Egyptian communists no longer believed that peace was possible.

Shmu'el Mikunis and Emile Habibi represented MAKI at the Twentieth Congress of the Soviet Communist Party, and Moshe Sneh and Tawfiq Tubi represented the party at the November 1957 Moscow conference of communist parties called to reassess the international movement's path following Khrushchev's revelations. According to Berl Balti (formerly a leader of MAKI), after meeting with Khalid Bakdash and other Arab communists in Moscow, Habibi and Tubi began to argue that the decision to support the partition of Palestine was an error attributable to Stalin's cult of personality and that the 1948–49 war had in fact been an unjust anti-Arab war; they therefore returned to Israel demanding that MAKI declare nonrecognition of Israel's territorial acquisitions beyond the boundaries of the UN partition plan.[93] When questioned about this, however, Habibi responded with the opposite contention: that some Jewish members of the party (most notably Balti) had begun to argue that Stalin's errors had caused the international communist movement to adopt a historically negative attitude toward Zionism.[94] Neither claim is supported by documentation, and it is possible both are correct.

The most direct result of the Twentieth Congress in MAKI was the expulsion of Hanokh Bzozah for Jewish national deviations on April 4, 1956, the day Mikunis returned from Moscow. Bzozah, a former member of Hashomer Hatza'ir and a founder of Kibbutz Ein Shemer before he joined the PCP in 1930, had a history of Jewish national opinions. He was the leader of the PCP Jewish Section in 1937, and he had been an early critic of the Slansky trial and other manifestations of anti-Semitism in the Soviet Union, Bulgaria, Hungary, and Rumania. In a letter responding to his expulsion, he criticized the Central Committee for failing to reexamine MAKI's line in light of the revelations of the Soviet party congress.[95] He also criticized MAKI's opposition to the Israeli coalition government of 1955, since it was composed of the three workers' parties. After his expulsion, Bzozah, joined by former Hebrew Communists Me'ir Slonim and Simha Tzabari and several others, issued irregular publications calling for a renewal of Israeli communism, a closer alliance with the socialist-Zionist parties, and rejection of emphasis on Israeli aggressiveness in the Arab-Israeli conflict without equal attention to the Arab states' refusal to make peace with Israel. Bzozah was in touch with dissident Jews from the British and Canadian communist parties, and the general outlook of his group was similar to that of the British new left and the former communists around *Jewish Currents* in the United States.

In the post–Suez/Sinai War atmosphere, the Bzozah group's criticisms of MAKI for its one-sidedly pro-Arab positions and its consistent opposition to the government that launched the war were not entertained seriously within the party. MAKI did not suffer a large loss of membership following the Twentieth Soviet Party Congress. In 1957, only 7 percent of the MAKI members in the Tel Aviv district and 15 percent in the Haifa district left the party and were not replaced by new adherents; in the other four districts, although sixty-three resigned, they were replaced by fifty-seven new members.[96] The defections were concentrated among Jewish members. In the Jerusalem district, where the party was almost entirely Jewish, there were twenty-four resignations and only three new members; but in the all-Arab Nazareth district the three resignations were more than balanced by seventeen new enrollments. Most of the thirty-four members who resigned in the coastal plain district were probably Jews, while the thirty-seven new members there were likely mostly Arabs from Triangle villages like Tayyiba, where MAKI's strength was growing.

Whereas in Egypt a national communist perspective, reinforced by the Soviet party congress and the theory of the noncapitalist road of development, provided the theoretical basis for unifying the communist movement, in Israel the Bzozah group's Jewish national communism was actually delegitimized by the 1956 war, which inspired harsh conclusions in the party about Israel's aggressive and oppressive character. The Jewish defections from MAKI also enhanced the importance of the Arab membership in the demographic composition of the party. These Israeli developments, combined with the rising tide of Arab nationalism led by a militantly anti-imperialist Egypt and closer relations between the Soviet Union and the radical nationalist Arab states, informed a new Arab-centered orientation in MAKI, which replaced its earlier Jewish-centered problematic.

MAKI'S ARAB PERIOD

On October 29, 1956, when Israel launched its attack on Egypt in the Suez/Sinai War, border guards appeared at 4:00 P.M. in several Arab villages on the boundary with Jordan and announced that a curfew would go into effect at 5:00 P.M. Palestinian Arab workers from the village of Kafr Qasim near Petah Tikvah who had left that morning for their jobs did not know of the curfew. They returned home just as it was going into effect; the IDF shot dead forty-nine of these workers and wounded thirteen others. Two other Arabs were shot dead for violating curfew in Tayyiba and al-Tira. The military censor prohibited publication of news of the massacre for several weeks; only a partial account was given in the press on November 11. Ester Vilenska tried to raise the matter in the Knesset on November 13, but she was not given the floor, and the few words she managed to say were stricken from the record. Tawfiq Tubi visited Kafr Qasim on November 20 to investigate the matter; three days later he published a report of the incident—including all the names of the dead and wounded—in an open letter in Hebrew, Arabic, and English, in which he called for support from all sectors of Israeli society and asked that the perpetrators be prosecuted.[97] Eventually the military officers responsible for the crime received a symbolic minimal punishment.

Following the 1956 war, the name Kafr Qasim became a rallying cry against Israel's oppression of its Arab citizens and denial of their national rights. It provided MAKI with a salient issue that could mobilize the Arab community and enabled the party to expand its influence in the villages of the southern Triangle. Kafr Qasim and the 1956 war linked the local issue of Palestinian national oppression to the regional threat that Israel posed to the entire Arab world. The prominence of these issues in the party's work after 1956 signified MAKI's adoption of an Arab-centered problematic that had been crystallizing since the conclusion of the Czech-Egyptian arms deal. The existence and security of the Jewish state was now regarded as an accomplished fact; at issue now was the danger that this state and its imperialist allies posed to the security, peace, and self-determination of the Arab world and its anti-imperialist allies.

The adoption of an Arab-centered orientation when the rest of Israeli society indulged in a festival of triumphalist nationalism increasingly isolated MAKI from the Jewish public. The party's basic assumptions—that Israel had been an aggressor in the war, that it was a fatal error for Israel to ally with imperialism against anti-imperialist Arab nationalism, that peace between Israel and its neighbors depended on repatriation of the Palestinian refugees and recognizing the Palestinian Arabs' right to self-determination, that the Palestinian Arab citizens of Israel were an oppressed national minority—now became almost unspeakable in the Israeli political arena. At the same time, many Arab citizens of Israel—including members and leaders of MAKI—buoyed by the meteoric rise of Nasserist pan-Arab nationalism and the formation of the UAR, pushed MAKI to adopt the rhetorical framework of Arab anti-imperialism. To the extent that the party did so, it became even further isolated from the Jewish majority in Israel.

MAKI totally opposed the Israeli-British-French war against Egypt, and its Knesset faction made a motion of no confidence in the government for launching the attack. The party demanded Israel's immediate and complete withdrawal to the armistice lines, an end to collusion with imperialism, and recognition of the Palestinian Arab people's right to self-determination.[98] It continued to view the Soviet statement of April 17, 1956, as indicating the correct basis for resolving the Arab-Israeli conflict and maintained, in response to charges that the Soviet Union was "pro-Arab," that this statement remained the guiding line of Soviet policy.[99]

Even while denouncing Israel's attack, MAKI tried to promote peaceful relations between Egypt and Israel. *Kol ha'am* quoted a Hebrew broadcast of Radio Cairo which stated that Egypt viewed imperialism, not Ben-Gurion, as the principal enemy of *all* the peoples of the Middle East.[100] An Arabic leaflet distributed in Tayyiba during the war condemned the military government's ban on political meetings and other acts of repression; it concluded with the slogans "Abolish the tyrannical military government," "Stop the war hysteria," "Long live peace between Israel and the Arab states."[101] The call for peace in the midst of war derived from MAKI's long-held view that the conflict served the interests not of the Israeli or the Arab peoples but only of imperialism. However, this call contrasted sharply with the Egyptian communists' enthusiastic call for national defense against the aggressors. While the stands of the Israeli and the Egyptian communists were easily explained by the differing circumstances on each side of the border, the war accelerated the divergence between the political lines and sensibilities of the two movements.

The 1956 war broke out just as MAKI was preparing for its Thirteenth Congress, which was to have convened in November. The war forced postponement of the congress and prompted the party to reevaluate its positions on Israeli-Arab relations. The original political theses of the Congress had been published in September;[102] after the war, in April 1957, the Central Committee published additions, explanations, and corrections to the original theses in preparation for the rescheduled congress which was to convene on May 29. Between September and the end of May, a sharp internal debate raged over Arab-Israeli issues.

At its Twelfth Congress, in 1952, MAKI had opposed discussion of the eventual borders between Israel and the Palestinian Arab state, to be established as an expression of the Palestinian people's right to self-determination. This refusal was a concession to the sentiments of the Jewish majority in Israel, which viewed the territorial status quo established by the 1949 armistices as the minimum (but not necessarily the maximum) borders of the Jewish state. MAKI's line thus deviated from that of the Arab communists, for whom the UN partition resolution of November 1947 defined Israel's legitimate borders.

Some Arab members of MAKI had apparently raised the border question even before the Twelfth Congress. According to Mikunis, in 1951 Habibi had demanded that in the territories occupied by Israel but designated by the UN as part of the Palestinian Arab state the communists should continue to function as the National Liberation League.[103] Acceptance of these terms would signify that MAKI did not recognize Israel's territorial conquests in the 1948–49 war. Since Mikunis made this claim in an interview given after the split in MAKI, when he would have been interested in emphasizing Habibi's "nationalist deviations," and since this issue had been resolved prior to MAKI's Eleventh Congress in 1949, there is reason to doubt Mikunis's account. Perhaps he simply shifted the date of Habibi's demand forward two years. Nonetheless, this issue was not a dead one among Arab cadres of the party. The Bandung conference resolution on the Arab-Israeli conflict indicated that the Arab states might be prepared to settle the dispute if Israel returned to the partition borders. Some Arab party members, therefore, sought to specify Israel's borders to facilitate resolution of the conflict on the terms of the Bandung resolution.

In September 1956, during the internal party debate over the original theses for the Thirteenth Congress, Fu'ad Khuri, a member of the Central Committee, wrote to the Political Committee insisting that the Palestinian Arab right to self-determination had to be connected to a specific territory and suggesting that the border question "could be solved in the light of the UN decision of 1947." Khuri believed his formulation was a compromise; he did not insist on the precise borders of the partition plan, yet reference to the UN partition resolution established the legitimacy of his proposal, which was intended to prevent "reactionary and pro-imperialist elements in the country" from popularizing "the status quo theory."[104] Mikunis rejected Khuri's formulation, arguing that such a program would encourage the separation of the Arabs of Nazareth and the Triangle, which he opposed, and that it made the question of Palestinian self-determination more difficult to explain to the Jewish public.[105] The original theses for the Thirteenth Congress, then, represented a compromise between Mikunis's and Khuri's positions, advocating a "compromise on the refugee question as well as a compromise on the question of frontiers" (i.e., between the status quo and the partition borders) and attacking the Israeli government's insistence that peace be based on the status quo.[106]

Israel's subsequent aggression against Egypt seemed to vindicate those within MAKI who advocated taking a harsher line against Israeli policies. The additions and corrections to the original theses declared that "the ruling circles of our country are dependent on imperialism, are its servants and an instrument in their hand against the cause of peace, against the national liberation movements of the peoples of the Arab East."[107] While harsh, this formulation was milder than Central Committee member Saliba Khamis's argument—which echoed the line of the Egyptian and other Arab communists—that the 1956 war led the Arab people to realize that "Israel [i.e., the entire state, not only its rulers] had become a base for imperialist aggression against them."[108]

The most controversial addition to the original theses was the determination that "Israeli-Arab peace demands the recognition by Israel of the right to self-determination, up to secession, of the Palestinian Arab people, including its part living in Israel."[109] In other words, not only were the Palestinian Arabs entitled to a separate state, but Arabs living in Israel (presumably those living in territorially contiguous areas of the Galilee and the Triangle) would also have the right to separate from Israel and join such a Palestinian state once it was established. This oblique formulation, which suggested that Israel might return to borders resembling those outlined in the partition plan, resulted from the intraparty struggle mentioned above, in which some Arab leaders (probably Fu'ad Khuri, Emile Tuma, Saliba Khamis, and possibly also Habibi) had insisted on specifying that a peaceful resolution to the conflict could come about only if the UN partition borders were adhered to. Emile Tuma, because of his opposition to the partition plan in 1947, had never been allowed to join MAKI's Central Committee, even though he was one of the party's most talented Arab cadres. Tuma therefore attended the congress as a member of the Haifa District Committee and, in a speech from the floor, announced that he regarded even the new theses as too moderate. He complained about MAKI's "insufficient consistency in opposing the policy of conquest of Israel's rulers. This error made it difficult for our party to struggle against the reactionary propaganda that these conquests were legal and just."[110] He then requested that the party remind the Israeli public that the Arab states were prepared to recognize Israel if it accepted the 1947 partition borders, a positive development that advanced the resolution of the Arab-Israeli conflict.

Some Jewish party members were dissatisfied with the new theses as well. Munya Gisis, of the Haifa District Committee, expressed his fear that the phrase "up to secession" might "encourage isolationist currents among the Arabs of Israel."[111] The juxtaposition of Tuma's and Gisis's remarks in MAKI's official record of the congress thus discreetly exposed the gap between "Jewish national" and "Arab national" positions in the party in the wake of the 1956 war.

As a result of MAKI's rather militant formulation of the Palestinian Arab right to self-determination, Jewish party members suffered intense pressures from their community. In the Hebrew press, MAKI was repeatedly excoriated for advocating the secession of the Arab citizens of Israel, even though the party had carefully defined this as a right, not an obligation. *Al hamishmar*'s report of the congress critically noted that Arab party leaders and members did not sing the Israeli national anthem, "Hatikvah," during the opening ceremony and that speakers referred to the "Gulf of ʿAqabah" rather than the "Gulf of Eilat." Ahdut Haʿavodah's *Lamerhav* (To the region) similarly reported that in delivering the political report of the Central Committee, Mikunis referred to "the war of 1948" and not "the War of Liberation."[112] In the postwar atmosphere, it was impossible to point out the absurdity of an Arab singing a national anthem that opens with the line, "As long as within a heart there yearns a Jewish soul." And the fact that for Israel's Palestinian Arab citizens the 1948–49 war was a national catastrophe, not a war of liberation, had no status in public discourse.

MAKI's isolation from the Jewish public, together with the strengthening of the alliance between the radical nationalist Arab states and the Soviet Union, translated into increased attention to the question of Palestinian Arab rights in Israel. In September 1957, after deliberations in its leading bodies, the party held a national conference to discuss intensifying its struggle against national oppression of the Arab population of Israel.[113] Shortly after this conference, MAKI initiated the formation of Kafr Qasim committees to mark the anniversary of the massacre. An

Arab general strike was called for October 29, 1957, and many memorial meetings were held. *Al-ittihad* published a special issue on October 28 dedicated almost entirely to Kafr Qasim and other aspects of Israel's national oppression of its Arab citizens. When the military government tried to prohibit commemorations in Arab villages, Arab sentiments were still further inflamed.

On October 26, 1957, Tawfiq Tubi and several other Arab MAKI members approached Kafr Qasim, where they were to participate in a memorial meeting, in a taxi. Although the riders held valid travel permits, civilian and military police prevented the vehicle from entering the village. As a member of the Knesset, Tubi had parliamentary immunity, and the police had no right to stop him without a determination that his presence posed a "security danger." While the police were inspecting the other passengers' permits, Tubi tried to run past the barricade and enter the village. He fell to the ground in a scuffle with the police just as a truck full of workers approached the barricade; it, too, was denied entrance. The workers were outraged and got out of the truck to confront the police. Tubi tried to calm them and reportedly said, "Don't be alarmed. In a little while we will destroy this state." *Ha'aretz* seized on this comment, uttered in a heated moment, as "proof" that MAKI's Arab leaders were hostile to the existence of the state of Israel. At the same time, *Ha'aretz* expressed no concern for the violation of Tubi's parliamentary immunity, an example of the growing gap in what was regarded as normal and reasonable by Jews on the one side and Arabs on the other.[114]

The General Security Services (SHABAK) attempted to use MAKI's growing isolation in the Jewish community and the discomfort this aroused among some of the party's Jewish members to exacerbate relations between Jewish and Arab party members. On February 6, 1958, the SHABAK met with the editors of all the newspapers except *Kol ha'am* and *Al-ittihad* and informed them that in January Arab leaders of MAKI had met in the home of Emile Habibi in Nazareth to discuss whether the Arabs of MAKI should secede and form a separate party. The papers broke the story the next day and, with the exception of Uri Avnery's *Ha'olam hazeh,* which denounced the information as fraudulent, universally condemned MAKI for its disloyalty. The *Jerusalem Post*'s exaggerated and unselfconscious comment was typical: "In calling on Israel's Arabs to fight colonialism and imperialism, Mr. Habibi is in fact preaching rebellion on the Algerian model."[115] *Al hamishmar*'s unsigned articles and editorials contained the sharpest attacks on

MAKI, while its Arab affairs correspondent, Amnon Kapeliuk, offered the most detailed account of the political differences between Arab and Jewish members of the party. According to Kapeliuk, Emile Habibi and Saliba Khamis led the Arab nationalist faction in MAKI.[116] His analysis combined correct information about tensions within MAKI with gossip about the religious background of Arab party leaders, personal rivalries, the Jewish wives of Khamis and Tuma, and insulting explanations of Tubi's opposition to a separate Arab party because of his lack of daring. By accusing MAKI's Jewish leaders of responsibility for this affair because of the party's advocacy of "self-determination up to separation," Kapeliuk implied that the Jews in the party were responsible for disciplining their Arab comrades (as was the custom in MAPAM).

Neither SHABAK nor any newspaper provided hard evidence that the alleged meeting actually occurred. Some reports stated that the meeting was taped, but no tape was ever produced. Jewish ex-party members have repeated the story both in their memoirs and orally, but these accounts are no more solid than the stories that appeared in the press.[117] Nonetheless, Israeli scholars have unquestioningly accepted the account of Jews who subsequently became political opponents of the Arabs involved in this incident.[118]

MAKI's Central Committee denounced the entire affair as a police provocation; *Kol haʿam,* for its part, defended the theses of the Thirteenth Party Congress.[119] According to Emile Habibi, the incident resulted from an informal meeting of Arab party members in his house at which political topics were discussed, including the fact that young Palestinians in Cairo were thinking of establishing an armed movement. There was some excessive drinking, and at one point Habibi and Hanna Naqqara picked up the telephone, which they assumed was tapped, and shouted curses against the Jewish state into the receiver.[120] Habibi's version of the incident reflects badly on the discipline and moral stature of the Arab party leaders and for that reason may be at least partly true. It also reveals the frustration and outrage that politically aware Palestinians in Israel must have felt: when the rest of the Arab world, including Palestinians outside Israel, appeared to be uniting and marching toward liberation, they were isolated, left behind in a Jewish state where any expression of Palestinian national sentiment was regarded as illegitimate. Habibi later expressed this outrage in a brilliant tragicomic novel, *The Secret Life of Saeed, the Ill-fated Pessoptimist: A Palestinian Who Became a Citizen of Israel,* which many regard as one of the finest works of Arabic fiction in the post-1967 period.

The wave of Nasserist pan-Arab nationalism that swept the Arab world after the Suez/Sinai War crested with the formation of the UAR in February 1958. To many contemporary observers, pan-Arab unity seemed destined to drive out the vestiges of imperialist influence in the Middle East. The apparent strength of pan-Arabism emboldened the Arab leaders of MAKI to speak out more militantly than they ever had before. Jewish communists, too, although they employed a different rhetorical style, adjusted their evaluation of the regional and local situation in light of this nationalist upsurge.[121] While the result was hardly a journalistic call to insurgency, as Greilsammer contended, that was how the Jewish community, including MAPAM, perceived MAKI's new militancy and pro-UAR sympathies.[122]

The anti-imperialist Arab nationalist sentiment that brought the UAR into existence now seemed to be the rising political force in the Middle East, and the Arab members of MAKI no longer felt isolated and intimidated. Thus, after the storm over the alleged meeting of Arab party leaders had passed, Habibi, speaking in the village of ʿArrabah, took the offensive against "those who oppress the Arab people, stole their lands, occupied their lands, and deny their right to self-determination." He also took the occasion to hail the formation of the UAR.[123] *Al hamishmar*, reflecting the terror Abdel Nasser inspired in the Jewish community, editorially attacked this speech as signaling a resurgence of mufti-like incitements against the Jews (a reference to al-Hajj Amin al-Husayni) and linked its condemnation of Habibi with condemnation of Abdel Nasser.[124]

Fu'ad Khuri was even bolder than Habibi. When the government tried to get the Nazareth city council to sponsor a celebration for Israel's tenth anniversary, he warned the council members not to commit "treason." After recalling the various ways in which Israel's Arab citizens were oppressed, he concluded:

> The Arab people of Israel have the right to full equality with all the Jewish citizens because they are living in their own country. The Arab people have the right to self-determination and the right to unite with the rest of the Arab peoples. The Arab people in Israel respect the right of the Israeli people to independence and therefore will never concede their own right to self-determination. The Arab people have the right [to demand] that the rulers of this country respect their national rights and national existence and patriotic dignity.[125]

Khuri's suggestion that Israel's Arab citizens had the right to join the UAR exceeded even the formulation of MAKI's Thirteenth Congress. A more frightening prospect for the majority of Israeli Jews could not have been imagined.

The growing tensions between MAKI and the state burst into a violent confrontation during the 1958 May Day celebration in Nazareth.[126] When MAPAM and MAPAI rejected the MAKI-initiated May Day committee's offer to hold a joint demonstration, it decided to hold its own.[127] After initially approving the plan, the military governor rejected MAKI's request for a permit to conduct a march in the morning, the traditional time for this event. The local party leaders then decided to demonstrate without a permit.[128] In the days before the demonstration, dozens of Arabs were placed under preventive detention by the military government. Emile Habibi and Saliba Khamis were arrested in MAKI's Nazareth office on April 30. On May Day itself, the army and police prevented hundreds of people from outlying villages from entering Nazareth and attacked MAKI's demonstration. Tawfiq Tubi was arrested while speaking to a crowd and taken off to Haifa, even though he had a license to enter Nazareth. Mikunis was lifted onto the demonstrators' shoulders, where he continued to speak. Police arrested 129 Arabs in Nazareth that day, with 16 sent to internal exile in Safed. Altogether, over 300 Arabs were arrested before and after May Day.

The violence in Nazareth prompted intensified criticism of the military government among many Jewish political forces outside the communist party.[129] In response to the May Day clash and arrests, MAKI formed a Public Committee to Free the Prisoners of the Military Government, which attracted the support of such prominent noncommunist Arab nationalist figures as the mayor of Kafr Yasif, Yani Yani (three members of Kafr Yasif's local council were arrested in the Nazareth demonstration); the mayor of Shafa 'Amr, Jabbur Jabbur; and the lawyer Ilyas Kusa. By the end of May the committee expanded into a Public Action Committee to Abolish the Military Government and to Free the Prisoners of the Military Government.[130]

This committee was the organizational precursor of the Arab Front, subsequently renamed the Popular Front, which came into being on July 6, 1958. Until early 1959 the Popular Front functioned as an alliance between Arab members of MAKI and noncommunist nationalists. Its program called for (1) returning "absent-present" Arabs to their villages, (2) stopping the theft of lands and returning confiscated lands, (3) abolishing the military government and all forms of national oppression, (4) guaranteeing equality and ending discrimination, (5) establishing Arabic as an official language in all government offices, and

(6) returning the refugees.[131] Despite continual harassment by the government, the Popular Front established local committees in many towns and villages, and together MAKI and the Front became the leading political forces in the Arab community.[132] Ultimately, however, internal dissension as a result of the breakup of the Nasserist-communist alliance—not repression by the Israeli government—destroyed the Popular Front and severely damaged MAKI's standing in the Arab community for several years.

CHAPTER VII

The Triumph of Nationalism: 1959–1965

The emergence of Nasserist pan-Arab nationalism as the leading anti-imperialist force in the Middle East redrew the political and strategic map of the region, just as the creation of the state of Israel had done nearly a decade earlier. Abdel Nasser's personal charisma and political daring captured the enthusiasm of the Arab masses, perhaps even more so in Lebanon, Syria, and Jordan than in Egypt itself. Egypt's transformation of military defeat into political victory in 1956, the formation of the UAR in 1958, and the military coup that overthrew the notoriously pro-Western Hashemite monarchy of Iraq on July 14, 1958, convinced even its most determined opponents that pan-Arab unity was the wave of the future. Not until 1967 did the internal contradictions of the pan-Arab movement and the misperceptions it promoted about the Arab-Israeli conflict transform its early successes into massive defeat.

Although the Israeli and Egyptian communists soon abandoned their early illusions about Israel's anti-imperialist potential, they remained able, as long as all the Arab states maintained their status as socially backward autocracies linked to the West, to preserve the stand toward the Palestinian/Arab–Israeli conflict they had adopted in 1947–48. From 1956 on, however, Abdel Nasser's presence set the political agenda of the Arab world and to a great extent of Israel as well. The Marxists were forced to reposition themselves and recognize his regional stature, even when they were critical of it.

BREAKUP OF THE NASSERIST-COMMUNIST ALLIANCE

In Egypt, CPE unity was destroyed by internal differences over the party's relationship to the Nasserist regime.[1] Because persisting political disagreements had not been resolved before the three organizations had fused, it was not long before differences between former members of the DMNL and their comrades in the united party emerged and rekindled the historic distrust of the "Curielists." As is often the case, the first clashes were over organizational questions: Kamal 'Abd al-Halim's withdrawal from the Permanent Committee shortly after the CPE's formation (he was replaced by Mahmud Amin al-'Alim) and the reduction in the number of paid party functionaries (who were disproportionately former DMNLers). The core of the political differences lay in the extent to which the Nasserist regime should be supported: the erstwhile DMNL members advocated complete and uncritical support; the other components of the party, although they did support Abdel Nasser and the establishment of the UAR, reserved the right to criticize its internal regime and to express their solidarity with the Arab communist parties. There was unease in the party ranks about the dissolution of the Communist Party of Syria and the continuing lack of democracy in the UAR, especially the government's ruling that only members of the National Union could run for office in trade union elections, a decision that effectively eliminated the communists from an arena in which they had a special interest.

Following the Iraqi military coup in July 1958, the former members of al-Raya and the WPCP began to look toward that country, where the Communist Party of Iraq was now a major component of the antimonarchist coalition led by 'Abd al-Karim Qasim, as a more desirable model for a national anti-imperialist front than the UAR, where the communists were permitted only limited freedom of action at Abdel Nasser's sufferance. Some CPE members appeared at demonstrations greeting the overthrow of the Iraqi monarchy and other mass meetings chanting, "Like Qasim, oh Gamal" and "Front, front, like Iraq"—calls for Abdel Nasser to cooperate more fully with the communists. Many former DMNL members, however, considered these slogans provocative attacks on national unity and continued to advocate unreserved support for Abdel Nasser and the UAR.

The Communist Party of Iraq was against Iraq joining the UAR because the party would then be declared illegal, as the Communist Party of Syria had been. Qasim agreed with the communists for his own reasons, and this became a point of friction between Qasim and Abdel Nasser, who feared that the new Iraqi regime would threaten his leadership of the pan-Arab movement, especially as the communist-nationalist alliance in Iraq was regarded with greater favor by the Soviet Union. Days after the Iraqi coup, all four former DMNLers in the CPE Political Bureau—Kamal 'Abd al-Halim, Shuhdi 'Atiyya al-Shafi'i, Ahmad al-Rifa'i, and Fu'ad Habashi, the leaders of the most pro-Nasser tendency in the party—were expelled from the CPE. Party members from both factions later agreed that the leadership of the Communist Party of Iraq encouraged these expulsions to insure the Egyptian communists' wholehearted support for their opposition to Iraq's entering the UAR.[2] Most of the DMNLers (but not their partners in the former UECP), amounting to about one-third of the CPE, rallied around their expelled leaders and, toward the end of 1958, formed the CPE-DMNL, essentially a reconstitution of the historic DMNL.

The CPE continued to support Qasim as the conflict between him and Abdel Nasser intensified. Still, the party was willing to cooperate with the National Union, which it regarded not as a national front but as the party of the national bourgeoisie, if a programmatic agreement could be reached. Mahmud Amin al-'Alim was delegated by the Political Bureau of the CPE to propose such an alliance to the National Union's general secretary, Anwar al-Sadat, when they met in September 1958. The CPE, however, refused to consider al-Sadat's proposal that the party dissolve and direct its members to enter the National Union as individuals.[3] In a comprehensive criticism of the CPE's "left opportunism" on this occasion, the four expelled DMNL members rejected the Political Bureau's characterization of the National Union; instead they described the Union as a broad alliance of forces whose leadership included some communists and that was "open to workers and peasants ... as citizens"—which suggested that the four were willing to accept al-Sadat's proposal.[4]

Abdel Nasser apparently did not understand the significance of the split in the CPE and, based on the CPE Political Bureau's refusal to authorize party members to join the National Union unconditionally, as well as on criticisms of his regime published by the Communist Party of Syria, decided that he had no choice but to liquidate all the Egyptian communists. After several arrests in the fall, the Nasserist-communist alliance was shattered on December 31, 1958, when hundreds of communists were seized in the middle of the night. On March 13, 1959, Khalid Muhyi al-Din and twelve other editors were removed from their positions at *Al-masa'* because they refused to support a rebellion against the Qasim regime led by Nasserist officers. By the end of the year, two to three thousand left-wing opponents of the regime were jailed, including one to two thousand members of both the CPE and the CPE-DMNL.

From 1959 to 1964 the main arena for communist political action in Egypt was inside the walls of the prisons and detention camps, where almost every known communist and many other leftist opponents of the government were incarcerated. The prisoners were humiliated, tortured, and pressured to repudiate their political credo. While a few did recant, most resisted and sustained themselves through political, cultural, and social activities: oral magazines, dramatic performances, a farm to grow vegetables and improve the quality of the food. Newspapers and radios were smuggled in, and political discussions were conducted on domestic and international issues. The prisoners constantly struggled to defend their health and human dignity through hunger strikes and other protests. Several died from beatings by prison guards, denial of medical attention, or other mistreatment. The best known of those murdered in jail was Shuhdi 'Atiyya al-Shafi'i, who was beaten to death in Abu Za'bal prison camp on June 15, 1960.[5] The international scandal thus aroused terminated the worst of the tortures; this easing of abuses permitted some of the communists to begin considering a reconciliation with the regime, which ultimately led to the dissolution of the two parties in 1965.

In Israel, the Popular Front was the local expression of the pan-Arab Nasserist-communist alliance. Consequently, the government saw the Front as a serious threat. When that alliance began to unravel in Egypt the reverberations were also felt in Israel. In early 1959, the Popular Front split between pro-Nasser Arab nationalist elements and those who remained loyal to MAKI. The Arab nationalists went on to establish the al-Ard (The Land) movement,[6] while Front members who were still willing to cooperate with MAKI continued their activity, though on a much diminished scale.

The breakup of the Nasserist-communist alliance brought an end to MAKI's Arab period. The party still considered the Arab nationalist movement to be the leading anti-imperialist force in the Middle East, but after early 1959 criticism of this movement became increasingly acceptable. Nonetheless, Israel's continuing alliance with France and West Germany, the military threat this posed to the radical nationalist Arab regimes, the continuing oppression and expropriation of the Palestinian Arab citizens of Israel, and the way these issues were represented in the hegemonic Zionist discourse following the post-1956 celebration of Israel's military prowess prevented MAKI from simply returning to the Jewish problematic that had informed its activity from 1948 to 1955. In addition, although this was not yet apparent in 1959 because of the temporary loss of support in the Arab community, the Arab component of the party was growing significantly in number; moreover, by expanding its presence in the Muslim communities of the Triangle, MAKI was becoming ever more solidly identified as the tribune of the Palestinian Arab citizens of Israel, while its position in the Jewish community had stagnated or declined. These structural tensions ultimately resulted in the split in MAKI along largely national lines in 1965.

MAPAM responded to the rise of Nasserist pan-Arabism and the crisis in Nasserist-communist relations by intensifying its attempts to organize in the Arab community. But these efforts coincided with the party's rejection of Marxism-Leninism as its ideological foundation at its Third Congress in 1958 and its continued participation in the ruling coalition dominated by Ben-Gurion; as a result, MAPAM's appearance in this chapter is a postscript to rather than an integral part of the history of the Marxist political forces. MAPAM still used Marxist terminology even after 1958, but from 1956 on the party's practice diverged ever more sharply from its nominal positions and a wide and permanent gap opened between its Arab and Jewish members. Riftin and Peri remained in the party until 1969, when they led a very small group out of MAPAM in protest over the formation of the MAPAM–Labor Party Alignment. Except among their circle, for most party members by the late 1950s Marxism had become either an embarrassment or an object of nostalgia.

DISSOLUTION OF THE EGYPTIAN COMMUNIST PARTIES

If the documentary evidence for the history of Egyptian communism before 1959 is thin and scattered, after the mass arrest of the communist activists it is nearly nonexistent. This was precisely the government's intention: to erase all traces of Marxism from the political map of Egypt. The principal sources of information on the period of internment are several volumes of prison memoirs published during the relaxation of political censorship that accompanied Anwar al-Sadat's de-Nasserization campaign following the October 1973 war.[7] These memoirs are marked by the enduring political commitments and imperfect memories of their ex-communist authors. Despite their bitter experiences in prison, these writers all defended the fundamental thrust of the Nasserist regime, as opposed to al-Sadat's turn toward private enterprise, a pro-American international orientation, and a separate peace with Israel, and they defended the communist movement in terms of its nationalist stand.

Although the prison memoirs are full of details about the hardships and daily routine of prison life and the intellectual and political issues that occupied the prisoners, they are conspicuously silent about the Arab-Israeli conflict. Apparently this was no longer an issue that inspired any significant disagreement either among the communists or between the communists and the government. The memoirs also observe a noticeably loud silence about the Jewish communist prisoners. By 1959 few Jews were left in Egypt, and only a handful of these were communists: Yusuf Darwish, Ahmad Sadiq Sa'd, Raymond Douek (all of the CPE), Albert Arie, Shihata Harun (of the CPE-DMNL), and a few others less well known. They were, of course, arrested with their comrades in 1959; but none of their names appear among the dozens mentioned in the published memoirs.

It was undoubtedly uncomfortable for former communists in the 1970s, attempting to defend the nationalist legitimacy of their political past and at the same time oppose the Egyptian government's effort to conclude a separate peace agreement with Israel, to remind their readers of their historic stand on the Arab-Israeli dispute and the Jewish contribution to the communist movement. By the late 1950s, moreover, the conflict with Israel was evidently not a major political issue for the communists: they were principally occupied with the establishment of the UAR and its breakup, the nationalization of Bank Misr and other major industrial and commercial enterprises, the adoption of Arab socialism as the new ideology of the regime, and the struggle against internal opponents of the government.

The CPE-DMNL gave full support to Abdel Nasser throughout the period of the communists' incarceration, despite the tortures and the murders. At first it characterized the UAR as a petty bourgeois nationalist regime; yet by late 1959, as a result of the institution of economic planning, nationalization of property of foreign nationals, and much talk of socialism by the government, party leaders adopted the view that a group of socialists led by Abdel Nasser held power in Egypt. As for the CPE, in late 1958 it adopted Fu'ad Mursi's view that the Nasserist regime represented the interests of the national bourgeoisie and should be supported on that basis. The following May, though, the CPE general secretary, Abu Sayf Yusuf—one of the few party leaders who escaped arrest—initiated a reassessment of the regime. Given the mass arrests and torture of the communists, the CPE now sought to build a national democratic front against the government, which, seen in this new light, seemed to serve the interests of the monopoly capitalist bourgeoisie.[8] By late 1962 or early 1963, however, the differences between the CPE and the CPE-DMNL diminished. The CPE returned to its pre–May 1959 stand, and both parties began to express a more favorable attitude toward the regime; its new party, the Arab Socialist Union; and the Charter of National Action. After many delays the last communists were released from prison in April 1964, just as Abdel Nasser was preparing to receive Nikita Khrushchev in Cairo.

Did the communists agree to dissolve their parties before their release from prison? One of the former inmates, Tahir 'Abd al-Hakim, argued yes, but when Ahmad Sadiq Sa'd asked him if he had any evidence he replied that he only inferred it from what happened afterward.[9] Another ex-prisoner, Fathi 'Abd al-Fattah, claimed that the CPE-DMNL actually dissolved itself in jail in late 1963.[10] Most former communists agree with Abu Sayf Yusuf, however, who asserted that although the communists were pressured to disband before being released from jail, they refused to do so.[11] Probably the communists discussed dissolving the parties in jail, and although they refused to take this action under duress, the leaders at least understood that they would likely do so after their release.

Western observers have argued that the dissolution of the Egyptian communist parties was a tactical maneuver dictated by the requirements of Soviet foreign policy.[12] By contrast, Abu Sayf Yusuf insisted that the decision was entirely an Egyptian initiative.[13] In the absence of documentary evidence there can be no decisive answer to this question. In any case, the movement of the Egyptian communists toward accommodation with Nasserism predated the decision to dissolve the parties by several years, and this was ultimately more significant than the specific organizational decision. Even before the unification of the CPE Fu'ad Mursi, in his September 1957 article "Marxism: The Living Theory" that theorized a highly Egyptian exceptionalist road to socialism, established the ideological justification for dissolving the communist parties (see Chapter 6). This is apparent only in retrospect, and Mursi certainly did not envision the end of the CPE before it was formed. Nonetheless, the CPE was ideologically disarmed by Mursi's version of Egyptian national communism. Had it not been for the imprisonment of the communists and the regime's gratuitous brutality toward them, the Egyptian parties might have voluntarily taken the path of the Algerian communists, who dissolved their party in 1963. The ideological continuity between Mursi's Egyptian exceptionalist road to socialism and the disbanding of the parties was apparent in a report of the CPE Central Committee issued in August 1964, only months after the communists' release from prison, which anticipated the CPE's dissolution.

This report mentioned Palestine and the Arab-Israeli conflict only in passing, expressing the party's approval of the "powerful assistance" the Egyptian regime was providing to the Palestinian people (probably a reference to Abdel Nasser's support for the establishment of the PLO). The report also stated that the Americans "have officially affirmed that they give Israel their support and protection, as it is a base of aggression and as it is their advance outpost."[14] These brief references suggest a continuity with ʿAbd al-Munʿim al-Ghazzali's positions of 1958: Israel was characterized simply as a base for American imperialism, not as a legitimate expression of the Israeli Jewish people's right to self-determination; moreover, no criticism was offered of the Egyptian government's approach to the Arab-Israeli conflict, though even in some parts of the Arab world the establishment of the PLO was regarded as an effort by the Arab states (especially Egypt) to contain and control the Palestinian national movement. (The oft-quoted proclamation of the PLO's first chairman, Ahmad al-Shuqayri, that the Arabs would "throw Israel into the sea" probably did more harm to the Palestinian cause than anything since al-Hajj Amin al-Husayni's collaboration with the Nazis.) This report is the only available documentary evidence on the Egyptian communists' view of the Arab-Israeli conflict from 1959 until the dissolution of the two communist parties in March and April 1965. The dissolution resolutions do not mention the conflict, and it was not a factor in the decision to disband.[15]

The August 1964 CPE Central Committee report and Mursi's 1957 article indicate that despite the still-continuing debate among former communists about the relative "rightism" or "ultraleftism" of the three tendencies, the ideological distance between Mursi (whose al-Raya tendency is most often characterized as leftist) and the majority of the DMNL (generally characterized as rightist) was not very great. Both had long regarded the struggle for national independence as the fundamental issue in Egyptian politics, and both adopted a pan-Arab outlook from about 1954 on. This reorientation was in part a reaction to the Egyptian nationalist intelligentsia's rejection of the communist stand on the Palestine question in the late 1940s and early 1950s and the prominent role of Jews in the communist movement during those years. Pan-Arab nationalism drew the communists away from their earlier stand on Palestine and limited the role of Jews in the communist movement. By removing the Jewish leadership, the parties opened the way for the rise of indigenous intellectual leaders like Fu'ad Mursi, Shuhdi ʿAtiyya al-Shafiʿi, Mahmud Amin al-ʿAlim, and ʿAbd al-ʿAzim Anis—the theorists of the new orientation.

NASSERISM, MAPAM, MAKI, AND THE PALESTINIAN ARAB CITIZENS OF ISRAEL

MAPAM's Third Congress convened in January 1958, on the eve of the proclamation of the UAR. The congress eliminated from the party lexicon the notion of "removing the barriers between MAPAM and the world of revolution" (the joint slogan of Sneh-Riftin-Peri in the early 1950s). The Soviet Union and the communist parties were no longer to be considered the center of the international socialist movement, and MAPAM declared that it would no longer be constrained by orthodox Marxism-Leninism:

> While maintaining our ideological independence based on Zionist pioneering realization and class struggle integrated with the construction of our country, and on Borochov's doctrine as the Marxist formulation of the solution for the national question of the Jewish people, MAPAM will devote itself to undogmatically adapting the fundamentals of Marxism and Leninism as the theoretical basis of revolutionary international socialism, to the conditions of our people and country.[16]

This terminology had enough Marxist flavor to placate party traditionalists, but the "undogmatic adaptation" of the "fundamentals of Marxism and Leninism" rapidly became a justification for abandoning all but a formalistic Marxism, especially as the party had already made a historic shift from opposition to government by joining the cabinet several years earlier.

The ideological eclecticism (some might say opportunism) unleashed by the resolutions of MAPAM's Third Congress was nowhere more apparent than in the Arab community, where the clash between communism and Nasserist pan-Arabism gave the party an opportunity to enhance its strength. Fifty Arab delegates attended the congress, representing some fifteen hundred party members.[17] This was four to five times the number of Arab members of MAKI, although of course there was no comparison between the level of ideological commitment and organizational discipline or the relative importance of the Arab members in the two parties.

At the congress, Arab delegates and Jewish members of the Arab Affairs Department spoke about the return of the Palestinian refugees, Palestinian self-determination, the military government, and related grievances. Their positions on these issues were more radical than those of most Jewish party members.[18] Indeed, Ya'ari and Hazan avoided these questions altogether, preferring to focus on the ideological reorientation of the party. In a speech addressed "to our Arab comrades," Hazan admitted that Arab-Israeli issues were not MAPAM's primary concern. He disagreed with statements by leading Arab party members Rustum Bastuni and Jamil Shihada, and he directly opposed returning all the Arab refugees, speaking instead of the possible return of "tens of thousands."[19]

MAPAM's Arab Affairs Department was reorganized after the congress under new leadership (seven Jews and seven Arabs) and began to issue a new information bulletin.[20] Simha Flapan, a secondary leader of the MAPAM left in the early 1950s who founded the English monthly *New Outlook* in 1957, joined the department secretariat, becoming its director after the 1959 Knesset elections. Arabs and Jews with a radical outlook tended to become compartmentalized in this marginal party institution.

The formation of the UAR led to a debate in MAPAM over Nasserist pan-Arab nationalism. Ya'ari, summarizing a discussion in MAPAM's Political Committee, set the guidelines for party deliberation of the question by describing the UAR as an anti–working class military dictatorship and an enemy of Israel. He explicitly criticized Flapan's recent proposal for a federal union between Israel and Jordan.[21] MAPAM's Arab members and Jews close to *New Outlook* had a more positive initial assessment, emphasizing the anti-imperialist and socially progressive potential of the UAR and other steps toward Arab unity. MAPAM was the main organizational force behind *New Outlook;* nevertheless, since it was not officially a party journal and its editorial board included political independents and supporters of other parties, the magazine could express more radical positions on Arab-Israeli affairs than were approved by MAPAM's leading bodies. Thus, inspired by the formation of the UAR, *New Outlook* published articles discussing how Israel might integrate into the Middle East by joining a regional federation based on an economic union.[22]

The articles in *New Outlook* also revealed a widening gap between MAPAM's Arab and Jewish members, even Jews regarded as leftists, on Arab-Israeli issues. Bastuni, consistent with his views of the early 1950s, advocated resolving the conflict on terms similar to those advocated by MAKI: recognizing the right of the Palestinian and Jewish people to self-determination; a territorial compromise between the partition borders and the status quo; the right of the Palestinian refugees to chose between return and compensation. Another Arab member of MAPAM, Na'im Makhul, although he was more pessimistic about the immediate possibilities for resolution than Bastuni and did not explicitly address the border question, held essentially the same position regarding self-determination and the refugees.[23]

Simha Flapan and Eli'ezer Be'eri responded to their Arab comrades' articles.[24] Both rejected any alteration of Israel's boundaries; both opposed the creation of a Palestinian state and regarded Jordan as the repository of Palestinian self-determination; both rejected the principle that the Palestinian refugees had a right to choose between return and compensation. The difference between the views of these two leading members of MAPAM's Arab Affairs Department—which corresponded to the difference between the (Jewish) "right" and "left" in MAPAM—was that Be'eri opposed repatriating any substantial number of refugees and went on to criticize Makhul for attributing too much Israeli responsibility for the refugee problem and for his "pessimistic" description of the situation of Israel's Arab citizens. For Be'eri, borders and a Palestinian state were not topics for discussion; his article therefore contained no reference to these points raised by his Arab comrades. In contrast, Flapan, although he opposed the idea of a Palestinian state, was willing at least to argue with Bastuni about it (but not about borders). He looked forward to an economic union with Jordan and favored allowing some, but not all, of the refugees to return if they wished. He later suggested that five to ten thousand refugees a year could be admitted before a comprehensive peace settlement was reached, as an Israeli gesture of goodwill.[25] The refugee question assumed particular prominence in these exchanges because the UN General Assembly discussed the matter in its autumn 1958 session; Jews were generally apprehensive that Israel's refusal to repatriate the refugees would be censored, as indeed it was.[26]

By 1959 MAPAM's central bodies were regularly criticizing Nasserist pan-Arab nationalism, but in the Arab community MAPAM continued to support Abdel Nasser and the UAR, hoping to benefit from the widespread disaffection from MAKI due to the split between Abdel Nasser and the communists. *Al-mirsad* and MAPAM's new Arabic monthly, *Al-fajr* (The dawn), both published pro-Nasserist articles, and *Al-fajr* reprinted the work of popular Egyptian authors identified with the regime, including Ahmad Baha' al-Din, Ihsan 'Abd al-Quddus, and Kamil Zuhayri; *Al hamishmar*, though, took the opposite course, criticizing Abdel Nasser and supporting Qasim. MAPAM's Arab Book Company, established in September 1958, reprinted books previously unavailable to Israel's Arab citizens; the works of Egyptian authors, including prominent supporters of the Nasserist regime, were the mainstay of the company, until it was closed down by pressure from Eli'ezer Be'eri. Bulus Farah, Rashid Hussein, and Fouzi El-Asmar wrote frequently in *New Outlook* and in MAPAM's Arab press. Hussein served as literary editor of *Al-fajr*, and El-Asmar was employed by the Arab Book Company, which published Farah's social history of the Arab world.[27] In many respects these intellectuals' views on Arab-Israeli issues were similar to those MAPAM had long excoriated MAKI for. MAPAM even flirted briefly with al-Ard before Flapan realized that the group would not restrict itself to the limits of Zionist political discourse.[28]

While MAPAM championed Nasserism in the Arab community, MAKI and its Arab leaders enthusiastically welcomed the Iraqi revolution, regarding it as the "beginning of the end" of the era of imperialist domination of the Middle East, the "dawn of comprehensive Arab unity," and further proof that the victory of Arab nationalism was imminent.[29] When relations between Qasim and Abdel Nasser reached a crisis level, the overwhelming majority of Arab MAKI members loyally criticized Abdel Nasser, despite the immediate loss of public support this entailed in the Arab community, especially in Nazareth.[30] *Al-ittihad* published a poem by Tawfiq Zayyad, then a Nazareth city councillor, criticizing the rebellion of Nasserist officers in Mosul against the Iraqi regime. Although Zayyad was slapped in the face in the streets of Nazareth while selling this issue of the party paper, he did not alter his stand.[31] The immediate and dramatic drop of support for MAKI in the Arab community is apparent from the sales figures of *Al-ittihad* in Nazareth and surrounding villages, MAKI's stronghold in the Arab community, before and after the Mosul rebellion (Table 4).

TABLE 4 SALES OF *AL-ITTIHAD*

District/Branch	Dec. 1958		Feb. 1959		Mar. 1959	
	Tues.	Fri.	Tues.	Fri.	Tues.	Fri.
Tayyiba	150	158	120	131	—	—
Umm al-Fahm	0	16	—	—	—	—
Baqa al-Gharbiyya	20	40	20	40	20	40
Haifa (city)	255	315	239	307	226	297
Acre	99	112	—	—	—	—
al-Tira	6	7	6	7	6	7
Nazareth (city)	446	662	446	662	377	559
Nazareth (district)	577	806	577	806	535	753

SOURCE: "Al-wad' bayna al-jamahir," an undated (but probably April 1959) and unsigned political report that gives a frank assessment of the party's losses following the Nasserist-communist split. KM 35 Pe'ilut bemigzar ha'aravi.

NOTE: The figures for the localities except Nazareth and Haifa are inconclusive because of incomplete reporting (and those for Baqa al-Gharbiyya and al-Tira suggest that those responsible for distributing *Al-ittihad* simply paid for the papers out of their own pockets).

The license to dissent from Nasserism also permitted significant differences to appear between the political lines of the Arab and Jewish sections of MAKI, because most Arab members criticized only reluctantly (as the Egyptian communists did), while many Jews did so with enthusiasm and a sigh of relief. To mark Israel's tenth anniversary, MAKI planned to publish a comprehensive account of the conditions of the Palestinian Arab population. Saliba Khamis submitted a draft in English entitled "The Truth About the Arabs in Israel: On the Tenth Anniversary of the State of Israel." Its characterization of the areas beyond the UN partition plan boundaries annexed by Israel as "occupied territory," along with other militant expressions of Palestinian national sentiment, may explain why it was not published. Instead Vilner, as editor of the party theoretical journal, *Zu haderekh* (This is the way), asked Tubi to prepare an article entitled "Ten Years of National Oppression," which was scheduled to appear in 1959. Khamis's draft was attached to Vilner's request, and his passages on the 1948–49 war as well as those insisting on the right of all the Palestinian refugees to return and the right of the Palestinian Arabs to establish an independent state were editorially marked for deletion by a fluent Hebrew speaker.

The article requested from Tubi was never published, and it is uncertain if he ever wrote it.[32]

Since at least January 1958 MAKI had forthrightly denounced the increasingly common tendency in radical Arab nationalist discourse to characterize Israel as an "imperialist base." That month the Conference of Asian and African Peoples convened in Cairo; although the Central Committee regarded the meeting as a generally positive event, it sharply criticized one of its resolutions on the Arab-Israeli conflict:

> Very severe is the resolution which determines that Israel is serving as an imperialist base endangering the security and progress of the Middle East and comprising a danger to the peace of the world. The deep and fundamental reason for this formulation can be found first and foremost in the anti-national pro-imperialist policies of the Ben-Gurion government which has placed the state of Israel at the service of the imperialists and their aggressive plans against the struggle for national liberation of the Arab peoples, in the policy of cruel national oppression of the Arab population [of Israel], in the policy of complete disregard for the just national rights of the Palestinian Arab people.
>
> This policy, fraught with danger, has isolated the state of Israel from the peoples of Asia and Africa in general and the Arab peoples in particular, especially since the war of aggression against Egypt in alliance with British and French colonialism.[33]

Jewish opinion perceived the difference between an "imperialist base" and a state "at the service of the imperialists" as inconsequential and regarded either formulation as motivated solely by a sinister desire to destroy Israel. But for those trained in Marxist theory, this nuance signified the difference between declaring that Israel was or was not a legitimate state, and MAKI never wavered from the stand that it was. As Sneh wrote in *Kol ha'am*, "Israel's right to exist, like that of any other state, is not dependent on its policies or its rulers."[34]

The importance of such minor formulaic subtleties was highlighted by an August 1959 leaflet of the Communist Party of Syria criticizing the anticommunist repression in the UAR. As reported in Hebrew in *Kol ha'am*, the Syrian communists explained that "the only way out of the serious situation and to remove the oppression of the masses is to correct the policies of the Republic in the Arab and international arenas and to turn once again toward a policy of correct Arab solidarity against imperialism and its agents." The Arabic version of the leaflet (probably true to the original) quoted in *Al-ittihad*, however, called for "Arab solidarity against imperialism and its prop Israel."[35] Thus, the editors of *Al-ittihad* accepted a formulation that came close to contradicting the stand of the MAKI Central Committee, whereas *Kol ha'am* "corrected" the sister party's leaflet to avoid a phrase that might sting the ears of its Jewish readers.

DEFEAT OF THE LEFT IN THE 1959 KNESSET ELECTIONS

Elections to the Ninth Congress of the Histadrut were held in May 1959, followed by Knesset elections in November, and a campaignlike atmosphere prevailed for most of the year. Amnon Kapeliuk brought the discrepancy between the two versions of the Syrian leaflet to the attention of the Hebrew reading public in *Al hamishmar* as part of MAPAM's electoral assault on MAKI.[36] As has been noted, the gap between MAPAM's Arab and Jewish members was substantial by 1958, and the party made no effort to unify its stand; moreover, MAPAM had always avoided emphasizing the central component of its platform—Zionism—in the Arab community. But during this Knesset campaign MAKI, too, presented different faces to the Jewish and Arab public. Not only did the rift between Abdel Nasser and the communists pose a difficult problem for MAKI in the Arab community, but MAPAM was also challenging MAKI's status as the staunchest defender of Palestinian Arab rights by posing as the nationalist alternative.

For the Jewish community the main issues in the Knesset elections were the sale of Israeli arms to West Germany, which had brought about Ben-Gurion's early resignation on July 5, and the oppressive conditions in the Oriental Jewish community, now receiving serious public attention for the first time because of a riot in the Haifa slum district of Wadi Salib, which then spread to other parts of the country. Both MAPAM and MAKI opposed the Israeli–West German arms deal and campaigned hard on the issue; this allowed them to cultivate a Jewish-patriotic, antifascist image that avoided the charges of being "soft on security," "pro-Arab," and linked to the unpopular policies of the Soviet Union. They also championed the cause of the Oriental Jews, though without much success beyond MAKI's preexisting support among Iraqi Jews. MAKI's most senior Iraqi-Jewish leader, Ya'akov Kujman, was given the tenth place on its Knesset list, the highest ever for an Oriental Jew, but in view of the party's dim electoral prospects this had no real impact.

These issues were minor concerns in the Arab community, where the election campaign became a proxy contest between Qasim and the communists on the one hand and Abdel Nasser on the other. MAPAM circulated a cartoon showing "Arab nationalism" embracing "Zionism" and both cooperating against communism.[37] *Al-fajr* and *New Outlook* published articles by Rashid Hussein so critical of Qasim and supportive of Abdel Nasser that one found its way into the Egyptian weekly *Akhir sa'a* (Latest hour).[38] *Al-fajr* continued to reprint articles by pro-Nasser Egyptians, and *Al-mirsad* opened its pages to non-MAPAM members who praised Arab nationalism.[39]

MAKI responded by viciously satirizing the contradiction between MAPAM's proclaimed policy of full equality for Arab citizens of Israel and its practice as a member of the ruling coalition.[40] For example, MAPAM opposed the military government and had campaigned hard against it, especially before joining the government in 1955; yet it refused to cooperate with MAKI in this effort, voting against MAKI's motions in the Knesset to abolish the military government in December 1955, February 1956, and July 1957. MAPAM's Arab MK, Yusuf Khamis, was the special object of MAKI's scornful humor, which portrayed him as a sycophant manipulated and controlled by the Jewish party leaders. MAKI also accused Khamis and MK Faris Hamdan, of a MAPAI-affiliated Arab list, of having known the details of Kafr Qasim but failing to expose them.

Whereas MAKI's Arabic propaganda during the early 1950s almost always included slogans like "Long live the friendship of the Jewish and Arab toilers" and calls for Arab-Israeli brotherhood and peace, its Arabic election literature in 1959 often omitted these slogans and instead emphasized the party's nationalist stand. The concluding passage from a leaflet issued by the MAKI Triangle District Committee (an all-Arab district) the day before the Knesset vote emphasized the party's appeal to purely Arab national sentiment:

> All the conscious nationalists from among the sons of our Arab people who cling to their national rights and who struggle for their land and to live freely in the land of their fathers and grandfathers have one path in this election campaign. That path is to repudiate the Zionist parties and their hirelings. It is to support the Communist Party, carrier of the banner of the steadfast and ultimately victorious struggle against the rapacious Ben-Gurion government and its aggressive aims.
>
> Brothers! Remember that increasing the strength of the communists means raising the voice of our oppressed people and the voice of the struggle for its rights.[41]

The elections were a devastating defeat for the entire left in the Jewish community, while in the Arab community MAPAM significantly increased its strength, mainly at MAKI's expense (Table 5). The combined

TABLE 5 FOURTH KNESSET ELECTION RESULTS
(NOVEMBER 3, 1959)

	Total Votes	%	Jewish Votes	%	Arab Votes	%	Jewish Vote as % of Total	Arab Vote as % of Total	Seats
MAPAI	370,585	38.2	364,735	40.1	5,850	7.5	98.4	1.6	47
MAPAI Arab lists	34,353	3.5	—	—	34,353	44.2	—	100.0	5
MAPAM	69,469	7.2	58,469	6.6	11,000	14.1	84.2	15.8	9
MAKI	27,374	2.8	18,212	2.2	9,162	11.8	66.5	33.5	3
Total valid votes for all parties	969,337	100	891,337	100	78,000	100	92.0	8.0	120

SOURCES: Israel, Halishkah hamerkazit lestatistikah, *Totzaʾot habehirot lakneset bahamishit*, Sidrat pirsumim meyuhadim, no. 166 (Jerusalem, 1962); Zeʾev Schiff, "Israel's Fourth Elections," *New Outlook* 6, no. 11 (Jan. 1964); Jacob M. Landau, *The Arabs in Israel: A Political Study* (London, 1969).

NOTE: MAKI received 8,097 votes and MAPAM 10,363 votes in all-Arab localities. The total Arab vote for these parties includes my estimate of the vote in mainly Arab polling places in the mixed cities.

strength of MAPAM, MAKI, and Ahdut Ha'avodah—twenty-five seats in the third Knesset—declined to nineteen seats in the fourth. MAPAI unexpectedly increased its strength from forty to forty-seven seats. Moreover, MAPAI's electoral campaign had been characterized by a significant shift to the right. Moshe Dayan and Shimon Peres, enthusiastic executors of Ben-Gurion's activist military policy and leading members of the technocratic, pragmatic young guard of the party who wanted to liberate MAPAI "from Marxist nostalgia," won Knesset seats for the first time;[42] Dayan entered the cabinet as minister of agriculture, and Peres became deputy minister of defense.

MAPAM retained its nine seats, mainly because its Arab vote had increased by 120 percent, from five thousand in 1955 to eleven thousand in 1959. Indeed, over 85 percent of MAPAM's total vote gain was due to increased support in the Arab community, without which the party would have lost a seat. MAKI, in contrast, lost 50 percent of its Knesset representation, which declined to three seats, with support for the party diminishing by roughly the same degree in both the Arab and the Jewish communities. In the Arab community MAKI won only 11.8 percent of the vote, dropping to third place behind MAPAI and MAPAM; nonetheless, very substantial gains in al-Tira and Qalansuwa, where the party had no branches, prepared the ground for future advances in the Muslim villages of the southern Triangle.[43]

At the meeting of the MAKI Central Committee convened to analyze this electoral debacle, the main topics of discussion were the party's line on the Arab-Israeli conflict and the extent of anti-Semitism in the Soviet-bloc countries. Mikunis argued that MAKI's line was correct and emphasized the objective reasons for the rightward drift of the electorate.[44] He and Ester Vilenska both claimed that MAKI's greatest stability was in the working-class vote, though this assessment was based on incorrectly equating urban and working-class voters. Moreover, Mikunis admitted that there were serious weaknesses in the party's workplace organizing and that MAKI had been late in addressing the questions posed by the Wadi Salib riots. In reality, MAKI's position in the Jewish working class was so tenuous that Avraham Hass thought the formation of a new cell of Jewish workers at the Friedman refrigerator plant in Jerusalem during the elections was notable enough to merit reporting to the Central Committee.

Yehoshu'a Irga noted that many Jewish workers who voted for MAKI did not accept the party's stand on Arab-Israeli issues:

> People don't care that there is a military government, that there was Kafr Qasim. *All the Zionist parties* dream of conquests, and it is acceptable. The

people are convinced that they beat the Arabs in two wars and they can continue to beat them. . . . If there was an "activist" competition in the elections, this is [because of] the atmosphere existing among the people.

Uzi Burstein, the secretary of BANKI, reported that a comrade in the BANKI secretariat, Ya'ir Tzaban, favored not telling the people everything MAKI believed about the Arab-Israeli issue and other "delicate" questions (probably a reference to the status of Jews in the Soviet bloc). Several Jewish members of the Central Committee—Ester Vilenska, Berl Balti, David Henin, Adolph Berman, and Fishel Hertzberg—criticized the party for excessive support for Abdel Nasser during 1958 and for advocating the right of the Palestinian Arabs to self-determination "up to separation." Sneh was deeply depressed by the election results. Nonetheless, he did not believe they were due to MAKI's identification with the policies of the Soviet Union, and he argued that the problems created by Stalin's cult of personality had already been overcome by new Soviet advances. Sneh thought that the underlying reason for the rightward drift in Israel was the influx of foreign capital and that MAKI's defeat came about chiefly because of "Jewish nationalism to extremist proportions."[45]

All the Arab members of the Central Committee whose remarks were recorded—Tawfiq Tubi, Zahi Karkabi, Saliba Khamis, and Fu'ad Khuri—declared full support for the line of the Thirteenth Party Congress on the Arab-Israeli conflict, with Khuri expressing in addition some pessimism about the revolutionary potential of the Jewish working class.

A definitive assessment regarding the differences of opinion expressed at this meeting is impossible because the minutes of adjacent Central Committee sessions are not available for comparison. Moreover, the opinions quoted above are based on Mikunis's personal notes, which do not reflect the full weight of his own leading role in the discussion. Nonetheless, several conclusions seem warranted. Clearly, differences of opinion occurred to some extent along national lines, motivated primarily by the exigencies of political work in the two national communities. Most Jewish party leaders had little grasp of the realities of the Arab community, or even of the Arab sections of the party. About 75 percent of MAKI members were Jews, and the central bodies of the party saw the Jewish community as their primary constituency. It was difficult enough to acclimatize new immigrants, who constituted a large percentage of the Jewish members, to Israeli Jewish society, let alone to Arab society. For Arab party leaders, conversely, their community was naturally the center of their political lives. Many were not fluent in Hebrew (Khuri and Khamis always reported to the Political Committee in English), and their knowledge of and sensitivity to conditions in the Jewish community were only marginally better than the Jews' knowledge of Arab conditions.

The political differences, which had existed historically in the Palestinian-Israeli communist movement, were naturally exacerbated by MAKI's electoral defeat. But the divisions among the Jewish communists in the postelection reassessment were drawn differently than they eventually would be in the split of 1965. Some of Sneh's followers who entered MAKI from the LSP (Berman, Hertzberg, and Tzaban, the last of whom did not attend the Central Committee meeting but was represented by Burstein's report of his position) united with a PCP veteran (Balti) and a future member of RAKAH (Henin) in drawing back from the political line of MAKI's Arab period. Sneh himself remained an unshakable tower of orthodoxy and pro-Soviet loyalism, perhaps even more so than Mikunis. Only the Arab members of the Central Committee rivaled Sneh in pro-Sovietism, as reflected in their lack of concern over the question of Soviet-bloc anti-Semitism: after loyally accepting the consequences of Soviet support for Qasim and the break with Abdel Nasser, they saw no purpose in criticizing the Soviet Union for its treatment of Jews. Vilenska and Hass, looking to their primary political responsibilities, were mainly concerned with improving the party's trade union and working-class organizing; hence, they were less critical of the party's line on the Arab-Israeli conflict than other Jewish leaders. This approach seemed to offer the best hope for the future; in addition, since the Histadrut had just decided to allow Arabs to become full members, it provided a basis on which Jews and Arabs could unite to overcome MAKI's defeat and isolation.

A NEW BEGINNING— OR THE BEGINNING OF THE END?

Between the 1959 and 1961 Knesset elections the political atmosphere in Israel appeared to change dramatically, raising MAKI's hopes not only for improving its own fortunes but also for breaking the grip of MAPAI hegemony and creating new possibilities for the workers' movement and the parties of the left. The new situation unfolded around a crisis in MAPAI during 1960–61 ignited by the accidental public exposure of some details concerning Israel's abortive sabotage campaign in Egypt in July 1954. Ben-Gurion insisted that Lavon, minister of defense at the time, assume full responsibility for the "security mishap" and refused to permit any attribution of responsibility to his political followers or IDF officers, who had actually ordered the sabotage without Lavon's knowledge. Ben-Gurion succeeded in having Lavon cast as the villain in what became known as the "Lavon affair," and forced MAPAI to oust Lavon as general secretary of the Histadrut. Many members of MAPAI recoiled from the old man's dictatorial tactics. Some rallied behind a movement to reform the party, which, though it initially appeared to have considerable potential, subsequently fell flat.

MAKI regarded this crisis, which toppled the government and necessitated the calling of an early election on August 15, 1961, as "the most powerful and deepest the Ben-Gurionist regime has known since the establishment of the state."[46] The party was optimistic that broad sections of the Israeli people would realize the contradiction that Ben-Gurion's policies posed to "the real national interests of Israel and the economic and social interests of the working people." Hoping to make the most of MAPAI's weakness, MAKI suggested to MAPAM and Ahdut Ha'avodah that the three parties form a "workers' front for the defense of democracy." The two Zionist parties, however, summarily rejected this proposal.[47]

MAKI also believed that the half-hour warning strike organized on January 23, 1961, by workers' action committees in Tel Aviv, Ramat Gan, and Haifa to protest the high cost of living and increased taxes, followed by workers' demonstrations in Tel Aviv, Haifa, Jerusalem, and Petah Tikva on March 15, marked a resurgence of class struggle after the ebb in trade union militancy since the 1956 war. The working-class upsurge was initiated by a new form of organization: action committees unsanctioned by the Histadrut. Such rank-and-file–initiated collective action seemed to indicate a radicalization of Jewish workers around economic issues.

The Arab community was less concerned with these questions than with the continuing efforts of the state to expropriate their lands. The consolidation of Jewish National Fund and state-owned lands under a unified Israel Lands Authority in 1960 effectively prohibited Arabs from owning, leasing, or being employed on 92 percent of all the land in the state of Israel. The same year, Minister of Agriculture Dayan proposed a Consolidation of Lands Law to the Knesset that would have allowed the state to declare "areas of concentration" (that is, areas of exclusively Jewish holdings) and seize Arab lands in exchange for other lands or monetary compensation.

In this matter, unlike the crisis within MAPAI and the workers' actions, MAKI was able to demonstrate political initiative and leadership by organizing a successful mass struggle against enactment of the law. Sneh spoke in the Knesset demanding that the item be struck from the agenda, thirteen Arab local councils passed resolutions opposing the law, and several protest meetings were held. The largest such meeting, on February 5, 1961, was attended by representatives from forty-three Arab towns and villages; it was convened in a cafe in Acre to denounce the law after official pressure first prevented the organizers from renting a hall in Haifa and then forced the owner of an Acre movie theater to cancel his rental agreement with them. On February 28, Hanna Naqqara and other participants in the Acre meeting presented their protest to the Knesset, and on the same day strikes and demonstrations were held in Tayyiba, Kafr Yasif, 'Ilabun, and al-Rama.[48] In response to the well-organized protest, the government abandoned the proposed legislation. This was the Palestinian Arab community's first legal victory in defense of its rights and a signal that it had learned the rules of the Israeli political system well enough to play the game and perhaps even succeed.

This campaign on rural land issues was followed by a conference of intellectuals in Haifa on March 19 (once again the authorities intervened to block the rental of the desired hall), which was attended by many noncommunists as well. The meeting called on the government to expand employment possibilities for educated Arabs, raise the level of education in the villages, and halt the campaign of intimidation against Arab teachers; it also extended the hand of solidarity to democratic Jewish elements.[49]

MAKI completed the circuit of its bases of support in the Arab community by calling a workers' conference in Haifa on April 22. Over three hundred workers from thirty villages attended and demanded that the Histadrut act speedily to insure complete equality for Arab workers regarding wages and working conditions, open medical clinics, and establish labor councils in Arab localities. Representatives of the Histadrut and the labor Zionist parties, though invited, did not attend the meeting; consequently, it was the most solidly communist in composition of the three meetings in the Arab community. Nevertheless, the conference delegates resolved to function within the Histadrut as the organization of the Israeli working class (Jews and Arabs alike) and issued a call for Jewish-Arab brotherhood.[50] Together, these meetings indicated that MAKI had broken its isolation in the Arab community and returned to a position of strength and respect.

The crisis in MAPAI, the upsurge in the workers' movement, and the flurry of activity in the Arab community gave MAKI a new sense of confidence as it approached its Fourteenth Congress, which convened shortly before the Knesset elections. In preparing for the congress, the party modified the traditional style of its precongress theses to make them simpler and "closer to the understanding of the masses." The formulations of the Thirteenth Congress theses, which had recognized the right of the Palestinian people, including the part living in Israel, to self-determination "up to separation," were therefore abandoned. This last phrase had created great obstacles for MAKI, since it openly challenged a fundamental component of the hegemonic Zionist discourse: that the 1949 armistice lines represented Israel's minimum borders. Mikunis argued that "the new formula" implied "no change of principle" but was simply an attempt "to bring the problem closer to the understanding of the broad public by simplifying the argumentation." [51] Hence, the theses emphasized general principles and were intentionally vague:

> The point of departure for our communist party on the solution of the problem of Israeli-Arab relations is the right of self-determination of nations. It is a fact that Eretz Israel in its historical development became the homeland of two nations: the Jewish and the Arab. It is necessary and possible to guarantee the legitimate national rights of both nations. . . .
>
> A Leninist approach, a democratic approach to solving the problem in question . . . requires *reciprocal* recognition of the legitimate national rights of both nations. Therefore we demand an Israeli policy that will recognize the legitimate rights of the Palestinian Arab people and its obligation to rectify the historic injustice that was caused to it by the negation of these rights. The people of Israel also need recognition of the state of Israel from the Arab states, including: recognition of the right to free navigation in the Suez Canal and the Red Sea straits, abolition of the Arab boycott, an agreed-upon resolution of the question of the waters of the rivers common to Israel and the neighboring countries, establishing normal relations with Israel. In order to attain this recognition from the Arab nations the Israeli side must recognize the right of the Arab refugees to return to Israel, insure proper compensation for those who will decide not to return, and show willingness to convert the temporary cease-fire lines, through mutual agreement, to permanent borders of peace. . . .
>
> Our communist party will encourage *any* peace agreement reached between Israel and the Arab countries that will take into consideration the legitimate national rights of nations.[52]

Despite Mikunis's insistence that this formulation represented historical continuity with the party's principles, it contained several new features. The programmatic content of the Palestinian right to self-determination was unspecified. No Palestinian state was mentioned, although the repeated insistence on the principle of self-determination of peoples did not exclude it. Israel's final borders were not specified. The language of the theses suggested that the armistice lines should become permanent but left open the possibility of their alteration through mutual agreement. The emphasis on reciprocal recognition between Israel and the Arab states was a theoretical innovation, and for the first time MAKI presented a detailed list of the components of Arab recognition of Israel.

Sneh, too, when asked by a journalist about the reason for the change, asserted that there was no difference in the meaning of the theses of the Thirteenth and Fourteenth Congresses, because "any self-determination, whether the words 'up to separation' are added or not, includes the possibility of separation." This exegetical device and Sneh's avoidance of the issue of whether the right of self-determination applied to any of Israel's Arab citizens (the main controversy generated by the Thirteenth Congress) may explain why MAKI had little difficulty uniting Arab and Jewish members around the new line. Sneh went on to explain, "Just as we oppose militaristic declarations and actions by Israel, we denounce all provocative declarations by Arab leaders that they will destroy Israel."[53] In principle, this juxtaposition was not an innovation, but the new tendency to "balance" criticism of Israeli policies with criticism of the policies of the Arab states, like the term "reciprocal recognition," reintroduced a symmetry into MAKI's analysis of the conflict that had been eliminated during the party's Arab period and that had proved unacceptable to Arab members of the party and to the other Arab communist parties after the 1956 war.[54]

Still, Emile Tuma's articles in *Al-ittihad* revealed no objections to the theses. Although he had been one of the most militant among those who had favored explicitly advocating the 1947 partition borders before and during the Thirteenth Congress, he now argued that what separated MAKI from the Zionist parties was that MAKI insisted the Palestine question still existed—a minimalist (but true) expression of the outstanding difference between the Zionist discourse and the party's stand on the Palestinian/Arab–Israeli conflict.[55] Tuma's abandonment of his former militant nationalist position was probably the reason for his election as a candidate member of the Central Committee at the congress. Fu'ad Khuri, who had argued for explicit endorsement of the partition boundaries before the Thirteenth Congress, now supported the vaguer new formulation of the party line.[56]

The intentionally ambiguous character of the new approach was underscored by Mikunis's summation of the Political Committee's discussion of the MAKI electoral program shortly after the congress: "We won't put the question of borders into the election program. We talk about the right of the refugees to return without going into arguments about numbers."[57] This statement indicates a conscious decision at the highest leadership levels to soften the presentation of the party's distinctive positions on the Arab-Israeli conflict in an effort to win support in the Jewish community. Although since shortly after the 1948–49 war MAKI's ideology prevented the party from appealing directly to Jewish nationalism, it now tried at least to avoid antagonizing Jewish national sentiment whenever possible.

This approach, however, was the mirror image of MAKI's propaganda line in the Arab community in the 1959 elections, when it defended itself by engaging in nationalist competition with MAPAM. And once this style was established as successful (by the relative standards of the overall electoral defeat of MAKI in 1959), it was difficult not to repeat it, especially since the breach between Abdel Nasser and the communists was not healed by 1961. Thus, MAKI's electoral campaign in the Arab community was marked by sharp attacks of MAPAM for remaining in the coalition and of the cabinet's decision of July 9, 1961, not to repatriate any Arab refugees.[58] MAPAM's official stand was that "a certain and agreed-upon number of refugees" should be permitted to return in the context of a peace settlement, and MAKI countered by emphasizing its commitment to give all the refugees a choice between return and compensation. As in 1959, MAKI attacked MAPAM for posing as a supporter of Arab nationalism in the Arab community, pointing out the differences between the political lines of *Al hamishmar* and *Al-mirsad,* which were perhaps even greater in 1961 than they had been in 1959.

The differential turn toward the two national communities during the election campaign caused disagreements in the Political Committee. Habibi criticized *Kol ha'am* for giving too much attention to the Eichmann trial, then in progress, and argued that the paper should place more emphasis on the election campaign. He also complained that the party's propaganda was too generous to MAPAM. Sneh replied by objecting to the propaganda line in the Arab community and stated unequivocally that the question of democracy (raised by the Lavon affair), not the refugee question, was the central election issue. The Political

Committee compromised by adopting resolutions criticizing both the party's Arab and Jewish propaganda organs. An Arabic election pamphlet was declared faulty for not emphasizing the reciprocal rights of the Palestinian and Jewish people, and *Kol ha'am* was instructed to strengthen its coverage of the election campaign.[59]

The political differences between the Jewish and Arab leaders that emerged during the election campaign were mitigated by the party's success. MAKI, with 4.2 percent of the votes, increased its Knesset representation from three seats to five; MAPAI and its associated Arab lists lost six seats; and MAPAM retained its nine seats (Table 6). MAKI's Political Committee was elated by the results. Mikunis was so encouraged that he proposed the party set itself the goal of doubling its membership by the next congress.[60] However, even in the Political Committee's analysis of the electoral results, differences between leading Jewish and Arab party members reappeared because of the nature of the success itself.

Traditionally, MAKI's vote had been two-thirds Jews and one-third Arabs, but in 1961 it was nearly evenly divided between Jews and Arabs, with the party receiving only 3,899 more Jewish votes than it had in 1959—about half the number required for a single Knesset seat. MAKI's support in the Arab community more than doubled from 9,162 in 1959 to about 20,000 and provided most of the votes necessary to increase its Knesset faction. MAKI again became the second strongest party in the Arab community, after MAPAI's Arab lists, and seemed well positioned to challenge MAPAI's preeminence. The party's electoral strength was now largely dependent on the support of Arabs who were not party members (there were about four hundred Arab party members at this time) or even readers of *Al-ittihad* (about two thousand on Tuesdays and three thousand on Fridays), support based on the party's consistent defense of Palestinian Arab civil and national rights, not its global ideology. While this support could be expanded if the party emphasized its distinctive stand on the Arab-Israeli conflict, it might dissipate if the party moderated its positions. Yet the party would likely lose Jewish support if it followed the first course. Mikunis's voluminous informal notes on MAKI leadership meetings from June 1961 on do not indicate that this issue was ever discussed in such unequivocal terms. But every member of the party's leading bodies must have been aware of it, and the contradiction was below the surface of many discussions both before and after the 1961 Knesset elections.

TABLE 6 FIFTH KNESSET ELECTION RESULTS
(AUGUST 15, 1961)

	Total Votes	%	Jewish Votes	%	Arab Votes	%	Jewish Vote as % of Total	Arab Vote as % of Total	Seats
MAPAI	349,330	34.7	335,200	36.6	14,130	15.7	96.0	4.0	42
MAPAI Arab lists	35,376	3.5	—	—	35,376	35.1	—	100.0	4
MAPAM	75,654	7.5	65,154	7.1	10,500	11.7	86.1	13.9	9
MAKI	42,111	4.2	22,111	2.4	20,000	22.2	52.5	47.5	5
Total valid votes for all parties	1,006,964	100	916,964	100	90,000	100	91.1	8.9	120

SOURCES: Israel, Halishkah hamerkazit lestatistikah, Totza'ot habehirot lakneset hahamishi, Sidrat pirsumim meyuhadim, no. 166 (Jerusalem, 1962); Moshe M. Czudnowski and Jacob M. Landau, *The Israeli Communist Party and the Elections for the Fifth Knesset, 1961* (Stanford, 1965); Jacob M. Landau, *The Arabs in Israel: A Political Study* (London, 1969).

NOTE: MAKI received 17,287 votes and MAPAM 9,232 votes in all-Arab localities. The total Arab vote for these parties includes my estimate of the vote in mainly Arab polling places in the mixed cities.

MAKI AND JEWISH NATIONAL COMMUNISM

During the preparations for the congress and the subsequent election campaign, MAKI tried to break away from its traditional norms based on the political and cultural style of Eastern Europe, the birthplace of most Jewish party veterans, and adopt a more popular Israeli style. After the years of isolation and defeat following the 1956 war, the party felt a need to move into the Israeli cultural mainstream if it was to make best use of the new political conditions in the country. The relaxation of discipline in the international communist movement following the Twentieth Congress of the Soviet Communist Party, the Moscow conferences of communist parties in 1957 and 1960, and the theoretical innovations of Italian Communist Party leader Palmiro Togliatti, the leading advocate of polycentrism and specific national roads to socialism in the communist movement, raised the question of the Israeli road to socialism in MAKI. The champion of Togliatti's ideas in MAKI was Eli'ezer Feiler, Mikunis's personal secretary and a candidate member of the Central Committee. Feiler was responsible for the party's international relations, and he had represented MAKI at the Italian party's Tenth Congress in December 1962.[61]

MAKI members hesitated much longer than the Egyptian communists before discussing their national road to socialism, and they never developed the concept theoretically because Mikunis and the entire Political Committee regarded Togliatti's line as too anti-Soviet. A committee appointed to elaborate an Israeli program for socialism after the 1961 Knesset elections never completed the task.[62] The deep attachment of MAKI's Eastern European Jewish veterans to the Soviet Union partly explains the party's exceptionally dogmatic political style and reluctance to embrace polycentrism. In addition, orthodoxy had a positive social and political function within MAKI. Just as the disbanding of the Comintern in 1943 had licensed various forms of national communism and been a factor in the split in the PCP, so too the concept of polycentrism threatened to undermine the authority of many ideological tenets that, though formulated in overly abstract terms and indulgent of some wishful thinking, maintained Jewish-Arab unity in MAKI.

One difficulty in developing an Israeli road to socialism was that Israeli culture was still in the process of formation, and no Israeli "nationality" existed, even in the narrow legal sense; identity as a Jew or Arab was decisive. A socialist program rooted in the national cultural traditions of Israel would almost inevitably have emphasized Eastern

European Jewish culture. Arab culture, including that of Jews from the Arab world, was marginal by definition in Israel, while manifestations of Arab national sentiment were considered offenses against the security of the state. An attempt to specify an Israeli road to socialism might—and eventually did—destroy the binational unity of the party.

In principle, MAKI could have tried to promote a binational Israeli identity, one connected to but distinct from its international Arab and Jewish components. Anton Shammas announced his support for such an identity in his Hebrew autobiographical novel, *Arabesques*. But in the early 1960s there was even less social foundation for this project than the slender one on which Shammas's literary venture was based. No Palestinian Arab was then capable of writing a novel in Hebrew. And while Iraqi Jews had been important figures in the literary history of Iraq, and several, including MAKI members Shimon Balas, Sami Michael, and Sasson Somekh, continued to write in Arabic after arriving in Israel, they all succumbed to heavy social pressure to shift to Hebrew. Theoretically, the Iraqi-Jewish members of MAKI might have been able to provide the cultural leadership to unite Jews and Arabs around a Middle East–centered identity, but at the time this was no more practically possible in MAKI than in any other Israeli political party, for Oriental Jewish culture had not yet begun to assert itself, as it has more recently.

The former members of MAPAM and the LSP who joined MAKI with Sneh in 1954 were a valuable resource for MAKI in its pursuit of an Israeli orientation. These party members had passed through the Zionist youth movements and the kibbutzim; some had served with distinction in the Palmah, the Haganah, and the IDF. They shared common educational and life experiences with many left Zionists and were part of the fabric of Israeli society in a way that most Jewish veterans of the PCP never could be. Sneh's followers had been regarded with suspicion by some veterans when they first entered MAKI;[63] now they emerged as the party's hope for the future.

MAKI's effort to reinvigorate the Young Communist League was a salient expression of its desire to embrace Israeli national culture, and the BANKI leadership became a center of Jewish national communist sentiment in the party. In late 1961, Ya'ir Tzaban, a follower of Sneh whose opinion that MAKI ought not to tell the Israeli public everything it believed about the Arab-Israeli conflict had already been brought to the attention of the Central Committee, replaced Uzi Burstein as secretary of BANKI. Under Tzaban's leadership BANKI adopted many of the practices of other Israeli youth movements, which, with their emphasis on pioneering, rural settlement, and armed defense, were part of the institutional structure of labor Zionism and expressed its ethos. It was impossible to adopt their norms and yet to avoid accepting (impossible at least to continue to struggle against) the national construction project as envisioned and implemented by the Zionist movement. But since the Zionist movement was the wellspring of Israeli-Jewish national culture, any effort to integrate into that culture was by definition potentially offensive to Arab party members and supporters.

In 1961, BANKI published a Hebrew songbook containing many songs sung in the labor Zionist youth movements as well as songs for several Jewish holidays. Despite the title's proclamation that the book contained "songs of nations," it included no Arabic songs, while there were several in Russian.[64] Next Tzaban suggested that BANKI accept new members on May Day and Hanukkah, rather than the traditional May Day and November 7, and that the ceremony awarding neckerchiefs (symbols of advancement through the ranks common to all Israeli youth movements) take place at Masada, where Jewish rebels made their last stand against the Romans. BANKI also established a NAHAL (Noʻar Halutzi Lohem—Fighting Pioneer Youth) unit—a group of high school graduates who entered the IDF and underwent basic training together before being sent to a border kibbutz, where they performed agricultural labor and continued military training simultaneously. BANKI's NAHAL groups went to Kibbutz Yad Hanah, most of whose members had joined MAKI with Sneh.[65] Clearly, Tzaban and other Jewish BANKI leaders ignored the probability that an Arab youth would find little significance in receiving a neckerchief at Masada during Hanukkah or that Arab BANKI and MAKI members would be upset by party sponsorship of a NAHAL unit. When Avraham Juri, the secretary of the NAHAL unit at Yad Hanah, was killed by gunfire from across the border in December 1964, Shoshana Katz, a member of the BANKI secretariat, declared at his funeral that there was a need for "more patriotism" in MAKI.[66]

National communist practices such as those BANKI introduced were not new in the history of the Palestinian-Israeli communist movement. They had been advocated both by the NLL and the Hebrew Communist Party in the 1940s and by Hanokh Bzozah and his group in the mid-1950s. By the 1960s, however, most of the former Hebrew Communist leaders were no longer members of MAKI, and Bzozah and his supporters, including several ex–Hebrew Communists, had been expelled from MAKI and sharply denounced by Sneh as advocates of Israeli national communism during 1956–58. In the shadow of the 1956 war, such an orientation was not viable. By contrast, many veterans of the NLL remained in MAKI despite their failure to develop a Palestinian Arab national communism, having joined MAKI after undergoing a self-criticism and accepting the party's predominantly Jewish orientation in the early 1950s. Still, MAKI's Arab period indicated that there was significant potential in the Arab community for a communist-nationalist front. Although the Nasserist-communist split in 1959 blocked its realization, by 1962–63, with the split repaired, the opportunity arose to reconstruct the alliance under the banner of pro-Soviet loyalism and ideological orthodoxy.

Previously, the Jewish communists had criticized the NLL's lack of orthodoxy on the national question; now, though, the Arab leaders of MAKI had become the staunchest defenders of orthodoxy, while some Jewish leaders were the main advocates of flexibility and renewal. But flexibility could not cut in only one direction. If MAKI was to be more open to cooperation with the Zionist left and to adapting its line and work to Jewish national culture, the party also had to be willing to allow its Arab cadres the freedom to be creative and innovative in their own community. This requirement created an internal contradiction that the party could not manage.

After their expulsion from MAKI, Bzozah and his colleagues tried to theorize a Jewish national communism through their ephemeral publications and international contacts; yet because this orientation did not develop a permanent organizational form, its theoretical efforts had little impact. The Jewish national communists of the 1960s, in contrast, confined by the discipline of remaining in a party whose line, unlike that of the Italian party, opposed national communism, never did develop a comprehensive theoretical justification for their position. They relied instead on tactical evaluations of political circumstances (overemphasizing, for example, the opportunities for political change represented by the Lavon affair) and stylistic modifications in the party's work—altering the party's tactics in the 1961 election campaign, introducing changes in BANKI, or adopting a more popular tone for the theses of the Fourteenth Congress without criticizing the line of the Thirteenth—while avoiding ideological reassessments. Consequently, when the internal party debate over these issues finally erupted, it was characterized by stereotypically wooden orthodox expressions that obscured much of what was at stake.

TOWARD THE SPLIT IN MAKI

Following the 1961 Knesset elections MAKI had two contradictory options for further growth: a "Jewish national" orientation or an "Arab national" orientation. After defending the flag of orthodoxy throughout the 1950s, Sneh became the most articulate representative of the Jewish national orientation. He expressed this change in direction at the Political Committee's discussion of the election results by proposing to approach MAPAM and explain that if the two parties had cooperated they would both have done better. He also wanted to undertake a public campaign to make MAPAM, Ahdut Ha'avodah, and the Liberals uphold their promise that they would not enter a new government headed by Ben-Gurion.[67] (MAPAM and the Liberals kept their word; Ahdut Ha'avodah did not.)

Habibi was the champion of the Arab national orientation. He argued that MAKI should have been more aggressive in its campaign attacks on the parties of the Zionist left, to lay the basis for an anti–Ben-Gurion front. He reported that the Arab intelligentsia rejected MAPAM's effort to pose as Nasserist: "The Arab population has chosen the path of struggle and not MAPAM's path of accommodation to the regime." According to Habibi, the principle campaign issue in the Arab community was the refugee question (here he continued the earlier argument with Sneh), and in its vote the Arab public demonstrated its support for MAKI's approach to resolving the Arab-Israeli conflict. Habibi also proposed that *Al-ittihad* become a daily. Although the Political Committee approved this proposal, it was not implemented because of lack of funds.[68]

The major disagreement between Sneh and Habibi at this point was the extent to which MAKI should strive to cooperate with MAPAM. MAKI had always sought such cooperation, but the MAPAM of 1961 was a very different entity from the MAPAM of 1948–52, and MAPAM's support for the 1956 war, its capitulation to the Zionist consensus on the Arab-Israeli conflict, and its tactics in the Arab community disgusted the Arab communists, especially Habibi. At the core of the argument was an evaluation of the direction in which Israeli politics was going. If the Lavon affair signified the bankruptcy of Ben-Gurionism and all it stood for, then it was reasonable to propose that MAKI make common cause with all who opposed Ben-Gurion to hasten his demise. But if the crisis in MAPAI was only superficial and did not create prospects for a fundamental political realignment, then blurring the distinctions between MAKI and the Zionist left could lead to the party's ideological capitulation and loss of support in the Arab community. Even Sneh admitted that while the election results were a sign of leftward movement, the government formed by Ben-Gurion was a move to the right.[69] It is therefore not surprising that he could not convince Habibi to support his new enthusiasm for an alliance with the Zionist left.

Ben-Gurion's resignation as prime minister for the last time on June 16, 1963 (prompted by the revelation that West German scientists were working on developing missiles for Egypt), and his replacement by Levi Eshkol marked the beginning of sharp national contention and ultimately division within the MAKI leadership. Mikunis, Sneh, and other Jewish leaders saw Ben-Gurion's demise as the delayed fruition of the hopes they had placed in the crisis of MAPAI in 1960–61, with Mikunis arguing that MAKI should concentrate its attacks on Ben-Gurion's supporters in the MAPAI young guard (Dayan, Peres, and Yosef Almogi). Vilner, however, was relatively unoptimistic about the significance of Ben-Gurion's departure, and the Arab leaders tended to agree with him.[70] Yet because Vilner was particularly outspoken in his reservations about Eshkol, the party leadership did not immediately divide along national lines in assessing Ben-Gurion's resignation.

Clashes on the border between Syria and Israel in the summer of 1963 intensified the disagreements in the Political Committee and made it clear that the Arab-Israeli conflict, not merely differing assessments on the significance of Ben-Gurion's departure, was the central issue at stake. Tensions had always been high on the Syrian border because of unresolved differences over the demilitarized zones and Israel's construction of a national water carrier that diverted part of the Jordan River. On July 13, the Syrians seized three Israelis and three Belgian tourists whose boat had blown against Syrian territory on the northeastern shore of the Sea of Galilee. The Belgians were released, but not the Israelis. On August 20, two Israelis were ambushed and killed by Syrians near Nahal Almagor on the northern tip of the Sea of Galilee. The general sense among the Jewish leaders of MAKI was that these Syrian actions were unjustified and unnecessarily provocative, despite recognition that the unresolved status of the border and Israel's boycott of the Syrian-Israeli Mixed Armistice Commission since 1951 were the root cause of the problem.

Sneh opened the Political Committee's discussion of the border clashes, at which only he, Vilenska, and Tzvi Breitstein (who was not a member of the Political Committee but attended most of its meetings during this period) were present; Mikunis, Vilner, Henin, Tubi, and Habibi were on summer vacation. The Eshkol government had decided to take the matter to the UN Security Council, which Sneh regarded as a significant improvement over Ben-Gurion's scornful disregard of international opinion. Sneh and Vilenska agreed that Syria was responsible for the latest incidents and that the Syrian response to what it considered a violation of the demilitarized zone was excessive. Sneh's stand was even more "pro-Israeli" than that of his two comrades.[71]

After the Soviet Union, on September 3, vetoed an Anglo-American draft Security Council resolution condemning Syria, the Political Committee discussed the matter again (with Mikunis and Vilner still on vacation). Vilenska reported that the Soviet veto had created a very hostile attitude toward (Jewish) party members in their workplaces; she carefully expressed her dismay with the Soviet action by emphasizing its tactical rather than its principled nature. As editor of the party daily, *Kol ha'am,* Sneh publicly supported the Soviet Union in that journal.[72] Tubi, however, criticized the newspaper's cool endorsement of the Soviet action and argued that the party's criticism of the government should be intensified (whereas Sneh had moderated his criticism because he supported the government's decision to turn to the Security Council). Habibi, noting that the veto had enabled the Soviet Union to regain lost influence in the Arab world, argued that the party should demand that Israel resume participation in the Mixed Armistice Committee and resolve the dispute over the demilitarized zone there.

This disagreement prefigured the 1965 split in the party and contained most of the components that caused it. The key issue was, Should MAKI loyally support the policy of the Soviet Union, which was based on the assessment that the Arab nationalist movement led by Abdel Nasser was the leading anti-imperialist force in the Middle East, or did the need to fashion an Israeli road to socialism require distancing the party from Soviet stands that were regarded in Israel as excessively and uncritically "pro-Arab"? Advocates of the first position (subsequently crystallized as opinion A) argued that if the radical Arab nationalist states did in fact constitute the leading anti-imperialist force in the Middle East, then in any dispute between them and Israel, an ally of imperialism, MAKI ought to support the Arab states, which in any case posed no concrete danger to Israel despite their verbal threats. This group upheld the party's traditional view that just as the imperialist powers had encouraged Arab reactionaries to attack Israel in 1948, so had they encouraged Israel to attack Egypt in 1956 and continued to encourage Israeli activism and aggression against the anti-imperialist Arab states. Advocates of the second position (opinion B) emphasized that the radical nationalist Arab states were military dictatorships, exercised repression against their working classes and communist parties, refused to recognize Israel, called for its destruction, and excepted it from the call for peaceful coexistence—which became the principal Soviet foreign policy slogan following the conclusion of the partial nuclear test ban treaty with Britain and the United States on August 5, 1963.

Supporters of the Israeli national communist orientation developed the new theory that the Arab-Israeli conflict was distinct from the battle between imperialist and anti-imperialist forces in the Middle East. The seeds of this concept were already present in the theses of the Fourteenth Party Congress, but because of the imprecision of those theses and a certain amount of apathy within the party ranks before the congress, MAKI did not conduct the thorough ideological discussion that could have sharpened this question. The dispute over just how much of a change the Eshkol government represented relative to Ben-Gurion's activist policies precipitated the more fundamental disagreement over the character of the Arab-Israeli conflict and the degree of support that undemocratic Arab nationalist regimes should be given. This latter debate had repercussions on MAKI's attitude toward the Zionist movement and the extent to which its anti-Zionist ideological principles should be emphasized. If the difference between Eshkol and Ben-Gurion was minimal (opinion A), then little could be gained by moderating the party's criticism of the government and the entire Zionist movement; if it was substantial (opinion B), then MAKI ought to encourage the forces in MAPAI and the other labor Zionist parties that opposed activism.

Several detailed studies in English, French, and Hebrew have described the evolution of the Political Committee dispute from the fall of 1963 through the public disclosure of the two contending opinions in *Kol ha'am* on May 19, 1965, and the split in the party in August, although none used Mikunis's minutes of these meetings, which have only recently become available to researchers.[73] All these studies have approached the question from within the Zionist discourse, assuming that Israel's stand in the Arab-Israeli conflict was fully justified and that the nationalist sentiment of the Arab members of MAKI was what caused the split, while the Jewish party members were true internationalists. This approach is obviously unsatisfactory, but I will not try to rectify it by constructing a revised narrative of the argument. Because the debate was confined to the Political Committee and later the Central Committee, with the party cadre remaining largely unaware of it until late 1964, a detailed reconstruction says little about MAKI's real effectiveness and the social conditions in which the party operated.

Was there an opportunity to challenge MAPAI's hegemony in the early 1960s? Did MAKI have a real prospect of growth among Jewish workers? Was there a substantial basis for unity between Jews and Arabs in Israel without a radical assault on the institutional structures of Jewish privilege? These questions must be answered in the negative, which suggests that there were in fact no realistic prospects for a Jewish national road to socialism in the 1960s. Earlier episodic disagreements between Jewish and Arab members began to crystallize along mainly national lines in late 1963; Arab party leaders came to understand the limited political potential of the Jewish community and to argue for an Arab-centered approach as the only one that could produce further gains for the party. Most Jewish communists were understandably reluctant to accept this orientation, and until the demise of Jewish national communism in the 1970s many continued to entertain illusions about radicalizing the Jewish working class in Israel. The 1965 split in MAKI is best understood as an expression of these conditions and not as the result of the "opportunism" or "nationalist deviation" of one or another faction.

DECLINE OF MAKI'S INFLUENCE IN
THE JEWISH WORKING CLASS

Although MAKI always supported the economic demands of the working class, by the late 1950s Jewish workers were so alienated from the party because of its stand on the Arab-Israeli conflict that it could make few long-term advances, even during the two-year period of exceptionally intense economic struggle that began with the strike of January 23, 1961. In February 1962, the government introduced a New Economic Policy aimed at attracting foreign investment, reducing consumption of imported consumer goods, stimulating exports, and freezing wages. The central component of the policy was a 41 percent devaluation of the Israeli pound that reduced wage earners' ability to purchase imported goods. Workers responded by organizing action committees independent of the Histadrut leadership and holding four militant general strikes during the year, as well as many smaller protests. Both MAKI and MAPAM participated energetically in the action committees, and for a time there were two networks of rival committees in which each party had influence.

MAKI registered only minimal advances among Jewish workers during these two years. Ester Vilenska lectured to the Central Committee on April 24, 1962, on the party's workplace organizing efforts and was able to give exactly four recent examples of successful work.[74] One was the same story of the formation of a party cell in the Friedman plant in Jerusalem that Avraham Hass had reported to the Central Committee in late 1959. In addition, a party member had recently been elected secretary of the workers' committee at the Hamaniʿa plant in Tel Aviv (a major center of activity during the 1962 strikes); the same party member who failed to win a seat on the Ata workers' committee in 1958 had since been elected; and MAKI members received 13 and 15 percent of the vote for the workers' committees in two departments of the Haifa port.

Yet in its report for 1963, the MAKI branch in Haifa informed the Central Committee that it had no cells of industrial workers in Israel's main industrial city.[75] Many party members who were once workers had become self-employed, and the only large-scale enterprises in which party members worked were the port, Rambam Hospital, the Haifa municipality, the government hospital in Nahariyya, and Bank Leʾumi. The absence of basic industries from this list is striking. The branch had done little workplace organizing and did not take part in the campaign for increased wages that year.

The decline of MAKI's influence among Jewish workers was the main reason for the overall stagnation or decline of its Jewish membership. As Table 7 indicates, the number of party members in mainly Jewish districts (Tel Aviv–Yafo, Haifa, Jerusalem, Shfelah, South, Negev) declined slightly from 1961 to 1965, while membership in entirely Arab districts (Nazareth, Triangle) nearly doubled. It is likely that the decline in the number of Jewish members in the Haifa district was even more pronounced than the table indicates because the Acre party branch, located in that district and composed mainly of Arabs, grew rapidly during 1962.[76] From 1958 on there was a secular decline in membership in all districts where Jews were a majority except Tel Aviv–Yafo and South/Negev (where the increase was marginal and may well have been due to new Arab members in Lydda and Ramle).

A broader indication of MAKI's declining influence among Jews and its expanding influence among Arabs in the 1960s may be seen in cir-

TABLE 7 MAKI MEMBERSHIP, 1958–65
(candidates in parentheses)

District	1958	1959	1961	1965
Tel Aviv–Yafo[a]	460 (+ 30)	455 (+25)	540	532
Haifa	256 (+ 22)[b]	235 (+ 18)	224	219
Nazareth	165 (+ 95)	214 (+ 47)	240	444
Shfelah	246 (+ 22)	245 (+ 16)	194	69
Sharon[c]	—	—	—	77
Triangle[d]	—	—	41	81
Jerusalem	65 (+ 8)	77 (+ 7)	75	65
South	96 (+ 16)	100 (+ 11)	91	75
Negev[e]	—	—	35	41
Central Committee & Control Commission	—	—	—	32
TOTALS	1,288 (+ 193)	1,326 (+ 124)	1,440	1,635

SOURCES: Party censuses, KM 35 Ve'idot 20.1, 20.2, 20.4.
NOTES: These figures are much smaller than those given in all other studies of MAKI, but since they rely on the unpublished party censuses conducted before the Fourteenth and Fifteenth Congresses (with retrospective comparisons based on the annual renewal of membership cards in 1958 and 1959), they are undoubtedly more accurate.
[a]Includes members of the Central Committee and Central Control Commission except in 1965.
[b]Includes some branches transferred to Nazareth in 1959.
[c]Part of Shfelah until 1965.
[d]Part of Shfelah until 1961.
[e]Part of South until 1961.

culation of the party press (Table 8). After the Suez/Sinai War, the party press readership declined in both communities: in the Jewish community because of the war and the surrounding circumstances, in the Arab community because of the break with Abdel Nasser in 1959. But neither *Kol ha'am* nor any of the party weeklies (read exclusively by Jews) ever regained the circulation they had before the war (the Polish weekly is exceptional because it was begun in response to the large immigration from Poland in 1961). In contrast, the readership of *Al-ittihad* had nearly recovered its 1956 level by early 1961, and it climbed steadily afterward. (The unusually high circulation in August 1961 was due to the Knesset elections that month.) As a result, by 1961, even though Arabs had a much lower literacy rate than Jews and constituted only 11.3 percent of Israel's population, there were twice as many readers of the Friday issue of *Al-ittihad* than readers of *Kol ha'am*—a proportion

TABLE 8 CIRCULATION OF MAKI PRESS, 1956–63

	8/56	4/61	8/61	12/61	6/62	12/62	6/63	12/63
Kol ha'am	1,834	1,413	1,420	1,431	1,553	1,595	1,663	1,651
Al-ittihad								
Tues.	1,837	1,734	2,181	2,012	1,908	1,874	1,929	2,142
Fri.	2,788	2,616	3,451	2,915	3,010	3,076	3,120	3,299
Weeklies	7,806	5,289	6,177	5,509	5,609	5,898	6,083	5,921
Yiddish	2,764	1,712	1,790	1,772	1,720	1,785	1,794	1,756
Rumanian	1,761	724	843	818	907	1,039	1,094	1,085
Bulgarian	2,331	1,098	1,171	1,146	1,104	1,132	1,188	1,157
Hungarian	347	330	352	324	303	320	323	293
French	603	496	513	463	480	508	535	514
Polish	—	929	1,058	986	1,095	1,114	1,149	1,116

SOURCE: KM 35 Mazkirut hamiflagah, Mazkirut, Inyanim shotfim 1964.
NOTE: Several slightly varying sets of circulation figures are in the file from which these numbers are taken, but all display the same trend.

MOBILIZATION OF THE PALESTINIAN ARAB CITIZENS OF ISRAEL

The rapid proletarianization of the former Arab peasantry after the easing of some work and travel restrictions by the military government in 1959 and expansion of secondary and university education were the main social processes that broke down the authority of the clan heads, mobilized the Arab community in the 1960s, and led to increased support for MAKI.[77] In 1954, 58.2 percent of the employed Arab citizens of Israel were engaged in farming, forestry, and fishing. By 1961 that figure was only 38.2 percent. The proletarianization of the Arab population had an immediate political impact, especially on the Histadrut. In 1965 the construction industry employed 21.6 percent of the Arab labor force and was the second largest economic sector in the Arab community after agriculture. This fact explains MAKI's impressive showing in the vote for the Congress of the Federation of Construction Workers held on January 31, 1965, the first Histadrut election in which Arabs participated: MAKI won 17.7 percent of the Arab votes and became the third strongest party after MAPAI and MAPAM; moreover, it won 4.3 percent of the total votes (as opposed to 3.1 percent in 1959), the first significant increase for the party in a Histadrut election in a decade.[78]

The young men who commuted daily from their villages to work in the cities, together with high school (and later university) graduates, became the principal bases of support for MAKI in the Arab community. Because the social mobilization of this community—by its very nature an irreversible process—has continued at an accelerating pace until the present, the Communist Party and other radical political forces have steadily increased their strength among Palestinian Arab citizens of Israel since the early 1960s.

The 1965 split in MAKI was fundamentally an expression of the party's shifting social base and the poor prospects for a radical reorientation in Israeli politics. The Jewish working class was moving toward the right, and the party's activity in the trade union struggles of the early 1960s failed to attract new Jewish members or readers of the party press. In contrast, the number of Arab members and supporters of the party was growing rapidly, and the political weight of the Arab community and their share of the general population was increasing. While admission of Arabs to the Histadrut was an important breakthrough, the expropriation of Palestinian lands continued in the 1960s as the government implemented plans to "Judaize the Galilee"; the military government also remained in force until 1966. Neither the Lavon affair nor Ben-Gurion's resignation resulted in a political realignment in Israel or diminished Israeli dependence on the West. Israel's balance of payments deficit increased steadily throughout the 1950s and 1960s, and its reliance on capital imports from the West intensified. In September 1962, the Kennedy administration agreed to sell Israel short-range Hawk missiles, the first time the U.S. government consented to provide Israel with advanced weaponry directly. This sale, followed by the supply of tanks in 1964 and Skyhawk jets in 1966, initiated the far-reaching U.S.-Israeli military relationship that has become a central feature of Israeli society. Although Eshkol tried to restrain the activists in the military establishment (as reflected by his decision to bring the Syrian violations of the armistice before the UN Security Council in 1963), activism was so entrenched as the only viable politico-military policy that public pressure forced Eshkol to follow their lead in launching the 1967 war.

The split in MAKI and subsequent establishment of two communist parties—the entirely Jewish MAKI, led by Mikunis and Sneh, and the overwhelmingly Arab RAKAH, headed by Vilner and Tubi—was an expression of the inability of the Jewish working class to keep its part of the bargain reached when the Jewish and Arab communists united to form MAKI in 1948. The Arabs agreed to recognize Israel and operate in its political system; in exchange, they expected that the class solidarity of Jewish and Arab workers in alliance with other democratic forces in both communities would achieve full democratic rights for Israel's Arab citizens and win Jewish recognition for the right of the Palestinian people to national self-determination in the form of an independent state. By the early 1960s, the prospects for this outcome appeared very remote. Thus, to avoid becoming hopelessly isolated within the Jewish community, MAKI stepped back from speaking about the Arab-Israeli conflict in the terms it had employed in the 1950s. For Arab party members this retreat was unacceptable, not only because it damaged the party's prospects for future growth in their community, but also because the anti-imperialist impulses of Nasserist pan-Arabism were not yet exhausted. Consequently, it was still possible to envision a political strategy based on a Nasserist-communist alliance. The weaknesses of the Arab nationalist movement were not fully exposed until the defeat of the Arabs in the 1967 war, but by then MAKI had already split and most of the Jewish party veterans had traveled so far along the road toward Zionism that reconstruction of the party on its old basis was impossible.

CHAPTER VIII

Conclusion

In July 1964, delegations from MAKI, represented by Shmu'el Mikunis and Emile Habibi, and from the Communist Party of Jordan, represented by Fu'ad Nassar and "Farid," met secretly in Moscow for three days to exchange views and coordinate political positions.[1] A historic tie existed between the Jordanian communists and the Arab component of MAKI because both had roots in the mandate-era National Liberation League. The Jordanian party was still mainly composed of Palestinians: refugees from 1948 and native West Bankers. Habibi and Nassar knew each other well because they had both been leaders of the NLL; Mikunis and Nassar were the main spokespersons for their respective parties.

After the exchange of formal expressions of solidarity, the most important point on the agenda was the Palestine question. Nassar's formulation of his party's line was close to the common communist line of 1947–48. Yet although the Jordanian party argued that the Zionist movement had always been an ally of imperialism, it had no regrets about supporting the 1947 partition plan, and it recognized the Jewish people's right to self-determination in Israel. The basis for a peaceful resolution of the conflict remained the UN plan and, in addition, recognition of the Palestinian refugees' right to return and the establishment of a Palestinian Arab state. It was true that radical Arab states had issued calls for the destruction of Israel (which the Communist Party of Jordan denounced), but there were no actual military plans to

Conclusion

attack Israel or to "throw the Jews into the sea." The Jordanian communists defended MAKI and regarded it as a worthy Marxist-Leninist party; they were anxious to coordinate positions with it, if not in the same verbal form, then in essence and content.

In his opening statement, Mikunis expressed concern about the founding conference of the PLO, convened in May 1964 in East Jerusalem (then under Jordanian rule), and the extreme anti-Israeli rhetoric of the organization and its leader, Ahmad al-Shuqayri. Although MAKI recognized the refugees' right to organize and demand their rights, Mikunis felt that al-Shuqayri's statements harmed the cause of peace. According to MAKI, it was up to Israel to take the first step toward resolving the conflict, by recognizing the national rights of the Palestinian Arabs. Mikunis surveyed the history of MAKI's position on the Palestine question through the texts of the political reports adopted at party congresses, whereupon he concluded that there was no "difference in principle or essence between our slogans for the solution of the Palestinian problem and what the Central Committee of your party has decided."

Further exchanges clarified that while the Jordanians did not insist on the precise borders of the UN partition plan, those were more or less what they had in mind as the territorial basis for a peace settlement. The Jordanians regarded lands annexed by Israel beyond the partition boundaries as "occupied territory," as MAKI did in 1948–49. Nassar insisted that there had to be a specified territorial basis for Palestinian national self-determination if this concept were to have any real content. Mikunis painstakingly explained why it was not productive to advocate these stands in Israel and that MAKI had to denounce Arab expressions of hostility to Israel. He reiterated that he did not believe this situation meant that any contradiction or substantive difference existed between the positions of MAKI and the Jordanian party.

In essence, Mikunis was acknowledging that MAKI could not speak the same language as the Jordanian and other Arab communists. In Israel, the notion that a peaceful settlement of the conflict had to be based on the terms of the 1947 UN partition resolution was already at the time of the 1955 Bandung conference considered to be evidence of aggressive, not peaceful, intentions. This was all the more true in 1964. It was precisely for this reason that MAKI revised its formulation of the requisites for settling the issue between the Thirteenth Party Congress in 1957 and the Fourteenth in 1961. The need to participate in the Israeli national political discourse had made slogans commonly used by Arab communists out of bounds for MAKI. The Arab communists, too, no longer spoke the same language they had before 1955. I have tried to argue, in opposition to Mikunis, that on both sides this reformulation was not simply linguistic but political.

However much Mikunis may have denied it, the exchange between MAKI and the Communist Party of Jordan confirmed that the positions of MAKI and, not just the Jordanian, but all the other Arab communist parties differed on this issue in a very important way. As Fu'ad Nassar hinted, the gap between MAKI and the Jordanians was narrower than that between MAKI and the other Arab communists, including the Egyptians. In fact, the Marxists of the Middle East no longer had a unified position on the Palestinian/Arab–Israeli conflict. In Israel, the transcript of this meeting became one factor leading to the split in MAKI because most of the Arab and some Jewish party members did not want to adopt positions at variance with those of the sister Arab parties—a question that had ceased to concern MAPAM. In Egypt, the dissolution of the communist parties meant that the Marxists would no longer make even a formalistic effort at coordination with MAKI. In both countries, national communism prevailed, eroding the common internationalist position on the Palestine question shared by most Arab and Jewish Marxists in the late 1940s and 1950s.

This situation was not the result of "errors" or "opportunism," as the classical communist lexicon would put it. Neither was it merely a minor tactical difference reflecting the need to adjust to different local conditions. Although the process had begun in the Popular Front period, the decline of the Soviet Union as the center of the international communist movement after 1956 and the elaboration of the theory of polycentrism accelerated the development of national communisms. Although internationalism was not abandoned, Marxist parties increasingly sought to legitimate themselves in national rather than internationalist terms. Since MAPAM always defined itself primarily in national terms even when it saw the Soviet Union as the leader of "the world of revolution" in the late 1940s and early 1950s, it accommodated to the Israeli national political arena more quickly and thoroughly than the communists.

MARXISM, ZIONISM, AND ARAB NATIONALISM

The Egyptian and Israeli Marxists did not ultimately regard nationalism as a social idea with the potential to mobilize forces beyond the interests of the particular classes that led a given national movement. National struggles—those that could be supported, at any rate—were considered to be fronts in the struggle against imperialism, and as such they were unproblematically perceived as a stage in the struggle for socialism. Consequently, the Marxists pursued a tactical and instrumental approach to nationalism that enabled them to be very flexible in the rapidly changing circumstances of the post–World War II period. Such tactical flexibility was often perceived as opportunism by observers whose consciousness was shaped by the cold war or nationalism, whether Arab or Zionist. The undisputed leading role of the Soviet Union in the international communist movement was certainly a major factor in determining the positions of the Middle Eastern Marxists; indeed, perhaps they were able to shift their positions so rapidly in 1947–49 precisely because they were motivated by internationalism and did not regard national sentiment as compelling.

In addition to the theoretical inability of Marxism to explain the power of nationalism to construct a hegemonic alternative to class politics, its particular incapacity to explain the character of Zionism led to political disorientation and fragmentation as well. The Marxist analytical armory could not adequately theorize both the nationalist—and hence, in the postwar conjuncture, anti-imperialist—and settler-colonial components of Zionism. The Zionist movement was allied with British imperialism until 1939. In the middle of World War II, Ben-Gurion and MAPAI shifted the movement toward an American orientation. At the same time, most non-Zionist Jews who were motivated by either orthodox religious or left-wing political sentiment were annihilated by the Nazis. As the emblematic victims of European fascism, Jews had a strong moral claim on the progressive forces of the postwar world. The Zionist movement, in the absence of plausible alternatives and the capitalist countries' unwillingness to provide refuge for the Jewish survivors of Hitlerism, became the sole legatee of this claim. Moreover, despite its early dependence on British imperialism, a Jewish national community had been formed in Palestine during the period of the British mandate, and it launched a struggle to expel the British from Palestine. Marxist theory did not have categories to explain this complex and contradictory trajectory.

The Soviet Union's decision to support the partition of Palestine created a moment of fusion between the communist and Zionist movements. The Soviet Union saw partition primarily as a tactic to defeat British imperialism in the Middle East and perhaps also as an expression of sympathy for the victims of Nazism. Many Marxists—not only members of MAPAM and Jewish members of MAKI—proceeded from the original tactical decision to support establishment of a Jewish state to imagine that the state of Israel embodied great progressive potential.[2] In Egypt, this tendency was represented by Voice of the Opposition/ MISHMISH. For a Jewish state to be a historically progressive force in the Middle East would have required it to disengage from the entire history of the nationalist movement that created it. While such a course was abstractly possible, in practice it was most unlikely. Instead Zionism—indeed, Ben-Gurion's aggressive, activist Zionism—shaped the political culture and social practice of the new state. For the communists, the fact that the state of Israel continued to be guided by the same theory and practice that had guided the Zionist colonization of Palestine was a constant source of unresolved problems; MAPAM, for its part, began to abandon Marxism when it became clear that it could not be loyal to both Zionism and Marxism.

Pan-Arab nationalism, too, was historically regarded by the international communist movement with great suspicion, and all the more so by MAPAM. Pan-Arab unity was considered to be a romantic, idealist vision promoted by the British as a stratagem to maintain their hegemony in the region. These attitudes changed when Gamal Abdel Nasser emerged in the second half of the 1950s as the anti-imperialist leader of the Arab world. Except for Henri Curiel and his followers (who have rarely been given full credit for this insight), the Egyptian and Arab communists were slow to grasp the anti-imperialist potential of Nasserism; as for MAPAM, it could claim legitimate Marxist antecedents for its predominantly negative attitude.

In the 1960s, the Egyptian and other Arab Marxists were abetted in their endeavor to enhance the image of Nasserism by the Soviet-sponsored theory of the noncapitalist road of development. This theory elegantly justified Soviet foreign policy in Egypt, Algeria, and other parts of the third world; it may also have been an expression of what Samir Amin has called the natural affinity between the economic systems of Soviet Marxism and the state interventionist development strategy of Arab socialism—which was, in fact, a form of state capitalism.[3] The historical trajectory of Arab nationalism, no less than that of Zionism, was not adequately explained by Marxist theory. Many Marxists found themselves minimizing the undemocratic and anti–working class aspects of the Egyptian regime and emphasizing its pro-Soviet international orientation, as though this would in and of itself transform the regime's character. Some Arab communists, especially the Syrians, resisted this tendency; yet no Arab Marxists found this approach to Egypt as problematic as the Jewish members of MAKI did.

So far, these concluding comments have been situated in the realm of ideas. But the inability of Marxist parties to develop an adequate theory of nationalism and to deflect its challenge was fundamentally rooted in the political weakness of the social forces on which they were based. I argued in Chapter 3 that the numerically small and organizationally and politically undeveloped Egyptian working class could not aspire to establish social hegemony. During the period discussed here, the anti-imperialist thrust of Arab nationalism obscured the extent of Nasserist repression of the working class and allowed the Marxist intelligentsia to represent its interests in a manner that ultimately led to accommodation with Nasserism. In Israel, the strength of the Jewish working-class movement, despite its organizational sophistication and political experience, was always undercut by the settler-colonial aspect of the Zionist project and its dependence on Western capital. The movement was, therefore, incapable of playing the revolutionary role that both MAPAM and MAKI envisioned for it. The fate of the Marxist political forces after 1965 and the development of the political economy of Egypt and Israel since then only reinforce this argument.

The lack of a social base for Jewish national communism in Israel was further demonstrated by the liquidation in 1975 of the Mikunis-Sneh tendency. This faction fused with the socialist-Zionist Moked group, which in turn, before the 1977 Knesset elections, joined SHELI (Shalom leyisra'el—Peace for Israel), a peace list that did not advocate explicitly socialist positions. SHELI won two seats in those elections, but then it too collapsed. Today no political organization in Israel claims the historical legacy of the old Mikunis-Sneh faction.

In contrast, the social base for a communist movement rooted in the Arab community of Israel continued to expand after 1965. In 1977, RAKAH and its allies in the Democratic Front for Peace and Equality won a majority of the Knesset vote among Arabs. Although it subsequently lost its majority status, the Front, dominated by the communists, remained the largest electoral force in the Arab community, which provided the list with over 90 percent of its total electoral support in the 1980s. RAKAH reclaimed the MAKI name and continued to demonstrate its commitment to internationalism by assigning to Jews at least two of the Knesset seats the Front had won in Knesset elections—far more than would be justified by the number of Jewish voters for the Front.

After their release from prison, the Egyptian communist intellectuals benefited from the regime's strategy of co-opting the communist movement. Many were admitted to the Arab Socialist Union, the regime's new party established in 1962; erstwhile communist workers, however, generally were not.[4] The intellectuals returned to their former jobs or assumed new positions of responsibility in the mass media and cultural apparatus of the regime; again, though, workers usually were not rehired in their old workplaces. The economic grievances that had helped to radicalize the intelligentsia in the 1930s and 1940s were alleviated by the regime's new policy of providing a job in the public sector to all college graduates otherwise unable to find employment. While many young intellectuals may have been dissatisfied by sitting at desks all day with little meaningful work to perform, their physical survival was secure, at least until the wave of inflation that accompanied the open door economic policy of the 1970s. The former communists, especially the intellectuals, had little direct experience of the actual relations of production under Arab socialism, a fact that undoubtedly contributed to their illusions about its character. The differential treatment of the intelligentsia and the workers also indicated which social component of the communist movement the regime regarded as the more significant threat.

Following the 1967 war the managers of the public sector, who were the most privileged beneficiaries of Arab socialism, sought to resolve Egypt's economic crisis by moving away from populist consumptionism, strengthening the power of the bureaucrats and technocrats in the name of efficiency, reducing the scope of the public sector, denationalizing some enterprises, and encouraging the adoption of free market criteria in the management of the public sector.[5] Later they joined with elements of the former ruling class and individual profiteers to prepare the ground for reintegration of Egypt's economy with the world capitalist market, even as former communists Fu'ad Mursi and Isma'il Sabri 'Abd Allah became ministers in the government of Anwar al-Sadat in the early 1970s. Because the Nasserist regime never undertook a revolutionary dismantling of the old regime, it was not difficult for the old and new privileged classes to reorient Egypt toward the West, turning Arab socialism into a transitional stage between a colonial and a neocolonial economy.

While all this was occurring, there was no Marxist politics in Egypt to speak of. The Communist Party of Egypt was reestablished in 1975, after Anwar al-Sadat's open door economic policy and Egypt's reorientation toward the United States were accomplished facts. Many former party members did not rejoin the party and restricted their political activity to the framework of the legal left opposition, the National Progressive Unionist Party (Tagammuʿ), a national united front combining Marxists, Nasserists, and others. Neither the Communist Party nor the Tagammuʿ has been as successful organizing workers as were the Marxists in the 1940s. The Tagammuʿ has been kept on the margins of political life by periodic repression, restrictive electoral laws, and a political style that appeals mainly to the radical intelligentsia, while the Communist Party remains illegal, as it has been since 1946.

POLITICAL DISCOURSE AND POLITICAL ACTION

The Communist Party of Italy has interpreted Antonio Gramsci's theoretical legacy as a justification of its strategy of "historic compromise." The entire Eurocommunist tendency, of which the Italian Party's orientation was an early expression, draws its inspiration from Gramsci's emphasis on the importance of national culture and the need to fight a "war of position" in the advanced capitalist countries over a protracted period of time. The richness of Gramsci's work and the Aesopian style imposed on him by his imprisonment make possible other readings that may illuminate a connection among political discourse, material conditions, and the limits of political action.

The Gramscian strategy for combating the hegemony of the ruling class is to create a counterhegemonic bloc. Political and cultural struggle shifts the balance of power from the hegemonic to the counterhegemonic forces, enabling the insurgent bloc to broaden its social power and emerge as the new representative of the interests of the entire nation. In order to create a historic bloc capable of assuming this role, problems of intellectual and moral reform must be linked with economic reform; a counterhegemonic bloc must construct its own interpretive order and provide a persuasive alternative representation of the meaning of national culture. The construction of this counterhegemonic bloc is both a discursive-cultural and a historico-political project. The subaltern groups must struggle to create a new form of consciousness and a new epistemology. As Gramsci put it, "The realisation of a hegemonic apparatus, in so far as it creates a new ideological terrain, determines a reform of consciousness and of methods of knowledge."[6]

Gramsci clearly believed that only the working class could form the core of the counterhegemonic bloc. And precisely this was impossible in Egypt and Israel. The Marxists pursued only part of the Gramscian strategy: they were attentive to the need to operate within the context of their national culture, but they could not construct a counterhegemonic bloc around themselves. This was not because of a moral failure, but because the political economy, social structure, and international orientation of Egypt and Israel set very severe limits on the potential and efficacy of this kind of political action. The task of elaborating a counterhegemonic discourse was abandoned. No political issue illustrates this more clearly than the stand of the Marxists toward the Palestinian/Arab–Israeli conflict.

Communist parties operating in difficult conditions have often believed that their most fundamental political task was to survive to fight another day. This perspective, rooted in both bureaucratic conservatism and Marxist teleology, has a certain indisputable logic in terms of normal politics. Gramsci opposed such a strategy, arguing that it sprang from a mechanical determinism "like religion or drugs (in their stupefying effect)"; nonetheless, he recognized that "when you don't have the initiative in the struggle and the struggle itself comes eventually to be identified with a series of defeats, mechanical determinism becomes a tremendous force of moral resistance, of cohesion and of patient and obstinate perseverance."[7] The Marxists' accommodation to the hegemonic political discourse in Egypt and Israel was part of an overall strategy designed to insure their survival and maximize their ability to achieve a modicum of political reform. It is easy to understand why this strategy was adopted, but its costs should also be recognized. If conditions for Marxist politics were difficult in the 1950s and 1960s, they subsequently became even more so.

It is very possible that a more determined rejection of the hegemonic political discourse by the Marxists in these two countries would have isolated the Marxists even more, further reduced their political influence, and led to even more repression against them. Perhaps only individuals and groups who are somewhat detached from their society, like Henri Curiel and the Rome group, can uphold a radically oppositional vision with little apparent social basis for its immediate realization. During the period discussed in this book, such a vision was no more capable of restructuring society than the path the Egyptian and Israeli Marxists actually did take in the 1950s and 1960s. But this may not be the only measure of its value.

Radical rejection of the hegemonic discourse, in addition to its existential and moral value, serves a necessary political function. An alternative politics cannot be realized unless it can be articulated and elaborated as a viable interpretive order. Yet such articulation and elaboration alone do not guarantee success; ultimately, success depends on whether an alternative political vision corresponds to the interests of social forces that can be united in a counterhegemonic bloc and mobilized for effective political action.

EPILOGUE: TOWARD A PALESTINIAN STATE AND BEYOND

Few realistic prospects for implementing the UN partition plan of 1947 actually existed; the Marxists were the only organized political force in the Middle East thoroughly committed to recognizing the right of self-determination of the Jewish and Arab communities in Palestine, yet their social base was too weak to defend partition politically and militarily. Subsequently, the Marxists' accommodation to their national political culture inhibited them from defending their original discursive terms. On the eve of the establishment of the PLO in 1964, then, the concept of the Palestinian people's right to self-determination had become an obscure notion with no status in international politics.

Ever since Israel occupied the West Bank and the Gaza Strip in 1967, all its governments without exception have denied the Palestinian national identity of the occupied population; indeed, the notion that Arab citizens of Israel are part of the Palestinian people (not merely "Israeli Arabs") remains so disturbing to the overwhelming majority of Israeli Jews, including many opponents of government policy, that it can hardly be mentioned. These and associated representations, which allowed Israel to maintain the occupation for many years without substantial international challenge, achieved extraordinary acceptance in the West as part of a powerful discursive formation constituted in the context of the U.S. defeat in Vietnam and the subsequent Nixon-Kissinger strategy of promoting regional surrogates to maintain U.S. positions in the third world, assimilation of the Arab-Israeli conflict to the global contention between the Soviet Union and the United States, fear of radical Arab nationalism, concern to insure the continued supply of low-priced petroleum, and envious amazement at Israel's rapid and apparently effortless military victory in 1967. In addition, Christian millenarianism and a sense of obligation toward the survivors of Nazism continued, as before, to immunize Israel from criticism of its actions against the Palestinians and other Arabs. Partly as a result of these forces and partly because resurgent American Jewish ethnicity came to be expressed as uncritical pro-Israelism, the domestic Zionist lobby in the United States gained uncommon power, including the ability to reinforce this discourse and obscure the complex of material factors in which the discourse was embedded.

The Palestinian people's desperation at confronting a world that denied their very existence, a fetishization of armed struggle (a complement to Israel's obsession with military might, and an understandable error for people who felt themselves otherwise powerless), and the lack of any stable territorial base from which to conduct their national struggle were prominent among the factors that made attacks on unarmed civilians a salient part of early PLO strategy against Israel. As a manifestation of the power of the Zionist discourse, Palestinian attacks on civilians (and even on armed soldiers) were widely described as terrorism by international opinion and the media, whereas far more devastating and more frequent Israeli attacks against Palestinian civilians (in refugee camps in southern Lebanon, for example) rarely received public attention, let alone condemnation. Although politically and psychologically significant, the PLO's military strategy was a failure. Nonetheless, Israel did not succeed in crushing the resistance of the Palestinian people.

After years of political stalemate, the Palestinian uprising (*intifada*) in the West Bank and the Gaza Strip beginning in December 1987 and the Palestine National Council's November 1988 decision to seek an independent Palestinian state alongside Israel have created a new balance of forces in the Palestinian-Zionist conflict. As a result, mutual recognition and self-determination for both peoples have reemerged as the only internationally agreed upon principles for resolving the conflict, though as of this writing rejection of this international consensus by Israel and the United States has blocked its implementation. The Palestinian people now assert their right to no more than what the Jewish people of Israel claim for themselves: a sovereign state at peace with its neighbors. This assertion of equality is both a rhetorical repudiation of the colonialist thrust of the Zionist project and the Palestinians' primary weapon of resistance. The Palestinians' claim to equality of status and the capacity of the *intifada* to assert that claim convincingly have undermined the stability of Israel's occupation of the West Bank and the Gaza Strip and made it very likely that Palestinian national aspirations will ultimately be realized.

What has been the role of the Marxist left in this process? Despite its regional collapse as an organized political force, the solution posed

Conclusion

by the Marxist left to the Palestinian-Zionist conflict has gained more widespread credibility than it has had since the early 1950s. Indeed, the communist parties and their supporters claim that recent developments constitute a historic vindication of their position on the conflict since 1947. The organized strength of Marxist political formations has not, however, been a major factor in the reemergence of the two-state solution, although Soviet support for this program was important in convincing the PLO leadership to adopt it. Rather, the single most important reason for the new prominence of the two-state compromise is the persistent resistance of the Palestinian people on the West Bank and the Gaza Strip and their acceptance of this program. The *intifada* has become such an integral part of the details of daily life and social organization for so many Palestinians that it is difficult to imagine how any state could obliterate the consciousness it embodies.

If it cannot be said that the new prominence of the two-state solution is a political victory for organized Marxist forces, it may still legitimately be claimed as a moral victory for the internationalist principles they historically espoused. To be sure, it is not an unproblematic moral victory. The main line of argumentation by both Palestinian and Israeli proponents of the two-state solution is pragmatic and national: that it alone can insure the national survival of the Israeli-Jewish people or the Palestinian people. Such a discursive strategy is probably necessary if this program is to have any chance of being realized. But national political discourse cannot resolve the deeper issues of the conflict: Will Israel acknowledge the historic injustice it has committed against the Palestinian people? Can Israel survive as a European cultural transplant in the Middle East? Is it possible for a state to be both Jewish and democratic? Can the Palestinian Arab people be territorially reconstituted, and what will be the relations between residents of the Palestinian state and those of the diaspora? Can Arab nationalism find a way to accommodate non-Arab and non-Muslim minorities in the Middle East and their need for political and cultural expression? Can economic relations between the state of Palestine and the state of Israel be established without perpetuating the structural subordination of the Arab economy to the Jewish economy? Can the liberation of women, hitherto subordinated to the nationalist political struggle by all parties to the conflict, be realized? In the current conjuncture, these issues are not at the top of the political agenda. But it is not too soon to begin articulating them or to begin thinking about how to construct a historic bloc of social forces that will seek to address them.

Notes

CHAPTER I. INTRODUCTION

1. Eric Hobsbawm, "Problems of Communist History," *New Left Review*, no. 54 (Mar.–Apr. 1969), p. 85.

2. Henri Curiel, "Pour une lutte conséquent pour l'unité des communistes égyptiens," Mar. 1953 (Curiel papers).

3. For example, see A. B. Magil, *Israel in Crisis* (New York, 1950). This book, published by the Communist Party of the United States, indicates that overoptimism about the revolutionary potential of Jewish workers was common even among non-Zionists (although Magil was Jewish, and Zionist "deviations" were widespread among the predominantly Jewish New York district of the party). In fact, even some elements of the Egyptian communist movement shared this perspective (see below, Chapter 4).

4. This approach can be seen in Walter Laqueur, *Communism and Nationalism in the Middle East* (London, 1961); G. Z. Yisra'eli (Laqueur's pseudonym), *M.P.S.–P.K.P.–MAKI: Korot hamiflagah hakomunistit beyisra'el* (Tel Aviv, 1951); Yehudah Lahav, *The Soviet Attitude Towards the Split in the Israeli Communist Party, 1964–1967*, Hebrew University of Jerusalem Soviet and East European Research Center, Research paper no. 39 (Jerusalem, June 1980); Leonard Binder, "The Failure of the Egyptian Left," *Asian and African Studies* 14 (1980): 20–34; Shimon Shamir, "The Marxists in Egypt: The 'Licensed Infiltration' Doctrine in Practice," in *The U.S.S.R. and the Middle East*, ed. Michael Confino and Shimon Shamir (Jerusalem, 1973), pp. 293–319. The seminal works emphasizing the national political context of Middle Eastern communist movements are Hanna Batatu, *The Old Social Classes and the Revolutionary Movements of Iraq* (Princeton, 1978); and Ervand Abrahamian, *Iran Between Two Revolutions* (Princeton, 1980). For Egypt and Palestine,

Marie-Dominique Gresh, "Le P.C.F. et l'Égypte: 1950–1956" (Mémoire de maîtrise, Université de Paris I, 1976–77); Selma Botman, *The Rise of Egyptian Communism, 1939–1970* (Syracuse, N.Y., 1988); and Musa Budeiri, *The Palestine Communist Party, 1919–1948: Arab and Jew in the Struggle for Internationalism* (London, 1979), give analytical priority to the national framework of communist political action.

5. This is the Arab nationalist critique of the Arab communist parties as exemplified by al-Hakam Darwaza, *Al-shuyuʿiyya al-mahalliyya wa-maʿarakat al-ʿarab al-qawmiyya* (Beirut, 1963). In Palestine/Israel one of the recurrent debates is whether the Jewish or Arab communists were "true" internationalists and which of the two groups were national deviationists. Those who see the Jews as internationalists and the Arabs as nationalists include Alain Greilsammer, *Les communistes israéliens* (Paris, 1978); Berl Balti, *Bamaʾavak al hakiyum hayehudi: Ledmuto shel Moshe Sneh* (Jerusalem, 1981); and Sondra Miller Rubenstein, *The Communist Movement in Palestine and Israel, 1919–1984* (Boulder, Colo., 1984). Dunia Nahhas, *The Israeli Communist Party* (London, 1976); and Samih Samara, *Al-ʿamal al-shuyuʿi fi filastin: Al-tabaqa waʾl-shaʿb fi muwajahat al-kuluniyaliyya* (Acre, 1980), portray communism as part of the Arab national movement and emphasize the disruptive Zionist impulses of the Jewish communists. Budeiri, *The Palestine Communist Party*, offers a more nuanced emphasis on the dynamic struggle for an internationalist orientation in very difficult circumstances. The analogous issue in the history of Egyptian communism is whether the Jewish communists undermined the national character of the movement by virtue of their Zionist "deviation." Rifʿat al-Saʿid, a prolific chronicler whose relevant works include *Al-yasar al-misri waʾl-qadiyya al-filastiniyya* (Beirut, 1974), *Taʾrikh al-munazzamat al-yasariyya al-misriyya, 1940–1950* (Cairo, 1977), *Munazzamat al-yasar al-misri, 1950–1957* (Cairo, 1983), and *Taʾrikh al-haraka al-shuyuʿiyya al-misriyya: Al-wahda, al-inqisam, al-hall, 1957–1965* (Cairo, 1986), generally defends the Jewish communists without addressing the issue squarely, as might be expected from someone whose work has the character of an official party history of the DMNL. Gilles Perrault's admiring biography of Henri Curiel, *Un homme à part* (Paris, 1984), adopts the same approach. ʿAbd al-Qadir Yasin, *Al-qadiyya al-filastiniyya fi fikr al-yasar al-misri* (Beirut, 1981), is less laudatory of Curiel but makes clear that the Jewish communists were not Zionists. Saʿd Zahran, *Fi usul al-siyasa al-misriyya* (Cairo, 1985), pp. 135–44, is polemically critical of the Jewish role in the movement, while Muhammad Sayyid Ahmad (Mohamed Sid-Ahmed), in *Mustaqbal al-nidal al-hizbi fi misr* (Cairo, 1984), pp. 112–15, and his article written in response to the publication of Henri Curiel's papers in Arabic, "Al-yahud fi al-haraka al-shuyuʿiyya al-misriyya waʾl-siraʿ al-ʿarabi al-israʾili," *Al-hilal* 66, no. 6 (June 1988): 21–27, offers the most sophisticated and historicized approach to this issue.

6. Perry Anderson, "Agendas for Radical History," *Radical History Review*, no. 36 (Sept. 1986), p. 36.

7. For a trenchant analysis of the sociology of knowledge of Israeli historical revisionism, see Zachary Lockman, "Original Sin," in *Intifada: The Pales-*

tinian Uprising Against Israeli Occupation, ed. Zachary Lockman and Joel Beinin (Boston, 1989).

8. Simha Flapan, *The Birth of Israel: Myths and Realities* (New York, 1987).

9. See Benny Morris, *The Birth of the Palestinian Refugee Problem, 1947–1949* (Cambridge, 1988); as well as the following articles by Morris: "The Crystallization of Israeli Policy Against a Return of the Arab Refugees: April–December, 1948," *Studies in Zionism* 6, no. 1 (1985); "The Causes and Character of the Arab Exodus from Palestine: The Israel Defence Forces Intelligence Branch Analysis of June 1948," *Middle Eastern Studies* 22, no. 1 (1986); "Operation Dani and the Palestinian Exodus from Lydda and Ramle in 1948," *Middle East Journal* 40, no. 1 (1986); "Yosef Weitz and the Transfer Committees, 1948–49," *Middle Eastern Studies* 22, no. 4 (1986); and "The Harvest of 1948 and the Creation of the Palestinian Refugee Problem," *Middle East Journal* 40, no. 4 (1986). See also Avi Shlaim, "Husni Zaʿim and the Plan to Resettle the Palestinian Refugees in Syria," *Journal of Palestine Studies* 15, no. 4 (Summer 1986): 68–80; and idem, *Collusion Across the Jordan: King Abdullah, the Zionist Movement, and the Partition of Palestine* (New York, 1988). Tom Segev's *1949: The First Israelis* (New York, 1986) also contains a chapter on Arab-Israeli relations that corroborates some of Flapan's arguments.

10. Sabri Jiryis, *The Arabs in Israel* (Beirut, 1968).

11. Jacob M. Landau, *The Arabs in Israel: A Political Study* (London, 1969).

12. Elia Zureik, *The Palestinians in Israel: A Study in Internal Colonialism* (London, 1979); Ian Lustick, *Arabs in the Jewish State: Israel's Control of a National Minority* (Austin, Tex., 1980); Charles S. Kamen, "After the Catastrophe: The Arabs in Israel, 1948–51," *Middle Eastern Studies* 23, no. 4 (1987), and 24, no. 1 (1988) (an expanded translation of "Aharei haʾason: Haʿaravim bemedinat yisraʾel, 1948–1950," *Mahbarot lemehkar ulebikoret,* no. 10 [Dec. 1984]). For a personal account corroborating these scholarly studies, see Fouzi El-Asmar, *To Be an Arab in Israel* (London, 1975).

13. For details, see Moshe Sharett, *Yoman ishi,* 8 vols. (Tel Aviv, 1978); and Livia Rokach's translation and exegesis of selected passages, *Israel's Sacred Terrorism* (Belmont, Mass., 1980); Avi Shlaim, "Conflicting Approaches to Israel's Relations with the Arabs: Ben-Gurion and Sharett, 1953–1956," *Middle East Journal* 37, no. 2 (Spring 1983): 180–201; Ehud Yaʿari, "Mitzrayim vehafedaʾin, 1953–1956," Arab and Afro-Asian Monographs, no. 13 (Givʿat Haviva, 1975); Gabi Sheffer, "Sharett, Ben-Gurion umilhemet habrerah be-1956," *Medinah, mimshal veyahasim beinleʾumiyim,* no. 26 (1987): 1–27; Elmore Jackson, *Middle East Mission: The Story of a Major Bid for Peace in the Time of Nasser and Ben-Gurion* (New York, 1983); Michael Scott Bornstein, "From Revolution to Crisis: Egypt-Israel Relations, 1952–1956" (Ph.D. diss., Princeton University, 1986); Jean Mandelstam, "La Palestine dans la politique de Gamal Abdel Nasser, 1952–1955" (Ph.D. diss., Université de Paris, 1970); Saadia Touval, *The Peace Brokers: Mediators in the Arab-Israeli Conflict, 1948–1979* (Princeton, 1982).

14. They are analyzed, not unproblematically, in Mandelstam, "La Palestine dans la politique de Gamal Abdel Nasser." Some are also discussed in Aharon Cohen, *Israel and the Arab World* (New York, 1970).

15. On the political role of the army in Israel, see Yoram Peri, *Between Battles and Ballots: Israeli Military in Politics* (Cambridge, 1983).

16. According to Ben-Gurion's speech in the Knesset on January 2, 1956, quoted in *My Talks with Arab Leaders* (Jerusalem, 1972), p. 272, the number of Israelis killed and wounded by saboteurs was 137 in 1951 (111 by Jordanian-based forces); 147 in 1952 (114 by Jordanian-based forces); 162 in 1953 (124 by Jordanian-based forces, 26 by Egyptian-based forces); 180 in 1954 (117 by Jordanian-based forces, 50 by Egyptian-based forces); 258 in 1955 (37 by Jordanian-based forces, 192 by Egyptian-based forces). These figures appear to include both civilian and military casualties. It is clear that until after Israel's raid on Gaza in February 1955 most acts of sabotage came from Jordan, while Israel directed reprisals at both Jordan and Egypt. That is to say, Israel's contention that it attacked Egypt in 1956 to prevent acts of terror and sabotage is not supported by Ben-Gurion's account of the source and timing of such acts.

17. *Ha'aretz*, Aug. 28, 1953, quoted in A. Yisra'eli [Moshe Machover and Akiva Orr], *Shalom, shalom—ve'ein shalom: Yisra'el arav, 1948–1961* (Jerusalem, 1961), p. 161.

18. E. H. Hutchison, *Violent Truce: A Military Observer Looks at the Arab-Israeli Conflict, 1951–1955* (New York, 1956), pp. 43–45. Ben-Gurion denied IDF responsibility in a radio speech on October 19, 1953; quoted in A. Yisra'eli, *Shalom, shalom*, p. 163. See also Kennett Love, *Suez: The Twice Fought War* (New York, 1969), p. 57. For the IDF's responsibility, see the semiofficial history of the paratroop corps *Sefer hatzanhanim* (Tel Aviv, 1969), p. 77.

19. This interpretation of the effects of the Gaza raid is advanced by Love, *Suez*; and Donald Neff, *Warriors at Suez: Eisenhower Takes America into the Middle East* (New York, 1981).

20. For a succinct summary of these events, see Rokach, *Israel's Sacred Terrorism*, pp. 37–40. Avri El-Ad, an Israeli agent in this affair, argued in his autobiography, *Decline of Honor* (Chicago, 1976), that the operation was intentionally exposed by the director of the Mossad, Ben-Gurion loyalist Isser Harel, in order to end indirect Israeli-Egyptian talks about a peaceful resolution of the conflict, which were then in progress. Whether intended or not, the Israeli sabotage and its exposure did diminish the prospects for an Egyptian-Israeli accommodation.

21. Love, *Suez;* Neff, *Warriors at Suez*.

22. A. Yisra'eli, *Shalom, shalom*.

23. Letter to Amos, October 5, 1937, in David Ben-Gurion, *Letters to Paula* (London, 1971), p. 157. On this point see also Baruch Kimmerling, *Zionism and Territory: The Socio-territorial Dimensions of Zionist Politics* (Berkeley and Los Angeles, 1983).

24. For example, see Zachary Lockman, "The Left in Israel: Zionism vs. Socialism," *MERIP Reports*, no. 49 (July 1976): 3–18; Peretz Merhav, *The*

Israeli Left: History, Problems, Documents (San Diego, Calif., 1980); [Israeli Socialist Organization], "The Left in Israel," in *The Other Israel: The Radical Case Against Zionism,* ed. Arie Bober (New York, 1972).

25. In an interview on Israeli television in the summer of 1987 Hazan said that this remark was the only thing he regretted about his political past.

26. See, for example, his characterization of the seamen's strike quoted in Chapter 3; and S.[aba] sh.[el] Yariv [David Ben-Gurion], *Al hakomunizm vehatzionut shel hashomer hatzaʿir* (Tel Aviv, 1953).

27. Benedict Anderson, *Imagined Communities: Reflections on the Origin and the Spread of Nationalism* (London, 1983).

28. Gareth Stedman Jones, *Languages of Class: Studies in English Working Class History, 1832–1982* (Cambridge, 1983).

29. Antonio Gramsci, "The Modern Prince," in *Selections from the Prison Notebooks,* ed. and trans. Quentin Hoare and Geoffrey Nowell Smith (New York, 1971), p. 151.

30. Tony Judt, *Marxism and the French Left* (Oxford, 1986), p. 18.

31. Hayden White, "The Value of Narrativity in the Representation of Reality," in *On Narrative,* ed. W.J.T. Mitchell (Chicago, 1981), pp. 1–23.

CHAPTER II. THE CREATION OF ISRAEL

1. Mordechai Bentov, *The Case for a Bi-national Palestine: Memorandum Prepared by the Hashomer Hatzair Workers' Party of Palestine* (Tel Aviv, Mar. 1946).

2. For a discussion of one example, the "crisis of the fifth *aliyah*" in 1929–31, see Elkanah Margalit, *Hashomer hatzaʿir: Meʿedat neʿurim lemarksizm mahapkhani, 1913–1936* (Tel Aviv, 1985), pp. 189–96.

3. Mazkirut mifleget poʿalim hashomer hatzaʿir, "Din veheshbon miyeshivat merkaz hamiflagah (27.11.47)," *Yediʿot,* no. 5 (Dec. 28, 1947), p. 3, Hashomer Hatzaʿir archive (hereafter cited as HH) 90.10 (3).

4. Ibid., p. 11.

5. *Al hamishmar* (hereafter cited as *AM*), Jan. 25, 1948.

6. *Yediʿot,* no. 5, p. 12, HH 90.10 (3).

7. Ibid., pp. 15–16.

8. "Matzaʿ ha'ihud," HH 90.31 (1).

9. "Hishtatfutanu bamemshalah hazmanit (midiyunei hamerkaz ba-7 bemartz 1948)," *Igeret lepeʿilim,* no. 1 (Mar. 16, 1948), HH 90.31 (2 gimel).

10. Morris, "Crystallization of Israeli Policy," p. 86.

11. Morris, "Yosef Weitz."

12. Morris, "Causes and Character." Morris argued that the report understated direct expulsions, which he judged to be at least 5 percent. See also his "Operation Dani."

13. Aharon Cohen, "Mediniutenu haʿaravit betokh hamilhamah: Ptihah leberur bevaʿadah hapolitit," HH 90.10.10 (4); "Mediniutenu klapei haʿaravim: Hahlatot havaʿadah hapolitit me 15.6.48," *Miyoman hamazkirut,* no. 4 (June 23, 1948), HH 90.31 (2 gimel).

14. Morris, "Crystallization of Israeli Policy," pp. 93, 104–6.

15. Interpellation of Tzvi Luria to Ben-Gurion and Shitrit, July 13, 1948; letter of Y. Peterzeil to M. Bentov, A. Tzizling, and M. Erem, Aug. 2, 1948; letter of Tzvi Luria to Ben-Gurion, Aug. 3, 1948; HH 90.32 alef (1).

16. Morris, "Causes and Character," p. 18n.1, noted that the copy of the IDF report he saw in Cohen's private papers at the Hashomer Hatza'ir archive has a notation in Cohen's writing "sent 8/7/48 received 11/7/48." When I asked to see this document I was told that the Israeli security services forbade the archive to release this document and that it had been a mistake to allow Morris to see it, as the original was still classified. The document was apparently removed from Cohen's papers after the publication of Morris's article.

17. Flapan, *Birth of Israel*, p. 114.

18. Aharon Cohen, "Nokhah hapinui ha'aravi," *Le'ahdut ha'avodah* 1, no. 1 (June 1948): 45.

19. Aharon Cohen, "Hava navhir dvarim le'atzmenu: Sihah 'im haverim bemadim," *Basha'ar*, nos. 10 and 11 (Aug. 5 and 19, 1948).

20. Ya'akov Hazan, speech in Tel Aviv, July 25–26, 1948, quoted in Yossi Amitay, "Mapam 1948–1954: Emdot besugiyat araviyei eretz yisra'el" (M.A. thesis, Tel Aviv University, 1986), pp. 30–31. According to Morris, "Operation Dani," pp. 88–89, the official Israeli accounts of the "rebellion" of Lydda, on which Hazan undoubtedly relied in making this distinction, were exaggerated to justify the expulsion.

21. Morris, "Yosef Weitz," p. 539.

22. Morris, "Harvest of 1948," p. 675.

23. Amitay, "Mapam 1948–1954," p. 41.

24. Quoted in ibid., p. 37. Amitay correctly noted that Tabenkin was more concerned about the moral effect on the Jews of looting than the injustice committed against Arabs.

25. For example Galili, Alon, Sneh, and Riftin, quoted in Amitay, "Mapam 1948–1954," pp. 19, 44–45; and Cohen, *AM*, Jan. 13, 1950.

26. Resolution of MAPAM Center, Oct. 7, 1948, in *Miyoman hamazkirut*, no. 7 (Oct. 1948), HH 90.31 (2 gimel).

27. HH 95.10.10 (6), quoted in Amitay, "Mapam 1948–1954," p. 72.

28. Minutes of the 27th Mo'etza of Kibbutz Artzi, Dec. 10–12, 1948, HH 5.20.5 (4). Published version in *Yedi'ot hakibutz ha'artzi*, Jan. and Feb.–Mar. 1949.

29. Ibid.

30. For details, see Budeiri, *The Palestine Communist Party*, pp. 162–65.

31. "Hahlatot have'idah ha-IX shel hamiflagah hakomunistit hafalestina'it," *Kol ha'am* (hereafter cited as *KA*), Sept. 23, 1945.

32. Me'ir Vilner, "Haderekh leshihrur (mediniut hamiflagah hakomunistit hafalestinit)," Oct. 1946, pp. 5, 42–43, Kibbutz Me'uhad archive (hereafter cited as KM) 35 Ve'idot 1.2.

33. *Mishmar*, Oct. 20, 1947.

34. For details on the Hebrew Communists, see the unclassified file "Komunistim ivrim" in the Jewish National Library (Jerusalem) manuscript collection, vol. 1272, which includes the Yehudit Buber papers. Membership figure is based on "Communist Activity in Palestine, January 1–July 31, 1947," U.S.

National Archives (USNA) RG 84, Cairo Embassy General Records, 1947, 169/800-C.

35. For details of Farah's activity and his influence over the young Haifa Arab intellectual party members, see Tubi's autobiography in KM 35 Tawfiq Tubi papers.

36. Budeiri, *The Palestine Communist Party,* p. 160.

37. Ibid., p. 164; Yehoshua Porath, "The National Liberation League, 1943–1948," *Asian and African Studies* 4 (1968): 4. The slightly variant texts are due to different translations into Hebrew.

38. Budeiri, *The Palestine Communist Party,* pp. 212–13.

39. E. Tuma, "Report on Palestine," Shmu'el Mikunis and MAKI Papers, Arkhion Ha'avodah Vehehalutz (hereafter cited as AA) IV 104.91. The quote is from Ronald Storrs, *Orientations* (London, 1937), p. 405.

40. "Report on Palestine by S. Mikunis," pp. 5, 6–7, AA IV 104.34.

41. "First Meeting of All Delegations to the Empire Communist Parties Conference on Palestine Problems," p. 2, AA IV 104.34.

42. "Intervention at the Meeting on Palestine and Unity of the Party, 13 March 1947," AA IV 104.34.

43. The Communist Party of Palestine, *We Fight for Freedom: Evidence Given to the UNSCOP,* Jerusalem, July 13 and 15, 1947, pp. 23, 43, KM 35 P.K.P. 1941–1948.

44. *KA,* Oct. 12, 1947.

45. Ibid., Oct. 14, 1947.

46. S. Mikunis, "For Genuine Independence," speech to the Central Committee meeting on Oct. 16, 1947, *KA,* Oct. 17, 1947; translated in *Palestine (PCP) News,* no. 10 (1947).

47. "Hoda'at hava'ad hamerkazi shel hamiflagah hakomunistit," Nov. 30, 1947, AA IV 425.34.

48. "Hamandat habriti met!" May 15, 1948, AA IV 425.35.

49. *KA,* July 22, 1948.

50. "Mikhtav el hakader," Nov. 15, 1947, AA IV 104.95.

51. Arnold Krammer, *The Forgotten Friendship: Israel and the Soviet Bloc, 1947–53* (Urbana, Ill., 1974), pp. 77–78. In his lecture at the memorial ceremony on the fifth anniversary of Mikunis's death (Lavon Institute, Tel Aviv, June 25, 1987), military historian Me'ir Pa'il confirmed Krammer's account of Mikunis's role in securing Czech military aid and argued that without this aid the Israelis would probably have lost the war.

52. *Al-ittihad* (hereafter cited as *I*), Oct. 19, 1947.

53. This account is based on a history of the NLL prepared by the organization in the West Bank before it became the Communist Party of Jordan: "Qararat al-lajna al-markaziyya li'usubat al-taharrur al-watani fi filastin," May 1951; reprinted in Samara, *Al-'amal al-shuyu'i,* pp. 347–63. The Jewish National Library manuscript collection, vol. 1272, box 34, file 2, contains a summary English version of the document prepared for MAKI. Laqueur, *Communism and Nationalism,* and Greilsammer, *Les communistes israéliens,* in their zeal to show that the Arab communists were not internationalists, do not do justice to the seriousness of the debate within the NLL. Their accounts should

be compared to Budeiri, *The Palestine Communist Party*, pp. 233–34. Tawfiq Tubi's version of the internal struggle, quoted by Samara, *Al-'amal al-shuyu'i*, p. 293, is homogenized and sanitized, probably to protect the reputation of Emile Tuma, who rejoined MAKI only in 1951.

54. Porath, "The National Liberation League," p. 16.
55. Ibid., p. 17.
56. "Qararat al-lajna al-markaziyya."
57. Kamen, "After the Catastrophe II," p. 72.
58. "Mikhtav el hakader al hitpathut haligah leshihrur le'umi," KM 35 Shonot, Haliga leshihrur le'umi, 1943–48.
59. *KA*, Jan. 23, 1948, quoting (slightly inaccurately) *Al-jamahir*, Jan. 18, 1948.
60. *AM*, July 11, 1948; *KA*, July 11, 12, 1948; Amitay, "Mapam 1948–1954," p. 28.
61. "Qararat al-lajna al-markaziyya."
62. "La situation à Haifa deux semaines après la conquête de la région arabe de la ville par la 'Hagana': Memorandum présenté à la Direction Populaire et au Quartier Général de la Hagana par le Comité Central du Parti Communiste Israélite," KM 35 P.K.P. 1941–1948. Kamen, "After the Catastrophe II," confirms that the charges in this memorandum were substantially correct.
63. Z. Bernard [Dov Bar Nir] to Behor Shitrit, July 21, 1948, HH 90.32 alef (1).
64. *KA*, Aug. 20, 1948.
65. Ibid., Aug. 19, 1948.
66. "Bayan ila al-shu'ub al-'arabiyya," Awa'il tishrin al-awwal, KM 35 Yehudi-'aravi.
67. Quoted by Shmu'el Mikunis, "Haderekh lenitzahon," *KA*, Oct. 24, 1948.
68. Ibid.
69. Yusuf Darwish, letter to Gamal Abdel Nasser, Dec. 3, 1956 (Yusuf Darwish papers), and Yusuf Darwish, interview, May 12, 1986. The book was Otto Heller, *La fin du judaïsme* (Paris, 1933), translated from the German original.
70. For example, Ahmad Sadiq Sa'd's (unsigned) "Kifah filastin al-watani al-dimuqrati," *Al-fajr al-jadid*, June 16, 1945, and "Yuqawimuna al-hijra ila filastin," ibid., Dec. 6, 1945 (reprinted from *I*). See also *Al-damir*, Oct. 17, 24, 1945. On the anti-Zionist demonstrations of November 2, 1945, see the articles and letters in several subsequent issues of *Al-fajr al-jadid*.
71. Ahmad Sadiq Sa'd, interview, Apr. 29, 1986; and Ahmad Sadiq Sa'd, *Filastin bayna makhalib al-isti'mar* (Cairo, 1946), pp. 2, 113–14.
72. Yasin, *Al-qadiyya al-filastiniyya*, pp. 73–98; Albert Arie, interview in al-Sa'id, *Al-yasar al-misri wa'l-qadiyya*, pp. 294–99; *Sawt al-umma*, Apr. 26, 1947; *Al-jamahir*, June 23, 1947.
73. Shuhdi 'Atiyya al-Shafi'i and 'Abd al-Ma'bud al-Jibayli, *Ahdafuna al-wataniyya* (Cairo, 1945), pp. 36–37. Latifa al-Zayyat gave a similarly moderate anti-Zionist presentation in her lecture at Iskra's intellectual forum, Dar al-Abhath al-'Ilmiyya, in early 1946: "Ma hiyya al-sihyuniyya," in al-Sa'id, *Al-yasar al-misri wa'l-qadiyya*, pp. 95–98.

74. "Le problème palestinien," Oct. 22, 1945 (Curiel papers), translated in al-Saʿid, *Al-yasar al-misri waʾl-qadiyya*, pp. 130–74). Although no author is indicated, it is almost certainly Curiel, as the French original is among his papers.

75. "La lutte du Mouvement Égyptien de Libération Nationale [MELN] puis du Mouvement Démocratique de Libération Nationale [MDLN] depuis leur fondation jusqu'à la déclaration de la loi martiale [Mai 1948]" (rapport adressé par Henri Curiel à ses camarades du MDLN en Septembre–Octobre, 1951?), unpaginated appendix to Henri Curiel, *Pages autobiographiques* (typescript, 1977).

76. Rifʿat al-Saʿid, interview, May 22, 1986.

77. "Les principales étapes de la lutte intérieure qui s'est déroulée autour du MDLN durant l'année: Mai 1947–Juin 1948, dite année de l'unité" (rapport adressé par Henri Curiel à ses camarades du MDLN à la fin de 1955), appendix to *Pages autobiographiques*, p. 11.

78. Raʾuf ʿAbbas and ʿIzzat Riyad have performed a great service by publishing an Arabic translation of a large selection of Curiel's papers, including his autobiography and a portion of his letters and reports to Egypt, in *Awraq Hinri Kuriyal waʾl-haraka al-shuyuʿiyya al-misriyya* (Cairo, 1988), making these documents available to the Egyptian public for the first time. The introductory essays of ʿAbbas and Riyad summarize the charges against Curiel made by former comrades, rivals, and opponents. Unfortunately, they also contain many exaggerations and errors of fact and interpretation, reflecting the uncritical anti-Zionist sentiment (which can be insensitive to the distinction between anti-Zionism and anti-Semitism) now prevalent among nationalist Egyptian intellectuals—an understandable, but nonetheless pernicious, reaction to the Camp David agreement and its failure to secure Palestinian national rights. The most flamboyant insinuations of ʿAbbas and Riyad—that the breakup of the DMNL in 1948 was planned by the Jewish communists (p. 23) and that Curiel was concerned for the welfare of the Egyptian Jewish saboteurs arrested in July 1954 and that this indicated that he was an Israeli intelligence operative (p. 69)—are unsupported by any evidence. For the record, the "young foreign researcher" (p. 9) who gave copies of these documents to Professor ʿAbbas is this writer. Since he chose to hint strongly at my identity, it seems best to abandon the anonymity I originally requested. The reason for my request was not that Curiel's friends in Paris forbade me to show the documents to others, as ʿAbbas wrote, suggesting that publishing them was a conspiratorial act; rather, I preferred to avoid appearing to be a partisan party in the inevitable disagreements among Egyptian leftists that would result from publication of these papers. In fact, their publication did generate an extended exchange in *Al-hilal* during 1988 as well as a book by Ibrahim Fathi, *Hinri Kuriyal didd al-haraka al-shuyuʿiyya al-ʿarabiyya: Al-qadiyya al-filastiniyya* (Cairo, 1989), whose arguments I did not have a chance to consider fully before completing this text. This debate, unlike previous ones on issues in the history of the Egyptian communist movement, has been informed by the common access of the contestants to a body of documentary evidence—which was my purpose in making the Curiel papers available in Egypt.

79. *Al-jamahir*, May 19, 1947.

80. Ibid., Oct. 19, 1947.

81. *Al-waʿy,* Dec. 20, 1947; facsimile in Darwaza, *Al-shuyuʿiyya al-mahalliyya,* appendix.

82. *Al-jamahir,* Oct. 19, Nov. 23, Dec. 21, 1947; Jan. 18, Feb. 29, 1948.

83. Interview in al-Saʿid, *Al-yasar al-misri wa'l-qadiyya,* p. 284.

84. So he wrote in his "Letter to Dr. Ra'uf ʿAbbas," which appeared in the second printing of the Arabic translation of Gilles Perrault's *Un homme à part.* ʿAbbas replied to Hazan's defense of Curiel and the Jewish communists (in my opinion unconvincingly) in "Hinri Kuriyal bayna al-ustura wa'l-waqiʿ al-ta'rikhi," *Al-hilal* 66, no. 11 (Nov. 1988): 42–47.

85. Mustafa Tiba, "Hawla awraq Hinri Kuriyal: Matlub taqyim mawduʿi li'l-ta'rikh al-hadith," *Al-hilal* 66, no. 11 (Nov. 1988): 57.

86. Letter of Mahmoud El Nabawi to the editor of *Kol ha'am,* Sept. 1, 1947, AA IV 104.91.

87. Curiel, "Les principales étapes de la lutte"; Albert Arie, interview, July 3, 1986; Yusuf Hazan, interview, June 24, 1986; Raymond Stambouli and Yusuf Hazan, quoted in Perrault, *Un homme à part,* p. 198.

88. Curiel, *Pages autobiographiques,* p. 57. The partial rendition of this passage in the English translation of Perrault, *Un homme à part—A Man Apart: The Life of Henri Curiel,* vol. 1 (London, 1987), p. 146—gives "rather chauvinist," conveying more hostility than the original French.

89. Botman, *The Rise of Egyptian Communism,* pp. 94–95. Zahran, *Fi usul al-siyasa al-misriyya,* p. 139, also attributes anti-Zionist motives to al-Shafiʿi.

90. Rifʿat al-Saʿid, interview, May 22, 1986.

91. Quoted in Darwaza, *Al-shuyuʿiyya al-mahalliyya,* pp. 149–50.

92. Ahmad Sadiq Saʿd, interview, Apr. 29, 1986; Yusuf Darwish, interview, May 12, 1986; Abu Sayf Yusuf, interview, May 9, 1986. No copies of *Al-hadaf* survive.

93. Ahmad Sadiq Saʿd, interview, Apr. 29, 1986; Raymond Douek, interview, June 26, 1986.

94. Hilmi Yasin, interview, May 25, 1986.

95. This was MAKI's position from mid to late 1948.

CHAPTER III. THE POLITICAL ECONOMY OF HEGEMONY

1. According to Israeli scholars including Morris, *Birth of the Palestinian Refugee Problem,* pp. xiv–xviii; Kimmerling, *Zionism and Territory,* p. 123; and Kamen, "Aharei ha'ason," p. 9, the number of abandoned (i.e., destroyed) villages is between 350 and 370. In addition, the cities of Majdal, Beersheba, Tiberias, Safed, and Beisan and the western section of Jerusalem were emptied of their Arab inhabitants. The Palestinian historian ʿArif al-ʿArif compiled a list of 385 destroyed villages, reprinted in Uri Davis and Norton Mezvinsky, eds., *Documents from Israel, 1967–1973: Readings for a Critique of Zionism* (London, 1975), pp. 43–54. Most of the discrepancy between the lists is due to Israeli scholars' reliance on the unpublished *Village Statistics, 1946* compiled by the mandatory government, which did not officially recognize all inhabited localities.

2. Statistics in this paragraph are drawn from Don Peretz, *Israel and the Palestine Arabs* (Washington, D.C., 1958), pp. 140–47.

3. The classic critical study of capital imports to Israel is Glenn Yago, "Whatever Happened to the Promised Land? Capital Flows and the Israeli State," *Berkeley Journal of Sociology* 21 (1976): 117–46.

4. Michael Wolffsohn, *Israel: Polity, Society, and Economy 1882–1986* (Atlantic Highlands, N.J., 1987), p. 267. The share of capital imports from the United States dropped to a historic low of 19 percent during 1961–65 but climbed to over 80 percent during some years of the 1970s and 1980s, leading Wolffsohn to conclude, "The importance of the United States as a source of capital imports . . . can hardly be overemphasized" (p. 264).

5. Henry Rosenfeld and Shulamit Carmi, "The Privatization of Public Means: The State-made Middle Class and the Realization of Family Value in Israel," in *Kinship and Modernization in Mediterranean Society*, ed. J. G. Perstiany (Rome, 1976), p. 137n.

6. Wolffsohn, *Israel*, p. 263.

7. Ibid., p. 212.

8. Michael Shalev, "The Political Economy of Labor Party Dominance and Decline in Israel" (forthcoming in a volume edited by T. J. Pempel to be published by Cornell University Press).

9. Deborah Bernstein and Shlomo Swirsky, "The Rapid Economic Development of Israel and the Emergence of the Ethnic Division of Labour," *British Journal of Sociology* 33, no. 1 (1982): 64–85.

10. Rosenfeld and Carmi, "The Privatization of Public Means." See also the statistical evidence of the social promotion of the (mainly Ashkenazi) veterans in Nadav Halevi and Ruth Klinov-Malul, *The Economic Development of Israel* (New York, 1968), p. 73.

11. This figure, given by Bernstein and Swirsky, "The Rapid Economic Development of Israel," p. 74, is based on data published in Halevi and Klinov-Malul, *Economic Development of Israel*. It is slightly higher than the official figures because it includes potential workers in *ma'abarot* (new immigrant camps) and (apparently) some correction for undercounting of Arab unemployment.

12. Shimshon Bichler, "He'arot letkufat hatzena'" (seminar paper, 1987), pp. 5–10. For the orthodox view, see Halevi and Klinov-Malul, *Economic Development of Israel*, pp. 272ff.; and Don Patinkin, *The Israeli Economy: The First Decade* (Jerusalem, 1969), pp. 38–40.

13. Yish'ayahu Etkin, "Shishim shnot shvitah beyisra'el, 1921–1980" (M.A. thesis, Tel Aviv University, 1982), pp. 176–88.

14. Tzvi Segal "Igud hayama'im, 1935–1953: Me'agudah mekomit le'igud artzi" (M.A. thesis, Tel Aviv University, 1976).

15. *Divrei hakneset*, Dec. 10, 1951, quoted in ibid., p. 88.

16. Israel's decision to recognize the People's Republic of China and to vote for its admission to the United Nations is an exception to this trend motivated by the strategy of courting the new states of Asia. Although this initiative succeeded in the case of Burma, it generally failed and was not pursued.

17. Shmu'el Mikunis, *Shvitat hayama'im, hahitpathut vehalekah*, quoted in Segal, "Igud hayama'im," p. 180.

18. Re'uven Kaminer and Dafna Kaminer, interview, August 31, 1985.
19. Shalev, "Political Economy of Labor Party Dominance and Decline."
20. *KA,* Feb. 16, 1958.
21. Election poster of Ahdut hapoʻalim joint MAKI/LSP list, KM 35 Behirot le'igudim miktzoʻiyim vetotza'otayhen, 1952–1972; Balti, *Bama'avak al hakiyum hayehudi,* p. 25.
22. MAKI. Havaʻad hamerkazi, *Hozer,* no. 38 (Apr. 9, 1959), KM 35 Hitkatvut 1.5. It may have been "the first time" in several years, but this was not an unusual phenomenon in the early 1950s.
23. Based on leaflets signed by these cells in KM 35 Hapeʻilut besnif haifah, 1950–1961.
24. "Aryeh," *Histadrut Hashomer Hatzaʻir beyisra'el,* no. 5, quoted in S[aba] sh.[el] Yariv, *Al hakomunism vehatzionut,* p. 3.
25. Eliyahu Kanovsky, *The Economy of the Israeli Kibbutz* (Cambridge, Mass., 1966), pp. 22, 41, 92–95, 138.
26. Amitay, "Mapam 1948–1954," pp. 143–44.
27. Kanovsky, *Economy of the Israeli Kibbutz,* p. 34.
28. The kibbutzim of Kibbutz Artzi established on formerly Arab lands after 1948 include Barʻam, Barkai, Bet Nir, Karmiah, Dvir, Ein Dor, Gaʻaton, Gazit, Givʻat Oz, Har El, Lahav, Lehavot Havivah, Magen, Megido, Mei Ami, Metzer, Nahshon, Nir Oz, Revadim, Saʻar, Sasa, Shomrat, and Zikim. This list, which may be incomplete, constitutes 30 percent of Kibbutz Artzi's members today.
29. Jon Kimche and David Kimche, *Both Sides of the Hill* (London, 1960), pp. 82–84. The account published by Hashomer Hatzaʻir justified the attack on the grounds that Saʻsa had been a conduit for armed infiltrators from Syria; see *Sefer hashomer hatzaʻir* (Merhavia, 1964), 3:74–76.
30. Morris, *Birth of the Palestinian Refugee Problem,* p. 230.
31. Diary entry for Jan. 16, 1949, in Kibbutz Sasa, the Secretariat, *The Launching: Sasa's First Year* (Tel Aviv, 1951; repr. 1984), p. 20.
32. Ibid., Jan. 21, 1949, p. 21.
33. Yak Matek, "The Mosque," in *Sasa 35, 1949–1984: Founders' Gathering, July 6–8, 1984* (mimeograph, Sasa, 1984), p. 19.
34. S.L., letter to Sasa comrades in America, Jan. 13, 1949, in *The Launching,* pp. 17–18.
35. Diary entry, Feb. 8, 1949, in *The Launching,* p. 21.
36. Ibid., Feb. 17, 1949, p. 26.
37. Information about Lahav is based on HH 101.6, an interview with David Shoshani, Dec. 18, 1988 and my nine-month residence there in 1970–71.
38. Mahmoud Abdel-Fadil, *Development, Income Distribution, and Social Change in Rural Egypt, 1952–1970* (Cambridge, 1975), p. 4 (1 feddan = 1.038 acres). The following synopsis of the nationalist movement and postwar political developments is based primarily on Shuhdi ʻAtiyya al-Shafiʻi, *Tatawwur al-haraka al-wataniyya al-misriyya, 1882–1956* (Cairo, 1957); Tariq al-Bishri, *Al-haraka al-siyasiya fi misr, 1945–1952* (Cairo, 1972); ʻAsim Ahmad al-Disuqi, *Kibar mallak al-aradi al-ziraʻiyya wa-dawruhum fi al-mujtamaʻ al-misri, 1914–1952* (Cairo, 1975); Anouar Abdel-Malek, *Egypt: Military Society* (New York, 1968); Eric Davis, *Challenging Colonialism: Bank Misr and*

the Political Economy of Industrialization in Egypt, 1920–1941 (Princeton, 1983); and Joel Beinin and Zachary Lockman, *Workers on the Nile: Nationalism, Communism, Islam, and the Egyptian Working Class, 1882–1954* (Princeton, 1988).

39. On the radicalization of the young intelligentsia, see the book by a Greek-Egyptian former member of Popular Democracy, Raoul Makarius, *La jeunesse intellectuelle d'Égypte au lendemain de la deuxième guerre mondiale* (Paris, 1960).

40. The classic account of American support for the coup is that of former CIA operative Miles Copeland, *The Game of Nations* (London, 1969). While there is little doubt that his story is generally true, it cannot be fully verified as the files of the U.S. embassy in Cairo relating to this matter, which should have been opened several years ago, have not been declassified.

41. Explanatory Note on the Land Reform Law of September 9, 1952 (mimeographed English translation from the Arabic).

42. For details, see Beinin and Lockman, *Workers on the Nile*, pp. 418–31.

43. From the point of view of the capitalist market, dismissing a worker because of production cutbacks (for example) is not "arbitrary." Egyptian workers judged this matter by a different standard, however, and I have employed the term they used for this practice.

44. Khalid Muhyi al-Din, Letter to Gamal Abdel Nasser, Mar. 31, 1953, published in *Al-ahali*, July 24, 1985; Amin ʿIzz al-Din, *Taʾrikh al-tabaqa al-ʿamila al-misriyya mundhu nushuʾiha hatta sanat 1970* (Cairo, 1987), pp. 817–20.

45. Not all the unions supported Abdel Nasser; some textile and transport workers' unions with a history of left-wing militancy supported Naguib. See Beinin and Lockman, *Workers on the Nile*, pp. 437–43.

46. Ulfat Mahmud ʿAtif, "Al-ʿummal waʾl-haraka al-ʿummaliyya fi misr: 1942–1961" (M.A. thesis, Cairo University, 1985), pp. 247, 249–50; Fathi Kamil, *Maʿa al-haraka al-niqabiyya fi nisf qarn: Safahat min dhikrayat Fathi Kamil* (Cairo, 1985), pp. 139–49; ʿIzz al-Din, *Taʾrikh al-tabaqa al-ʿamila*, pp. 820–26.

47. "Taqrir ʿan milaff maktab al-ustadh Yusuf Darwish al-muhami" (Yusuf Darwish papers).

48. Yusuf Darwish, Letter to Gamal Abdel Nasser, Dec. 3, 1956, and "Asmaʾ al-munazzamin fi al-muqawama al-shaʿbiyya—Shubra al-Khayma" (Yusuf Darwish papers); *Al-masaʾ* (hereafter cited as *M*), Dec. 9, 1956. Darwish's Jewish identity was probably another factor motivating the government's action against him.

49. See, for example, Lufti al-Khuli, "Taʾmim al-qanah waʾl-tabaqa al-ʿamila," *M*, Oct. 7, 1956; and Muhammad ʿAli ʿAmir, "Khatt al-difaʿ al-awwal," *M*, Dec. 27, 1956.

50. Fathi Kamil, Ahmad Fahim, Sayyid ʿAbd al-Wahhab Nada, and Nur Sulayman, *Al-tabaqa al-ʿamila fi al-maʿraka didd al-istiʿmar* (Cairo, 1957), p. 7. Many of the events mentioned in the first paragraph of this section are described in this book.

51. Patrick O'Brien, *The Revolution in Egypt's Economic System* (London, 1966), p. 100.

52. *Budget Report, 1957–58,* p. 13, cited in ibid., p. 102.

53. See *M,* Nov. 25, 1957, for a letter criticizing Mar'i on this issue. Fernand J. Tomiche, *Syndicalisme et certains aspects du travail en République Arabe Unie (Égypte), 1900–1965* (Paris, 1974), p. 43, interprets publication of the letter as proof of increased freedom of expression, but criticism of a single government minister was not a new phenomenon in the Egyptian press. Moreover, in the context of a discussion of the government's labor policies it seems more significant that a minister opposed the formation of a union than that a worker criticized the minister for doing so. Unions of agricultural workers were eventually established.

54. *M,* Feb. 15, 1959.

55. O'Brien, *Revolution in Egypt's Economic System,* p. 103.

56. For statistical evidence of the increase in industrial conflict, see Joel Beinin, "Labor, Capital, and the State in Nasserist Egypt," *International Journal of Middle East Studies* 21, no. 1 (Feb. 1989).

57. *M,* July 30, Nov. 7, 1957.

58. Ibid., Aug. 19, 1958.

59. Ibid., Oct. 28, 1957.

60. Ibid., Sept. 2, 1957.

61. Ibid., Jan. 20, 1958.

62. Tahir al-'Amiri, "Ana al-'amil," *Nashrat ittihad niqabat al-ghazl wa'l-nasij bi-jumhuriyat misr,* no. 3 (probably Sept. 1955), p. 14.

63. A convenient translation of Bayram al-Tunisi's poem, which first appeared in English in a book published by Egyptian leftists in 1942 to introduce Egypt to British troops, is available in Botman, *Rise of Egyptian Communism,* pp. 18–19.

64. For a discussion of the fate of this concept and its application in Egypt, see Esmail Hosseinzadeh, *Soviet Non-capitalist Development: The Case of Nasser's Egypt* (New York, 1989).

65. "Hikayat awwal mayu," *M,* May 21, 1957.

66. Ahmed Abdalla, *The Student Movement and National Politics in Egypt* (London, 1985), pp. 101–10.

67. Abdel-Fadil, *Development, Income Distribution and Social Change,* pp. 23, 41–49; idem. *The Political Economy of Nasserism: A Study in Employment and Income Distribution Policies in Urban Egypt, 1952–1972* (Cambridge, 1980), p. 33.

68. The Kamshish affair symbolized the absence of an agrarian revolution; see Hamied Ansari, *Egypt: The Stalled Society* (Albany, N.Y., 1986).

69. Gouda Abdel-Khalek, "The Open Door Economic Policy in Egypt: Its Contribution to Investment and Equity Implications," in *Rich and Poor States in the Middle East: Egypt and the New Arab Order,* ed. Malcolm Kerr and El-Sayyid Yassin (Boulder, Colo., 1982), pp. 263, 268.

CHAPTER IV. A WINDOW OF OPPORTUNITY?

1. These women included Latifa al-Zayyat, Soraya Adham, Fatma Zaki, Inge Aflatun, Aimée Setton, and Odette Hazan Solomon (the last two were Jewish).

2. Mohamed Sid-Ahmed, interview, May 11, 1986. For more anecdotes about Iskra's social style, see the biographical sketch of Albert Arie in Selma Botman,"Oppositional Politics in Egypt: The Communist Movement, 1936–1954" (Ph.D. diss., Harvard University, 1984), pp. 505–6.

3. Curiel, *Pages autobiographiques,* p. 54 and appendix, "Les principales étapes," p. 7.

4. Ibid., p. 55, and appendix, "Les principales étapes," pp. 5, 24.

5. Caffery to State, September 18, 1950, USNA RG 84, Cairo Embassy General Records, 1950–52, 231/350.21(E–L). Ambassador Caffery offered no evidence to support his implicit allegation.

6. Hilmi Yasin, interview, May 25, 1986; Mahmud Amin al-ʿAlim, interview, May 1, 1986; Fuʾad Mursi, interview, May 19, 1986.

7. Fuʾad Mursi, interview, May 19, 1986.

8. Ibid.

9. "De l'élargissement," Mar. 31, 1951 (Curiel papers).

10. Figures for the size of the organizations are based on estimates given by several former communists.

11. "Au C.C. du M.D.L.N.," May 25, 1953 (Curiel papers).

12. *Bulletin d'études et d'information sur l'Égypte et le Soudan,* no. 17 (Aug. 1952). For Curiel's personal statement of support for the new regime despite his realistic assessment of the army's limitations, see "H.C. lettre à l'Égypte," Aug. 27, 1952 (Curiel papers).

13. "Reports of Anti-Jewish Activities in Egypt," Embassy to State, Apr. 21, 1954, USNA RG 84, Cairo Embassy General Records, 1954, 258/350.21

14. Amin Shakir, Saʿid ʿAryan, and ʿAli Adham, *Haqiqat al-shuyuʿiyya* (Cairo, 1954), p. 180. This volume appeared in the *Ikhtarna laka* (We Have Chosen for You) series sponsored by the government to direct information to a mass audience.

15. Mahmud Amin al-ʿAlim, interview, May 1, 1986.

16. Philip Gallab, interview, May 14, 1986.

17. Rifʿat al-Saʿid, interview, May 22, 1986.

18. Fuʾad Mursi, interview, May 19, 1986.

19. Ibid. Mursi quoted his pamphlet from memory, as no copies of the original are available. Similar sentiments were expressed by Rifʿat al-Saʿid, Mahmud Amin al-ʿAlim, and Philip Gallab.

20. Mahmud Amin al-ʿAlim and ʿAbd al-ʿAzim Anis, *Fi al-thaqafa al-misriyya* (Beirut, 1955).

21. Taha Husayn, *The Future of Culture in Egypt* (Washington, D.C., 1954).

22. al-ʿAlim and Anis, *Fi al-thaqafa al-misriyya,* p. 6.

23. Ahmad Taha and ʿAbd al-Munʿim al-Ghazzali, interviews in ʿAbd al-ʿAzim Ramadan, *ʿAbd al-Nasir wa-azmat maris* (Cairo, 1976), pp. 309–10, 351.

24. For details of this affair, see Gresh, "Le P.C.F. et l'Égypte"; and Perrault, *Un homme à part,* pp. 240–55.

25. Perrault, *Un homme à part,* p. 255.

26. Among them was Sayyid Sulayman Rifaʿi, an air force mechanic recruited by Curiel to the communist movement with the first group of Egyptians

in 1943, who loyally upheld Curiel's line when he succeeded him in the DMNL leadership. In August 1953, Rifa'i split from the DMNL to lead the DMNL–Revolutionary Current, which rejected the DMNL's continuing support for the military coup. In February 1954, the internal bulletin of Rifa'i's group stated that "the international movement considers Yunis a doubtful element" (quoted in "À propos de l'article du 'cadre' du MDLN-CR," early 1954 [Curiel papers]).

27. "Résolution du groupe de Rome du MDLN à la suite de la création du PCEU: Au CC du PCEU—Juin 1955" (Curiel papers).

28. "Correspondance et rapports concernant le cas de Jacques [another nom de guerre of Curiel]," 1955–56 (Curiel papers).

29. Henri Curiel, letter to Naomi Canel in prison, May 10, 1957 (Curiel papers).

30. In an interview on June 24, 1986, Yusuf Hazan expressed enthusiastic support for the partition plan (in contrast to the organization's reluctant acceptance). By this time, though, his opinions may well have been different from his views in 1948. Moreover, Hazan was one of the first Jewish DMNL members to leave Egypt, arriving in Paris in 1949, after which point he had little influence.

31. *Sawt al-brulitariyya,* no. 2 (Nov. 2, 1948), organ of Voice of the Opposition, partial facsimile in Darwaza, appendix to *Al-shuyu'iyya al-mahalliyya;* full text pp. 151–53. For a fuller exposition of the general line of this tendency, see "Here Is the Egyptian Communist Organization That We Wish to Create," a programmatic document probably written in May 1948, acquired and translated by the U.S. Embassy in Cairo. No author is indicated on the document itself, but its line is consistent with that of Voice of the Opposition/MISHMISH, since the only reference to Palestine is a statement that "fascist parties and organizations [i.e., Young Egypt and the Muslim Brothers] are being militarized under the benevolent eye of reaction and imperialism (especially since the events of 21 February 1946, and above all lately under cover of the defense of Palestine)" (Controlled American Source to the Ambassador, Aug. 30, 1948, USNA RG 84, Cairo Embassy General Records, 1948, 193/800C).

32. Mohamed Sid-Ahmed, interview in Botman, "Oppositional Politics in Egypt," p. 294. For further information on this tendency, see also pp. 289–94.

33. *Nouvelles d'Égypte,* no. 8 (Oct. 31, 1953): 13–15.

34. Ibid., no. 19 (July 14, 1954): 9–11.

35. Khalid [Fu'ad Mursi], *Tatawwur al-ra'smaliyya wa-kifah al-tabaqat fi misr* (Cairo, 1949 or 1950), pp. 48–50, facsimile reproduction in appendix to Darwaza, *Al-shuyu'iyya al-mahalliyya.* No full copies of the original are available.

36. *Rayat al-sha'b,* no. 31 (1952), quoted in Darwaza, *Al-shuyu'iyya al-mahalliyya,* p. 164.

37. *Rayat al-sha'b,* Nov. 3, 1953, facsimile in Darwaza, *Al-shuyu'iyya al-mahalliyya.*

38. "Deux analyses—deux politiques: La situation actuelle en Égypte" (Rodinson papers). My dating of the document relies on internal evidence.

39. Albert Arie, interview, July 3, 1986.

40. The exchanges between the two parties are contained in "Mapam. Hamerkaz. Tik ksharim im hamiflagah hakomunistit hayisra'elit (1948)," HH 90.31 alef (1 bet). Some of the letters between the party leaderships were later published in the party dailies and other organs.

41. In Israel's single-constituency proportional system, voters choose one party list of 120 candidates. Candidates win Knesset seats in proportion to the party's national vote in the order their names appear on the list. A joint list would consist of candidates from both parties in an established order and proportion.

42. El'azar Peri, "Tzionut: Tnai lehazit me'uhedet," *Igeret lemasbir,* Nov. 17, 1948, HH 90.31 (2 gimel).

43. Aharon Cohen, speech at the Council of Kibbutz Artzi, Dec. 10–12, 1948, HH 5.20.5 (4).

44. Peri, "Tzionut."

45. Mifleget hapo'alim hame'uhedet, *Sihah 'im haboher* [1949].

46. Hamahlakah lepe'ulah 'aravit, "Hozer el kol hevrei mapam haba'im bemaga' 'im 'aravim," Jan. 14, 1949, HH 90.31 (2 bet).

47. Mapam, Hamerkaz, "Bulitin hamahlakah lepe'ulah 'aravit," nos. 5 (Feb. 20, 1949) and 6 (Aug. 10, 1949); "Likrat mo'etzet hamiflagah (prakim leberur)—hartza'at Aharon Cohen be'ishur hamahlakah lepe'ulah 'aravit," July 31, 1949; "Hozer lehevrai hamo'etzah veva'adot snifim," Oct. 4, 1949; all in HH 90.31 (2 alef).

48. *I,* Jan. 10, 17, 1949.

49. The text of the speech is reprinted in Hanna Ibrahim, ed., *Hanna Naqqara: Muhami al-ard wa'l-sha'b* (Acre, 1985), pp. 323–33, where it is incorrectly identified as having been delivered in the 1951 election campaign. The speech was reported in *I,* Dec. 26, 1948.

50. *I,* Jan. 17, 24, 1949.

51. Results for the first three Knesset elections are based on Israel, Halishkah hamerkazit lestatistikah, *Totza'ot habehirot lakneset harishonah, hashniyah vehashlishit ulerashuyot hamekomiyot be 1950 ube-1955,* Sidrat pirsumim meyuhadim, no. 51 (Jerusalem, 1957).

52. Ze'ev Tzur, *Bein shutafut le'oppozitziah: She'elat shitufah shel mapam bamemshalah, 1949–1954* (Efal, 1983), pp. 7–10.

53. *KA* and *AM,* Apr. 5, 1949.

54. *KA,* Feb. 21, 25; Mar. 24; Aug. 8; Sept. 14, 17, 1949.

55. *KA,* Aug. 2, 1949; *AM,* July 7, 1949.

56. *KA,* Apr. 28, 1949.

57. *AM,* June 22, Sept. 6, 1949.

58. Me'ir Vilner, *Internatzionalizm proletari mul natzionalizm burgani,* p. 19, KM 35 Ve'idot 1.3.

59. Shmu'el Mikunis, "Ne'um hatshuvah levikuah haklali," *Hahlatot, divrei ptihah, tshuvah levikuah, brakhot,* p. 18, KM 35 Ve'idot 1.3.

60. "Duah hava'ad hamerkazi shel MAKI leve'idah ha-11," *Hahlatot, divrei ptihah, tshuvah levikuah, brakhot,* p. 75, KM 35 Ve'idot 1.3.

61. Emile Habibi, interview, July 21, 1987.

62. *KA*, Mar. 9, 1949.
63. *KA*, June 13, 14, 1949; *AM*, June 16, 1949; and also the pamphlet of MAKI's Central Committee, "Hodaʿat havaʿad hamerkazi shel hamiflagah hakomunistit hayisraʾelit beʿinyan hitztarfutam shel 28 hevrei 'Zikim' lemaki."
64. *KA*, Oct. 23, 1949.
65. Membership figure is based on the number of votes for delegates to the Second Congress. A U.S. diplomatic dispatch—"Israel-Prague Trials," Dec. 27, 1952, USNA RG 84, Tel Aviv Embassy Classified General Records, 1950–52, 7/350—estimated that Sneh and Riftin had the support of 25–30 percent of MAPAM.
66. Elʿazar Peri, *Anahnu veʿolam hamahapekhah* (Tel Aviv, May 1, 1950). See also Yaʿakov Riftin, "Anu vehakomunizm," *AM*, Apr. 30, 1950; and Aharon Cohen, "ʿOlam hamahapekhah vehatzionut," *Mahbarot lemarksizm*, no. 2 (Feb. 1951). These constitute the classic texts of the Kibbutz Artzi left.
67. For example, a joint demonstration was held in front of the American embassy in Tel Aviv on the second anniversary of the outbreak of the Korean War, on June 25, 1952 (reported in USNA RG 84, Tel Aviv Embassy General Records, 1950–52, 6/350.21).
68. "Likrat moeʿtzet hamiflagah (prakim leberur): Hartzaʾat A. Cohen beʾishur hamahlakah lepeʿulah ʿaravit," HH 90.31 (2 alef); Aharon Cohen to Meʾir Yaʿari, July 1, 1950, HH 90.38 (2).
69. "El tzirei hamoshav hashlishi shel moʿetzet mapam," HH 90.31 (2 alef).
70. R. Bastuni to A. Cohen, Jan. 12, 1951; R. Bastuni to Y. Vashitz, Feb. 20, 1951—both in HH 95.10.11 (7). E. Beʾeri to R. Bastuni, Oct. 28, 1952, HH 90.37 (7).
71. Elʿazar Peri, *Bameh nivdalim shloshet hamatzaʿim zeh mizeh*, Feb. 25, 1951, HH 90.39 (1).
72. "Gilui daʿat shel haveʿidah harishonah shel hahativah haʿaravit, 13–14 April 1951," HH 90.39 (1).
73. Mifleget hapoʿalim hameʾuhedet, *Likrat veʿidat mifleget hapoʿalim hameʾuhedet: Hanahot leberur* [Tel Aviv, 1951], p. 7.
74. Hehazit lelikud hamiflagah, *ʿAl mah beʾemet havikuah?* HH 90.39 (1).
75. *Matzaʿ hamiflagah* (the Haifa program) [Tel Aviv, 1951], p. 16.
76. *Davar*, June 3, 1951.
77. *AM*, Nov. 23, 1952.
78. "Yeshivot havaʿadah hapolitit vehamedinit," Nov. 23, 1952, HH 90.66 bet (8).
79. Minutes of MAPAM's Eighth Council, Dec. 24, 1952, HH 90.69 (1).
80. Hativat hasmol bemifleget hapoʿalim hameʾuhedet, "Gilui daʿat," Jan. 17, 1953, HH 90.37 (5).
81. "Hodaʿat hahativah haʿaravit," HH 90.32 bet (5 gimel).
82. Tzvi Lubliner to Sneh, Berman, and Tubin, Jan. 21, 1953, HH 90.31 alef (2 heh); Sneh, Berman, Tubin, and Bastuni to Central Committee, Jan. 25, 1953, HH 90.31 alef (1 bet).
83. Sneh, Berman, Rubin, and Bastuni, "El hevrei moʿetzet hamiflagah," Jan. 27, 1953, HH 90.32 bet (5 gimel).

84. "Parashat mishpat Prag," Y. Riftin to M. Ya'ari, June 18, 1953, HH 95.2.1 (4 dalet).
85. Y. Riftin and E. Peri to M. Ya'ari, July 27, 1953, HH 95.2.1 (4 chet).
86. Isser Harel, *Bitahon vedemokratiah* (Tel Aviv, 1989), p. 214.
87. *AM*, Jan. 8, 1953.
88. This is the figure reported in MAKI's *Information Bulletin*, no. 3 (Mar. 15, 1953). It is consistent with Kibbutz Artzi's record (in HH 5.6 [4]) of the vote in the first thirty-five kibbutzim (of a total of sixty-seven) in alphabetical order, in which 17.6 percent voted no or abstained. The second half of the record has not been preserved, but since Ein Shemer and Shuval, which had a large number of no votes, are in that section of the list, a total of 20 percent is not unreasonable.
89. Tz. Lubliner to F. Ilanit, A. Lipsker, G. Levi, E. Peri, E. Preminger, S. Flapan, Y. Riftin, and H. Rubin, Jan. 18, 1954, HH 95.2.1 (4 tet).
90. Me'ir Ya'ari, *Kibutz galuyot be'aspeklariah shel yamenu* (Merhavia, 1954).
91. "Hatza'ot beyeshivat hava'ad hapo'el shel hakibutz ha'artzi be'ein shemer hugshu al yedei El. Peri," Jan. 27–28, 1954, HH 95.2.1 (4 tet).
92. *Hashavu'a bakibutz ha'artzi*, Apr. 16, 1954.
93. El'azar Peri, "Dvarim bemo'etzet hakibutz ha'artzi, Giv'at Havivah," Apr. 3, 1954, HH 95.2.1 (4 tet).
94. Quoted in *Smol*, Feb. 18, 1954. *AM*'s October 19, 1953, editorial indirectly supported the raid using activist language typical of Ahdut Ha'avodah. The October 20 editorial expressed mild reservations but did not challenge Ben-Gurion's version of the incident. Both editorials criticized the UN for acting one-sidedly against Israel.
95. "Lesiyum haparasha ha'aguma," *Hashavu'a bakibutz ha'artzi*, Apr. 9, 1953.
96. Quoted in *Smol lakibutz* (supplement to *Smol*), July 27, 1953.
97. "Parashat Har El," Oct. 27, 1955, HH 5.6 (4).
98. Shmu'el Amir, interview, Aug. 21, 1985.
99. *Smol*, Mar. 30, 1953.
100. Shmu'el Amir (expelled from Shuval), interview, Aug. 21, 1985; Re'uven Kaminer and Dafna Kaminer (expelled from Sa'ar), interview, Aug. 31, 1985.
101. Ibid.
102. "Matza' hayesod shel mifleget hasmol hasotzialisti hayisra'eli," *Smol*, Apr. 16, 1953.
103. *Smol*, Feb. 12, 1953.
104. M. Vilner, "Im hakamat mifleget hasmol hasotzialisti beyisra'el," *KA*, May 22, 1953.
105. Lecture notes (Shmu'el Amir papers).
106. Shmu'el Amir, interview, Aug. 21, 1985.
107. Sneh's own account of his political development is contained in his "political will," *KA*, Mar. 15, 1972. Balti, *Bama'avak al hakiyum hayehudi*, adopted the perspective of this document in portraying Sneh as having been

motivated primarily by Jewish national sentiment throughout his life. While there is undoubtedly some truth to this characterization, it does not explain why Sneh was a champion of Soviet loyalism and Marxist theoretical orthodoxy in the 1950s and early 1960s. It is difficult to believe that his consistent positions during these years did not represent his deep convictions.

108. *Smol*, Feb. 12, 1953.

109. Balti, *Bamaʾavak al hakiyum hayehudi*, p. 21.

110. Protocols of the Council of the Left Socialist Party, Jan. 15–16, 1954 (Shmuʾel Amir papers).

111. Moshe Sneh, *Sikumin basheʾelah haleʾumit leʾor hamarksizm-leninizm* (Tel Aviv, Aug. 1954).

112. My account of MAKI's activity in defense of Arab rights is based mainly on the many Arabic leaflets in KM 35 Peʿilut bemigzar haʿaravi and other mostly unclassified boxes of Arabic material.

113. Ibrahim, *Hanna Naqqara*, p. 275; "Latasqut muʾamarat al-sultat didd qadat idrab ʿummal al-zaytun," MAKI Acre District Committee, n.d., KM 35 Kruzim leʾigudim miktzoʿiyim, 1950–1971.

114. See, for example, the wall poster of the Nazareth and Haifa-Acre District Committees against the Majdal expulsions of August 19, 1950, KM 35 Peʿilut bemigzar haʿaravi.

115. E. Tuma to MAKI Secretariat, Oct. 9, 1955, KM 35 Zekhuyot hamiʿut haʿaravi, 1950–1964, Havaʿad lehaganat zekhuyot haʾukhlusiyah haʿaravit.

116. KM 35 Peʿilut bemigzar haʿaravi.

117. *I*, Mar. 28, Apr. 11, 1949.

118. A. Cohen, "Yoman shvitat ovdei hatabak" (1949), HH 95.10.11 (6); *I*, Sept. 25, 1948.

119. *I*, Oct. 16, 1949.

120. Ibid. Dec. 10, 1950.

121. "Tivutal haʾisur al veʿidat kongres hapoʿalim benatzeret," AWC leaflet, Sept. 24, 1950, 35 KM Zekhuyot hamiʿut haʿaravi, 1950–1964, Kongres hapoʿalim haʿaravim; *I*, Apr. 27, 1951.

122. Havaʿad hamerkazi, *Hozer*, no. 6 (July 7, 1952), KM 35 Hitkatvut (Mazkirut havaʿad hamerkazi—hozrim lamhozot ulesnifim, 1950–1961) 1.1; Letter of E. Drukman to MAPAM, July 14, 1952, KM 35 Hamahlakah hamiktzoʿit hamerkazit (Pniyot lemiflagot hahistadrut vehuleh); Havaʿad haʾartzi hatziburi lemaʿan histadrut ahidah lekhol haʿovdim beyisraʾel, KM 35 Vaʿadei peʿulah, kruzim—1952; Yeshivot havaʿadah hamedinit, July 3, 1952, HH 90.66 bet (8).

123. "Ila ikhwanina al-ʿummal al-ʿarab," leaflet of MAKI Haifa committee, Feb. 22, 1955, KM 35 Tubi papers; *I*, Dec. 23, 1955, and Jan. 3, 1956.

124. Various unclassified leaflets in KM 35 Yehudi-ʿAravi and Homer beʿaravit; Halishkah haʾirgunit, *Hozer*, no. 12 alef, (Nov. 1952), KM 35 Hitkatvut 1.1.

125. "Nidaʾ li-ʿaqd muʾtamar shaʿbi liʾl-mutalaba bi-ilghaʾ al-hukm al-ʿaskari wa-anzimat al-tasrih," KM 35 Peʿulah bemigzar haʿaravi.

126. See Eliʿezer Beʾeri's polemic against MAKI in *AM*, Jan. 14, 16, 20, 1955.

127. *I*, Jan. 31, 1949.
128. MAKI program adopted at the Twelfth Congress, May 29–June 1, 1952, chap. 2, art. 6, pp. 109, 114.

CHAPTER V. INTERNATIONALISM IN PRACTICE

1. Acheson to Tel Aviv, May 2, 1949; Webb to Tel Aviv, June 1, 1949—both in USNA RG 84, Tel Aviv Embassy General Records, Israel (1949) 3/350.21.
2. *Al-misri*, July 21, 22, 1949.
3. See ʿAbd al-Qadir Yasin, *Hizb shuyuʿi zahruh ila al-haʾit: Shahada taʾrikhiyya ʿan al-haraka al-shuyuʿiyya fi qitaʿ ghazza, 1948–1967* (Beirut, 1978).
4. Mohamed Sid-Ahmed, interview, July 4, 1989.
5. *Bulletin d'information sur l'Égypte et le Soudan*, no. 1 (Feb. 15, 1951), and its successor, *Bulletin d'études et d'information sur l'Égypte et le Soudan*, no. 6 (June 20, 1951).
6. *AM*, July 21, 1950; and Mar. 20; Apr. 6, 27; May 1, 1951.
7. Rifʿat al-Hariri, "Harakat al-ʿummal fi misr," *I*, May 1, 1950; the source was W. J. Handley, "The Labor Movement in Egypt," *Middle East Journal* 3 (July 1949): 277–92.
8. *KA*, Sept. 18, 1951; Menahem Dorman, *Lamerhav*, Dec. 9, 1955; Aharon Cohen, "Yusuf Hilmi," in *Yad leyedidim—bamaʾavakam leshalom vehavanah yehudit-ʿaravit* (Givʿat Haviva, 1982), pp. 60–61; *AM*, Oct. 19, 1951.
9. Emile Habibi, *KA*, Sept. 21, 1951; *Haderekh*, no. 3 (Dec. 1951): 16.
10. *Bulletin d'études et d'information sur l'Égypte et le Soudan*, no. 10 (Nov. 1951).
11. This interchange is reconstructed from fragmentary notes in a very disorganized notebook, KM 35 Tawfiq Tubi papers.
12. Gila Cohen, interview, July 22, 1986; Henri Curiel, "Pour une lutte conséquente pour la paix" (1957), in *Pour une paix juste au Proche-Orient* (Paris, 1979), p. 45.
13. Yusuf Hazan, interview, June 24, 1986.
14. Curiel, "Note sur les relations entre Israël et les pays Arabes" (Aug. 1953), in *Pour une paix juste*, pp. 30–31. The source of the Mikunis quote is a polemic against MAPAM following the expulsion of the Left Section in *Zu haderekh*, no. 7 (June 1953): 32. The text of the DMNL's letter to MAKI is unavailable.
15. According to a French translation, the DMNL's draft program of 1951 (which was never formally adopted) called for "the creation of a democratic Arab state in Palestine and application of the UN resolutions of November 1947 regarding the partition of Palestine" (Curiel papers).
16. Curiel, "Note sur les relations entre Israël et les pays Arabes," pp. 26–29, 33–34.
17. Perrault, *Un homme à part*, p. 533.
18. Yusuf Hazan, interview, June 24, 1986; Gila Cohen, interview, July 22,

1986; Curiel, "Pour une lutte conséquente pour la paix," p. 46; "Eli Lobel," *Khamsin*, no. 7 (1980): 5–6.

19. A.K. [Amnon Kapeliuk], "Youssouf Hilmi: Fighter for Peace," *New Outlook* 7, no. 6 (July–Aug. 1964): 27.

20. In Curiel, *Pour une paix juste*, pp. 102–4.

21. "Hilukei hade'ot shebeinenu levein ha'oportunistim mesi'at 'degel ha'amelim' shel hatzer hamalkhut," *Zu haderekh*, no. 10 (June 1954): 38–41.

22. Hamiflagah hakomunistit hayisra'elit, Hava'adah hamerkazit, *Hama'avak leshalom be'artzot ha'araviot* (Tel Aviv, June 23, 1954).

23. Perrault, *Un homme à part*, p. 534; Uri Avnery, *My Friend, the Enemy* (Westport, Conn., 1986), p. 30.

24. Ahmad El Kodsy and Eli Lobel, *The Arab World and Israel* (New York, 1970).

25. For an egocentric and idiosyncratic description of these contacts and their significance, see Avnery, *My Friend, the Enemy*.

26. Anri Kuri'el [Henri Curiel], *Al mizbeah hashalom* (Jerusalem, 1982).

27. Shimon Balas, *Horef aharon* (Jerusalem, 1984).

28. Yusuf Hazan, interview, June 25, 1986.

29. Full text in A. W. Singham and Tran Van Dinh, eds., *From Bandung to Colombo: Conferences of the Non-aligned Countries, 1955–75* (New York, 1976), pp. 8–9.

30. *Newsweek*, May 30, 1955. Abdel Nasser's interview was reprinted in the government-sponsored daily *Al-jumhuriyya* on May 23, 1955.

31. Letter from Yusuf Hilmi to Gamal Abdel Nasser, May 25, 1955 (mimeographed English text published by the Rome group).

32. Hilmi's remarks appeared in *Kifah shu'ub al-sharq al-awsat*, no. 9 (Nov. 1955) (published by the Rome group); translated and reprinted in *KA*, Oct. 11, 1955, and in a pamphlet.

33. Published in Arabic in *Kifah shu'ub al-sharq al-awsat*, no. 9 (Nov. 1955), and in French as annexes to *Nouvelles d'Égypte*, n.s., no. 2 (Dec. 1955).

34. The main basis for comparison is the UECP's article "The Israeli Question" in *Kifah al-sha'b* (Dec. 1955), translated as "La question israélienne," *Nouvelles d'Égypte*, n.s., no. 5 (June 1956). It is possible that the article in *Kifah al-sha'b* was intended as a response to Yusuf Hilmi's activities. See Chapter 6 below for more detailed analysis and comment.

35. Al-Sa'id, *Al-yasar al-misri wa'l-qadiyya*, p. 256.

36. *Lamerhav*, Dec. 9, 1955.

37. *AM*, Dec. 16, 1955.

38. Ibid.

39. See resolution in *I*, Dec. 27, 1955.

40. It is unclear when and how regularly MAKI received materials from the Rome group. There are scattered Arabic and French publications in KM 35 Yehudi-'aravi, Homer al 'artzot 'arav, dating mainly from 1957–59. Materials from 1954–55 are scattered in other boxes of unclassified Arabic material.

41. "Note concernant l'établissement des relations entre le PCEU et certains partis ouvriers" (Oct. 6, 1956?) (Curiel papers).

CHAPTER VI. THE CONSOLIDATION OF
NATIONALIST POLITICS

1. Election data are based on Israel, Halishkah hamerkazit lestatistikah, Totza'ot habehirot lakneset harishonah, hashniyah vehashlishit.
2. Greilsammer, Les communistes israéliens, p. 187, based on an interview with Mikunis.
3. Chronology prepared for the Thirteenth Party Congress, AA IV 104.19.
4. Nessia Shafran, Shalom lekha komunizm (Tel Aviv, 1983), p. 24.
5. For examples, see KM 35 Homer be'aravit.
6. On statism, see Mitchell Cohen, Zion and State: Nation, Class, and the Shaping of Modern Israel (Oxford, 1987), pp. 201–59.
7. Ibid., pp. 238–49.
8. Material in this paragraph is drawn from Joel Beinin, "The Communist Movement and Nationalist Political Discourse in Nasirist Egypt," Middle East Journal 41, no. 4 (1987): 575–76.
9. Quoted in Hasan al-Masilhi, Qissati ma'a al-shuyu'iyya (Cairo, 1979), p. 104.
10. "Deux analyses—deux politiques: La situation actuelle en Égypte" in Gresh, "Le P.C.F. et l'Égypte," annexes, pp. 60–67; original in Rodinson papers.
11. Published in Le monde, June 19, 1956.
12. Yusuf Hilmi, "Khitab ila Jamal 'Abd al-Nasir," Kifah shu'ub sharq al-awsat, no. 9 (Nov. 1955).
13. Quoted in Communist Party of Israel, Information Bulletin, no. 1(17) (May 1955).
14. KA, Apr. 22, 24; May 6, 1955.
15. I, May 20, 1955.
16. Emile Habibi, Internatzionalizm proletari mul sotzial shovinizm: Tshuvah lehasatat "al hamishmar" al ma'avakah shel hamiflagah hakomunistit hayisra'elit neged hadiku'i hale'umi (Tel Aviv, [1955]). Of course, judged by the standards of the hegemonic Zionist discourse, this pamphlet was an unrestrained expression of nationalist extremism, since it demanded recognition of the national rights of the Palestinian Arabs.
17. KA, Oct. 6, 1955.
18. Full text in Keesing's Contemporary Archives, Jan. 21–28, 1956, p. 14655.
19. KA, Jan. 20, 27, 1956.
20. Decisions of the Central Committee meeting of December 14–16, KA, Dec. 27, 1955.
21. KA, Jan. 27, 1956.
22. I, Jan. 31, 1956.
23. Greilsammer, Les communistes israéliens, p. 214.
24. Ibid., p. 234. Greilsammer does not read Arabic, however, and his book contains no indication that he has actually studied the contents of Al-ittihad.
25. Ibid., pp. 196, 206.

26. *KA,* Oct. 11, 1953. For similar arguments, see Oct. 30, 1953 (on Qibya); Mar. 18, 1954 (on Maʿale Akrabim); Apr. 23, 1954 (on Nahalin); and *I,* Mar. 19, 1954 (on Maʿale Akrabim).

27. "La question israélienne," *Nouvelles d'Égypte,* n.s., no. 5 (June 1956).

28. Curiel, letter to Egypt, July 22, 1957, in *Pour une paix juste,* pp. 84–85.

29. Ibid.

30. Moshe Sneh, "Hakol lemaʿan hizuk hashalom, hakol lemaʿan hakhshalat britot hamilhamah," *Zu haderekh,* no. 14 (Nov. 1955): 3–12.

31. See, for example, his interview in the *New York Times,* Oct. 6, 1955; see also Love, *Suez,* p. 98.

32. Yaʿari, *Mitzrayim vehafeda'in.*

33. "Bekohenu leholel et hatmurah," *AM,* July 8, 1955.

34. See, for example, Riftin's speech in the Knesset on December 7, 1953, in which he discussed Qibya, proceeding from the intention "to help the government get out of the trouble it is in."

35. *AM,* May 4, 8; June 29, 1951; Oct. 19, 1953; Apr. 4, 1954; Mar. 2, May 22, 1955.

36. *AM,* July 22, 1955.

37. E.L.M. Burns, *Between Arab and Israeli* (New York, 1963), p. 101.

38. Moshe Dayan, *Diary of the Sinai Campaign* (London, 1966), p. 12.

39. Richard Weintraub, "Bein hametzarim," *Hedim,* no. 48 (Jan. 1956): 3–8.

40. Mifleget hapoʿalim hame'uhedet, Hamerkaz, *Lekonenut bithonit, miniʿat hamilhamah, nyutraliyut uma'avak al hashalom: hahlatot merkaz mapam meyom 19.1.1956* (Tel Aviv, Feb. 1956).

41. Touval, *Peace Brokers,* pp. 106–33.

42. Love, *Suez,* p. 107.

43. *AM,* Oct. 11, 12, 14, 16, 28, 29, 1956.

44. Ibid., Oct. 30, 1956.

45. "Hahlatot havaʿadah hamedinit shel mifleget hapoʿalim hame'uhedet beshe'elot hashaʿah," Nov. 26, 1956, HH 90.34 (1).

46. *AM,* Jan. 24, 30; Feb. 3, 4, 7, 8, 1957.

47. Ibid., Feb. 24, 1957.

48. Ibid., Mar. 7, 1957.

49. "L'ennemi principal est l'impérialisme," *Nouvelles d'Égypte,* n.s., no. 5 (June 1956): 3; Arabic original in Rodinson papers.

50. "Activités progressistes dans la littérature, le cinéma et l'art," *Nouvelles d'Égypte,* n.s., no. 3 (Apr. 1956).

51. "La question israélienne," *Nouvelles d'Égypte,* n.s., no. 5 (June 1956): 13.

52. Ibid., p. 16.

53. See Curiel's reference to the Syrian positions in *Pour une paix juste,* p. 93.

54. "Le 1er Mai: Commémoration de la lutte des ouvriers," *Nouvelles d'Égypte,* n.s., no. 5, June 1956.

55. *Ruz al-yusuf,* Apr. 23, 1956, p. 8.

56. *M*, Oct. 6, 1956.
57. Editorial, ibid., Oct. 11, 1956.
58. Letter from the Committee (in Arabic), Aug. 9, 1956, KM 35, Pe'ilut bemigzar ha'aravi, Pirsumim vehomer pnimi mehamiflagot hakomunistiot be'artzot 'arav.
59. Yusuf Hilmi, "Nida' jadid ila al-sha'b al-isra'ili," KM 35, Pe'ilut bemigzar ha'aravi, Pirsumim vehomer pnimi mehamiflagot hakomunistiot be'artzot 'arav.
60. As reported in *Le monde*, Aug. 5–6, 1956.
61. Hilmi, "Nida' jadid."
62. Mustafa Tiba, *Rasa'il sajin ila habibatihi* (Cairo, 1978–80), 1:201–6.
63. 'Ahmad al-Rifa'i and 'Abd al-Mun'im Shatla, *Ayyam al-intisar* (Cairo, 1957); "Bayan ila al-sha'b al-misri min al-lajna al-wataniyya li'l-muqawama al-sha'biyya" (Yusuf al Mudarrik papers); Amina Shafiq, interview, May 17, 1986.
64. *M*, Dec. 9, 1956.
65. Ibid., Jan. 9, 1957.
66. Ibid., Jan 10, 1957.
67. Ibid., Nov. 1, 1956.
68. Ibid., Dec. 3, 1956.
69. Curiel, "À propos des relations israélo-arabes," in *Pour une paix juste*, pp. 88–99; letter to Naomi Canel in prison, June 7, 1957 (Curiel papers).
70. "Lettre aux camarades," Aug. 25, 1957 (Curiel papers).
71. Fu'ad Mursi, interview, May 19, 1986.
72. *M*, Mar. 11, 1957.
73. See Layla al-Jibali (a member of the UECP), "Ma'sat filastin takshif siyasat amrika," *M*, May 13, 1957; and Philip Gallab (a former member of al-Raya), "15 mayu, yawm filastin," *M*, May 15, 1958.
74. Yusuf Darwish, interview, May 12, 1986.
75. Hilmi Yasin, interview, May 25, 1986.
76. Mahmud Amin al-'Alim, interview, July 10, 1986. According to Albert Arie (interview, July 3, 1986), the report advocated excluding Jews from the party entirely; this was apparently al-Raya's original demand. 'Abd al-'Azim Anis belonged to both the UECP and al-Raya, a fact that caused some consternation when al-Raya proposed him as one of its candidates for the Political Bureau of the united party.
77. "Khitab ila al-maktab al-siyasi," Jan. 12, 1958; and "Résolution du Parti Communiste Égyptien," second week of March 1958 (Curiel papers).
78. Fu'ad Mursi, interview, May 19, 1986.
79. Al-Sa'id, *Ta'rikh 1957–1965*, pp. 87–88. The fact that this decision was actually adopted by al-Muttahid before unity with the WPCP was effected underscores the correctness of this judgment.
80. "Khitab ila al-maktab al-siyasi."
81. "Lettre sur la nature du régime nasserien et le rôle de Nasser" (text in Arabic), Sept. 20, 1956; "Analyse (très court) de l'intervention franco-anglaise," Jan. 1957; "Lettre à Philippe," Feb. 14, 1957; and "Lettre à Noémie Canel en prison," May 10, 1957 (Curiel papers).

82. Hilmi Yasin, interview, May 25, 1986.
83. Fu'ad Mursi, interview, May 19, 1986.
84. Ahmad Sadiq Sa'd, interview, Apr. 29, 1986; Hilmi Yasin, interview, May 25, 1986. Fu'ad Mursi confirmed Spano's critical role in the unity talks, interview, May 19, 1986.
85. "Les peuples arabes sur la voie de l'indépendance: La lutte des communistes égyptiens pour l'unité," French translation of article in *L'unità*, Dec. 5, 1957 (Rodinson papers).
86. Members of the three components of the CPE still disagree on their size at the time of unity. In my judgment, the division of seats in the united Central Committee accurately reflects their relative size. The figure for the total number of party members is my best estimate.
87. *Hayat al-hizb* (internal bulletin of al-Muttahid), no. 1 (Aug. 1957), quoted in al-Sa'id, *Ta'rikh 1957–1965*, p. 53.
88. "Les positions générales des communistes égyptiens," *Documents d'Égypte*, no. 2 (Oct. 1957) (translated from *Al-wahda*).
89. "Bayan ila al-sha'b 'an al-wahda," Jan. 28, 1958, quoted in al-Sa'id, *Ta'rikh 1957–1965*, p. 136.
90. 'Abd al-Mun'im al-Ghazzali, *Isra'il qa'ada li'l-isti'mar wa-laysat umma* (Cairo, 1958).
91. Khalid, "Al-markisiyya al-nazariyya al-hayya," *Hayat al-hizb*, no. 2 (Sept. 1957): 3–12 (Rodinson papers).
92. *M*, Sept. 12, 1957.
93. Balti, *Bama'avak al hakiyum hayehudi*, pp. 49–50.
94. Emile Habibi, interview, July 21, 1987.
95. Hanokh Bzozah to the Central Committee of MAKI, April 30, 1956, National Library (Jerusalem) manuscript collection, vol. 1271, box 34.2, file 82. All information on Hanokh Bzozah and his group is based on this collection.
96. Tawfiq Tubi's notes on report of Rut Lubitz to the Central Committee meeting of April 17, 1957, on the organizational situation of the party (in Arabic), KM 35 Tubi papers.
97. Copies of the privately circulated letter are in KM 35 Homer be'aravit; a printed Hebrew version appeared in *Zu haderekh*, no. 18 (Jan. 1957): 29–33.
98. Resolution of the Political Bureau, *KA*, Jan. 4, 1957.
99. Report of the Central Committee meeting of January 24–27, 1957, ibid., Jan. 29, 1957.
100. Ibid., Oct. 30, 1956. This article also shows that Rubenstein's claim in *The Communist Movement in Palestine and Israel*, p. 331, that MAKI originally supported the war is incorrect.
101. "Falyasqut al-irhab, layaquf al-ta'ammur 'ala al-tayyiba wa-qura al-muthallath" (date determined by internal evidence), KM 35 Homer be'aravit.
102. *Zu haderekh*, no. 17 (Oct. 1956); Arabic version in *I*, Sept. 18, 21, 25, 1956. References to the additions and corrections of the theses are based on a Hebrew insert in the copy of *Zu haderekh* that I consulted. They were published in *I* on April 9, 1957, and also in *KA*.

103. Me'ir Edelstein, "Lepilug bemaki beshnat 1965," *Me'asef*, no. 5 (Mar. 1973): 166.
104. Letter of Fu'ad Khuri to the Political Committee (in English), Sept. 1, 1956, KM 35 Ve'idot 2.4.
105. Mikunis's position is outlined by an unidentified Arab member of the Political Committee (either Habibi or Tubi, but probably Tubi because the text is in perfect Hebrew and Tubi's Hebrew was better than Habibi's) in a discussion paper prepared before the publication of the congress theses; KM 35 Ve'idot 2.4.
106. *Zu haderekh*, no. 17 (Oct. 1956): 10.
107. Additions to sec. A, para. 7.
108. *I*, May 10, 1957.
109. Clarifications and addition to chap. 3, "Israeli-Arab Relations."
110. Hamiflagah hakomunistit hayisra'elit, Hava'adah hamerkazit, *Hava'eidah ha-13 shel hamiflagah hakomunistit hayisra'elit, Tel Aviv–Yafo 29.5–1.6.1957* (Tel Aviv, 1957), p. 180.
111. Ibid.
112. Both reports are from May 30, 1957.
113. "Mikhtav hozer shel hava'ad hamerkazi," Sept. 11, 1957, KM 35 Zekhuyot hami'ut ha'aravi, 1950–64, Hava'ad lehaganat zekhuyot ha'ukhlusiyah ha'aravit.
114. *Ha'aretz*, Oct. 28, 1957; *I*, Oct. 28, 1957. Edelstein, "Lepilug bemaki," p. 165, uncritically adopting the hegemonic Zionist discourse, accepted the evidence of the *Ha'aretz* report without question.
115. *Jerusalem Post*, Feb. 11, 1958.
116. *AM*, Feb. 7, 14, 1958.
117. Balti, *Bama'avak al hakiyum hayehudi*, pp. 60–61; Shafran, *Shalom lekha komunizm*, p. 192. There is an interesting contradiction between these two accounts. Shafran, who as a youthful member of the Young Communist League could not have been privy to reliable firsthand information about the incident, repeated the most extreme allegations of the Israeli press, that the Arab communists were discussing forming a separate party and launching an Algerian-style guerrilla war. As a member of the Central Committee, Balti may have been in a position to know what happened. He alleged only that the leading Arab communists had met to discuss political issues among themselves, a breach of democratic centralism, but hardly a threat to Israel's security. In a letter to me dated February 14, 1989, Amnon Kapeliuk wrote, "As far as I can recall my sources were from within MAPAM, that is to say antagonistic to MAKI. One of them, I remember with certainty, was MK Yusuf Khamis, who recently died. This does not mean that the information was not correct. Nonetheless, it is possible that there were party interests. It is difficult for me to believe that a guerrilla war in the Galilee was mentioned . . . perhaps someone thought out loud and it was blown up."
118. Edelstein, "Lepilug bemaki," p. 166; Greilsammer, *Les communistes israéliens*, p. 206.
119. *KA*, Feb. 11, 14, 1958.
120. Emile Habibi, interview, July 21, 1987.

121. For an expression of Jewish opinion within MAKI very supportive of Abdel Nasser and the UAR, see Mikunis's article in *KA*, Mar. 14, 1958.

122. Greilsammer, *Les communistes israéliens*, p. 204. As Greilsammer does not know in any detail what was written in *I*, his judgments are unreliable. Similarly, his assertion (p. 234) that after Kafr Qasim the ideological line of *I* and *KA* diverged significantly and that by the early 1960s *I* had become a nationalist journal cannot be accepted. Greilsammer's interpretation is rooted in the common Israeli assumption that militant insistence on the national rights of the Palestinian Arabs is fanatical nationalism (*le'umanut*).

123. *I* and *KA*, Feb. 11, 1958.

124. *AM*, Feb. 12, 1958.

125. *I*, Feb. 7, 1958.

126. The best description of these events in English is in Walter Schwarz, *The Arabs in Israel* (London, 1959), pp. 15ff. Further details are in "Gilui da'at leda'at hakahal," May 25, 1958, KM 35 Parshiot, Me'ora'ot natzeret 1958.

127. *KA*, May 4, 1958.

128. According to Balti, *Bama'avak al hakiyum hayehudi*, pp. 62–63, this decision was taken without the approval of the Political Committee or the Secretariat; he therefore considered it an adventurist action. His claim that it cost MAKI Arab votes in Nazareth, however, has no foundation.

129. See, for example, the editorial in *AM*, June 11, 1958; Aharon Meged's article in *Lamerhav*, June 20, 1958; Shabtai Tevet's article in *Ha'aretz*, May 7, 1958. Others who called for the abolition of the military government included the poet Natan Alterman; P. Bernstein, the leader of the General Zionist Party; and the Progressive Party.

130. "Ha'emet al me'ora'ot ha-1 bemai benatzeret," MAKI Central Committee, May 1958, KM 35 Parshiot, Me'ora'ot natzeret 1958.

131. "Dustur al-jabha al-sha'biyya fi isra'il," KM 35 Zekhuyot hami'ut ha'aravi, 1950–1964, Hehazit ha'amamit.

132. The government refused to give permits to supporters of the Popular Front to attend the founding meeting in Nazareth, so separate meetings in Nazareth and Acre were held. On October 2, 1958, the government refused to register the Popular Front as a legal association. For reports of harassment of Front activists, see *KA*, July 7; Oct. 12, 19, 1958. The political success of the Front and MAKI's ascendancy within the Arab community as a result of its activity in the Front were confirmed by one of MAKI's political opponents in the Front, Sabri Jiryis (*The Arabs in Israel*, p. 126).

CHAPTER VII. THE TRIUMPH OF NATIONALISM

1. Information in the following paragraphs is based on interviews with Mahmud Amin al-'Alim, May 1, 1986; Abu Sayf Yusuf, May 9, 1986; Mohamed Sid-Ahmed, May 11, June 10, 1986; Fu'ad Mursi, May 19, 1986; Ahmad al-Rifa'i, May 29, 1986; and al-Sa'id, *Ta'rikh 1957–1965*, pp. 114–50. Kamal 'Abd al-Halim declined to be interviewed.

2. Ahmad al-Rifa'i, interview, May 29, 1986; Mohamed Sid-Ahmed, interview, June 10, 1986.

3. The Political Bureau's response to al-Sadat, "Hawla al-ittihad al-qawmi: Radd ʿala al-sayyid Anwar al-Sadat," Sept. 19, 1958, is reprinted in al-Saʿid, *Taʾrikh 1957–1965,* pp. 287–306.

4. "Haqaʾiq al-azma allati tuʿarrad laha hizbuna wa-allati tuhaddid bi-tasfiyatihi tasfiya kamila," late Aug. or early Sept. 1958, quoted in al-Saʿid, *Taʾrikh 1957–1965,* p. 128. Even al-Saʿid, who generally defends his former comrades, obliquely criticized the four for formulating their position so as to leave open this interpretation.

5. The documents relating to the investigation of his death were published in Rifʿat al-Saʿid, *Al-jarima* (Cairo, 1984).

6. The story of al-Ard will not be pursued here. For a sympathetic account, see Jiryis, *The Arabs in Israel,* pp. 130–40; for a discussion reflecting the official Israeli perspective, see Landau, *The Arabs in Israel,* pp. 92–107.

7. Fathi ʿAbd al-Fattah, *Shuyuʿiyyun wa-nasiriyyun* (Cairo, 1975); ʿAbd al-ʿAzim Anis, *Rasaʾil al-hubb waʾl-huzn waʾl-thawra* (Cairo, 1976); Ilham Sayf al-Nasr, *Fi muʿtaqal abu zaʿbal* (Cairo, 1977); Tahir ʿAbd al-Hakim, *Al-aqdam al-ariyya* (Beirut, 1978); Tiba, *Rasaʾil sajin ila habibatihi.*

8. Until Abu Sayf Yusuf was apprehended on December 23, 1960, he and other CPE members at liberty issued sharp denunciations of the regime; see, for example, a leaflet signed by Abu Sayf Yusuf, Ismaʿil al-Mahdawi, and Ahmad Salim denouncing the brutalization of the communist prisoners, published in *Al-akhbar* (Beirut), Dec. 11, 1960, and translated as an appendix to Adel Montasser, "La répression anti-démocratique en République Arabe Unie," *Les temps modernes,* no. 183 (July 1961): 184–90.

9. Al-Hakim, *Al-aqdam;* Ahmad Sadiq Saʿd, interview, Apr. 29, 1986.

10. ʿAbd al-Fattah, *Shuyuʿiyyun wa-nasiriyyun,* p. 251.

11. Abu Sayf Yusuf, interview, May 9, 1986.

12. Richard Lowenthal, "Russia, the One-Party System, and the Third World," *Survey* (London), no. 58 (Jan. 1966): 45; Walter Laqueur, *The Struggle for the Middle East: The Soviet Union in the Mediterranean, 1958–1968* (London, 1969), pp. 201–3, 208–12; Shamir, "The Marxists in Egypt"; Binder, "Failure of the Egyptian Left."

13. Abu Sayf Yusuf, interview, May 9, 1986.

14. Parti communiste d'Égypte, Comité central, "Pour assurer l'adoption de la voie non-capitaliste, pour l'écrasement des forces de la contre-révolution, pour l'unité des forces, de toutes les forces du progrès et du socialisme," Aug. 19, 1964, pp. 6, 7. A copy of this document was given to me by Abu Sayf Yusuf, who confirmed that the French version is faithful to the Arabic original, which is unavailable.

15. The resolutions are reproduced in al-Saʿid, *Taʾrikh 1957–1965,* pp. 323–28, 330–48.

16. Mifleget hapoʿalim hameʾuhedet, *Hahlatot haveʿidah hashlishit shel hamiflagah* (Haifa, Jan. 3–6, 1958), p. 13.

17. *Al-mirsad,* Jan. 2, 1958. The official claim of thirty-two thousand MAPAM members at the time of the Third Congress is ridiculously high. The party reported that ten thousand participated in precongress discussions—a more realistic indication of MAPAM's real strength, though even that figure

probably includes all the members of kibbutzim, only a fraction of whom may have participated in political discussion. The total number of congress delegates was inflated by one-quarter, since all members of the party Center were appointed as delegates in addition to the 640 elected delegates, a procedure that diminished the weight of the Arab members and the remnants of the left in the party.

18. *Al-mirsad,* Jan. 9, 1958.
19. Ibid., Jan. 16, 1958.
20. Hamahlakah lepeʿulah aravit, *Bulitin informativi,* no. 1 (May 19, 1958), HH 90.34 (1).
21. *AM,* Apr. 18, 1958.
22. See, for example, the editorial in *New Outlook* 1, no. 8 (Mar. 1958): 3–4; and Haim Darin-Drabkin, "Israel and the Arab Unions," *New Outlook* 1, no. 9 (Apr. 1958): 3–8, 15.
23. Rustum Bastuni, "Jewish-Arab Agreement Is Possible," *New Outlook* 1, no. 10 (May 1958): 41–45; Naʿim Makhoul, "A Just Peace," *New Outlook* 1, no. 12 (July–Aug. 1958): 35–38.
24. Simha Flapan, "Palestinian Arabs at the Crossroads," *New Outlook* 1, no. 10 (May 1958): 46–51; Eliʾezer Beʾeri, "A 'Just Peace' Must Be Just," *New Outlook* 1, no. 12 (July–Aug. 1958): 39–40, 59.
25. Simha Flapan, "One More Step Is Needed," *New Outlook* 2, no. 5 (Jan. 1959): 9–13.
26. Expressions in *New Outlook* of willingness to allow some refugees to return resulted in the resignation of some editorial board members and prompted Golda Meʾir to call for MAPAM's resignation from the cabinet in 1960, whereas *Al hamishmar* claimed that articles in the journal represented only the opinions of their authors. See *I,* Sept. 20, 1960.
27. Bulus Farah, *Muqaddimat fi taʾrikh al-ʿarab al-ijtimaʿi* (Tel Aviv, 1962).
28. El-Asmar, *To Be an Arab in Israel,* pp. 63–72.
29. *I,* July 15, 1958, especially Emile Habibi's editorial.
30. See ibid., Jan. 2, 9, 1959.
31. Ibid., Mar. 20, 1959; *Haʿolam hazeh,* Apr. 1, 1959.
32. Letter from Vilner to Tubi, Jan. 7, 1959, and enclosure, KM 35 Tubi papers.
33. Communist Party of Israel, *Information Bulletin,* no. 2–3 (Feb.–Mar. 1958).
34. *KA,* July 28, 1959.
35. *I,* Aug. 18, 1959; *KA,* Aug. 24, 1959.
36. *AM,* Aug. 30, 1959.
37. Emile Habibi, "Hadith shahr," *Al-jadid* 7, no. 2 (Feb. 1960): 1–2.
38. Rashid Hussein, "Ila Hanna Abu Hanna," *Al-fajr,* Apr. 1959, pp. 19–23; idem, "The Middle East Between Nasser and Kassem: The Case Against Kassem," *New Outlook* 2, no. 9 (June 1959): 37–40.
39. *Al-mirsad,* Oct. 15, 1959.
40. For example, "Amatat al-sham ʿan hizb al-mabam: Masrahiyya zajaliyya," Feb. 1959, and "Ahl al-kahf al-judad" (n.d., but obviously an election propaganda piece), KM 35 Peʿilut bemigzar haʿaravi.

41. MAKI, Triangle District Committee, leaflet addressed to the residents of al-Tira, Nov. 2, 1959, KM 35 Peʿilut bemigzar haʿaravi.
42. This was how Yosef Almogi, the boss of the Haifa Labor Council and Peres's rival in the MAPAI young guard, critically characterized Peres's views; quoted in M. Cohen, *Zion and State*, p. 225.
43. For a detailed account of MAKI's vote in the Arab community, see "Al-jamahir al-ʿarabiyya tatahaddi al-irhab fi al-intikhabat wa-tatamassik bi-hizbina al-shuyuʿi raghma al-tadlil wa'l-rashwa wa'l-tahrid min al-dakhil wa'l-kharij," *I*, Nov. 6, 1959. This article's emphasis on the vote in the Arab community and neglect of the nationwide vote are further evidence of the party's appeal to Arab national sentiment in the campaign.
44. Shmu'el Mikunis, "Nekudot lesihot ha-tz.k.," Nov. 11, 1959, AA IV 104/41.
45. Comments of Irga, Burstein, Sneh, and others at this meeting, all in ibid.
46. Resolutions of the Central Committee meeting of March 15–17, 1961, *I*, Mar. 24, 1961.
47. *I*, Mar. 31, 1961.
48. Ibid., Nov. 11, 1960; Feb. 7, Mar. 3, 1961; Ibrahim, *Hanna Naqqara*, pp. 288–89, 354–61; Jiryis, *The Arabs in Israel*, p. 82.
49. *I*, Mar. 21, 1961.
50. Ibid., Apr. 6, 25, 1961.
51. Shmu'el Mikunis, report to the Central Committee, KA, Mar. 24, 1961.
52. "Rashei haprakim likrat haveʿidah ha-14," *Zu haderekh*, no. 29 (Apr. 1961): 10.
53. Moshe Sneh, interview in *Maʿariv*, May 31, 1961.
54. Balti (*Bamaʾavak al hakiyum hayehudi*, p. 87) claimed that in the permanent committee of the congress, Habibi, Tubi, and Khamis struggled to eliminate references to "reciprocal recognition," but, typically, he gave no evidence for the assertion. This claim is suspicious because if the Arab party leaders had any intention of opposing this language, the congress itself (as Balti well knew) was the last place they could have hoped to win their struggle. Balti's own political stand was revealed by his claim that all references that could be interpreted as impinging on the territorial integrity of Israel were eliminated from the report of the Central Committee to the congress. While this may have been his desire, in fact the report used the same language as the theses—that Israel must be prepared "to convert the temporary cease-fire lines, through reciprocal agreement, to permanent borders of peace," leaving open a possible alteration of borders; see Hamiflagah hakomunistit hayisra'elit, Havaʿadah hamerkazit, *Haveʿidah ha-XIV, Tel Aviv–Yafo, 31.5–3.6.1961* (Tel Aviv, 1961), p. 36.
55. "Al-tariq li-taswiyyat al-ʿalaqat al-isra'iliyya al-ʿarabiyya," *I*, Apr. 21, 1961; see also "Al-umumiyya al-brulitariyya . . . min muqawwamat nasr sabil al-hizb al-shuyuʿi al-isra'ili," *I*, May 30, 1961.
56. Hamiflagah hakomunistit hayisra'elit, *Haveʿidah ha-XIV*, pp. 205–6. At a meeting of the Political Committee after the congress, Mikunis confirmed that Khuri supported the line of the report; see "Protokolim miyeshivot ha-

merkaz vehalishkah, yuni 1961–yanu'ar 1963," meeting of Nov. 26, 1961, AA IV 104.55.

57. Sh. Mikunis, "Sikum hadiyun al matza' habehirot," Political Committee meeting, June 19, 1961, AA IV 104.55.

58. "Hukumat Bin Ghuryun tathbit mujaddadan siyasat 'wa-la laji'" (leaflet), July 1961, AA IV 425.45.

59. "Protokolim miyeshivot hamerkaz vehalishkah," Political Committee meeting, July 2, 1961, AA IV 104.55.

60. Ibid., Aug. 21–22, 1961.

61. Eli'ezer Feiler, interview, Aug. 3, 1987. See also Feiler's articles in *KA* praising the theses of the Italian party.

62. "Protokolim miyeshivot hamerkaz vehalishkah," Political Committee meeting, Nov. 26, 1961, AA IV 104.55.

63. Shafran, *Shalom lekha komunizm*, p. 139.

64. Brit hono'ar hakomunisti hayisra'eli, *Shir nashirah: Kovetz shirei am umoledet, shirei amal uma'avak veshirei amim* (Tel Aviv, 1961).

65. Shafran, *Shalom lekha komunizm*, pp. 121, 137–39.

66. As reported by Yehoshu'a Irga at the Eighteenth Plenum of the Central Committee, Jan. 19, 1965, AA IV 104.29.

67. "Protokolim miyeshivot hamerkaz vehalishkah," Political Committee meeting, Aug. 16, 1961, AA IV 104.55.

68. Ibid., Aug. 21–22, 1961.

69. Ibid., Nov. 1, 1961.

70. Ibid., June 30, 1963. See also Sneh's article in *KA*, Aug. 16, 1963.

71. "Protokolim miyeshivot hamerkaz vehalishkah," Political Committee meeting, Aug. 25, 1963.

72. *KA*, Sept. 5, 1963.

73. Balti, *Bama'avak al hakiyum hayehudi*; Greilsammer, *Les communistes israéliens*; Edelstein, "Lepilug bemaki beshnat 1965"; Eli Rekhess, "Leshe'elat hayahasim bein yehudim ve'aravim bemaki," *Medinah, mimshal veyahasim beinle'umiyim*, no. 27 (1987): 67–95; Lahav, *Soviet Attitude Towards the Split in the Israeli Communist Party*. I have also consulted an unpublished paper by R. R. Kaminer, "Opinion A and Opinion B: The Inner Party Debate in the Communist Party of Israel, 1965," which does not employ the same terms of reference as the works cited above. Mikunis's minutes are contained in "Protokolim miyeshivot hamerkaz vehalishkah," AA IV 104.55.

74. E. Vilenska, "Avodatenu ha'igud miktzo'it vehapolitit bamkomot avodah," KM 35 Hava'ad hamerkazi (mikhtavim veyeshivot), 1957–1965.

75. "Din veheshbon al pe'ulat snif haifa beshnat 1963," KM 35 Mazkirut, Inyanim shotfim 1963.

76. "Din vehesbon va'ad mehoz haifa al bitzu'a tokhnit hape'ulah lehodashim martz–detzember 1962," KM 35 Mehoz haifa.

77. See Elana Kaufman, "The Electoral Basis of the Communist Party (RAKAH) Among the Arabs in Israel" (Ph.D. diss., UCLA, in progress).

78. "Totza'ot artziot labehirot leve'idat po'alei binyan bashetah ha'aravi," AA IV 219.108; *Lamerhav*, Feb. 2, 1965.

CHAPTER VIII. CONCLUSION

1. The following account is based on a transcript of the meetings, "Hasihot bein mishlahat maki umishlahat hamiflagah hakomunistit hayardenit," KM 35 Yehudi-ʿaravi, Homer al ʾartzot ʿarav. Other copies of the transcript are in the Shmuʾel Mikunis papers. On some copies the names of the Arab participants are indicated, on others they are not. Details of the meeting were confirmed in an interview with Emile Habibi, July 21, 1986.

2. For an American example, see Magil, *Israel in Crisis*.

3. Samir Amin, *The Arab Nation: Nationalism and Class Struggle* (London, 1978), p. 109.

4. ʿAbd al-Fattah, *Shuyuʿiyyun wa-nasiriyyun*, p. 267.

5. Mark Cooper, *The Transformation of Egypt* (Baltimore, 1982).

6. Gramsci, "The Study of Philosophy," in *Selections from the Prison Notebooks*, p. 365.

7. Ibid., p. 336.

Chronology

late 1943 — NLL splits from PCP
1945 — AWC established
September 1946 — New Dawn reorganized as Popular Vanguard for Liberation
late 1946 — Jewish Anti-Zionist League established
June 1947 — EMNL and Iskra fuse to form the DMNL
November 29, 1947 — UN General Assembly votes to partition Palestine
December 1947 — PCP becomes MAKEI; then MAKI
January 1948 — Hashomer Hatza'ir Workers' Party and Ahdut Ha'avodah–Po'alei Tzion fuse to form MAPAM
May 15, 1948 — Proclamation of the State of Israel; Arab invasion
June 1948 — Splintering of DMNL begins
October 22, 1948 — Unity of NLL and MAKI
January 1949 — End of the Palestine War of 1948–49; elections for first Knesset
mid-1949 — Popular Democracy formed by unity of Popular Vanguard for Liberation and smaller groups
December 1949 — al-Raya established
August 1950 — Henri Curiel expelled from Egypt, establishes Rome Group on reaching Paris
June 1951 — Second Party Congress of MAPAM; factions consolidated
July 30, 1951 — Elections for Second Knesset
November–December 1951 — Israeli seamen's strike
May 1952 — Twelfth Party Congress of MAKI
July 23, 1952 — Free Officers' coup
September 7, 1952 — Execution of Kafr al-Dawwar strike leaders
January 1953 — Sneh and Left Section expelled from MAPAM; purge in kibbutzim

May 1953 — LSP formed
March 1954 — Abdel Nasser consolidates his rule
July 1954 — Jewish saboteurs apprehended in Egypt; France begins to supply arms to Israel
August 1954 — Ahdut Ha'avodah–Po'alei Tzion splits from MAPAM
September 1954 — LSP joins MAKI
October 1954 — Anglo-Egyptian evacuation agreement ratified
February 1955 — UECP formed
February 28, 1955 — Israeli raid on Gaza
April 1955 — Bandung conference
July 26, 1955 — Elections for Third Knesset
November 1955 — MAPAM and Ahdut Ha'avodah join government for first time
February 1956 — Twentieth Congress of the Communist Party of the Soviet Union
July 23, 1956 — Nationalization of the Suez Canal
September 28, 1956 — Egypt announces purchase of Czech arms
October 29, 1956 — Outbreak of Suez/Sinai War; Kafr Qasim massacre
January 30, 1957 — GFETU formed
March 1957 — Popular Democracy becomes WPCP
April–May 1957 — Thirteenth Party Congress of MAKI
June 1957 — UECP and al-Raya fuse in Unified Egyptian Communist Party (al-Muttahid)
January 3–6, 1958 — Third Party Congress of MAPAM
January 8, 1958 — WPCP joins al-Muttahid, forming CPE
February 1, 1958 — UAR proclaimed
March 1958 — Dissolution of Rome Group
July 14, 1958 — Coup led by 'Abd al-Karim Qasim ousts Hashemite regime in Iraq
late 1958 — CPE-DMNL splits from CPE
January 1, 1959 — Mass arrest of Egyptian communists
November 3, 1959 — Elections for Fourth Knesset
May–June 1961 — Fourteenth Party Congress of MAKI
August 15, 1961 — Elections for Fifth Knesset
February 1962 — New Economic Policy in Israel; strike wave in response
July 23, 1962 — Charter of National Action adopted in Egypt
June 16, 1963 — Levi Eshkol replaces Ben-Gurion as prime minister of Israel
July 1963 — Clashes on Syrian-Israeli border; MAKI split begins
April 1964 — Last Egyptian communists released from jail
March–April 1965 — Dissolution of CPE-DMNL and CPE
August 1965 — Split in MAKI; formation of RAKAH

Glossary

AHDUT HA'AVODAH — Hatnu'a Lema'an Ahdut Ha'avodah—The Labor Unity Movement. First a faction in MAPAI; in 1944–46 and again in 1954–68, an independent party; in 1948–54, a component of MAPAM; since 1968, a component of the Labor Party

ALIYAH — Zionist immigration to Palestine/Israel

ERETZ ISRAEL — The Land of Israel, the Hebrew term for Palestine

HAGANAH — The militia created by the Histadrut (see below) during the Palestine mandate period

HASHOMER HATZA'IR — The Young Guard. A worldwide Zionist youth movement whose members were educated to emigrate to Israel and join kibbutzim; also used to designate Kibbutz Artzi (see below)

HASHOMER HATZA'IR WORKERS' PARTY — Created in 1946 by the fusion of Kibbutz Artzi (see below) and its urban ally, the Socialist League

HISTADRUT — Hahistadrut Haklalit Shel Hapo'alim (Ha'ivriyim) Be('eretz) Yisra'el—The General Federation of the (Hebrew) Workers in (the Land of) Israel. A trade union federation established by Zionist workers in 1920 with a wide-ranging network of economic and cultural institutions; Arabs were permitted to become full members in 1965

KIBBUTZ — A collective agricultural settlement

KIBBUTZ ARTZI — Hakibutz Ha'artzi Hashomer Hatza'ir—The National Kibbutz Federation of Hashomer Hatza'ir (see above)

KIBBUTZ ME'UHAD — Hakibutz Hame'uhad—The United Kibbutz Federation, affiliated with Ahdut Ha'avodah (see above)

KNESSET — The Israeli parliament

LEFT PO'ALEI TZION — Po'alei Tzion Smol—Left Workers of Zion. A small

Marxist Zionist formation that united with Ahdut Ha'avodah in 1946 and then joined MAPAM in 1948

PALMAH — The elite strike force of the Haganah (see above)

WAFD — Delegation. The overwhelmingly popular Egyptian nationalist party from 1919 to 1952

YISHUV — The Jewish settlement in Palestine

Bibliography

ARCHIVES AND PRIVATE PAPERS

Shmuʾel Amir papers, Tel Aviv
Henri Curiel papers, Paris (courtesy of Joyce Blau)
Yusuf Darwish papers, Cairo
Hashomer Hatzaʿir archive, Merkaz teʿud veheker shel hashomer hatazaʿir, Givʿat Haviva, Israel
Jewish National Library, Jerusalem, manuscript collection vol. 1272—includes "Komunistim Ivrim" and the Yehudit Buber papers
MAKI papers, Yad Tabenkin Kibbutz Meʾuhad archive, Efal, Israel
Shmuʾel Mikunis and MAKI papers, Arkhion haʿavodah vehehalutz, Lavon Institute for Labor Research, Tel Aviv
Yusuf al Mudarrik papers, Cairo (courtesy of Rifʿat al-Saʿid)
Maxime Rodinson papers, Paris
U.S. National Archives
    Diplomatic Post Files (RG 84)
        Cairo Embassy General and Classified Records, 1947–54
        Tel Aviv Embassy General and Classified Records, 1947–54
    State Department Central Files
        Egypt, Internal Affairs, 1945–49, 1950–54
        Palestine and Israel, Internal Affairs, 1945–49, 1950–54

INTERVIEWS

Yosef Algazi, Bat Yam, August 7, 1987
Mahmud Amin al-ʿAlim, Cairo, May 1, 1986
Shmuʾel Amir, Tel Aviv, August 21, 1986

Albert Arie, Cairo, July 3, 1986
Gila Cohen, Tel Aviv, July 22, 1986
Yusuf Darwish, Cairo, May 12 and June 10, 1986
Adib Dimitri, Paris, June 24, 1986
Raymond Douek, Paris, June 26, 1986
Eliʿezer Feiler, Yad Hanah, August 3, 1987
Philip Gallab, Cairo, May 14, 1986
Emile Habibi, Haifa, July 21, 1986
Yusuf Hazan, Paris, June 24, 1986
Michel Kamil, Paris, June 17, 1986
Reʾuven and Dafna Kaminer, Jerusalem, August 31, 1986
Amnon Kapeliuk, letter from Moscow, February 14, 1989
Yak Matek, Sasa, August 16, 1985
Fuʾad Mursi, Cairo, May 19, 1986
Ahmad al-Rifaʿi, Cairo, May 29, 1986
Ahmad Sadiq Saʿd, Cairo, April 29, 1986
Rifʿat al-Saʿid, Cairo, May 22, 1986
Amina Shafiq, Cairo, May 17, 1986
David Shoshani, Lahav, December 18, 1988
Mohamed Sid-Ahmed, Cairo, April 30, May 11, and June 10, 1986, and July 4, 1989
Hilmi Yasin, Cairo, May 25 and July 14, 1986
Abu Sayf Yusuf, Cairo, May 9, 1986

UNPUBLISHED MATERIALS

Amitay, Yossi. "Mapam 1948–1954: Emdot besugiyat araviyei eretz yisraʾel." M.A. thesis, Tel Aviv University, 1986.
ʾAtif, Ulfat Mahmud. "Al-ʿummal, waʾl-haraka al-ʿummaliyya fi misr: 1942–1961." M.A. thesis, Cairo University, 1985.
Bornstein, Michael Scott. "From Revolution to Crisis: Egypt-Israel Relations, 1952–1956." Ph.D. diss., Princeton University, 1986.
Botman, Selma. "Oppositional Politics in Egypt: The Communist Movement, 1936–1954." Ph.D. diss., Harvard University, 1984.
Curiel, Henri. *Pages autobiographiques.* Typescript, 1977.
Etkin, Yishʿayahu. "Shishim shnot shvitah beyisraʾel, 1921–1980." M.A. thesis, Tel Aviv University, 1982.
Geffner, Ellen Joyce K. "Attitudes of Arab Editorialists in Israel, 1948–1967: An Analysis of *Al-ittihad, Al-mirsad,* and *Al-yawm.*" Ph.D. diss., University of Michigan, 1973.
Gresh, Marie-Dominique. "Le P.C.F. et l'Égypte: 1950–1956." Mémoire de maîtrise, Université de Paris I, 1976–77.
Kaminer, R. R. "Opinion A and Opinion B: The Inner Party Debate in the Communist Party of Israel, 1965." Typescript, [1984?].
Kaufman, Elana. "The Electoral Basis of the Communist Party (RAKAH) Among the Arabs in Israel." Ph.D. diss., UCLA, in progress.

Mandelstam, Jean. "La Palestine dans la politique de Gamal Abdel Nasser, 1952–1955." Ph.D. diss., Université de Paris, 1970.
Parti communiste d'Égypte, Comité central. "Pour assurer l'adoption de la voie non capitaliste, pour l'écrasement des forces de la contre-révolution, pour l'unité des forces, de toutes les forces du progrès et du socialisme." Photocopy, Cairo, Aug. 19, 1964.
"Sasa 35, 1949–1984: Founder's Gathering, July 6–8, 1984." Mimeo, 1984.
Segal, Tzvi. "Igud hayama'im, 1935–1953: Me'agudah mekomit le'igud artzi." M.A. thesis, Tel Aviv University, 1976.
Shalev, Michael. "The Political Economy of Labor Party Dominance and Decline in Israel." Forthcoming in a volume edited by T. J. Pempel to be published by Cornell University Press.

PERIODICALS

Al hamishmar
Bulletin d'études et d'information sur l'Égypte et le Soudan
Bulletin d'information sur l'Égypte et le Soudan
Communist Party of Israel *Information Bulletin*
Al-damir
Documents d'Égypte
Al-fajr
Al-fajr al-jadid
Al-ittihad
Al-jamahir
Kifah shuʿub al-sharq al-awsat
Kol haʿam
Lamerhav
Al-mirsad
Al-masaʾ
New Outlook
Nouvelles d'Égypte
Smol
Al-taliʿa
Yediʿot hakibutz haʾartzi
Zu haderekh (and its predecessor *Haderekh*)

BOOKS AND ARTICLES

ʿAbbas, Raʾuf. "Hinri Kuriyal bayna al-ustura waʾl-waqiʿ al-taʾrikhi" (Henri Curiel between the legend and the historical reality). *Al-hilal* 66, no. 11 (Nov. 1988).
ʿAbd al-Fattah, Fathi. *Shuyuʿiyyun wa-nasiriyyun* (Communists and Nasserists). Cairo, 1975.
ʿAbd al-Hakim, Tahir. *Al-aqdam al-ariyya* (Naked feet). Beirut, 1978.
Abdalla, Ahmed. *The Student Movement and National Politics in Egypt*. London, 1985.

Abdel-Fadil, Mahmoud. *Development, Income Distribution, and Social Change in Rural Egypt, 1952–1970.* Cambridge, 1975.

———. *The Political Economy of Nasserism: A Study in Employment and Income Distribution Policies in Urban Egypt, 1952–1972.* Cambridge, 1980.

Abdel-Khalek, Gouda. "The Open Door Economic Policy in Egypt: Its Contribution to Investment and Equity Implications." In *Rich and Poor States in the Middle East: Egypt and the New Arab Order,* edited by Malcolm Kerr and El-Sayyid Yassin. Boulder, Colo., 1982.

Abdel-Malek, Anouar. *Egypt: Military Society.* New York, 1968.

Abrahamian, Ervand. *Iran Between Two Revolutions.* Princeton, 1980.

Abu Ghosh, Subhi. "Communism in an Arab Village." In *Texts and Responses: Studies Presented to Nahum Glatzer on the Occasion of His Seventieth Birthday by His Students,* edited by Michael A. Fishbane and R. Flohr. Leiden, 1975.

Aharonson, Sholomo, and Dan Horovitz. "Ha'astrategiyah shel tagmul mevukar: Hadugmah hayisra'elit" (The strategy of controlled retaliation: The case of Israel). *Medina, mimshal, veyahasim beinle'umiyim* 1, no. 1 (Summer 1971).

al-'Alim, Mahmud, and 'Abd al-'Azim Anis. *Fi al-thaqafa al-misriyya* (On Egyptian culture). Beirut, 1955.

Amin, Samir. *The Arab Nation: Nationalism and Class Struggle.* London, 1978.

al-'Amiri, Tahir. "Ana al-'amil" (I the worker). *Nashrat ittihad niqabat al-ghazl wa'l-nasij bi-jumhuriyat misr,* no. 3 (Sept. 1955).

Anderson, Benedict. *Imagined Communities: Reflections on the Origin and the Spread of Nationalism.* London 1983.

Anderson, Perry. "Agendas for Radical History." *Radical History Review,* no. 36 (Sept. 1986).

Anis, 'Abd al-'Azim. *Rasa'il al-hubb wa'l-huzn wa'l-thawra* (Letters of love, sadness, and revolution). Cairo, 1976.

Ansari, Hamied. *Egypt: The Stalled Society.* Albany, N.Y., 1986.

Avnery, Uri. *My Friend, the Enemy.* Westport, Conn., 1986.

Bakr, 'Abd al-Wahhab. *Adwa' 'ala al-nashat al-shuyu'i fi misr, 1921–1950* (Light on communist activity in Egypt). Cairo, 1983.

Balas, Shimon. *Horef aharon* (Last winter). Jerusalem, 1984.

Balti, Berl. *Bama'avak al hakiyum hayehudi: Ledmuto shel Moshe Sneh* (In the struggle for Jewish existence: For the image of Moshe Sneh). Jerusalem, 1981.

Bar-Siman-Tov, Yaacov. "Ben-Gurion and Sharett: Conflict Management and Great Power Constraints in Israeli Foreign Policy." *Middle Eastern Studies* 24, no. 3 (July 1988).

Batatu, Hanna. *The Old Social Classes and the Revolutionary Movements of Iraq.* Princeton, 1978.

Beinin, Joel. "The Communist Movement and Nationalist Political Discourse in Nasirist Egypt." *Middle East Journal* 41, no. 4 (1987).

———. "Israel at Forty: The Political Economy/Political Culture of Constant Conflict." *Arab Studies Quarterly* 10, no. 3 (Fall 1988).

———. "Labor, Capital, and the State in Nasserist Egypt, 1952–1961." *International Journal of Middle East Studies* 21, no. 1 (Feb. 1989).
Beinin, Joel, and Zachary Lockman. *Workers on the Nile: Nationalism, Communism, Islam, and the Egyptian Working Class, 1882–1954.* Princeton, 1988.
Ben-Gurion, David. *Letters to Paula.* London, 1971.
———. *My Talks with Arab Leaders.* Jerusalem, 1972.
Ben Nahum, Yizhar. "Hashomer hatzaʿir veraʿayon haduleʾumit, 1942–1947" (Hashomer Hatzaʿir and the binational idea). *Meʾasef* 15 (1985).
Bentov, Mordechai. *The Case for a Bi-national Palestine: Memorandum Prepared by the Hashomer Hatzair Workers' Party of Palestine.* Tel Aviv, Mar. 1946.
Bernstein, Deborah, and Shlomo Swirsky. "The Rapid Economic Development of Israel and the Emergence of the Ethnic Division of Labour." *British Journal of Sociology* 33, no. 1 (1982).
Binder, Leonard. "The Failure of the Egyptian Left." *Asian and African Studies* 14 (1980).
al-Bishri, Tariq. *Al-haraka al-siyyasiyya fi misr, 1945–1952* (The political movement in Egypt). Cairo, 1972.
———. "Qiraʾa misriyya fi awraq Hinri Kuriyal" (An Egyptian reading of the papers of Henri Curiel). *Al-hilal* 66, no. 4 (Apr. 1988).
Bober, Arie, ed. *The Other Israel: The Radical Case Against Zionism.* New York, 1972.
Botman, Selma. *The Rise of Egyptian Communism, 1939–1970.* Syracuse, N.Y., 1988.
Brit hanoʿar hakomunisti hayisraʾeli. *Shir nashirah: Kovetz shirei am umoledet, shirei amal umaʾavak veshirei amim* (Let's sing: A collection of songs of the people and the homeland, songs of labor and struggle, and international songs). Tel Aviv, 1961.
Budeiri, Musa. *The Palestine Communist Party, 1919–1948: Arab and Jew in the Struggle for Internationalism.* London, 1979.
Burns, E. L. M. *Between Arab and Israeli.* New York, 1963.
Bzozah, Hanoch. *Dvarim levikuah* (Matters for argument). Tel Aviv, 1956.
Cohen, Abner. *Arab Border Villages in Israel.* Manchester, Eng., 1965.
Cohen, Aharon. "Hava navhir dvarim leʿatzmenu: Sihah ʿim haverim bemadim" (Let's clarify things for ourselves: A conversation with comrades in uniform). *Bashaʿar,* nos. 10 and 11 (Aug. 5 and 19, 1948).
———. *Israel and the Arab World.* New York, 1970.
———. "Maʿamad hapoʿalim vekohot hakidmah bamizrah haʿaravi" (The working class and the forces of progress in the Arab east). Reprinted from *Al hamishmar,* April 6, 27; May 1, 1951.
———. "Nohah hapinui haʿaravi" (In view of the Arab evacuation). *Leʾahdut haʿavodah* 1, no. 1 (June 1948).
———. "Olam hamahapehah vehatzionut" (The world of revolution and Zionism). *Mahbarot lemarksizm,* no. 2 (Feb. 1951).
———. *Yad leyedidim—Bamaʾavakam leshalom vehavanah yehudit-ʿaravit* (A

hand to friends—In their struggle for Jewish-Arab Understanding). Givʿat Haviva, 1982.
Cohen, Mitchell. *Zion and State: Nation, Class, and the Shaping of Modern Israel.* Oxford, 1987.
Cooper, Mark. *The Transformation of Egypt.* Baltimore, 1982.
Copeland, Miles. *The Game of Nations.* London, 1969.
Curiel, Henri. *Awraq Hinri Kuriyal waʾl-haraka al-shuyuʿiyya al-misriyya* (The papers of Henri Curiel and the Egyptian communist movement). Introduction by Raʾuf ʿAbbas; translated by ʿIzzat Riyad. Cairo, 1988.
———. *Pour une paix juste au Proche-Orient.* Paris, 1979. Published in Hebrew as *Al mizbeah hashalom.* Jerusalem, 1982.
Czudnowski, Moshe M., and Jacob M. Landau. *The Israeli Communist Party and the Elections for the Fifth Knesset, 1961.* Stanford, 1965.
Darwaza, al-Hakam. *Al-shuyuʿiyya al-mahalliyya wa-maʿarakat al-ʿarab al-qawmiyya* (Local communism and the Arab national battle). Beirut, 1963.
Davis, Eric. *Challenging Colonialism: Bank Misr and the Political Economy of Industrialization in Egypt, 1920–1941.* Princeton, 1983.
Davis, Uri, and Norton Mezvinsky, eds. *Documents from Israel, 1967–1973: Readings for a Critique of Zionism.* London, 1975.
Dayan, Moshe. *Diary of the Sinai Campaign.* London, 1966.
al-Disuqi, ʿAsim Ahmad. *Kibar mullak al-aradi al-ziraʿiyya wa-dawruhum fi al-mujtamaʿ al-misri, 1914–1952* (Large agricultural landowners and their role in Egyptian society). Cairo, 1975.
Ebon, Martin. "Communist Tactics in the Middle East." *Middle East Journal* 2, no. 3 (July 1948).
Edelstein, Meʾir. "Lapilug bemaki beshnat 1965" (Toward the split in MAKI in 1965). *Meʾasef,* no. 5 (Mar. 1973).
El-Ad, Avri. *Decline of Honor.* Chicago, 1976.
El-Asmar, Fouzi. *To Be an Arab in Israel.* London, 1975.
"Eli Lobel." *Khamsin,* no. 7 (1980).
El Kodsy, Ahmad, and Eli Lobel. *The Arab World and Israel.* New York, 1970.
Farah, Bulus. *Muqaddimat fi taʾrikh al-ʿarab al-ijtimaʿi* (Prolegomena to Arab social history). Tel Aviv, 1962.
Fathi, Ibrahim. *Hinri Kuriyal didda al-haraka al-shuyuʿiyya al-ʿarabiyya: Al-qadiyya al-filastiniyya* (Henri Curiel against the Arab communist movement: The Palestine question). Cairo, 1989.
Flapan, Simha. *The Birth of Israel: Myths and Realities.* New York, 1987.
Flores, Alexander. "The Arab CPs and the Palestine Problem." *Khamsin,* no. 7 (1980).
Ghali, Waguih. *Beer in the Snooker Club.* New York, 1987.
al-Ghazzali, ʿAbd al-Munʿim. *Israʾil qaʿada liʾl-istiʿmar wa-laysat umma* (Israel is an imperialist base and not a nation). Cairo, 1958.
Gramsci, Antonio. *Selections from the Prison Notebooks.* Edited and translated by Quentin Hoare and Geoffrey Nowell Smith. New York, 1971.
Greilsamer, Ilan. "Tziyunei derekh leshivato shel Moshe Sneh latzionut" (Pathmarks for Moshe Sneh's return to Zionism). *Medinah memshal veyahasim beinleʾumiyim* 10 (Spring 1977).
Greilsammer, Alain [Ilan Greilsamer]. *Les communistes israéliens.* Paris, 1978.

Habibi, Emile. "Hadith shahr" (Talk of the month). *Al-jadid* 7, no. 2 (Feb. 1960).

———. *Internatzionalizm proletari mul sotzial shovinizm: Tshuvah lehasatat "al hamishmar" al ma'avakah shel hamiflagah hakomunistit hayisra'elit neged hadiku'i hale'umi* (Proletarian internationalism against social chauvinism: An answer to *Al hamishmar*'s incitement against the struggle of MAKI against national oppression). Tel Aviv, [1955].

Habiby [Habibi], Emile. *The Secret Life of Saeed, the Ill-fated Pessoptimist: A Palestinian Who Became a Citizen of Israel.* New York, 1982.

Halevi, Nadav, and Ruth Klinov-Malul. *The Economic Development of Israel.* New York, 1968.

Harel, Isser. *Bitahon vedemokratiah* (Security and democracy). Tel Aviv, 1989.

Heller, Otto. *La fin du judaïsme.* Paris, 1933.

Hobsbawm, Eric. "Problems of Communist History." *New Left Review*, no. 54 (Mar.–Apr. 1969).

Hosseinzadeh, Esmail. *Soviet Non-capitalist Development: The Case of Nasser's Egypt.* New York, 1989.

Husayn, Taha. *The Future of Culture in Egypt.* Washington, D.C., 1954.

Hutchison, E. H. *Violent Truce: A Military Observer Looks at the Arab-Israeli Conflict, 1951–1955.* New York, 1956.

Ibrahim, Hanna, ed. *Hanna Naqqara: Muhami al-ard wa'l-sha'b* (Hanna Naqqara: Lawyer of the land and the people). Acre, 1985.

Idris, Yusuf. *Al-bayda'* (The fair one). Cairo, 1982.

Ismael, Tareq Y. "The Communist Movements in the Arab World." In *Law, Personalities, and Politics of the Middle East: Essays in Honor of Majid Khadduri*, edited by James Piscatori and George S. Harris. Boulder, Colo., 1987.

Isma'il, Ahmad. "Hiwar ma'a Marsil Isra'il: Al-haraka al-taqaddumiyya al-misriyya laysat min san' al-ajanib" (Dialogue with Marcel Israel: The Egyptian progressive movement is not the work of foreigners). *Adab wa-naqd*, no. 40 (Aug. 1988).

Israel. Halishkah hamerkazit lestatistikah. *Totza'ot habehirot lakneset harishonah, hashniyah vehashlishit ulerashuyot hamekomiyot be-1950 ube-1955* (Results of the elections for the First, Second, and Third Knessets and for local authorities in 1950 and 1955). Sidrat pirsumim meyuhadim, no. 51. Jerusalem, 1957.

———. *Totza'ot habehirot laknesset hahamishit* (Results of the elections for the Fifth Knesset). Sidrat pirsumim meyuhadim, no. 166. Jerusalem, 1962.

'Izz al-Din, Amin. *Ta'rikh al-tabaqa al-'amila al-misriyya mundhu nushu'iha hatta sanat 1970* (History of the Egyptian working class from its emergence to 1970). Cairo, 1987.

Jackson, Elmore. *Middle East Mission: The Story of a Major Bid for Peace in the Time of Nasser and Ben-Gurion.* New York, 1983.

Jiryis, Sabri. *The Arabs in Israel.* Beirut, 1968.

Judt, Tony. *Marxism and the French Left.* Oxford, 1986.

Kamen, Charles S. "After the Catastrophe: The Arabs in Israel, 1948–51." *Middle Eastern Studies* 23, no. 4 (1987); 24, no. 1 (1988).

———. "Aharei ha'ason: Ha'aravim bemedinat yisra'el, 1948–1950" (After the catastrophe: The Arabs in Israel). *Mahbarot lemehkar ulebikoret,* no. 10 (Dec. 1984).

Kamil, Fathi. *Ma'a al-haraka al-niqabiyya fi nisf qarn: Safahat min dhikrayat Fathi Kamil* (With the Egyptian trade union movement for half a century: Pages from the memoirs of Fathi Kamil). Cairo, 1985.

Kamil, Fathi, Ahmad Fahim, Sayyid 'Abd al-Wahhab Nada, and Nur Sulayman. *Al-tabaqa al-'amila fi al-ma'raka didda al-isti'mar* (The working class in the battle against imperialism). Cairo, 1957.

Kanovsky, Eliyahu. *The Economy of the Israeli Kibbutz.* Cambridge, Mass., 1966.

Kenan, Amos. *The Road to Ein Harod.* London, 1987.

Kibbutz Sasa. The Secretariat. *The Launching: Sasa's First Year.* Tel Aviv, 1951; repr. 1984.

Kimche, Jon, and David Kimche. *Both Sides of the Hill.* London, 1960.

Kimmerling, Baruch. *Zionism and Territory: The Socio-territorial Dimensions of Zionist Politics.* Berkeley and Los Angeles, 1983.

Krämer, Gudrun. *The Jews in Modern Egypt, 1914–1952.* Seattle, 1989.

Krammer, Arnold. *The Forgotten Friendship: Israel and the Soviet Bloc, 1947–53.* Urbana, Ill., 1974.

Lahav, Yehudah. "The Soviet Attitude Towards the Split in the Israeli Communist Party, 1964–1967." Hebrew University of Jerusalem, Soviet and East European Research Center, Research Paper no. 39. June 1980.

Landau, Jacob M. *The Arabs in Israel: A Political Study.* London, 1969.

Laqueur, Walter. *Communism and Nationalism in the Middle East.* London, 1961.

——— . *The Struggle for the Middle East: The Soviet Union in the Mediterranean, 1958–1968.* London, 1969.

Lockman, Zachary. "The Left in Israel: Zionism vs. Socialism." *MERIP Reports,* no. 49 (July 1976).

——— . "Original Sin." In *Intifada: The Palestinian Uprising Against Israeli Occupation,* edited by Zachary Lockman and Joel Beinin. Boston, 1989.

Love, Kennett. *Suez: The Twice Fought War.* New York, 1969.

Lowenthal, Richard. "Russia, the One-Party System, and the Third World." *Survey* (London), no. 58 (Jan. 1966).

Lustick, Ian. *Arabs in the Jewish State: Israel's Control of a National Minority.* Austin, Tex., 1980.

Magil, A. B. *Israel in Crisis.* New York, 1950.

Makarius, Raoul. *La jeunesse intellectuelle d'Égypte au lendemain de la deuxième guerre mondiale.* Paris, 1960.

Margalit, Elkanah. "Binationalism: An Interpretation of Zionism, 1941–1947." *Studies in Zionism* 4 (Oct. 1981).

——— . *Hashomer hatza'ir: Me'edat ne'urim lemarksizm mahapkhani, 1913–1936* (Hashomer Hatza'ir: From youth group to revolutionary Marxism). Tel Aviv, 1985.

al-Masilhi, Hasan. *Qissati ma'a al-shuyu'iyya* (My story with communism). Cairo, 1979.

Merhav, Peretz. *The Israeli Left: History, Problems, Documents.* San Diego, Calif., 1980.

Hamiflagah hakomunistit hayisra'elit. Hava'adah hamerkazit. *Hama'avak leshalom be'artzot ha'araviot* (The struggle for peace in the Arab countries). Tel Aviv, June 23, 1954.

———. *Have'idah ha-13 shel hamiflagah hakomunistit hayisra'elit, Tel Aviv–Yafo 29.5–1.6.1957* (The Thirteenth Congress of MAKI). Tel Aviv, 1957.

———. *Have'idah ha-XIV, Tel Aviv–Yafo, 31.5–3.6.1961* (The Fourteenth Congress of MAKI). Tel Aviv, 1961.

Mifleget hapo'alim hame'uhedet. *Hahlatot have'idah hashlishit shel hamiflagah* (Decisions of the Third Party Congress). Haifa, Jan. 3–6, 1958.

———. *Likrat ve'idat mifleget hapo'alim hame'uhedet: Hanahot leberur* (Toward the congress of the United Workers' Party: Assumptions for clarification). [Tel Aviv, 1951].

———. *Matza' hamiflagah.* [Tel Aviv, 1951].

———. *Sihah 'im haboher.* [1949].

———. Hamerkaz. *Lekonenut bithonit, mini'at hamilhamah, nyutraliut uma'avak al hashalom: Hahlatot merkaz mapam meyom 19.1.1956* (For security preparedness, prevention of war, neutralism, and the battle for peace: Decisions of the MAPAM Center). Tel Aviv, Feb. 1956.

Mikunis, Shmu'el. *Besa'ar tekufot* (In stormy times). Tel Aviv, 1969.

Montasser, Adel. "La répression anti-démocratique en République Arabe Unie." *Les temps modernes,* no. 183 (July 1961).

Morris, Benny. *The Birth of the Palestinian Refugee Problem, 1947–1949.* Cambridge, 1988.

———. "The Causes and Character of the Arab Exodus from Palestine: The Israel Defence Forces Intelligence Branch Analysis of June 1948." *Middle Eastern Studies* 22, no. 1 (1986).

———. "The Crystallization of Israeli Policy Against a Return of the Arab Refugees: April–December, 1948." *Studies in Zionism* 6, no. 1 (1985).

———. "The Harvest of 1948 and the Creation of the Palestinian Refugee Problem." *Middle East Journal* 40, no. 4 (1986).

———. "Operation Dani and the Palestinian Exodus from Lydda and Ramle in 1948." *Middle East Journal* 40, no. 1 (1986).

———. "Yosef Weitz and the Transfer Committees, 1948–49." *Middle Eastern Studies* 22, no. 4 (1986).

Muhyi al-Din, Khalid. Letter to Gamal Abdel Nasser, Mar. 31, 1953. *Al-ahali,* July 24, 1985.

Murqus, Ilyas. *Ta'rikh al-ahzab al-shuyu'iyya fi al-watan al-'arabi* (History of the communist parties in the Arab homeland). Beirut, 1964.

Nahhas, Dunia. *The Israeli Communist Party.* London, 1976.

Neff, Donald. *Warriors at Suez: Eisenhower Takes America into the Middle East.* New York, 1981.

O'Brien, Patrick. *The Revolution in Egypt's Economic System.* London, 1966.

Patinkin, Don. *The Israeli Economy: The First Decade.* Jerusalem, 1969.

Peretz, Don. *Israel and the Palestine Arabs.* Washington, D.C., 1958.

Peri, El'azar. *Anahnu ve'olam hamahapehah* (Us and the world of revolution). Tel Aviv, May 1, 1950.

Peri, Yoram. *Between Battles and Ballots: Israeli Military in Politics.* Cambridge, 1983.

Perrault, Gilles. *Un homme à part*. Paris, 1984. Published in English as *A Man Apart: The Life of Henri Curiel*, vol. 1. London, 1987.

Porath, Yehoshua. "The National Liberation League, 1943–1948." *Asian and African Studies* 4 (1968).

Ramadan, ʿAbd al-ʿAzim. *ʿAbd al-Nasir wa-azmat maris* (Abdel Nasser and the March crisis). Cairo, 1976.

Rekhess, Elie. "Jews and Arabs in the Israeli Communist Party." In *Ethnicity, Pluralism, and the State in the Middle East*, edited by Milton J. Esman and Itamar Rabinovich. Ithaca, N.Y., 1988.

———. "Lesheʾelat hayahasim bein yehudim veʿaravim bemaki" (On the question of relations between Jews and Arabs in MAKI). *Medinah, mimshal, veyahasim beinleʾumiyim*, no. 27 (1987).

al-Rifaʿi, Ahmad, and ʿAbd al-Munʿim Shatla. *Ayyam al-intisar* (Days of resistance). Cairo, 1957.

Riftin, Yaʿakov. "Anu vehakomunizm" (Us and communism). *Al hamishmar*, Apr. 30, 1950.

Rodinson, Maxime. *Israel and the Arabs*. Harmondsworth, Eng., 1968.

———. *Marxism and the Muslim World*. London, 1979.

Rokach, Livia. *Israel's Sacred Terrorism*. Belmont, Mass., 1980.

Rosenfeld, Henry, and Shulamit Carmi. "The Privatization of Public Means: The State-made Middle Class and the Realization of Family Value in Israel." In *Kinship and Modernization in Mediterranean Society*, edited by J. G. Perstiany. Rome, 1976.

Rubenstein, Sondra Miller. *The Communist Movement in Palestine and Israel, 1919–1984*. Boulder, Colo., 1984.

S.[aba] sh.[el] Yariv [David Ben-Gurion]. *Al hakomunizm vehatzionut shel hashomer hatzaʿir* (On the communism and Zionism of Hashomer Hatzaʿir). Tel Aviv, 1953.

Saʿd, Sadiq. *Filastin bayna makhalib al-istiʿmar* (Palestine between the claws of imperialism). Cairo, 1946.

al-Saʿid, Rifʿat. *Al-jarima* (The crime). Cairo, 1984.

———. *Munazzamat al-yasar al-misri, 1950–1957* (Organizations of the Egyptian left). Cairo, 1983.

———. *Taʾrikh al-haraka al-shuyuʿiyya al-misriyya: Al-wahda, al-inqisam, al-hall, 1957–1965* (History of the Egyptian communist movement: Unity, split, dissolution). Cairo, 1986.

———. *Taʾrikh al-munazzamat al-yasariyya al-misriyya, 1940–1950* (History of the Egyptian leftist organizations). Cairo, 1977.

———. *Al-yasar al-misri waʾl-qadiyya al-filastiniyya* (The Egyptian left and the Palestine question). Beirut, 1974.

Salima, ʿAyida. *Misr waʾl-qadiyya al-filastiniyya* (Egypt and the Palestine question). Cairo, 1986.

Samara, Samih. *Al-ʿamal al-shuyuʿi fi filastin: Al-tabaqa waʾl-shaʿb fi muwajahat al-kuluniyaliyya* (Communist action in Palestine: The class and the people confronting colonialism). Acre, 1980.

Sayf al-Nasr, Ilham. *Fi muʿtaqal abu zaʿbal* (In Abu Zaʿbal prison). Cairo, 1977.

Sayyid Ahmad, Muhammad [Mohamed Sid-Ahmed]. *Mustaqbal al-nidal al-hizbi fi misr* (The future of party struggle in Egypt). Cairo, 1984.

———. "Al-yahud fi al-haraka al-shuyu'iyya al-misriyya wa'l-sira' al-'arabi al-isra'ili" (The Jews in the Egyptian communist movement and the Arab-Israeli conflict). *Al-hilal* 66, no. 6 (June 1988).

Schnall, David J. "Notes on the Political Thought of Dr. Moshe Sneh." *Middle East Journal* 27, no. 3 (Summer 1973).

Schwarz, Walter. *The Arabs in Israel.* London, 1959.

Sefer hashomer hatza'ir. (The Book of Hashomer Hatza'ir). 3 vols. Merhavia, 1964.

Sefer hatzanhanim (The paratroopers' book). Tel Aviv, 1969.

Segev, Tom. *1949: The First Israelis.* New York, 1986.

al-Shafi'i, Shuhdi 'Atiyya. *Tatawwur al-haraka al-wataniyya al-misriyya, 1882–1956* (Development of the Egyptian national movement). Cairo, 1957.

al-Shafi'i, Shuhdi 'Atiyya, and 'Abd al-Ma'bud al-Jibayli. *Ahdafuna al-wataniyya* (Our national objectives). Cairo, 1945.

Shafran, Nessia. *Shalom lekha komunizm* (Goodbye communism). Tel Aviv, 1983.

Shakir, Amin, Sa'id 'Aryan, and 'Ali Adham. *Haqiqat al-shuyu'iyya* (The truth about communism). Cairo, 1954.

Shalev, Michael. "Jewish Organized Labor and the Palestinians: A Study of State/Society Relations in Israel." In *The Israeli State and Society: Boundaries and Frontiers,* edited by Baruch Kimmerling. Albany, N.Y., 1989.

Shamir, Shimon. "The Marxists in Egypt: The 'Licensed Infiltration' Doctrine in Practice." In *The U.S.S.R. and the Middle East,* edited by Michael Confino and Shimon Shamir. Jerusalem, 1973.

Shammas, Anton. *Arabesques.* New York, 1988.

Sharett, Moshe. *Yoman ishi* (Personal diary). 8 vols. Tel Aviv, 1978.

Sheffer, Gabi. "Sharet, Ben Gurion umilhemet habrerah be-1956" (Sharett, Ben-Gurion, and the war of choice in 1956). *Medinah, mimshal veyahasim beinle'umiyim,* no. 26 (1987).

Shlaim, Avi. *Collusion Across the Jordan: King Abdullah, the Zionist Movement, and the Partition of Palestine.* New York, 1988.

———. "Conflicting Approaches to Israel's Relations with the Arabs: Ben-Gurion and Sharett, 1953–1956." *Middle East Journal* 37, no. 2 (Spring 1983).

———. "Husni Za'im and the Plan to Resettle the Palestinian Refugees in Syria." *Journal of Palestine Studies* 15, no. 4 (Summer 1986).

Singham, A. W., and Tran Van Dinh, eds. *From Bandung to Colombo: Conferences of the Non-aligned Countries, 1955–75.* New York, 1976.

Sneh, Moshe. *Sikumin bashe'elah hale'umit le'or hamarksizm-leninizm* (Conclusions on the national question in light of Marxism-Leninism). Tel Aviv, Aug. 1954.

Stedman Jones, Gareth. *Languages of Class: Studies in English Working Class History, 1832–1982.* Cambridge, 1983.

Storrs, Ronald. *Orientations.* London, 1937.

Tiba, Mustafa. "Hawla awraq Hinri Kuriyal: Matlub taqyim mawdu'i li'l-ta'rikh al-hadith" (On the Henri Curiel papers: An objective evaluation of recent history is demanded). *Al-hilal* 66, no. 11 (Nov. 1988).

———. *Rasa'il sajin ila habibatihi* (Letters of a prisoner to his beloved). 2 vols. Cairo, 1978–1980.

Tomiche, Fernand J. *Syndicalisme et certains aspects du travail en République Arabe Unie (Égypte), 1900–1965*. Paris, 1974.

Touval, Saadia. *The Peace Brokers: Mediators in the Arab-Israeli Conflict, 1948–1979*. Princeton, 1982.

Tzur, Ze'ev. *Bein shutafut le'opozitziah: She'elat shitufah shel mapam bamemshalah, 1949–1954* (Between partnership and opposition: The question of MAPAM's participation in the government). Efal, 1983.

Volfenson, Avraham. *Kahol-lavan-adom: Toldot ha'orientatziah hapro-sovietit beyisra'el* (Blue-white-red: History of the pro-Soviet orientation in Israel). Tel Aviv, 1983.

Weintraub, Richard. "Bein hametzarim" (Between the straits). *Hedim*, no. 48 (Jan. 1956).

White, Hayden. "The Value of Narrativity in the Representation of Reality." In *On Narrative*, edited by W. J. T. Mitchell. Chicago, 1981.

Wolffsohn, Michael. *Israel: Polity, Society, and Economy 1882–1986*. Atlantic Highlands, N.J., 1987.

Ya'ari, Ehud. *Mitzrayim vehafeda'in, 1953–1956* (Egypt and the fedayeen). Arab and Afro-Asian Monographs, no. 13. Giv'at Haviva, 1975.

Ya'ari, Me'ir. *Kibutz galuyot be'aspeklariah shel yamenu* (The ingathering of the exiles in the mirror of our times). Merhavia, 1954.

Yago, Glenn. "Whatever Happened to the Promised Land? Capital Flows and the Israeli State." *Berkeley Journal of Sociology* 21 (1976).

Yasin, 'Abd al-Qadir. *Hizb shuyu'i zahru ila al-ha'it: Shahada ta'rikhiyya 'an al-haraka al-shuyu'iyya fi qita' ghazza, 1948–1967* (A communist party with its back to the wall: Historical testimony about the communist movement in the Gaza Strip). Beirut, 1978.

———. *Al-qadiyya al-filastiniyya fi fikr al-yasar al-misri* (The Palestine question in the thought of the Egyptian left). Beirut, 1981.

Yishai, Yael. "Integration of Arabs in an Israeli Party: The Case of MAPAM, 1948–54." In *Zionism and Arabism in Palestine and Israel*, edited by Elie Kedourie and Sylvia G. Haim. London, 1982.

Yisra'eli, A. [Moshe Machover and Akiva Orr]. *Shalom, shalom—ve'ein shalom: Yisra'el arav, 1948–1961* (Peace, peace—and there is no peace: Israel and the Arabs). Jerusalem, 1961.

Yisra'eli, Amihud. "Hamahapekhah hata'asukit bemigzar hami'utim beyisra'el" (The employment revolution in the minority sector in Israel). *Hamizrah hehadash* 26, no. 3–4 (1976).

Yisra'eli, G. Z. [Walter Laqueur]. *M.P.S.–P.K.P.–MAKI: Korot hamiflagah hakomunistit beyisra'el* (S.W.P.–P.C.P.–MAKI: History of the Communist Party in Israel). Tel Aviv, 1951.

Zahran, Sa'd. *Fi usul al-siyasa al-misriyya* (On the roots of Egyptian politics). Cairo, 1985.

Zureik, Elia. *The Palestinians in Israel: A Study in Internal Colonialism*, London, 1979.

Index

'Abd al-Fattah, Fathi, 210
'Abd al-Hakim, Tahir, 210
'Abd al-Halim, Kamal, 114, 166, 178, 185, 188, 205, 206
'Abd al-Quddus, Ihsan, 145, 215
'Abd Allah: Amir of Transjordan, 32, 36, 39, 64, 116, 118, 120, 123, 129; King of Jordan, 144
'Abd Allah, 'Amr, 185
'Abd Allah, Isma'il Sabri, 105, 109, 113, 187, 252
Abdel-Malek, Anouar, 57, 61, 97–98
Abdel Nasser, Gamal, 5, 111, 157; and Arab-Israeli conflict, 10, 102–3, 153, 154–55, 157–58, 170, 175, 181, 182, 184; and pan-Arab nationalism, 99, 164, 188, 204, 206; anti-imperialist foreign policy of, 97, 98, 156, 160–61; CPE stand on, 205, 209–10; CPE-DMNL stand on, 205–6, 209–10; communist reassessment of, 156, 160, 164–65, 166, 177–78, 179, 182, 187, 189, 191, 250; Curiel's view of, 186; economic policies of, 90, 93, 94, 162, 164; and Iraqi revolution (1958), 205–6, 215, 218–19, 223, 228; MAPAM's stand on, 201, 215; and PLO, 211; al-Raya's stand on, 160, 165; and the Soviet Union, 100, 232; and the United States, 86–87, 88, 100, 172. See also Arab socialism; pan-Arab nationalism
Abu Sinayna, 'Adnan, 150
academician's strike, 73, 76, 174
activism, 10, 11, 14–15, 26, 32, 37, 64, 75, 102, 161, 162, 163, 168, 172–73, 174, 175–76, 177, 222, 238, 244. See also IDF
Aflam al-Nur, 178
Aflatun, Inji, 178
Ahdut Ha'avodah, 26, 29, 41, 77, 78, 224; Arab policy of, 26, 27, 29, 36, 120, 128, 130, 158, 198; and Egyptian communists, 158, 184; electoral strength, 161, 173, 221; joins government, 174, 235; in MAPAM, 119, 128–29, 131, 132, 134; military policy of, 26, 36, 129, 172, 173, 174
'Ali, Salman, 95
Alignment, 22, 78, 208
al-'Alim, Mahmud Amin, 110, 112, 180, 185, 205, 206, 212
Allon, Yigal, 26, 34, 36
Almogi, Yosef, 236
Amin, 'Abd al-Mun'im, 89
Amin, Samir, 150, 152, 250
Amir, Shmu'el, 137
al-'Amiri, Tahir, 96
Amitay, Yossi, 80, 152
'Amr, Mukhlis, 48, 56
Anderson, Robert B., 175
Anis, 'Abd al-'Azim, 112, 185, 191, 212 283n76
al-'Aqqad, Mahmud 'Abbas, 112
Arab Book Company, 215
Arab Higher Committee, 33, 35, 44
Arab-Israeli Committee for Peace, 150
Arab-Israeli War of 1948–49, 1, 9, 19, 32, 168, 190; and Arab communists,

309

Arab-Israeli War of 1948–49 *(continued)* 53–54; and Egyptian communists, 49, 53, 62, 103, 104, 115, 116, 155, 156–57, 168, 204; and Egyptian domestic politics, 85–86; and MAKEI, 46–47, 48, 50; and MAKI, 54–55, 118, 168, 169, 184, 192, 198, 204, 228, 237; and MAPAM, 31–39; and NLL, 48, 49–51, 53–54

Arab-Israeli War of 1967, 101, 245, 255

Arab nationalism. *See* pan-Arab nationalism

Arab socialism, 99–101, 250, 252

Arab Socialist Union, 2, 88, 210, 252

Arab Workers' Congress. *See* AWC

Arafat, Yasir, 8

al-Ard, 207, 215

Arie, Albert, 209

al-Armani, Ya'qub, 42

Arnon, Ya'akov, 152

al-Ashhab, 'Awda, 50

Ata strike, 73, 76–77

Avidan, Shimon, 34

Avnery, Uri, 15, 151, 152, 159, 199

AWC (Arab Workers' Congress), 42–43, 48, 51, 121, 139–41; and New Dawn, 56

Baha' al-Din, Ahmad, 215

Bakdash, Khalid, 144, 183, 192

Balas, Shimon, 152, 232

Balti, Berl, 192, 222, 223, 289n54

Bandak, 'Abd Allah, 42

Bandung Conference of Asian and African States, 156, 160–61, 164, 165, 170, 182, 242; MAPAM's stand on, 166; resolution on the Arab-Israeli conflict, 153–54, 155, 156, 158, 166, 171, 196; MAKI's stand on, 166

BANKI (Young Communist League of Israel), 135, 148, 222, 232–33, 234

al-Baqri, Mustafa, 89

Bar Nir, Dov, 50, 51

Barkai (Kibbutz), 126, 270n28

Barzilai, Yisra'el, 150

Basisu, Mu'in, 166

Bastuni, Rustum, 127–28, 131, 135, 213, 214

Be'eri, Eli'ezer, 29–30, 39, 49, 84, 128, 214, 215

Be'eri, Yish'ayahu, 39

Begin, Menahem, 4, 61, 76

Ben-Gurion, David, 3, 4, 67, 162, 217, 218, 244; activist military policy of, 10, 11, 12, 28, 64, 71, 154, 161, 168, 172, 173, 221, 250; international orientation of, 69, 74, 75, 76, 164, 172, 175, 249; and Lavon affair, 11–12, 224; and MAKI, 16, 44, 219, 235, 236, 238; and MAPAM, 16, 25, 32, 122, 208; and Palestinian Arabs, 32, 34, 38, 54, 78, 103; and partition of Palestine, 14, 26, 27, 32, 38, 64; and RCC, 155, 166; statism of, 28, 163, 164. *See also* Suez/Sinai War, and Ben-Gurion

Bentov, Mordechai, 32, 129

Berman, Adolph, 119, 131, 134, 136, 222, 223

Bernadotte, Count Folke, 37, 64, 66, 118

Bet Alfa (kibbutz), 30

Biltmore Program, 27, 69

Binationalism, 28, 38, 103; and Ahdut Ha'avodah, 29; and Curiel, 58, 60; and Hashomer Hatza'ir, 24, 27–28, 29, 30, 41; and PCP, 40–41, 44, 45

al-Bindari, Kamil, 145, 147

Blau, Joyce, 107

Border incidents, 10, 11, 172, 173, 180, 191–92, 262n16; DMNL's stand on, 116, 170; MAKI's stand on, 170, 236–37; MAPAM's stand on, 133, 173, 175, al-Raya's stand on, 117

Borders of Israel, 9, 10, 12, 13, 14, 64; Communist Party of Jordan's stand on, 247; Egyptian communists' stand on, 184; Egypt's stand on, 153, 175; MAKI's stand on, 64, 122, 124–25, 142–43, 192, 196–98, 214, 216, 226–28, 247; MAPAM's stand on, 37, 64, 80, 120, 129, 158, 176–77, 214. *See also* Partition of Palestine

Breitstein, Tzvi, 236

al-Burayj, IDF raid on, 11, 116, 175

Burstein, Uzi, 148, 222, 223, 232

Bzozah, Hanokh, 192–93, 233, 234

Canel, Naomi, 109, 114, 166

capital imports to Israel, 68, 70–71, 72, 78, 222, 244, 251, 269n4

Carmel, Moshe, 34

CEA (Communist Educational Association), 40, 41

Cohen, Aharon, 27, 30, 36, 84, 133, 134; and Arab Affairs Department of MAPAM, 27, 31, 120–21, 127–28; and left in Arab world, 146; and Nazareth tobacco workers' strike, 139; and Palestinian Arabs, 33–35, 36, 37, 38, 55; and Yusuf Hilmi, 147

Cohen, Gila, 150, 152

Cohen, Shalom, 151

Comintern, 16, 25, 28, 42, 231

Communist Educational Association. *See* CEA

Communist Party of Algeria, 211

Communist Party of Egypt (1949). *See* al-Raya
Communist Party of Egypt (1958). *See* CPE
Communist Party of Egypt (1975), 252–53
Communist Party of Egypt–Democratic Movement for National Liberation. *See* CPE-DMNL
Communist Party of France, 16, 105, 113–14, 187
Communist Party of Great Britain, 45
Communist Party of Iraq, 6, 53, 150, 151, 205
Communist Party of Israel. *See* MAKI
Communist Party of Italy, 185, 231, 253
Communist Party of Jordan, 6, 151, 246–48
Communist Party of Lebanon, 6, 53
Communist Party of Syria, 6, 53, 144, 179, 183, 188–89, 205, 206, 217–18
Communist Party of the Land of Israel. *See* MAKEI
Communist Party of the Soviet Union, 192–93, 231
Communist Party of the Sudan, 150
Communist Party of the United States, 41, 259n3
Communist Student League (DMNL), 111
Communist Union of Palestine, 41, 58
Conference of Communist Parties of the British Empire (1947), 44–45, 56
CPE (Communist Party of Egypt, 1958), 20, 106, 187–90, 191–92, 205–7, 208–12
CPE-DMNL (Communist Party of Egypt–Democratic Movement for National Liberation), 20, 206, 207, 208–12
crisis of March 1954, 90, 113
Curiel, Henri, 2, 58, 62, 106, 190, 267n78; and Arab-Israeli peace, 110, 148–49, 170–71, 183–84; communist opposition to, 63, 113–15, 117, 180, 185, 187, 273–74n26; contacts with Israelis, 6, 148–53, 170; criticisms of Iskra, 57, 105; and Egyptian national struggle, 58, 107, 111, 112, 250; and partition of Palestine, 58, 60, 64; and Rome group, 6, 20, 107, 159, 254; and split in DMNL, 104, 110, 267n78; and Zionism, 59, 114–15
Curiel, Rosette, 113
Czech-Egyptian arms agreement, 154, 161, 164, 170, 180; Abdel Nasser's reasons for, 167, 171–72, 173; Egyptian communists' stand on, 117, 155, 156, 165; MAKI's stand on, 167, 168, 171, 194; MAPAM's stand on, 168, 174–75

Dajani, Musa, 48
Dar al-Fikr, 92, 178, 185, 190
Darwish, Yusuf, 55, 56, 91, 92, 106, 108, 182, 186–87, 209
Dayan, Moshe, 10, 12, 162, 173, 221, 224, 236
Deir Yasin, massacre of, 33
Democratic Front for Peace and Equality, 251
Democratic Movement for National Liberation. *See* DMNL
Democratic Movement for National Liberation–Revolutionary Current, 150, 273–74n26
DMNL (Democratic Movement for National Liberation), 16, 57, 58–59, 104, 107, 109; and Arab-Israeli peace, 116, 117, 190; communist criticism of, 103–4, 106, 107, 114–15, 116, 117; and CPE (1959), 185, 186, 211; and international peace movement, 145–46; Jews in, 60, 61, 63, 104–6, 107, 114–15; and MAKI, 116, 148–49, 150–51, 159; and RCC, 107, 111–12, 113, 114, 165, 186, 187, 250; split in (1947–48), 61, 62, 63, 104, 105, 106, 110, 267n78; and Zionism, 59–60, 64, 110, 114–17. *See also* CPE-DMNL; Rome group; UECP
Dorman, Menahem, 146, 147, 158
Douek, Raymond, 55–56, 106, 187, 209

Eden, Anthony, 175
Egyptian-Israeli Committee for Peace, 150
Egyptian Jews: in communist movement, 103–10, 114–15, 117, 185–88, 209, 212, 283n76; status of, 14, 182. *See also* Rome group
Egyptian Movement for National Liberation. *See* EMNL
Ehrenburg, Ilya, 119
Ein Shemer (Kibbutz), 133, 134, 192
Eisenhower doctrine, 100
El-Asmar, Fouzi, 215
Eliav, Lova, 152
EMNL (Egyptian Movement for National Liberation), 2, 57, 58, 59
Erem, Moshe, 29, 131
Eshel, Nimrod, 75
Eshkol, Levi, 12, 236, 237, 238, 244
ETZEL (Irgun Tzva'i Le'umi), 4, 33, 61

Fahim, Ahmad, 91, 92
Fahmi, ʿAziz, 145
Farah, Bulus, 42, 48, 56, 215
Faruq (King of Egypt), 84, 85, 116
Feiler, Eliʿezer, 152, 231
Flapan, Simha, 7–8, 9, 129, 133, 138, 140, 152, 213, 214
Free Officers, 2, 86, 87, 187

Galili, Yisra'el, 26, 36, 74, 81, 131
Gallab, Philip, 110
Gaza, IDF raid on, 11–12, 157, 161, 166, 171–72, 173, 262n16
General Federation of Egyptian Trade Unions (GFETU), 90–91, 99
Ghali, Waguih, 105
Ghazzali, ʿAbd al-Munʿim, 190, 211
Ghilan, Maxime, 151, 152
Gisis, Munya, 198
Givli, Binyamin, 12
Gojansky, Eliyahu, 47
Gramsci, Antonio, 17, 21, 253–54
Gromyko, Andrei, 45, 59, 60

Habashi, Fuʾad, 206
Habibi, Emile, 42, 123, 202, 246; and Egyptian communists, 146, 148; and Palestinian Arab national issues in MAKI, 125, 166, 170, 192, 196, 199–200, 201, 228, 235, 236, 237; and partition of Palestine, 47, 52–53, 169
Hacohen, Eliʿezer, 30
Haganah, 26, 32, 47, 48, 50, 68, 232
Haifa program, 129, 131
Hamdan, Faris, 219
Harari, Ezra, 57
Harari, Haya, 150
Har El (Kibbutz), 133, 134, 135, 270n28
Harun, Shihata, 182, 209
Hashomer Hatzaʿir, 26–28; and Arab-Israeli War of 1948–49, 35, 38–39; attacked by Curiel, 58; binationalism of, 24, 27–28, 29, 41; and kibbutzim, 79–84, 126, 134; in MAPAM, 29–31, 128, 129, 133, 134; and PCP, 41, 192
Hass, Avraham, 221, 223, 240
Hatata, Sharif, 183–84
Hazan, Yaʿakov: and Arab-Israeli War of 1948–49, 39; and international communist movement, 27; and intra-party struggle in MAPAM, 30, 128, 130; and Palestinian Arab refugees, 35–36, 213; and Slansky trial, 131, 132, 135; and Soviet Union, 15, 74; and Suez/Sinai War, 176
Hazan, Yusuf, 60, 61, 148

Hebrew Communist Party, 41, 42, 128, 132, 233
Henin, David, 222, 223, 237
Hertzberg, Fishel, 222, 223
Herut, 4, 161, 172, 173
Hilmi, Yusuf: contacts with Israelis, 146–47, 150, 151; and Egyptian peace movement, 145, 152, 153, 154; peace initiative of, 153–59, 165, 171, 179, 181–82, 184
al-Hilu, Radwan (Musa), 40, 42
Histadrut, 68, 73, 78, 123, 163–64, 218, 224; and PCP, 41, 58; and workers' action committees, 224, 239; and World Federation of Trade Unions, 56, 74. See also Palestinian Arab citizens of Israel, and Histadrut
Husayn, Taha, 112
al-Husayni, ʿAbd al-Qadir, 48, 54
al-Husayni, al-Hajj Amin, 35, 48, 201, 211
al-Husayni, Jamal, 44
Hussein, Rashid, 215, 219

IDF (Israel Defense Forces): and activism, 10, 14, 163; and Arab-Israeli War of 1948–49, 33, 34–35, 81, 83, 121, 123; and Lavon affair, 224; and MAKI, 123, 232, 233; and MAPAM, 10, 32, 34–35, 81; Unit 101, 11, 14, 162, 171. See also activism
Idris, Yusuf, 105
Ihud, 28, 41
Irga Yehoshuʿa, 221
Irgun Tzvaʾ i Leʾumi. See ETZEL
Iskra, 56–58, 61, 104–5, 115
Israel Defense Forces. See IDF
Israel Labor League, 140
Israel Peace Council, 15, 123, 132
Israel-Soviet Union Friendship League, 15, 74, 123, 132
Israel Workers' Party. See MAPAI
Israeli Committee for a Free Algeria, 151

Jabbur, Jabbur, 202
Jarjura, Munʾim, 53
Jasr, Nur Sulayman, 92
Jewish Agency, 3, 67, 79, 83
Jewish Anti-Zionist League, 57–58, 59
Jewish National Fund, 32, 36, 224
Joliot-Curie, Frederic, 145
Juri, Avraham, 233

Kafr al-Dawwar, strike and riot of, 89, 107
Kafr Qasim, massacre of, 194, 198–99, 219, 221

Index

Kamil, Fathi, 92
Kamil, Michel, 57
Kapeliuk, Amonon, 200, 218
Karkabi, Zahi, 222
Karmiah (Kibbutz), 133, 134, 270n28
Katz, Shoshana, 233
Katznelson, Berl, 38
Kenan, Amos, 150, 151, 152
Khalid, Khalid Muhammad, 145
Khamis, Mustafa, 89
Khamis, Saliba, 197, 200, 202, 216, 222, 223
Khamis, Yusuf, 138, 141, 219
Khrushchev, Nikita, 168, 175, 190, 192, 210
al-Khuli, Lutfi, 96
Khuri, Fu'ad, 196–97, 201, 222, 223, 227
Kibbutz Artzi, 26, 27, 32; Arab Department of, 27, 29; and Arab-Israeli War of 1948–49, 38–39; left in, 27, 31, 75, 84, 119, 129, 131, 132–36, 137; and MAPAM, 79, 80, 126, 134, 173, 174, 270n28; and Qibya raid, 133. *See also* kibbutzim
Kibbutz Me'uhad, 26, 31, 32, 36, 74, 133. *See also* kibbutzim
kibbutzim: 3; economy of, 27, 79, 80, 83, 135; and MAKI, 232, 233; and MAPAM, 20, 34, 36, 64, 78, 79–84, 132–36. *See also* Kibbutz Artzi; Kibbutz Me'uhad
Kujman, Ya'akov, 218
Kusa, Ilyas, 202

Labor Party, 22
Lahav (Kibbutz), 80, 83–84, 270n28
Lausanne Conference, 9, 66
Lavon, Pinhas, 12, 224
Lavon affair, 11–12, 103, 117, 157, 171, 223–24, 228, 234, 235, 244, 262n20
League for Arab-Jewish Rapprochement and Cooperation, 28
Left Po'alei Tzion, 26, 28–29, 58, 128
Left Socialist Party. *See* LSP
Lehavot Habashan (Kibbutz), 133, 134
LEHI (Lohmei Herut Yisra'el), 4, 33
Liberal Party, 235
Liberation Rally, 88, 90, 107, 165
Likud, 4, 22, 68, 76
Lobel, Eli, 150, 152
LSP (Left Socialist Party), 77, 135–37, 148, 150, 163
Luria, Tzvi, 34

Machover, Moshe, 13
al-Maghribi, Fathi, 96

al-Mahdawi, Isma'il, 287n8
Mahmud, Hifni, 145
Makarius, Raoul, 63
MAKEI (Communist Party of the Land of Israel), 46–47, 52; and DMNL, 60–61; and NLL, 48–49, 50, 51
Makhul, Na'im, 214
MAKI (Communist Party of Israel), 1, 103, 214; and Arab-Israeli War of 1948–49, 54–55, 118, 168, 169, 184, 192, 198, 204, 228, 237; and Communist Party of Jordan, 246–48; and Egyptian communists, 116, 146, 147, 148–49, 150–51, 152, 159, 166, 184, 186, 190, 248; electoral strength, 103, 121–22, 161, 162–63, 219–21, 229–30; Eleventh Party Congress, 124, 126, 196; former Hebrew Communist Party members in, 41; former LSP members in, 163, 223, 232, 233; Fourteenth Party Congress, 226–27, 234, 238, 247, 289n54; and Histadrut, 77–78, 243; Iraqi Jews in, 6, 151, 163, 218, 232; isolation after Suez/Sinai War, 20, 159, 194, 198, 231, 241; and Jewish workers, 73, 74, 77–78, 139, 142, 161, 221–22, 223, 224, 239–43, 251; and Lavon affair, 223–24, 228; and LSP, 77, 136, 137; and MAPAM, 15, 31, 117–19, 122–24, 125–26, 127, 131, 136, 138, 140, 202, 218–19, 224, 228, 235–36, 238–39, 248; and Nasserism, 165–66, 169, 174, 195, 201, 215–17, 218, 222, 234, 241, 244–45, 251; and national communism, 231–35, 238, 239; and NLL, 51–55, 65; relations between Jews and Arabs in, 166, 169–70, 213, 215–16, 217–18, 219, 222–23, 227, 228–29, 231–32, 233, 234, 235–45; and Soviet Union, 66–67, 74, 75, 117–18, 167–69, 218, 221, 222, 223, 231, 237; split in, 2, 78, 208, 235–39, 243–45, 248; and Suez/Sinai War, 172, 195, 197, 227, 238; Thirteenth Party Congress, 184, 195–98, 200, 201, 222, 226, 227, 234, 247; Twelfth Party Congress, 142, 196; and Twentieth Congress of the Communist Party of the Soviet Union, 192–93, 231. *See also* Borders of Israel, MAKI's stand on; Palestinian Arab citizens on Israel, and MAKI; Palestinian Arab refugees, MAKI's stand on; Partition of Palestine, MAKI's stand on
MAKI (Mikunis-Sneh), 2, 78, 244, 251
Mandur, Muhammad, 145

Mao Zedong, 2, 5, 178, 187
MAPAI (Israel Workers' Party), 26, 41, 64, 163; electoral strength, 161, 173, 220–21, 229–30; hegemony of, 15, 67–73, 76, 78, 162, 164, 223, 239; and Histadrut, 26, 67, 71–72, 76, 77, 243; international orientation of, 38, 69, 74, 75–76, 136, 172, 175, 177, 249; and Lavon affair, 224, 225, 226, 235, 236; and MAKI, 139, 202, 236, 238; and MAPAM, 2, 25–26, 32, 103, 128, 172, 174. See also Palestinian Arab citizens of Israel, and MAPAI; Palestinian Arab refugees, MAPAI's stand on
MAPAM (United Workers' Party), 1, 3, 4, 20, 103, 248, 287–88n17; and Ahdut Ha'avodah (post-1954), 172, 173; Arab Affairs Department, 27, 49, 120–21, 127–28, 140, 213, 214; Arab members of, 26, 29, 31, 127, 128, 131, 134, 200, 213, 214, 218; Arab Section, 127–28, 128–29, 131; and Egyptian communists, 146–47, 150, 155, 184; electoral strength, 103, 122, 161, 173, 219–21, 229–30; founding of, 25–26, 29–31; and Histadrut, 78, 243; and Jewish workers, 73, 77, 78, 140, 240, 251; Left Section, 15, 131–32, 135; left wing of, 16, 31, 36, 37, 39, 45, 65, 75, 79, 118, 119, 121, 125–36, 140, 208, 214; and MAKI, 15, 31, 117–19, 122–24, 125–26, 127, 131, 138, 140, 158, 202, 218–19, 228, 232, 235–36; and MAPAI, 2, 25–26, 32, 103, 128, 172, 174; and Nasserism, 67, 201, 208, 212, 213, 215, 218–19, 228, 235; and NLL, 49, 50–51; Second Party Congress, 128–30; and the Soviet Union, 15–16, 24, 27, 31, 39, 66, 74, 75, 117–18, 128, 130, 135, 136, 137, 168, 175, 212, 218, 248; and Suez/Sinai War, 2, 172–77; Third Party Congress, 208, 212–13; and Yusuf Hilmi's peace initiative, 158. See also Borders of Israel, MAPAM's stand on; Palestinian Arab citizens of Israel, and MAPAM; Palestinian Arab refugees, MAPAM's stand on; Partition of Palestine, MAPAM's stand on
Mar'i, Sayyid, 94
Marty Affair, 113–14, 117, 148, 273–74n26
Al-masa', 178, 180, 182–83, 184, 206–7
Matek, Yak, 82
Mayus, Ya'akov, 150, 158
Meir, Golda, 38, 54, 288n26

Mesilot (Kibbutz), 133, 134
Michael, Sami, 232
Mignot, Elie, 113
al-Mihi, Darwish Muhammad, 98
Mikunis, Shmu'el, 74–75, 124, 169, 192, 202, 221, 229; and Arab-Israeli War of 1948–49, 47, 51, 54, 55, 198; and borders of Israel, 196, 197, 226, 228; and Communist Party of Jordan, 246, 247, 248; and Egyptian communists, 144, 148, 170, 182; in PCP, 40, 44–45, 46, 49; and split in MAKI, 78, 236, 237, 238, 244; and Soviet Union, 74, 223, 231
military government, 70, 76, 121, 139, 140, 141, 199, 202, 213, 219, 221, 243, 244
Mishmar Ha'emek (Kibbutz), 39
MISHMISH (Egyptian Communist Organization), 105, 108, 115, 144, 250, 274n31
Moked, 251
Mudarrik, Yusuf, 56
Muhyi al-Din, 'Amr, 111
Muhyi al-Din, Khalid, 89, 152, 159, 180–81, 206
Murad, Zaki, 185
Mursi, Fu'ad, 105, 111, 113, 184, 185, 186, 187, 188, 191, 209–10, 210–11, 212, 252
Muruwwa, Husayn, 112
Musa, Salama, 146
Muslim Brothers, Society of, 55, 86, 111, 145, 274n31
al-Muttahid (United Egyptian Communist Party), 185, 188–89, 191

Nabrawi, Saiza, 145, 147
Nada, Sayyid 'Abd al-Wahhab, 92
Naguib, Muhammad, 90, 113, 160
NAHSHAM (Toward an Egyptian Communist Party), 105, 108
Naqqara, Hanna, 121–22, 200, 225
Nassar, Fu'ad, 43, 47, 50, 138, 246, 247, 248
Nassar, George, 29
National Democratic Front, 109, 111
National Liberation League. See NLL
National Progressive Unionist Party (Tagammu'), 253
National Union, 88, 189, 191, 205, 206
New Communist List. See RAKAH
New Dawn, 7, 16, 55–56, 58, 62, 91, 112
New Outlook, 213–14, 219
Nir, Nahum, 119
Nirim (Kibbutz), 150

NLL (National Liberation League), 7, 40, 42–43, 121, 125, 144, 151, 196, 233, 234, 246; and Curiel, 58; and MAPAM, 49, 50–51; and New Dawn, 56; and partition of Palestine, 47–51; unity with MAKI, 51–53
Nucleus of the Egyptian Communist Party, 110

Oren, Mordehai, 27, 47, 130, 134
Orr, Akiva, 13, 75

Pa'il, Me'ir, 152
Palestine Communist Party. *See* PCP
Palestine Labor League, 43, 51, 139, 140
Palestine Liberation Organization. *See* PLO
Palestinian Arab citizens of Israel, 8, 69–70, 76, 78, 122, 224, 255; and MAKI, 22, 121–22, 124–25, 137–43, 161, 193–203, 207–8, 215–16, 218–19, 222, 225, 228, 229, 234, 235–36, 243–45; and Histadrut, 3, 70, 78, 128, 129, 139, 140, 141, 223, 225, 243, 244; and MAPAI, 3, 70, 76, 140, 141, 219; and MAPAM, 33–39, 70, 76, 78, 120–21, 127, 129, 138, 139–40, 141, 215, 218–19. *See also* military government
Palestinian Arab refugees, 8, 9, 10, 11, 12, 32–39, 53, 69, 78, 80, 123, 138, 228, 268n1, 278n114; MAKI's stand on, 122, 123, 142, 214, 228, 235; MAPAI's stand on, 34, 38; MAPAM's stand on, 38, 123, 129, 213, 214, 228, 288n26
Palmah, 10, 26, 31, 32, 68, 81, 135, 232
pan-Arab nationalism, 99–100, 103, 162, 164, 201, 204, 250; and Egyptian communists, 112–13, 156–57, 178–80, 186, 188, 189, 191, 204–7, 212; and Palestinian Arab citizens of Israel, 195, 200
Partisans of Peace, 145–46, 147, 150, 159, 178
Partition of Palestine, 1, 3, 7, 8, 10, 19, 32, 33, 103, 247, 255; Ahdut Ha'avodah's stand on, 27, 36; Arab communist parties' stand on, 53–54, 63–64, 183, 246; Arab states' stand on, 171; Egyptian communists' stand on, 49, 59–63, 85, 178–79, 184, 189, 279n15; Hashomer Hatza'ir's stand on, 27, 29, 30; Israel's stand on, 8, 34; and MAKEI, 46–47, 49; MAKI's stand on, 122, 123, 124, 143, 192, 196–97, 250; MAPAM's stand on. 29. 31. 37. 64, 120, 129, 158, 250; NLL's stand on, 47–51; PCP's stand on, 45–46; Soviet Union's stand on, 24, 25, 37, 45, 47, 53, 60, 64, 65, 66, 184, 190, 249–50. *See also* Borders of Israel
PCP (Palestine Communist Party), 3, 7, 29, 40–41, 42, 46, 51, 52, 118, 192, 223, 231, 232; and Curiel, 58; and NLL, 43–45. *See also* Partition of Palestine, PCP's stand on
Peled, Matti, 152
Peres, Shimon, 10, 12, 221, 236
Peri, El'azar, 27, 31, 119, 126–27, 131, 133, 134, 158, 208, 212
Pineau, Christian, 181
PLO (Palestine Liberation Organization), 6, 8, 152, 211, 247, 255, 256, 257
Popular Democracy, 63, 106, 108, 109, 145, 185
Popular Front, 202–3, 207, 286n132
Popular Liberation Movement, 63
Popular Vanguard for Liberation, 62–63
Preminger, Eli'ezer, 132

Qasim, 'Abd al-Karim, 205, 206, 215, 218, 219, 223
al-Qaysuni, 'Abd al-Mun'im, 93
Qibya, IDF raid on, 11, 116, 133, 173

Rabin, Yitzhak, 34, 39
RAKAH (New Communist List), 2, 78, 223, 244, 251
al-Raya, 105–6, 108, 109, 111, 146, 150, 178, 187, 188, 211; and Arab-Israeli peace, 116–17, 184; and Jews in the Egyptian communist movement, 110, 116, 117, 185, 186, 187, 188; and RCC, 116, 160, 165, 166, 187
RCC (Revolutionary Command Council), 87–91, 93, 102, 107, 110, 150, 158
Revolutionary Bloc, 61, 109, 110, 114
Revolutionary Command Council. *See* RCC
Rifa'i, Ahmad, 206
Rifa'i, Sayyid Sulayman, 273–74n26
Riftin, Ya'akov, 27, 31, 36, 39, 119, 126, 130–31, 132, 133, 134, 135, 173, 208, 212
Rome group, 6, 107, 114, 178; contacts with Israelis, 145, 148–53, 159, 179, 181; dissolution of, 185, 186; and Yusuf Hilmi, 153, 156, 157, 171, 179
Rustum, Sayyid 'Ali, 96

Sa'd, Ahmad Sadiq, 55–56, 58, 62, 106, 187, 209, 210

al-Sadat, Anwar, 98, 206, 208, 252
Sadeh, Yitzhak, 74, 135
Sadiq, Mustafa, 63
al-Saʿid, Rifʿat, 62, 111, 186
Salama, Anwar, 99
Salim, Ahmad 287n8
Salim, Ovadia, 62
Sasa (Kibbutz), 80–83, 84, 270n28
Schwartz, Hillel, 57, 105, 106, 108, 110
Seamen's strike, 73–75, 76
Semitic Action, 15, 151
Setton, Aimée, 105
al-Shafiʿi, Shuhdi ʿAtiyya, 57, 58, 61, 206, 207, 212
Shahin, Rushdi, 48
Shamir, Yitzhak, 4
Shammas, Anton, 232
Shanir, Khalil, 43, 48, 49
Sharett, Moshe, 10, 11, 12, 154, 161, 162, 172, 173
Sharon, Ariel, 11
Shatta, Muhammad, 183, 185
SHELI (Shalom Leyisraʾel), 251
Shihada, Jamil, 213
al-Shuqayri, 211, 247
Shuval (Kibbutz), 84, 133, 134
Sid-Ahmed, Mohamed, 57, 61, 104, 108, 145
Slansky trial, 15, 103, 130–31, 132, 133, 135, 136, 137, 192
Slonim, Meʾir, 40, 192
Sneh, Moshe: and Curiel, 170; expulsion from MAPAM, 15, 75, 132, 135, 158; and Jewish-national tendency in MAKI, 227, 228, 234, 235, 236, 237, 244; as leader in MAKI, 192, 217, 225, 227; as leader in MAPAM, 31, 36, 119, 128, 129, 134, 137, 212; and LSP, 135, 137, 163, 223, 232, 233; and MAKI (Mikunis-Sneh), 78, 244, 251; and Slansky trial, 130–31, 132, 133, 136; view of Soviet Union, 74, 126, 137, 168, 222, 223, 277–78n107
Solomon, Odette, 106, 108, 115
Solomon, Sidney, 106, 108, 115
Somekh, Sasson, 232
Soviet Union, 3, 41, 238, 255; and Iraqi revolution (1958), 206; leading role in international communist movement, 4, 5, 16, 24, 25, 53, 54, 60, 210, 248, 249; relations with Egypt, 167–68, 169, 198; relations with Israel, 66, 75–76, 118, 168; stand on Arab-Israeli conflict, 177, 180, 183, 190, 195, 237, 257. *See also* Partition of Palestine, Soviet Union's stand on
Spano, Velio, 185, 187

Stalin, Joseph, 5, 18, 190, 192, 222
Stambouli, Raymond, 61
Stockholm appeal, 145, 155
Suez Canal, nationalization of, 75, 91, 99, 161, 165, 171, 178, 180, 181, 190
Suez Canal Zone, withdrawal of British forces from, 11, 102, 111, 160
Suez/Sinai War, 2, 9, 12, 14, 19–20, 67, 75, 99, 103, 114, 117, 190, 193, 195, 201, 204; and Ben-Gurion, 154, 161, 171, 173–74, 176, 195, 262n16; and Egyptian communists, 97, 182, 183, 184; and Egyptian Jews, 14, 182; and Egyptian workers, 91–93, 96; and MAKI, 172, 197, 227, 238; and MAPAM, 2, 172–77, 235; postwar atmosphere in Israel, 14, 15, 162, 193, 194, 198, 224; and Soviet Union, 177

Tabenkin, Yitzhak, 26, 36
Talʿat, Ibrahim, 145
Talmi, Meʾir, 119
al-Tamimi, Jabir, 145
Tiba, Mustafa, 60, 61
al-Tlimsani, ʿAbd al-Qadir, 150, 178
Togliatti, Palmiro, 231
Toward a Bolshevik Organization, 105
Toward an Egyptian Communist Party. *See* NAHSHAM
Trade Union Committee for Popular Resistance, 92
Tsarapkin, M. Semyon, 46, 47, 60
Tuʿayma, Ahmad ʿAbd Allah, 90
Tubi, Tawfiq: and Egyptian communists, 144, 145, 147; and Palestinian Arab national issues in MAKI, 122, 194, 199, 200, 202, 216–17, 222, 237; and partition of Palestine, 47–48, 192; in PCP, 42; and RAKAH, 78, 244
Tubin, Pinhas, 119, 131, 134
Tuma, Emile, 42–43, 44, 46, 47, 48, 49, 56, 138, 197–98, 200, 227
al-Tunisi, Bayram, 96
Tzabari, Simha, 40, 192
Tzaban, Yaʾir, 222, 223, 232, 233
Tzizling, Aharon, 32

UECP (Unified Egyptian Communist Party), 92, 114, 117, 165, 188; and MAKI, 159; and Rome group, 153, 156, 157, 179, 185–86; stand on Abdel Nasser and RCC, 117, 177–78, 181; stand on Arab-Israeli conflict, 116, 117, 156–57, 170, 179–80, 183–84. *See also* DMNL; al-Muttahid
Unified Egyptian Communist Party. *See* UECP

United Egyptian Communist Party. *See* al-Muttahid
United States: relations with Egypt, 86–87, 88, 100, 271n40; relations with Israel, 66, 70–71, 75, 171, 174, 175, 176, 177, 244
United Workers' Party. *See* MAPAM

Vashitz, Yosef, 127, 128
Victory League, 41
Vilenska, Ester, 40, 194, 221, 223, 236, 240
Vilner, Me'ir, 40–41, 45, 74, 78, 124, 166, 216, 236, 237, 244
Voice of the Opposition, 105, 115, 144, 250, 274n31

Wadi Salib, riot of, 218, 221
Wafd, 55, 85, 86, 87, 106, 111
Wafdist Vanguard, 63, 85, 86, 145
Weintraub, Richard, 174
Weitz, Yosef, 32, 35–36
women in Egyptian communist movement, 104–5, 106, 115
Workers and Peasants' Communist Party. *See* WPCP

Workers' Vanguard, 180
World Zionist Organization, 3, 29, 67, 79
WPCP (Workers and Peasants' Communist Party), 185, 186–87, 188, 189

Ya'ari, Me'ir, 27, 30, 38–39, 128, 130–31, 132, 133, 134, 135, 172, 213
Yad Hanah (Kibbutz), 133, 233
Yalin-Mor, Natan, 151
Yani, Yani, 202
Yaron (Kibbutz), 133
Yasin, Hilmi, 187
Yitzhaki, Yitzhak, 29, 128
Young Communist League of Israel. *See* BANKI
Young Egypt, 55, 56, 274n31
Yusuf, Abu Sayf, 188, 210, 287n8

Zahran, Sa'd, 187
Zayyad, Tawfiq, 215
al-Zayyat, Latifa, 57, 266n73
Zikim (Kibbutz), 133, 134, 136, 270n28
Zuhayri, Kamil, 215

Compositor:	Graphic Composition, Inc.
Text:	10/13 Sabon
Display:	Sabon
Printer:	BookCrafters
Binder:	BookCrafters

www.ingramcontent.com/pod-product-compliance
Lightning Source LLC
Chambersburg PA
CBHW031250230426
43670CB00005B/115